Transportation Management with SAP TM 9.0

A Hands-On Guide to Configuring, Implementing, and Optimizing SAP TM

Jayant Daithankar
Tejkumar Pandit

Transportation Management with SAP TM 9.0: A Hands-On Guide to Configuring, Implementing, and Optimizing SAP TM

ISBN-13 (pbk): 978-1-4302-6025-7

ISBN-13 (electronic): 978-1-4302-6026-4

Publisher: Heinz Weinheimer
Lead Editor: Saswata Mishra
Technical Reviewer: Shreekant Shiralkar
Editorial Board: Steve Anglin, Ewan Buckingham, Gary Cornell, Louise Corrigan, James DeWolf, Jonathan Gennick, Jonathan Hassell, Robert Hutchinson, Michelle Lowman, James Markham, Matthew Moodie, Jeff Olson, Jeffrey Pepper, Douglas Pundick, Ben Renow-Clarke, Dominic Shakeshaft, Gwenan Spearing, Matt Wade, Steve Weiss
Coordinating Editor: Mark Powers
Developmental Editor: Gary Schwartz
Copy Editor: Lisa Vecchione
Compositor: SPi Global
Indexer: SPi Global
Artist: SPi Global
Cover Designer: Anna Ishchenko

Distributed to the book trade worldwide by Springer Science+Business Media New York, 233 Spring Street, 6th Floor, New York, NY 10013. Phone 1-800-SPRINGER, fax (201) 348-4505, e-mail orders-ny@springer-sbm.com, or visit www.springeronline.com. Apress Media, LLC is a California LLC and the sole member (owner) is Springer Science + Business Media Finance Inc (SSBM Finance Inc). SSBM Finance Inc is a Delaware corporation.

For information on translations, please e-mail rights@apress.com, or visit www.apress.com.

Apress and friends of ED books may be purchased in bulk for academic, corporate, or promotional use. eBook versions and licenses are also available for most titles. For more information, reference our Special Bulk Sales–eBook Licensing web page at www.apress.com/bulk-sales.

Any source code or other supplementary material referenced by the author in this text is available to readers at www.apress.com/9781430260257. For detailed information about how to locate your book's source code, go to www.apress.com/source-code.

Contents at a Glance

Contents

About the Authors

Jayant Daithankar has 24 years of industry and SAP experience. He has held numerous consultancy engagements with global clients. He has strong domain experience in the financial area and multiple professional credentials, including certified SAP consultant for SAP Finance and Controlling, SAP delivery head for the SAP transportation unit, and driver for the SAP Transportation Management logistics practice and other business units. Jayant has also worked at the senior level in the delivery of business-process re-engineering in large enterprise resource planning projects, systems analysis, and application design of SAP processes for customer-specific requirements. He has been closely associated with the SAP Transportation Management product from version 6.0 through its latest release. Jayant currently serves as the Center of Excellence leader in global IT organization.

Tejkumar Pandit has worked for more than 20 years in areas such as supply chain management, customer relations management, transportation, retail, warehousing, and associated software technology. He has several years of varied, hands-on logistics-industry experience in critical roles, such as head of cargo & operations manager. Furthermore, over the past 11 years he has played critical roles in building technology solutions for areas such as transportation management, distribution management, and track and trace. As the practice lead for Logistics and Transportation, he plays a key role, interacting with customer's C-Suite officers in order to understand their organizations' needs and challenges. Tejkumar is currently a consultant, designing operational processes and associated technology landscapes that help firms meet their growth objectives.

About the Technical Reviewer

 **Shreekant Shiralkar** is a senior management professional with experience leading and managing business functions as well as providing technology consulting for major corporations. He is presently consolidating analytic practices for a leading technology company that provides IT services, consulting, and business solutions. He has established, expanded, and diversified businesses, both within India and globally for Fortune 500 firms. He has also authored several best-selling books and published white papers on technology. He holds a number of patents for innovations he has developed.

Acknowledgments

We would like to thank Punit Chheda for his assistance in the writing of this book. His knowledge of and experience with the logistics industry, and with SAP Transportation Management in particular, were invaluable.

Introduction

Globalization has played a crucial role in the expansion of supply chains across countries and continents into ever-changing worldwide networks. Manufacturers, driven by the desire to produce cost-effective, high-quality products are continuing to extend their supply-demand chains, introducing new challenges to these networks. This seismic shift has lead to the phasing out of internal logistics functions, and a move towards third-party logistics providers (3PLs), enabling manufacturers to focus on their core business areas. 3PLs are challenged daily by demanding customers, changing regulations, compliance standards, and gaps between their information technology (IT) maturity and customers' expectations. Hence, 3PLs have started to simplify, modernize, and standardize their IT systems. The aim is to build a system landscape that can address all of their requirements, while replacing most of the existing complex and fragmented systems with a robust platform. In particular, applications that deal with critical functional areas, such as order management, transportation planning, execution, warehousing, finance, billing, and pricing and costing are in need of attention. TMS (transportation management systems) has therefore emerged as one of the critical areas, if not the most critical one.

Implementation of a TMS is key. If executed well, a good TMS can deliver many benefits to an organization in terms of optimization, improved efficiency, reduced errors, and increased revenue. However, a number of projects fail to achieve these objectives for a host of reasons, including incorrect product selection, overcustomization of the system, lack of standardized processes, and little support from management. In realizing the maximum benefit from a TMS, the product selection process and implementation methodology play significant roles.

This book provides insights intended to make the SAP Transportation Management (SAP TM) journey more relevant and fruitful. With a proven evaluation framework and solid recommendations, the book is useful for executives, pre-sales teams, and implementation and rollout teams. Furthermore, it can help decision makers, such as chief intelligence officers (CIOs) and chief experience officers (CXOs), with the important tasks of selecting a product, creating a business case for management approval, and designing a future road map for the organization. Combining the results of research and analysis and knowledge gained from experience working with industry leaders, the book helps to advance the understanding of SAP TM, and it serves as a step-by-step implementation and rollout guide.

This book is structured as follows:

- Transportation Industry Overview: 3PL Perspective
- The Need for TMS: Challenges and IT Landscape
- TMS Product Landscape: Vendors, Product Overview, Plans, and Comparison
- SAP TM: Overview, Architecture, and Road Map
- TMS Selection Framework
- Industry Best Practices for Implementation, Rollout, and Maintenance of SAP TM
- Team Composition and Skill Matrix Required for TM Engagement and How to Build Competency in TM
- Transformation Impact of SAP TM Implementation
- New Dimension Products: HANA, Mobility, and Analytics—Their Impact on Transportation Management
- Process Mapping End-to-End Freight Life-Cycle Scenarios
- Step-by-Step Guide to Configuring and Implementing SAP TM 9.0

CHAPTER 1

■ ■ ■

Transportation Industry Overview: 3PL Perspective

In this chapter, we will discuss the following:

- How the third-party logistics provider (3PL) industry evolved

- Services offered by 3PLs

- Expectations of 3PLs' customers in terms of technology and service offerings

- The way forward

A few decades ago, it was normal practice for freight owners (manufacturers/shippers) to deliver their products to wholesalers and retailers using their own in-house fleet of vehicles. Often, products did not reach customers on time, owing to the unavailability of these vehicles, resulting in loss of opportunity and revenue, not to mention customer dissatisfaction. When manufacturers/shippers started selling their goods internationally, this issue became more serious. During this time, many organizations engaged local road carriers owning one or two trucks/trailers to supplement the work of their fleet. They discovered that such outsourcing was cost-effective and flexible and allowed them to be free of capital investment and the hassle of maintaining aging assets. Soon, using hired or contracted vehicles became a universally accepted method of inland transport. Furthermore, freight owners instituted use of long-term contracts with these types of carriers to avoid any uncertainty regarding services and transportation costs. Carriers owning one or two vehicles increased their fleet sizes and introduced different vehicle types to qualify for these long-term contracts that awarded them a committed volume of business.

As international trade flourished, products began crossing borders. Manufacturers/shippers recruited professionals with import/export and international ocean and airfreight-forwarding experience to manage the movement of their products. To obtain customs clearance, contact and book carriers, provide documentation, and handle the various legal aspects of international shipping, a team of tens to hundreds was required, depending on the size of the business and the location and nature of the freight. Yet, setting up transportation on other continents remained a major challenge. The unpredictable increase in business on some trade lanes and the laws of the importing country added to the complexity of the transportation business.

Globalization forced manufacturers/shippers and retailers to produce products that were cost-effective but high quality. Many well-known and established brands were being challenged by new brands in terms of lower customer prices because the new brands had operation costs comparatively lower than those of their competitors. All aspects of cost contribution that were increasing expenditures in the supply chain were analyzed. Extended supply chains, reduced inventories, shortened product life cycles, and increased freight cost and handling charges were a few factors leading to an increase in the cost of supply chain operations. Outsourced logistics was a new idea that emerged during this time. Manufacturers/shippers started focusing on their core areas, while transferring logistics functions to outsourced 3PLs.

As 3PLs took on these new clients, the greater freight and handling costs compelled the 3PLs to venture into organizing transportation activities, such as:

- Consolidation of small freight with freight from other manufacturers/shippers to build volume and thereby get better rates from air and ocean carriers

- Customs clearance

- Rate negotiation with inland carriers

- Carrying out part of the documentation

- Arranging for temporary storage of freight

Initially, manufacturers/shippers watchfully assigned 3PLs a relatively limited number of services, such as transportation needs and managing warehouses, but subsequently started employing 3PLs to do more. In this way, 3PLs gained experience and expertise in delivering core and associated services, thereby gaining customers' confidence.

Manufacturers/shippers that chose not to use 3PLs at that time did so for the following reasons:

- Logistics operation requires core competency and hence cannot be outsourced; furthermore, meeting level of service was perceived as a risk.

- Outsourcing was not seen as cost saving.

- Logistics experts in their organization did not want to lose their importance and control.

- Difficulty of integrating the organization's Internet technology (IT) systems with those of the 3PL.

- Freight security was their concern.

- Inhibition of relationships with 3PLs.

- Insufficient geographical coverage of 3PLs.

- Bitter experience in the past.

During the initial phases, 3PLs offered a maximum of two types of service, such that the manufacturer/shipper might get only trucking, only customs clearance, or only warehousing and rate negotiation with carriers. Geographical coverage was also limited. 3PLs were mostly local, proprietary firms with small teams. However, the demands of the manufacturing/shipping community and growing world trade soon created longer and more complex supply chains and their associated logistics processes. To address this demand, 3PLs began to partner with other logistics companies in different countries, with specialization and expertise. These arrangements gave the 3PLs time to establish themselves. However, differences in culture, level of development, and technology were major impediments in such relationships. 3PL industry leaders started phasing out these business relationships by opening their own offices in some countries. Moreover, increasingly global manufacturers/shippers wanted a single point of contact for their outsourced logistics. Large and global manufacturers/shippers were often looking for large, financially stable 3PLs that could provide all services and wider geographic coverage. Geographic and portfolio expansion, therefore, remained a priority for 3PLs. Large 3PLs began exploring opportunities to acquire partners where the 3PLs did not have a presence. The period 1996–2006 witnessed major acquisitions and mergers.

After a set of initial hiccups, parent 3PLs and acquired 3PLs started working together as a single company. Standardizing the process across the organization would remain a major challenge for many years. Business-process mapping, analysis, and automation helped achieve some movement toward standardization. Training helped standardize organizations further. Incorporating local requirements and ways of working into standard, global processes was a Herculean task. Today, most leading 3PLs have documentation regarding their processes. However, technology consolidation has continued to be a major problem area. 3PLs use different applications, most of which are homegrown. These applications not only have scalability and integration issues, but also are functionally poor. 3PLs are working on rationalizing their technology landscape to reduce the gap in IT expectation experienced by their customers, something that is being discussed in every logistics forum. Some 3PLs are looking at their technology landscape holistically, but in most cases, it is still project focused and more tactical. Manufacturers/Shippers want 3PLs to offer comprehensive and easily integrated solutions; to do so, 3PLs need to have a clearer picture of the manufacturer/shipper supply chain. A collaborative approach between manufacturer/shipper and 3PL remains the only way to improve manufacturer/shipper satisfaction with the 3PL's IT capabilities and the relationship between manufacturer/shipper and 3PL. Today, most manufacturers/shippers believe that their 3PLs should have the following execution-oriented enablers and tools:

- Network modeling and optimization

- Order management

- Collaboration portals for booking, tracking, and payment

- Collaboration tools (SharePoint, Lotus Notes, video conferencing, and so on)

- Electronic data interchange (orders, advance shipment notices, invoicing)

- Transportation management: planning, sourcing, and execution

- Yard management

- Warehouse management

- Event management and track and trace

- Supply chain event management

- Bar coding

- Radio frequency identification (RFID)

- Global trade management tools

- Advanced analytics and data-mining tools

The large 3PLs are expanding their portfolio and coverage. There are more than a dozen organizations globally, with annual turnover in excess of five billion dollars. The revenue of the 3PL industry has been growing continuously as a result of more and more manufacturers/shippers' opting for outsourcing rather than insourcing. Furthermore, manufacturers/shippers are also considering a reduction in the number of 3PLs engaged by them.

3PLs are major employers in many countries. 3PLs have been elevated to partner status, which essentially means that they have exceeded their customers' expectations. These 3PLs have visibility in the manufacturer/shipper supply chain, which helps them forecast and plan their resources/operations more effectively and offer cost advantage and superior service to their customers. Moreover, 3PLs play an important role in network planning and streamlining supply chain operation. Manufacturers/Shippers are satisfied with the updated information shared by 3PLs and regard these companies as sufficiently agile and flexible. Manufacturers/Shippers largely view these relationships as successful and have gained incremental benefits yearly.

Having spent time with many industries, in diverse locales, and experienced complexity in the supply chain, 3PLs forecasted a huge demand for their services. 3PLs learned, adopted, and built offerings that help manufacturers/shippers reduce their logistics costs, giving them time to market and increase the quality of their services. The 3PL advantage lies in its commitment to surpassing customer expectations and maintaining a can-do attitude.

Today, 3PLs have mature offerings in the following areas:

- Ocean and airfreight forwarding

- Transportation execution

- Freight bill payment

- Negotiation with carrier

- Merging freight while on the move

- Letters of credit

- Freight insurance

- Consolidation

- Deconsolidation, breaking bulk

- Nonvessel operating common carrier operations

- Track and trace

- Cross-border services

- Value-added services

- And more!

Some of the leading 3PLs have further elevated themselves to lead logistics service provider (4PL). These companies coordinate activities and monitor the performance and contracts of other logistics companies on behalf of manufacturers/shippers. 4PLs also provide technology know-how to manufacturers/shippers and, at times, undertake their business processes. 4PLs are seen as a partner that helps large manufacturers/shippers gain supply chain efficiency. More and more Fortune 100 organizations are using 4PLs.

In addition, growing prosperity in Southeast Asia is causing consumer markets to boom. Eyeing the opportunities, the leading global 3PLs from the rest of the world have already ramped up their operations in this region.

While the 3PL industry is trying to expand its portfolio, increase revenues, and move into different regions, it is under tremendous pressure to survive among growing competition. The industry is challenged by

- Demanding customers

- Changing regulations and compliance standards

- Lack of skilled/experienced labor resources

- Gap between IT maturity and customer requirements/expectations

Let's take a look at the industry's existing technology landscape. In many cases, it is the result of one or more of the following:

- Underdeveloped IT strategy, onboarding, system retention (of acquired organizations)

- Decentralized development responsibilities

- Deficient technology: multiple applications providing similar functionalities, old technology platforms, one-to-one integration, poor functional coverage

- High maintenance costs, lack of support

- Unavailability of systems, nonscalable transaction-capturing systems

- Merged entities' continuing on with individual legacy systems

- Poor return on investment

Summary

In this chapter, we explained the evolution of 3PLs and the problems and challenges they face. 3PLs need to focus on rationalizing their application landscape, particularly applications that deal with critical functional areas, such as order management, transportation planning, execution, pricing and costing, warehousing, finance, and billing. These applications have to be looked at holistically, as 3PLs do not have time to deal with them individually. Every day that goes by in which a company lacks integrated, technically sound, functionally rich, architecturally well-designed, user-friendly applications (preferably on a single platform) to address these critical functions is a day in which that company is falling behind the competition. A transportation management system (TMS) covering these business functionalities remains a top priority for 3PLs.

CHAPTER 2

■ ■ ■

The Need for TMS: Challenges, IT Landscape

In this chapter, we will cover

- The need for a transportation management system (TMS)

- Why third-party logistics providers (3PLs) should invest in TMS product selection

- Benefits of the software as a service (SaaS) model

- What TMS offers

- The role of software systems integrators (SIs)

The growth of the 3PL industry is dependent on the performance of overall trade. The 3PL industry has grown every time the trade industry has performed better. The present economy has created growth and profit challenges for the industry.

When asked, how they plan to expand their business, moving forward their responses usually include one or more of the following strategies:

- **Global expansion**: Asian markets are performing better than those on other continents. Increased consumption by Asians, ready availability of skilled resources at reasonable rates, and cost-effective production are among the primary reasons for the growth of these markets. In the past, European 3PLs looked to North America for growth, and vice versa. Today, all 3PLs have their sights set on Asia. Most of the leading 3PLs have created a wider network that provides all kinds of logistics services and value-added services that customers in European and North America regions enjoy.

- **Introduction of new lines of service**: In the last decade, most 3PLs have started offering a range of services as part of their growth strategy. This change is a result of consolidation and customer demand. Today, you will find warehousing organizations that have transportation services; freight forwarders that supply customs brokerage services; and road transport companies that furnish value-added services, warehousing, and freight forwarding by air, ocean, and rail.

- **Targeting new industry segments**: 3PLs that began their operations by serving a particular industry created expertise for that industry's needs over a period of time.3PLs are now looking to leverage their capabilities in order to grow in other industries with similar customer requirements.

- **Penetrating the small and medium-size markets**: The vast majority of companies that work with 3PLs are tier 1 enterprises (annual revenues exceeding one billion dollars). However, this market segment is almost saturated, so 3PLs have started offering logistics services to small and medium-size businesses as a means of sustaining growth. There was less reason for 3PLs to focus on this market segment years ago, when there were plenty of multiyear, multimillion dollar contracts available from large customers. But, such large-scale opportunities are relatively few these days; an increasing number of the requests for proposals (RFPs) received for services are smaller in scale and scope than in the past. To maintain their already slim profit margins, service providers have to offset these smaller revenue opportunities with lower operating costs.

- **Merger and acquisition**: There have been many mergers and acquisitions in the 3PL industry over the past decade. This allows 3PLs to continue to reach out to newer regions and industry segments and to acquire expertise in other services.

One of the key constraints in achieving merger and acquisition goals is the existing Internet technology (IT) landscape. However, many companies have started to simplify, modernize, and standardize their IT systems, recognizing that the existing landscape is becoming an impediment to their growth.

In 2001 we were a part of a team that developed a TMS for India's leading logistics company. Modules included registering business entities (customers, vendors, partners), contract capturing, order management, execution, billing, and reporting. Furthermore, we integrated these with SAP, FICO, SD, and vehicle-tracking systems. Work continued for more than a year, during which we followed the software development life cycle religiously. The team size at peak was close to seventy associates. After moving on to another project and subsequently to another organization, we remained in touch with some of our colleagues who were supporting the TMS we developed. One day, we heard that the management had decided to invest in a best-of-breed TMS product. They called a few product vendors for a demonstration. One of the vendors started carrying out a proof of concept for them. None of the products could meet the organization's requirements. However, this vendor agreed to bridge the gaps identified in its product during a joint evaluation. A road map was drawn. Then, we learned that the second attempt did not materialize and that the company had gone on to explore yet another option.

We were sad to know that the system we had built over several months was not being used. A lot of money and time were invested in a sincere effort by stakeholders and the project team to make a system that would go a long way—a system we had basically conceptualized as an enterprise resource planning (ERP) system for a road transportation business in India. So, what went wrong? Who should be held responsible? Why had the opportunity been lost? Many more unanswered questions troubled us for months, after which we attended a seminar on TMS. Our questions were answered as we consulted international logistics players. Whereas we had just started developing TMS for Indian companies, others had already been on a similar journey; our experiences were not any different from theirs. For many, the aim was to build a system that could address all the company's requirements and replace most of the existing landscape. In reality, many initiatives went on hold because of budgetary constraints; some kept missing deadlines, and others concluded with their scope reduced to less than half its original size. In contrast, a few developers took a narrow view, creating systems for their business unit, location, and functional areas. Others tried their hand at products. Partially available functionalities and unclear and sometimes noncommittal product road maps forced 3PL companies to live with whatever they got. They kept building systems around these products or continued doing many things manually or inefficiently.

3PLs are under tremendous pressure to survive among growing competition. They are challenged by demanding customers, changing regulations and compliance standards, a lack of skilled/experienced labor resources, and gaps between their IT maturity and their customers' requirements/expectations. In many cases, their existing technology landscape is the result of an underdeveloped IT strategy, onboarding, system retention (of acquired organizations), and decentralized development responsibilities. The current landscape therefore has characteristics such as deficient technology, multiple applications providing similar functionalities, old technology platforms, one-to-one integration, poor functional coverage, high maintenance costs, lack of support, unavailability of systems, and nonscalable transaction-capturing systems. Moreover, many product vendors did not invest in upgrading their products. Some discontinued support for them. Mergers and acquisitions added to the problem, with merged entities retaining their systems. Absence of a corporate IT strategy created a worsening of the situation as well: business and IT managers built systems for their needs; as a result, 3PLs have hundreds of systems in their inventory. Maintenance costs are high, and return on investment is very poor. In a landscape such as this, companies cannot achieve objectives such as these:

- Ability to manage transport logistics networks in a holistic fashion in order to reduce operational costs and ensure high use of assets and better multi-modal planning

- Understanding of cost structures

- Exceeding customer service levels

- Compliance with all regulations and policies

- Improved freight consolidation

- Efficient appointment management

- Greater partner collaboration

- Increased visibility throughout the freight life cycle

- Better decision making

- Tighter control across the entire transport management business, from quoting, to planning, to execution, to monitoring, to settlement

As discussed in Chapter 1, the 3PL industry has largely delayed its rationalization journey. The industry needs to makerationalizing its application landscape a priority. Applications that deal with critical functional areas, such as order management, transportation planning, execution, warehousing, finance, billing, and pricing and costing, are in particular need of attention. TMS therefore emerges as key. Without integrated, technically sound, functionally rich, architecturally well-designed, user-friendly applications (preferably on a single platform) to address these critical functions, 3PLs will find it difficult to compete.

In the last five years, we have seen midsize to large 3PLs undertake some big initiatives. Organizations have been gearing up to roll out TMS as the core system of their transportation business unit. There are still many functional gaps in the TMS offered as off-the-shelf products. However, road maps drawn by these 3PLs with TMS product companies appear realistic and within reach. If these initiatives are realized, many 3PLs can reduce their system inventory by tens to hundreds, depending on its current state.

Leading TMS products have functionally evolved and continue to evolve in breadth and depth. Gone are the days of buying individual pieces of TMS functionality from multiple vendors. You can now source solutions for your needs from a single source. Many vendors have begun offering tools for planning and execution. These tools were used by the shipping community for internally controlling and managing costs of the transportation of raw materials and finished goods. Over the years, these solutions found some relevance for transportation service providers, and current solutions are being used by 3PLs for order allocation, load consolidation, routing, transport mode selection, carrier selection, tendering, freight audit, track and trace, and payment and settlement. The newer add-ons are visibility; load building; and event, carrier, and performance management.

TMS is a category of software that deals with the planning and execution of the physical movement of goods across the supply chain. TMS is used by manufacturers/shippers, multimodal operators, assets, and non-asset–based 3PLs and 4PLs. TMS is expected to support all modes of transportation, including road, rail, intermodal, air, and ocean. Manufacturers/Shippers use TMS to manage freight sourcing, planning, execution, and settlement. 3PLs use it for planning and execution. Planning here involves load consolidation, routing, mode selection, and carrier selection; execution entails tendering loads to carriers, shipment tracking and tracing, and freight audit and payment.

Acquiring tools to reduce freight costs continues to be the main reason for investing in a TMS for both manufacturers/shippers and 3PLs. This, along with a desire to improve overall efficiency during the entire freight life cycle, has forced TMS vendors to expand their TMS suite (TMS Integrated with other required systems); offerings now include strategic planning, carrier selection, execution, visibility, performance management, freight payment services, and audit capabilities.

Multiple subcomponents make up comprehensive multimodal TMS solutions across sourcing, planning, optimization, execution, audit and settlement, track and trace/visibility, and performance management. These are some of the capabilities provided:

- Strategic network design and planning

- Tactical planning

- Multimodal, multileg transportation planning and optimization

- Transportation execution

- Freight rating and contract management

- Asset and freight routing, scheduling, and dispatching

- Freight audit, payment and settlement

- Visibility and event management/business activity monitoring

- Analytics, performance management, scorecards and management dashboards

- Global trade management

- Sound architecture, adaptability, flexibility, usability and deployment options

- Ease of use

- Enabled workflow

To accelerate implementation of TMS solutions, today's TMS vendors have established integration with leading ERP systems. Post implementation, these integrations mean less manual work and higher assured quality of data. Some of the common integrations are as follows:

- **Integration with ERP**: Performs transportation planning and execution of ERP orders and deliveries in TMS and invoicing and invoice verification of TMS settlement documents in ERP. Data are transferred using enterprise services. Also integrates TMS with ERP shipment processing.

- **Integration with track-and-trace application**: To help monitor the execution status of transportation.

- **Integration with global trade management (GTM):** Performs customs processing of TMS business documents (e.g., requesting export declarations for freight orders or freight bookings). Data are transferred using enterprise services.

- **Integration with environment, health and safety (EHS)**: To ensure the safe transportation of dangerous goods, in accordance with legal regulations.

- **Integration with business intelligence (BI)**: Makes use of integrated query and analytic tools for evaluating, analyzing, and interpreting business data.

- **Integration with a geographic information system (GIS)**: For data required from a location-based-services perspective.

Most of the customers implementing TMS have also built in integration between TMS and their portals. TMS gives freight status to portal users, and orders received from portals are planned and executed in TMS. Further notifications and approvals are managed between the two systems as well.

Recently, we asked 3PLs, which delivery and implementation approach is best suited to your organization? This question would have been unheard of five years ago. Increased maintenance costs and decreased margins have forced 3PLs to look outside purely traditional ownership models. 3PLs want to focus on their core business, leaving systems responsibility to systems experts. Many SIs and product vendors offer these next-generation services, such as on-premises service, hosting, on-demand service/SaaS, and TMS-managed services.

These models offer

- cost advantage

- minimal risk

- freedom from maintaining infrastructure

- easy availability of software upgrades

- tried and tested solutions

- access to best practices

(SIs play a big role in TMS implementation, rollout, integration with the ecosystem, and maintenance and enhancement. We recommend that you use SIs, as they bring best practices, accelerators, and tools to all these services. In addition, some SIs have created business-process outsourcing solutions with respect to these services. Service providers set up one or more business-process outsourcing (BPO) centers, depending on the number of customers, in countries where this is cost-effective. These centers, equipped with a TMS suite, receive/access customer orders, consolidate them, route them, book them with carriers, prepare documentation, report freight status, handle claim requests, audit freight, prepare invoices, process bills received from carriers/vendors, measure service levels, and generate reports. This gives 3PLs more time to concentrate on their core activities as well as providing savings in terms of labor resources and system ownership.

Manufacturers/Shippers' greater desire for supply chain optimization and visibility, and continual innovation on the part of TMS product vendors, together have been driving growth in the TMS market. C. H. Robinson Worldwide, one of the largest 3PL companies in the world, with global operations, has developed strong technology for use in its own transportation operations, and this has evolved into its Managed TMS offering, which is deployed by TMC (a division of C. H. Robinson). Other Leading TMS providers include SAP, Oracle, JDA Software Group, MercuryGate International, Manhattan Associates, IBM Sterling Commerce, TMW Systems, LeanLogistics, Transplace, and Interlogistics. See Chapter 3 for more details on these product vendors.

Prima facie, there are many options on the market, but finding which one meets the exact requirements of a given 3PL company requires analysis. Every company has a unique selling proposition (USP) that helps it grow and retain customers. Its processes are accordingly aligned. Therefore, 3PLs must do a careful assessment before deciding to invest in a TMS product. See Chapter 5 for further information on how to make a rational choice.

TMS is a core component of a 3PL's IT landscape. Most business activities are centered on this core component. Figure 2-1 shows how TMS is interrelated with other components of the IT landscape.

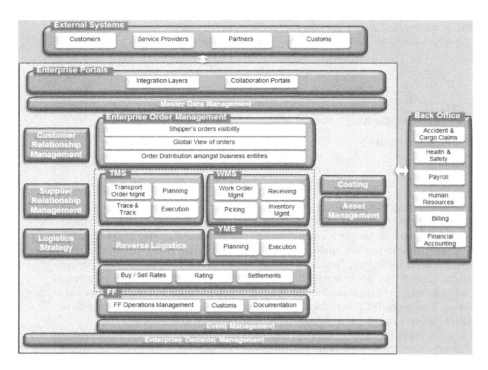

Figure 2-1. *Integrated IT landscape of a 3PL*

As you can see, TMS is integrated with enterprise order management, warehouse management systems (WMSs), customer relationship management (CRM), supplier relationship management (SRM), logistics strategy, costing, asset management, event management, and so on. Because TMS plays such an important role in managing a 3PL's operations, functionally and technically mature TMS helps 3PLs gain a competitive advantage.

Summary

In this chapter, we discussed the importance of integrated TMS for 3PLs and the need to do an accurate assessment before deciding to invest in TMS products.We also noted that 3PLs should also explore available deployment options and the outsourcing of TMS-related business processes in order to gain efficiencies. Finally, we looked at the role of SIs in driving transformation.

CHAPTER 3

■ ■ ■

TMS Product Landscape: Vendors, Product Overview, Plans, and Comparison

In this chapter, we will describe the following:

- The transportation management system (TMS) market

- TMS product vendors' strategies

- Key trends in the TMS market

- TMS vendors

The market for TMS is large and growing. Entities in the supply chain—raw material suppliers, traders, manufacturers, distributors, retailers, transport and warehousing 3PLs—all need TMS for their organization. A range of suppliers, from small boutiques to large enterprise resource planning (ERP) vendors, provides TMS products. Furthermore, the TMS market recently witnessed several acquisitions and mergers. Many product vendors started their journey with an additional customer or two, developing basic functionality. Then, together with their customers, they evolved and developed the missing functionalities. Soon, these product vendors started offering these functionalities in the marketplace using, in the initial phase of operation, one or several of the following product strategies:

- **Focus on subindustry**: Some product vendors remained focused on the vertical market with which they were experienced. This gave them reference to potential customers in the same vertical subindustry.

- **Focus on single process**: Emphasis here was on one or two process areas, as available capabilities were limited to capturing transactions in the system.

- **Focus on regions/countries in closer proximity**: These vendors concentrated all their efforts on the areas within their reach so that they could give extra attention and provide quick resolution. Often, this happened because different regions/countries were following their usual processes.

- **Perform everything with one's own resources**: To keep knowledge within the company, some TMS vendors performed all tasks, from development to rollout, on their own. This did not afford them any scale.

- **Give every customer a different TMS**: Certain vendors believed that every new customer required different TMS because each customer has a unique way of working/doing business. This called for a lot of bespoke development, resulting in a need for additional investment and a delay of return on investment of many years.

Soon, product vendors realized that there were markets for TMS in other industries, subindustries, regions, and process areas. In addition, vendors' customers wanted them to implement the same or similar solutions to their operations outside the current region or diversified industry or cater to the other processes in the transportation life cycle. The TMS market started growing, and so did the competition. This increased competition created challenges for these TMS product companies. To address their needs, TMS vendors have revisited their strategies for growth. These are some of their current strategies:

- **Acquire to grow**: TMS vendors are carrying out self-evaluation to identify gaps in their offerings. To bridge the gaps, many are building relationships with other vendors or acquiring them in order to reach larger regions and provide solutions to other industries, functions, and processes.

- **Offer products and services under one roof**: Many TMS vendors have built solutions for other functions of the supply chain, such as warehousing, yard management, and freight settlement, thereby giving customers a single platform for supply chain execution.

- **Target additional processes**: Build or enhance existing products to include more processes in the areas of planning, scheduling, optimization, multimodal operations, global trade compliance, and so on. Over time, product companies have developed a process repository, and subject matter content that the processes handle is more standardized. This helps 3PLs adopt industry best practices when TMS is implemented. For instance, SAP TM is enhancing processes such as air and ocean transportation for 3PLs' businesses.

- **Target a specific industry**: Build or enhance product for a particular industry. Product vendors have gained experience and subject matter understanding of their businesses—challenges, gaps (and hence opportunities), processes, key performance areas, potential to automate, existing technology landscape, and vision for growth. Having understanding of all this has helped many vendors build the most relevant products for specific industries. For example, MercuryGate TMS solutions is integrating with the Integrated Business Solution (IBS) Business Suite, serving customers in key vertical markets, such as 3PL, pharma, auto spare parts, and wholesale. Similarly, SAP is planning TM for railroads, given the company's experience with railroad customers worldwide.

- **Target technology and architecture**: TMS product vendors have identified opportunities in the areas of improving integration capabilities, migrating to a newer platform, use of mobile technology, and adopting service-oriented architecture (SOA). Integration with systems within and outside the organization has remained a priority.

- **Partner to gain scale**: TMS product vendors have begun establishing their businesses in newer regions. For example, Asian markets are increasing in importance for retailers and shippers, and to meet their logistics outsourcing needs, 3PLs have set up their operations in the pertinent countries. TMS vendors see this as a growth opportunity. Moreover, some of the local logistics players in these areas are gaining in size and maturity. They are the next set of target/potential customers for the product vendors. Some TMS vendors are expanding by using an implementation partner model. The vendors have appointed/partnered with systems integrators (SIs) to carry out rollouts and implementation services in these countries. This model provides the vendors scale and flexibility, and they need not have large, permanent teams. In addition, they can concentrate on product development and enhancement, leaving the implementation work to their partners, who are trained in using these products.

- **Offer a flexible costing model**: Besides the typical licensing model, some product vendors are offering software as a service (SaaS), on a pay-per-use or pay-per-transaction basis. This model is attracting many small to midsize 3PLs that were managing these functions either manually or with the help of outdated applications.

These growth strategies have helped TMS product vendors develop their business, while meeting industry expectations. SAP is investing a lot in enhancing the current supply chain execution platform to reach out to new markets, such as railroads, for which they already have a large customer base for their other products.

Key Trends in the TMS Market Affecting 3PLs

The 3PL industry evolved greatly in just a few years, from conceptualization to what it is today. We think that lack of development is one of the key reasons not many product companies paid a lot of attention in early years. But, the industry has grown severalfold and is being seen as having potential for transport management product adoption. However, the dynamics and local aspects of the business require highly flexible, functionally rich, technically sound products to meet industry needs. Here are some of the trends:

- **Custom-Built solutions will continue to be popular, along with TMS products**: TMS vendors still have a few gaps in their offerings when it comes to the requirements of 3PL customers. So long as there are gaps that must be bridged, 3PLs will continue to build solutions themselves. Potential TMS customers believe that if the solution is built in-house, it will take care of all their requirements; moreover, knowledge remains with them. This, however, is not entirely true. We have come across cases in which well before the solution could be developed in-house, the business requirements had changed. We believe that neither product nor bespoke can immediately address a customer's changing requirements. Yet, when it comes to selecting a product option or building a solution in-house, due diligence must be carried out to determine whether the product can cater to ever-changing needs. Also, with bespoke development, one must create an architecture that can accommodate such changes in the shortest possible time.

- **Niche TMS products will continue to find new 3PL customers, along with the leading vendors**: There are many small to midsize 3PLs operating worldwide. These companies have been managing their transportation management solution requirement by using a TMS product from a niche product vendor. Until the leading TMS vendors are able to offer customized solutions and pricing to suit these small to midsize 3PLs, the trend toward buying niche TMS that can cater to their business will continue to prevail.

- **TMS will gain center stage**: It is anticipated that transportation software will be at the center of the landscape and will be integrated with other enterprise solutions, such as global trade management (GTS), warehouse management systems (WMS), business reporting and business intelligence (BI), customer relationship management (CRM), portal, supplier relationship management (SRM), track and trace, ERP, and financial accounting systems. Soon, TMS will serve as the "hub" for all these "spoke" systems. TMS will have to share data both ways to ensure that nothing is deviating from the standard operating procedure.

- **Transportation software will first be used for transportation execution rather than optimization**: 3PLs will continue to leverage TMS for execution rather than optimization primarily for two reasons, the first being the absence of standardized processes at the enterprise level and the second being that these companies are still in the process of setting up the basic technology platforms needed to automate their processes. In the past, many 3PLs purchased TMS products for automatically planning and optimizing their networks, schedules, routes, and carrier assignments but failed and went back to manual planning. This has discouraged these 3PLs from taking a similar journey. Our understanding is that, in most cases, the 3PLs did not have standardized processes before embarking on such a journey. In addition, the 3PLs should have started by capturing execution, gained confidence, and gotten master data in place and processes streamlined and only then used the planning, scheduling, and optimization features.

- **3PLs will continue to invest in visibility and tracking technologies, along with TMS**: Customers serviced by 3PLs have evolved their technology landscape, implementing best-of-breed solutions for their business needs. These solutions have the ability to interface with 3PLs' systems for order sharing, monitoring status of orders, workflows, and payment. The customers therefore expect a total technology conversion between them and their vendors. As a result, 3PLs need to have the necessary technology platforms to provide data related to the order: bill of lading (BL), house bill of lading (HBL), house air waybill (HAWB), status of the order in the execution life cycle, freight costs, accessorial charges, claims, shortages, loss and damage, and any other deviation. In this context, 3PLs will continue to invest in mobility solutions; tracking with Global Positioning Systems (GPS); or item-level to box-level tracking, using radio frequency identification (RFID) or similar technology, along with TMS.

- **3PLs will continue to invest in business intelligence (BI) technologies, along with TMS**: Customers serviced by 3PLs have increased expectations of them. Customers look to 3PLs to work as one of the partners in running their business. This has forced a convergence. Reporting is one of the vital ways to build trust, confidence, and transparency in the business. 3PLs have therefore started investing in BI technologies both to know what is happening within their own organization and to give different views of the business to the customer. This, as well as monitoring key performance Indicators and creating dashboards and "what if?" scenarios, is helping 3PLs engage meaningfully with their customers to improve operations, stay cost competitive, and build healthy relationships for the long term. The majority of TMS products offer a few ready-made reports. However, the expectation is for more. Hence, TMS product vendors are also forming integrations with BI products, and when BI is not available, 3PLs are implementing it, along with TMS products, to gain maximum return on investment.

- **TMS vendors will increasingly provide SaaS solutions**: 3PLs, in their effort to optimize spending on technology, while avoiding noncore functions, such as running the technology function themselves, are looking for reliable partners who can take over these responsibilities from them. In this context, a few TMS vendors have begun providing TMS, using the SaaS model. Although the number of software vendors offering a full-scale SaaS solution is small, it is anticipated that increasingly these vendors will furnish this as a cost-effective solution to the 3PL industry.

- **SIs see TMS as a big and long-term opportunity**: Many leading SIs see the growth of TMS as one of the major opportunities in terms of number, size, and duration of deals with their customers. These SIs have created separate teams to focus on this line of business. They also have a clear go-to-market strategy to target customers. The initial focus is the possibility of picking up a ramp-up customer from their existing customers. In some cases, the solution and the commitment are offered jointly (product vendor and SI). Gaps identified during the blueprint phase are bridged through development of either a joint intellectual property (IP) or next-version system or a system retained for that customer only. Some SIs have moved a step further in closing the gap between them and product vendors. These SIs have identified use cases that the product vendors do not have in their road map and have proposed building these using product platforms, for example, TMS for the shipping industry using a TMS platform. SIs also viewed this as an opportunity to get the integration work required with TMS. Compared with product vendors, SIs are more versatile with regard to implementation and rollout of a product or system. SIs leveraged this capability by becoming implementation and rollout partners for TMS product vendors. SIs trained their teams in using the product and learned configuration and blueprinting by placing these teams as shadow resources with product vendors' teams during the implementation phase. Then, the SIs were on their own. Many 3PLs are present in more than 100 countries. SIs have some presence in most of these countries, and this is helping them gain an advantage over TMS product vendors when evaluated for implementation and rollout of TMS. Furthermore, the cost of engaging an SI vendor for implementation and rollout is lower than that required for using resources from product vendors. The next big opportunity SIs have an eye on is annual maintenance contracts for TMS as an ongoing revenue stream. Some SIs are also investing in creating TMS platform–based business-process outsourcing solutions.

- **Consolidation has begun**: Other large or similar-size vendors are acquiring TMS products or its vendors. For example, IBM recently acquired Sterling Commerce's TMS. Similarly, JDA acquired RedPrairie's TMS product, and Kewill acquired Foursoft. In the coming years, the 3PL industry is expected to benefit from this, because the acquiring companies are spending more and more money to increase the breadth and depth of their products. These companies have started offering them as a service or on a pay-per-use basis, which will free many 3PLs from up-front investment toward having TMS on the premises.

Product vendors see the potential in offering TMS to the 3PL industry and are working to bridge the gaps between their products and the business requirements and rules of the industry. SAP TM is leading the pack by putting together a comprehensive solution for this industry. Other product vendors are producing leading TMS products as well.

TMS Product Vendors

Following are some of the leading TMS product vendors (apart from SAP TM):

- Oracle
- IBM
- C. H. Robinson Worldwide
- Infor
- JDA
- Manhattan Associates
- MercuryGate International

These vendors offer some of the top products available. You may want to consult the company web sites for overviews as well as new features, acquisitions, and success stories, which are updated regularly. In addition, you can find relevant information on TMS products in "Gartner Magic Quadrant for Transportation Management Systems," an online survey conducted by Gartner every year and available for purchase on its web site (`www.gartner.com`). You can also refer to recent findings of the ARC advisory Group, which presents profiles of TMS vendors and their products on its web site.

Most product vendors support planning, optimization, and execution of multimodal business handled by the 3PL industry, with varying degrees of coverage. Control tower visibility, workflows, predictive analysis, decision-making ability, resource and network optimization, cost optimization, easy integration, and scalability are becoming some of the key capabilities requested of TMS products.

Summary

The TMS market has many small to large players. The leading ERPs, SAP and Oracle, both offer TMS. The TMS market is growing, and so, too, is the competition. TMS vendors have acquired other TMS vendors or their TMS platform in order to reach other regions/countries, subindustries, or process areas. This will continue until the market has three or four big names. TMS as SaaS or on an on-demand basis is an opportunity for small to midsize 3PLs to garner the benefits of using leading TMS product without the burden of capital costs—for building or buying a TMS or for its maintenance and enhancement. The next chapter looks at the details of the SAP TM solution, its architecture and road map.

■ ■ ■

CHAPTER 4

SAP TM : Overview, Architecture, Road Map

In this chapter, we will cover

- How SAP Transportation Management (SAP TM) has evolved

- The functional focus of every release

- SAP TM for 3PLs

- The use of new technologies, such as Floor Plan Manager (FPM), Business Rule Framework plus (BRFPlus), and Business Object Processing Framework (BOPF)

- Support for an air freight-forwarding scenario

The SAP TM platform has a long history. SAP TM started with shipment execution functionality, primarily for the manufacturing/shipping community, as part of SAP R/2, under Logistics Execution-Transportation (LE-TRA), to capture shipment execution-related transaction data. Then SAP TM was an enterprise-centric transportation solution used by manufacturers/shippers for freight cost and settlement, billing, freight auditing, and direct store delivery as well as simple planning and reporting. Next to arrive was Transportation Planning/Vehicle Scheduling (TP/VS), which provided shipment planning and optimization capabilities. Features such as vehicle scheduling and route guidance, along with enhanced carrier selection and continuous move optimization, gained industry acceptance. SAP Event Management (SAP EM) and and SAP Global Trade Services (SAP GTS) then further strengthened offerings in the area of event management across supply chains and border crossings, respectively.

SCM 5.0, an add-on to TM, was enhanced for capacity planning. Business partner collaboration was key, particularly for booking ocean vessel capacity. A subsequent pilot solution, strategic freight management (SFM), dealt with strategic collaboration and web-based collaboration and had a feature that allowed sharing of requests for quotation (RFQs) for ocean and land rates.

SAP TM 6.0 had many improved features: centralized/decentralized TM, adaptive planning, execution, re-planning, carrier allocation, single-and multiple stop planning, scheduling, routing and optimization, activity-based costing, freight billing, and payment and profit distribution. This solution also provided greater visibility for 3PL-based activities, such as freight quotation and buy-and sell-side visibility.

Enabling the user to make optimal use of existing resources, choose the best carrier and means of transport, determine the most efficient transport plan with the given constraints, and modify plans based on real progress were some of the improved capabilities of SAP TM 6.0. Key drivers for further investment in SAP TM are depicted in Figure 4-1.

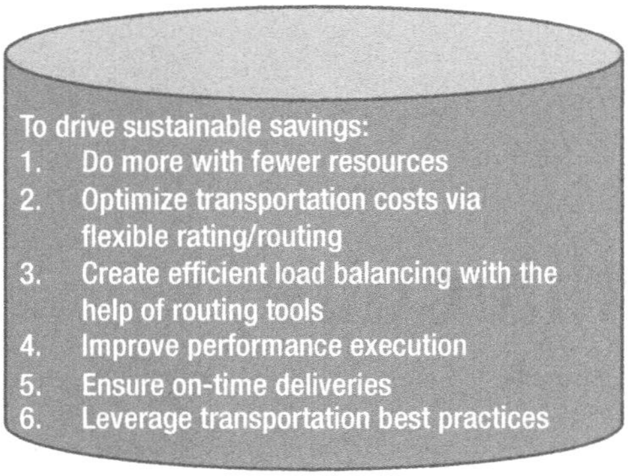

Figure 4-1. Key drivers for investing in SAP TM

In many ways, SAP TM 6.0 was a significant improvement over Enterprise Resource Planning Logistics Execution System (ERP LES), TP/VS, and SAP Advanced Planning and Optimization (SAP APO) put together.

The major improvements were

- A single system for transportation planning, execution, and transportation charge calculation

- Transportation planning and execution for shipments from multiple ERP systems

- Support for peer-to-peer broadcasting and being open to all tendering

- Support for the execution of both inbound and outbound transportation

- Support by transportation proposal/routing guide for the same constraints as in planning (e.g., compartments, trucks, trailers)

- Support for master data for standard routes, container, and driver

- Adaptive planning that can be done even after the execution of the transportation activities has begun (e.g., planning new transportation demands for existing shipments)

- No limit on the number of transshipment points, or hubs, used in the life cycle of a shipment

SAP TM 7.0

SAP TM 7.0 had several enhancements in functionality with respect to SAP TM 6.0. The following is a summary of these changes:

- **Shipment request (SRQ) approval:** Condition-based workflow; if SRQ exceeds a specific capacity, it must be approved before it can be processed further. The person who is responsible for approval gets a message in his or her SAP TM business workplace inbox. He or she can accept or reject the approval message.

- **Mode-Specific user interface (UI):** Additional SRQ entry screens for different types (intermodal, air, ocean, land) of shipment requests.

- **Adding existing SRQ to a freight request (FRQ):** Additional functionality to assign existing SRQ in a FRQ.

- **Parcel planning/Tariff planning:** Carrier rate integration with external systems and integration with external rating engines (SMC3, less than truckload [LTL]); tariff cost calculation in SAP TM or procurement of tariff costs from an external system.

- **Routing freight units (FUs) of a SRQ individually:** Proposals (planning profiles) can be created in such a way as to list all possible routes. Users can select different routes for different FUs within SRQ.

- **GTS integration:** Triggers export declaration. Custom status can be considered during the execution of shipments.

- **Inter-and intra-company cost and revenue distribution:** The sales organization is responsible for processing a SRQ and charging the customer (customer freight invoice request [CFIR]). The purchase organization is responsible for subcontracting transportation to a carrier (supplier freight invoice request [SFIR]). Internal charging between the sales organization and purchase organization is possible for profit sharing and cost surcharges.

- **Multi-resource scheduling:** Defining a resource with a means of transport (MTR) that can count available resources (e.g., ten trucks with a 20 ton capacity).

- **Graphical documentation presentation:** All business-related documents appear in graphical format under the Document Flow tab.

- **Customer fact sheet:** Contains a single screen for important customer data and relevant analytic content from business intelligence (BI).

- **Free fields in SRQ, BO, SO:** Custom fields in the aforementioned objects.

In addition to these key features, SAP TM 7.0 also had enhancements in terms of its tendering template (the creation of tendering information as master data), resource less schedule creation, addition of one-time manual stops during manual planning, and personal object work list (POWL) dynamic selection criteria.

SAP TM 8.0

SAP TM 8.0 entered the market in the ramp-up in November 2010 and reached general availability in June 2011. The new release provided these enhancements:

- Improved transportation planning

- Reduced transportation costs

- Improved freight consolidation

- Improved use of assets

- Efficient service-level fulfillment

- Improved partner collaboration

- Increased visibility throughout the freight life cycle

- Improved decision making capability

In SAP TM 8.0 the following product integrations occurred:

- **Integration of SAP ERP with SAP TM:** Performs transportation planning and execution for ERP orders, deliveries in SAP TM and invoicing and invoice verification in ERP for TM settlement documents. The data is transferred using enterprise services. Also integrates SAP TM with ERP shipment processing. In this case, data is transferred using enterprise services and intermediate documents (IDocs).

- **Integration of SAP TM with SAP EM:** To help track events to monitor the execution status of transportation.

- **Integration with GTS:** Performs customs processing for SAP TM business documents in a connected GTS system (e.g., requesting export declarations for freight orders or freight bookings). Data is transferred using enterprise services.

- **Integration with environment, health, and safety (EHS):** To ensure the safe transportation of dangerous goods in accordance with legal regulations.

- **Integration with BI:** Makes use of integrated query and analytic tools for evaluating, analyzing, and interpreting business data.

- **Integration with a geographic information system (GIS):** For data required from a location-based-services perspective.

With SAP TM integrated with SAP ERP, the manufacturing/shipping community finally got an integrated transportation management solution. The introduction of integrated order management made transport planners' lives easier, allowing them to cover order-to-cash (OTC) and procure-to-pay (PTP) processes associated with booking and moving freight, albeit with an emphasis still on ocean freight. The transport planner could now get a single view of the freight to be dispatched. Moreover, both manual and automatic planning and dispatching were made possible. Advanced and dynamic transportation optimization combined inbound and outbound planning features to help manufacturers/shippers optimize their transportation resources. This release came with some additional decision-supporting reports and views that helped manufacturers/shippers improve their service levels at reduced cost. With this release, management was also improved. Integrated global cross-border management and dangerous goods acquisition attracted manufacturers/shippers' attention. In the case of the scheduler workplace, new features were added, and some SAP TM 7.0 features were enhanced; new features included searching for replacement resources for an existing assignment, editing demand splits, automatic scheduling of multiday assignments, copying time allocations, confidentiality of resource names (displaced for authorized users only), connections to external GIS systems (enhanced), container positions saved in the scheduler by user, resource list re-sorting directly in the planning board, and separate dialog boxes for work lists. The planning board now contains a button that allows the user to align assignments.

The web-based planning board introduced resource planning, making optimization possible at the team level, as well as multiday planning, optimization, and appointment booking. A parts availability check was also added to the planning board, along with mass change and assignment.

The development focus for SAP TM 8.0 was customer co-innovation, deep-process integration (OTC, PTP, customs and compliance management, DGR), best-in-class functionality, collaboration, decision making, flexibility, simplicity, and performance.

SAP TM 8.1

The main focus of SAP TM 8.1 was to extend solutions to support 3PLs. SAP TM 8.1 entered ramp-up in August 2011. SAP TM 8.1 extends the core transportation processes covered by SAP TM 8.0 to support enhanced

- Ocean freight management

- Transportation network planning

- Quotation and forwarding order management

- Freight booking and service order management

- Cargo management

Furthermore, a new scenario was included: less than container load (LCL), for 3PLs. SAP TM 8.1 also delivers general enhancements for both manufacturers/shippers and 3PLs, including

- Advanced transportation planning

- Advanced charge management and settlement

- Enhanced analytics

A fragmented system landscape, point-to-point legacy systems for transport execution (often different ones for each mode of transport) without proper integration, old technology in need of replacement, a lack of experienced developers for legacy technology, the absence of a software vendor for transport execution with double-digit market share, a presence limited to the local or regional level, minimal innovation, and limited development and support capability were some of the challenges faced by supply chain convergence agents. Among 3PLs, challenges were great because of the increasing gap between their existing technology landscape and the expectations of their customers. -A growing need for network planning and cargo optimization to increase margins and compliance, along with the proactive monitoring of execution status visibility and collaboration, added to these issues.

With SAP customers' being responsible for 86 percent of the athletic shoes, 70 percent of the chocolates, 50 percent of the branded jeans, 72 percent of the beer, and 77,000 of the cars produced per day worldwide, SAP had a complete understanding of the widening expectation gap between industry leaders and their 3PL partners.

SAP continued investing in its goal of being the market leader in supply chain execution and sought leadership in supply chain convergence by creating best-in-class solutions (functionality, complete and comprehensive), integrated and connected processes (intra-and inter-enterprise solutions, end-to-end process integration, out-of-the-box connectivity), and vertical offerings (industry-specific functionality, but also multi-industry offerings). While moving forward in the journey of building solutions for freight forwarding and the 3PL industry, SAP did try, we believe, to answer some of the key questions of 3PL industry leadership, such as

- How can I manage my logistics network in a holistic fashion that is beneficial to both my customers and my profitability?

- How can I provide operational excellence to my customers without sacrificing my bottom line?

- How can I leverage my transportation network as 3PL and make informed decisions about the best use of purchased services from carriers/partners?

- How do I ensure high customer service levels and responsiveness to unexpected supply chain events?

- How do I ensure that I am compliant with all regulations?

- How do I implement Internet technology (IT) solutions quickly on a global and local scale as needed?

The industry was on the lookout for a system that could offer robust functionality to meet a diverse set of requirements, while enabling ease of business strategy execution, providing a platform for growth, and reducing risk to business continuity—a system that could become a catalyst rather than a hindrance and lower long-term total cost of ownership (TCO) through the elimination of the many legacy systems and multiple integrations to achieve higher return on investment (ROI) in every business unit/functional area. SAP continues to invest in TM for the 3PL industry. SAP TM 9.0 is a result of this initiative.

SAP TM 9.0

With SAP TM 9.0, SAP has released a much awaited solution that many manufacturers/shippers and 3PL industry members believe will go beyond any best-of-breed products available on the market. SAP TM 9.0 is a complete transportation management solution. It includes not only enhanced support for all means of transport (including ocean, air, road, and rail) for shippers and manufacturing industries, but also native collaborative scenarios between manufacturers/shippers and 3PLs. SAP TM 9.0 supports processes required for domestic and international freight forwarding and is compliant with international trade management and dangerous goods regulations. In addition, SAP TM 9.0 provides interactive transportation and shipment planning, along with collaborative tendering, integrated fulfillment, execution, visibility in the freight life cycle, complete freight cost management, and integrated freight and forwarding settlement.

With the SAP TM 9.0 implementation, support for end-to-end intermodal airfreight and ocean freight scenarios for small freight to container load was achieved. The end-to-end life cycle of freight begins as follows:

- Freight pick up from manufacturer/shipper

- Transport by truck to an origination terminal/ hub/station for processing/consolidation and onward planning

- Booking with main carriage

- Transfer by road to the container freight station (CFS)/airport hub for the main journey as applicable

- Customs clearance at the origin and destination gateways

- Transport between the port of destination to the destination terminal/hub/station for processing/deconsolidation and onward planning by road

- Delivery to the consignee by road

Also supported:

- Required documentation

- Data exchange

- Reporting and decision support

- Event tracking and monitoring

- Transportation cockpit

Major enhancements and new features include

- Integration with carrier schedule

- Carrier allocation

- Ocean and air schedule consolidation; conversion of schedules into bookings

- Confirmations with carriers

- Manual and automated planning and dispatching using a routing engine

- Security requirements for air and ocean

- Compatibility checks for special handling requirements; pre-booking with gateways

- Discrepancy handling

- Mode of transport–specific documentation and electronic data interchange (EDI) messaging

- Automated transportation charge calculations per mode of transport

- Audits and recalculation of freight agreements

- Support for industry standards, such as The Air Cargo Tariff and Rules (TACT) and Cargo Accounts Settlement Systems (CASS)

This, along with enhanced decision support and event tracking, particularly from an airfreight perspective, helped SAP look good in the TM space. SAP emerged as visionary, committed, and industry focused.

With SAP TM 9.0, SAP's extended communication and connectivity to the entire ecosystem of the supply chain–converging the elements and actors, enables effective collaboration among them. These ready-to-use integrations helped SAP gain mileage over its competition. E-mails and short message service (SMS) notifications requesting quotations from carriers, freight orders, or freight bookings to share with the carrier; event sharing on mobile and other modes; and data exchange for freight rates, schedules, and mode-specific transaction messages made users' lives simpler and minimized data errors, while sharing information and improving customer and partner experiences.

SAP TM uses this set of new technologies:

- SAP NetWeaver Process Integration (PI)

- SAP NetWeaver Business Client (NWBC)

- FPM

- BRFPlus

- BOPF

Descriptions of these technologies follow.

PI

- Formerly known as SAP Exchange Infrastructure (SAP XI)

- The primary integration tool for SAP-to-SAP and SAP-to-non-SAP environments

- Leveraged in case additional data elements need to be transferred from SAP ERP Central Component (SAP ECC) to SAP TM

NWBC

- A role-based single point of entry for SAP business applications, such as graphical user interface (GUI) applications and new applications based on Web Dynpro

- It is available in desktop and zero footprint versions, allowing flexible access for all user groups

- Lets users create their own queries, filters, and work lists

- Displays classic SAP GUI transactions simultaneously for one-stop access

FPM

- The framework for creating and configuring Web Dynpro Advanced Business Application Programming (Web Dynpro ABAP) applications

- Adopts standard SAP TM screens without code modifications

- Provides end users with the ability to configure their own screens

- Ensures consistency across applications by means of predefined elements

BRFPlus

- The business rules system available in SAP NetWeaver ABAP

- A comprehensive framework that helps business and IT end user model rules used for automatic decision support in business cases of all kinds

- Enables customers to leverage current practices and not have to rely on standard functionality

- Rule maintenance is done by end user

BOPF

- An architectural concept that the new SAP solution adopted

- Lets SAP TM model important transactional documents and master data elements in an object-oriented environment

- Makes these objects addressable via a standard access mechanism

- Allows for better enhancement options

Air freight as a New Scenario

Until now, TM was seen by 3PLs as applicable only to ocean business. The industry was unsure of airfreight support. However, SAP worked with its customers to build integrated solutions supporting air-and ocean freight in parallel. The journey from transportation management for manufacturers/shippers to internal transportation needs, to full-container ocean freight, to LCL volumes, to the airfreight business only proves the vision and commitment of SAP. Additional details on air freight are provided here for reference. SAP TM 9.0 supports air-freight-related activities, ranging from order taking to final billing and settlement, both at origin and destination stations as well as their respective gateways.

The air freight scenario in TM 9.0 covers

- Gateway consolidation/deconsolidation (import and export), with automatic import file creation

- Business unit consolidation (local), with automatic import file creation

- International Air Transport Association (IATA) direct shipments

- Back-to-back and cross-trade shipments

- Cost distribution and job costing for launch service providers (LSPs)

- Charge management

- Destination call off

- Partial shipment handling

- Co-load shipment handling

Document handling and event and status management are supported throughout the air freight scenario. Let's take a look at SAP TM capabilities in a little more detail.

Plan Capacity

- Capacity planning through schedule-based allocation

- Automated generation of operative flight schedules from master flight schedules

- Automated message-based airline booking and confirmation

- Relevant master data

- Master airway bill (MAWB) stock management
- XML message-based connectivity

Booking

- A forwarding order (FWO) references a forwarding agreement item, including a service product
- Automated population of fields from service products
- Automated business partner/text determination, compliance checks, air cargo security
- House airway bill (HAWB) stock management
- Commodity codes, dangerous goods handling, export customs data

Routing

- Optimizer-based E2E routing proposals, according to network, schedule, and capacities (optional)
- Manual definition or revision of routing
- Shortcut functions to create or select freight bookings; interaction with export gateways
- Pre-booking processes; pre-book against gateway capacity, status handling, auto confirmations
- Instruction work lists, with event-based tracking and alerting
- Execution status

Capacity Manager

- The transportation cockpit offering flexible and powerful features for observing capacity usage, optimizing weight-volume ratios, and confirming/rejecting/reassigning pre-bookings
- Manages and communicates capacity increases or decreases
- Preparation of load plans, receipt of loading reports, finalizing paperwork, and printing
- Trucking schedules for feeding and drayage transports
- Mixed unit load devices (ULDs); scenario-based validations
- Discrepancy handling and irregularity reporting; execution status handling
- Import/Export organization handling

Import/Recovery

- Import freight bookings and import forwarding orders to be prepared in order to allow prompt recovery from the airline and import customs upon confirmation of arrival
- Deconsolidation (actual, status) handling
- Manage local drayage/on-carriage/de-feeding subcontracted trucking freight orders
- Trucking schedules for de-feeding and drayage transports

Final Delivery

- Finalize import forwarding order

- Create freight orders for final delivery and send to subcontracted truckers

- Record proof of delivery

- Trucking schedules/tour building

Customer Billing

- Automated charge calculations, according to International Commercial Terms (Incoterms), profiles, and agreements

- Settlement of charges via forwarding the settlement documents through integration using an ECC (including intercompany settlements)

- Manual adjustments, revisions possible at all levels; credit note handling

- Internal agreements, templates, usability of transportation charge calculation sheets (TCCS) and rate table UIs

- Flexible ratings; quantity/ULD/counters/surcharges

- Rate lookup tools

Cost Settlement

- Automated charge calculation for freight orders and freight booking, according to agreement

- Settlement of charges via freight settlement documents through integration with ECC

- Intra-company costs settled on internal orders or cost centers via direct integration with an ECC

- Internal agreements for internal costs versus distribution from freight orders/bookings/ settlement documents

- Service-based costs in internal agreements

- Profitability view for forwarding orders

- TACT rating: general commodity rate (GCR)/specific commodity rate (SCR)/ULD; CASS integration

- Rate lookup tool

SAP TM Road Map

If you take a close look at the SAP transportation and logistics road map, it is very clear that transportation and logistics together form a major area of investment for SAP. To build a best-in-class TM solution with industry focus, SAP is working in close collaboration with industry leaders in supply chain convergence, making this its highest priority in the entire development life cycle. In addition to enriching current solution functionally, SAP is also investing in next-generation technologies, such as SAP High-Performance Analytic Appliance (SAP HANA), and is working to increase mobility and build a seamless integrated suite for supply chain execution.

Summary

SAP TM has evolved from being a collection of systems capturing transaction data to a single system that provides extended communication and connectivity to the entire ecosystem of supply chain–converging elements and actors, enabling effective collaboration among them. This has simplified users' lives and minimized data errors, while allowing for sharing of information and improving the customer and partner experience. SAP has shown commitment to further investing in this product to cover remaining modes and actors, introduction of new technologies, and improving ease of integration. There are many TM products on the market; however, we believe that SAP ooffers good value. To make your TM selection, we suggest that you make use of our product selection framework in Chapter 5.

CHAPTER 5

■ ■ ■

TMS Selection Framework

In this chapter, we will deal with

- The need for a structured and scientific selection process

- The value of a product selection framework

- Features of a product selection framework

- The importance of adopting industry best practices

- Preparation required before initiating product selection

The transportation management system (TMS) product market is crowded with the offerings of leading commercial off-the-shelf (COTS) product companies, boutiques, niche players, and segment specialists as well as enterprise resource planning (ERP) giants, such as SAP and Oracle. The majority of these products provide functionality of 50 percent or better of the full range of functionality one would hope for. Most were designed to cater to the needs of manufacturers/shippers. A few companies have also invested in solutions that address segment/vertical challenges better than those of other companies. However, many of the products still rely on older technology, have challenges in integration and scalability, and have not received an upgrade in decades. Some have remained conservative when it comes to creating a network of implementation and rollout partners. Implementations and rollouts carried out by such companies are therefore expensive and time-consuming. As a result, many buyers have lost patience and aborted their incomplete journey or suffered multifold cost overruns that did not justify investment, or both.

For several years, the 3PL industry did not draw the attention of many of these companies. 3PLs continued to invest in homegrown systems, with individual regions and profit centers building their own systems. Acquisitions and mergers further added to these complexities. Generally, mergers remained limited to high-level businesses, yet local systems remained The lack of corporate guidelines/direction concerning platform, technology, and integration resulted in these 3PLs' continuing on with hundreds or thousands of systems. Many leaders and tier 2 challengers have either drawn their IT landscape strategy or are in the advanced stages. A few are in talks with TMS product companies.

The potential benefits of using TMS products are increased reliability and stability, shorter development time, and reduced costs. Given the dynamic nature of the TMS marketplace, a number of parameters should be analyzed as 3PLs evaluate new TMS products and vendors. The success of a product largely depends on selection of the right product. Careful analysis of the capabilities and limitations of products is a must.

Selection should be made by a process of elimination. Eliminate products that do not meet your organization's requirements.

The objective of incorporating our TMS product selection framework in this book is to offer a comprehensive, easy-to-use, industry-proven guide that can help you select the most appropriate TMS product for your 3PL, one that can provide increased return on investment and long-term solutions.

The framework has the following core sections:

- Business Functionality

- Technical Compatibility

- Non-product Contributions

- Costs

The framework presents summaries by product and core section. The weight assigned to each core section is based on the experience of the authors in the area of logistics as well as corroboration by C-level executives of leading 3PLs.

The authors suggest a demonstration-based selection approach in which 3PLs, on their own or with the help of third-party experts or a consulting firm, prepare a profile that captures their current and future processes. The profile must include all exceptions and deviations as well as business rules and real data. Share the profile with product vendors, and ask them to demonstrate their product in terms of the profile. The demonstration plays an important role in the evaluation of business functionalities and most aspects of technical compatibility. It is highly recommended that internal agreement be reached as to the business processes to be mapped before contacting vendors.

Products offer best practice processes. Products represent a wealth of experience gained over years of implementation with different customers. Buyers should attempt to gain as much as they can from this experience. These best practices help buyers achieve operational efficiency, costs reduction, improved collaboration, and customer satisfaction. In the past, many buyers ignored this fact totally or partially, citing the expense entailed in alignment with best practice processes. These buyers therefore did not make use of most product functionalities. As a result, the buyers' return on investment was poor. Buyers should have a detailed understanding of these processes; carry out gap analysis between the industry best practices suggested for the selected product and their own current processes; prioritize these practices; and come up with a plan to implement them while the selected product is customized, configured, implemented, and rolled out. Implementation and rollout should follow the process changes, and not the other way around.

Business functionalities included in the framework capture an entire freight life cycle, from order to payment. In your analysis, you should include functionalities that are not presented here but that are typical of your business or your unique selling proposition (USP). Such functionalities may receive more weight, as they are critical to your business. If so, you will need to change the weight accordingly for the rest of the functionalities to keep the total at 100 percent. Emphasis must be given to your key and unique functional needs, while staying focused on capabilities to capture, using transactional data. Capability in the areas of planning, scheduling, reporting, visibility, event management, workflow, and notification must be analyzed with your own data.

Technical compatibility with the existing or proposed landscape plays a vital role in the selection of any product. The more specific you are (in terms of integration and technology), the smoother your future will be. Ignoring any aspect of technical compatibility may result in a major increase in maintenance costs, plus time taken to devise work-arounds.

Every aspect of non-product contribution is critical to implementation and thereafter.

The authors suggest the following steps before inviting product vendors for the product selection process:

- The sponsor identifies a core team.

- The core team, along with the sponsor, is to have a clear view of the changing business model and big-ticket changes that are part of your firm's vision.

- The core team includes technology and functional single points of contacts (SPOCs), in addition to other stakeholders.

- The core team identifies a functional SPOC from transportation planning, execution, customer service, finance, sales, and technology.

- The functional SPOC team details processes, including scenarios, deviations, exceptions, and business rules; this information is then shared with product vendors so that they have time to incorporate it in their product demonstration. The technology SPOC delineates platform-, environment-, and integration-related expectations for the new product.

- A short list no more than ten products for evaluation.

As part of the selection process, these steps are recommended:

- Invite shortlisted vendors to demonstrate how their product meets your requirements.

- Make use of the parameters of the TMS product selection framework for evaluation (see the tables in the section "TMS Product Selection Framework" later in this chapter).

- SPOCs evaluate each product separately.

- A summary of the evaluation is prepared.

- The product with higher scores is selected.

Business Functionality

Evaluation of business functionality is vital to the success of the product selection process. It is the tendency of product companies to create hype about their products' functionality. Never go by the company's promotional material; check things out on your own. The best way to do this is by inviting companies to demonstrate their offerings and clearly show how they are relevant to your business. Some products may have functionalities that are not required by your organization. Make sure you do not discount these wares simply because you are not yet ready for them or do not anticipate needing them. Your organization may change and evolve, either because of challenges it encounters or because of its vision and goals, and if your core team is not , and knowledgeable about the firm's mission, it may not give adequate attention to the product demonstration. As a result, your company may miss an opportunity for future growth.

TMS Product Selection Framework

The product selection framework that follows contains parameters with respect to the business and technical functionalities on which the product may be evaluated. The framework also has parameters for assessing the product company. These parameters will assist you in selecting a product that meets your organization's requirements (see Figures 5-1–5-5).

						Product 1		Product 2		Product 3		Product 4		Product 5	
Feature	Parameters	Rating Rationale	Scale	Weightage		Rating	Score	Rating	Score	Rating	Score	Rating	Score	Rating	Score
Transport Planning	Modes of transport	Ability to handle Road, Ability to handle Sea, Ability to handle Inland waterway, Ability to handle Rail, Ability to handle Air	0 - 1	1%											
	Multiple time zones support	Departure time in local time	0 - 1	1%											
	Types of Transport support	Groupage, Bulk, Distribution network Management	0 - 1	1%											
	Ability to store, update and maintain	vehicle, Driver, Service Provider details	0 - 1	1%											
	Mode selection and Optimisation	Consolidation of loads and decision on mode and carriage type, Assigning shipments to a truck based on service level agreements with customers	0 - 1	1%											
	Vendor Contract Management	Obligations of terms / conditions agreed in contract documentation handling, operational performance for carrier management	0 - 5	3%											
	Customer contract management	lane wise/ slab wise contracts - vehicle wise/ product wise, Basis of Freight Rate (Rate Matrix :- zone, lane, slab etc.)	0 - 5	3%											
	Route Planning & Scheduling	optimal transport routes for order delivery	0 - 1	1%											
	Trip Planning	Based on Geographical maps. Defines the actual roads that will be driven	0 - 1	1%											
	Automated carrier selection	Selects most suitable carrier to execute the trip	0 -1	1%											
	Vehicle and Driver scheduling	Allocation of vehicles and drivers to planned loads/ routes	0 - 1	1%											
	Simulation on cost/time options	simulations on performance indicators for distance costs, utilization of equipment, other resources	0 - 1	1%											
	Landed cost calculation	Direct transportation costs, legal costs(octroi, toll), handling (cross docking cost)	0 - 1	1%											
	Transport Planning with fleet planning	Synergies in Transport planning and fleet planning	0 - 1	1%											
	Transport Planning with warehouse planning	Synergies in Transport planning and warehouse planning	0 - 1	1%											
	Vehicle maintenance management	Maintenance Scheduling, Preventive and Breakdown maintenance	0 - 1	1%											

Figure 5-1. *Product Selection Framework: Business Functionality (Part 1)*

						Product 1		Product 2		Product 3		Product 4		Product 5	
Feature	Parameters	Rating Rationale	Scale	Weightage		Rating	Score	Rating	Score	Rating	Score	Rating	Score	Rating	Score
Transport Execution	Booking process	Indent receipt, Consignment Note Creation, Loading sheet	0 - 5	10%											
	Delivery process	Vehicle Arrival Information creation, Recording details of Condition of Received Goods etc..., Delivery runsheet	0 - 5	10%											
	Consignment Tracking	Tracking/ Tracing consignment across the distribution network	0 - 5	5%											
	Reverse Logistics / Repairs	Tracking/ Tracing returned goods across the distribution network, complaints processing, credit memo processing, warranty claim processing, complaints and returns analysis	0 - 5	8%											
	Transhipment of Cargo	Arrange first leg transport, Vehicle arrival, Shipment Receipt, Prepare Manifest / VHC, Transship goods, Transship hub records updation	0 - 5	8%											
	Workflow management	Support of business processes in triggering alerts / workflows for TMS events, Flexibility of configuring user defined alerts/ workflows	0 - 1	3%											
	Claims Management	Insurance documentation handling for accident/ fire/ damages	0 - 1	2%											
	Vendor / Service providers' Invoices	Compliance with TDS, VAT and other tax laws, Allocation of common costs on a shipment across consignment notes, Ability to track ATH and BTH against a VHC, Additional charges incurred at destination to be captured against shipment	0 - 5	3%											
	Customer Billing and Reports	Tax compliance on billing, Billing on confirmation of delivery, Option to schedule billing on a weekly/ daily basis, Fixed price billing to be done automatically each month. Report : Customer-wise sales, cost of sales and margins at each distribution terminal. Report : A single report stating consignment note number, customer invoice number, revenue, VHC doc number, vehicle hire charges, additional charges at destination, allocated common costs	0 - 5	3%											
	Preprinted documents issuance process and flow	BO creates requisitions, Central documents department to corporate for new documents, Corporate process team changes format based on needs, Layouts send to printer and documents received at CDD	0 - 1	3%											

Figure 5-2. *Product Selection Framework: Business Functionality (Part 2)*

Business Functionality					Product 1		Product 2		Product 3		Product 4		Product 5	
Feature	Parameters	Rating Rationale	Scale	Weightage	Rating	Score	Rating	Score	Rating	Score	Rating	Score	Rating	Score
Performance Monitoring and control	Trip auditor	Registration of preprinted stationery Allocation to the RO Allocation to the Terminal Allocation to the user	0 - 1	1%										
	Payment processing	Ability to handle user specific requirements (e.g. transportation rates, weight etc.)	0 - 1	1%										
	Tracking of cargo, truck	Ability of making the status information available to partners	0 - 1	2%										
	Transportation, cargo optimisation	Ability to perform (truck scheduling, route planning, cargo loading)	0 - 1	2%										
	Transport documentation	Export Cargo Shipment Instruction CMR forms (road consignment notes) CIM forms (rail consignment notes) Air Waybills (air consignment notes) Sea Waybills Bills of Lading Standard Shipping Note Dangerous Goods Note	0 - 5	6%										
	Customer interfaces	agreements on rates, charges invoice creation accounts receivable processing	0 - 1	1%										
	Transporter interfaces	Subcontracting invoices, charges	0 - 1	1%										
	Dashboard/ Performance Management	Flexible Operational reporting Key performance indicator reporting capability Business Intelligence for company wide reporting Support for wide array of chart types (bar, line, gauge, scatterplot, maps) Aggregate data from disparate systems into a single view Support for multiple data sources supports Multiple export formats: Excel, PDF, XML, HTML and CSV	0 - 5	10%										
New Roles	3PL in a 4 PL role	LSP may execute all the above logistics activities in-house, under subcontract, or outsource all activites and act as a Logistics Manager(4 PL) in the pursuit for completing a	0 - 1	1%										
			Total	100%										

Figure 5-3. *Product Selection Framework: Business Functionality (Part 3)*

Technical Compatibility					Product 1		Product 2		Product 3		Product 4		Product 5	
Feature	Parameters	Scale	Weightage		Rating	Score	Rating	Score	Rating	Score	Rating	Score	Rating	Score
Transportation Management System														
Architecture/Non functional Requirements	Customization support (provide details of tools / GUI	0 - 5	16%											
	SOA compliance	0 - 5	17%											
	Type of architecture (N Tier), Client support - Web / Client-server / Legacy	0 - 5	17%											
	Brief on redistribution of business component among technical architecture	0 - 5	10%											
	Performance benchmark details- workload profile, concurrent users	0 - 5	10%											
	Security provision - Data & functional	0 - 5	10%											
	Scalability approach - Ease of evaluation	0 - 5	10%											
	Disaster recovery approach	0 - 5	10%											
	Total		100%											
Hardware Support Range	Hardware support required / supported	0 - 5	20%											
	Recommended OS (product best runs on XX Platform with XX OS)	0 - 5	20%											
	Storage Requirements	0 - 5	15%											
	Software Infrastructure needed (App/ Web servers etc)	0 - 5	20%											
	Database supported	0 - 5	25%											
	Total		100%											
Integration	Integration approaches with Enterprise Applications (ERP etc)	0 - 5	18%											
	Integration Approach - Web service, EDI, XML	0 - 5	16%											
	Integration Approach - Details on readymade adapters	0 - 5	18%											
	Integration Approach - How many current installation has integration with leading	0 - 5	30%											
	ODBC compliance	0 - 5	18%											
	Total		100%											
Others	Multichannel support (Web & Mobile)	0 - 5	40%											
	Error Handling Approach	0 - 5	30%											
	Brief on Technical interoperability approach	0 - 5	30%											

Figure 5-4. *Product Selection Framework: Technical Compatibility*

	Parameter	Rating Rationale	Scale	Weightage	Product 1		Product 2		Product 3		Product 4		Product 5	
					Rating	Score	Rating	Score	Rating	Score	Rating	Score	Rating	Score
Transportation Management System														
Stability & Performance	Company's overall revenue (Global , country of interest)	Figure	0 - 5	40%										
	Total no of employees (Globally and country of interest)	Number	0 - 5	20%										
	Details of quality certifications (CMMi, ISO etc)	Details	0 - 5	20%										
	Awards WON in last five years	Details	0 - 5	20%										
	Total			100%										
Industry Experience	Number of years in TMS product business (global and country of interest))	Years	0 - 5	40%										
	Large customers (Global and country of interest) - TMS product specific	Number	0 - 5	30%										
	Implementation / reference sites available in the country of interest)	Names of client	0 - 5	30%										
	Total			100%										
Presence in country of interest	Location details in country of interest (HQ, Regional offices, support offices Etc)	Location	0 - 5	30%										
	Product support availability in country of interest	Yes/No	0 - 5	30%										
	TMS installation by country of interest-LSP clients	Number	0 - 5	40%										
				100%										
Ease of Use	Usability by operators and associates on the shop floor	Number	0 - 5	100%										

Figure 5-5. *Product Selection Framework: Non-product Contributions*

Summary

Selection of the TM product best suited to your organization is a priority and a major milestone in making your technology landscape more reliable, stable, and able to achieve higher return on investment. Before initiating the project journey, however, you need to have a clear idea of your organization's vision goals, and business case. The first step in your journey is the preparatory phase, in which you identify a core team and SPOCS to document your business's processes and establish an implementation and rollout strategy. When choosing a product (and afterward), keep in mind that products provide best-practice processes. Do not ignore them, or your firm may risk losing its competitive edge. By making use of our product selection framework, you are ensuring selection of an appropriate TM product. It is always advisable to add to the standard functionalities contained in our framework those functionalities that are unique to your business.

Now that you have selected a product, we will give you some tips on how to implement it. The next chapter serves as a guide to implementing TM, particulary SAP TM.

CHAPTER 6

Industry Best Practices for Implementation, Rollout, and Maintenance of SAP TM

In this chapter, we will discuss the following:

- Approaches for speedy and effective implementation of SAP TM

- The value of organizational preparedness

- The need for strong executive sponsorship

- The importance of documented processes, business case, and training

- Key success factors

- Living with SAP TM

Organizations planning on replacing legacy systems that are unable to keep up with growing business requirements with a state-of-the-art integrated solution, such as SAP TM, are always looking to find answers to a variety of questions relating to the solution, such as its necessity, its functionalities and, more important, how it can meet the firm's needs. Best practices and effective approaches for speedy and effective implementation are other considerations (see Figure 6-1).

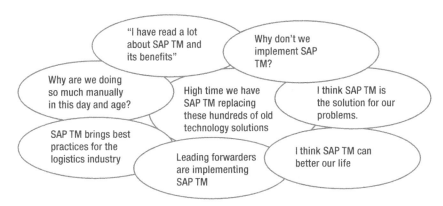

Figure 6-1. *A discussion on selection of SAP TM*

Having seen a few SAP TM implementations and rollouts, we believe that the process is a journey. The success of this journey depends on your firm's approach. Some organizations have come at it as an organizational transformation initiative. Other organizations have treated it as just one more information technology (IT) project. We believe that it is an important transformation initiative, not the responsibility of any one department or individual. The change involves a lot more than just installing a software product. SAP TM, as a supply chain execution platform, is a core system for 3PLs. The preparation required for such a large initiative may need to begin two to three years prior. Before implementing this system, organizations must have clear answers to fundamental questions such as these:

- Why is such a transformation required? Does this transformation align with our vision for the next decade?

- What are the key success factors?

- What does our competition look like?

- Do we have strong executive sponsorship?

- Do we have a sufficient budget planned for such a transformation?

- Do we meet all critical requirements in our functional areas for this implementation?

- Are all of the processes relating to our unique selling proposition (USP) documented?

- Are we equipped to handle such a large change at every organizational level?

- Do we need an expert's guidance for this journey? Do we have access to such an expert if needed?

- Have we identified key resources from each area, and can we spare them for this process?

- Do we have the bandwidth to manage training needs?

- Do we have a defined IT strategy?

Depending on the answers to these questions, you can judge whether your organization is ready for a transformation of this magnitude or if more preparation is needed. How the organization will keep moving forward after the transformation must be thought out before initiation of the preparatory phase of any transformation as well.

Poorly managed transformations tend to receive the kind of feedback illustrated in Figure 6-2.

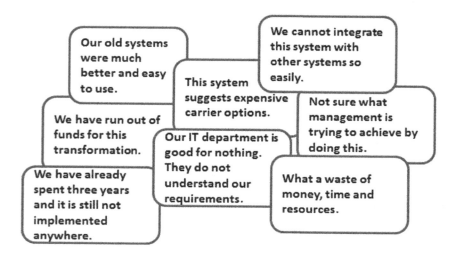

Figure 6-2. *Feedback on a poorly managed transformation*

It is our aim to help you avoid a situation that would invite comments such as these. We are hopeful that our suggestions in this chapter will ensure that your organization's journey is a smooth one.

Implementation is the act of accomplishing an objective. To begin, you have to know what your firm's goals are and how practical the aims are that you are trying to achieve.

Where does your organization want to go? How ready is it to embark on this journey? What are the practical steps that will enable it to reach its destination? How do you create an organization-wide culture of continual change in order to stay on top for the long haul?

In replacing your organization's systems approach, you want an integrated, functionally rich, growth-supportive business management solution that is capable of bringing about greater productivity and effective communication within the organization's ecosystem. The first step toward this end destination is the preparatory phase.

Preparatory Phase

When does your organization begin implementation? If your answer is today, it is doubtful that you will be successful. Implementation of this magnitude requires a great deal of preparation. Let's look at some of the key tasks.

Obtain executive commitment (directly proportional to success)

Is executive commitment important to this initiative? The answer is obviously yes, because otherwise nothing will progress. Executive commitment is crucial to delivering expected results on schedule and within budget. Knowing your project sponsor, and his or her managerial style, is critical.

Many project sponsors do not spend sufficient time on the project. As a chief information officer (CIO), however, you cannot afford to have a disconnected executive sponsor. Ensure that you engage the sponsor from the kickoff to the end—this can mean the difference between success and failure. Communicate clearly with your sponsor; the best project sponsors make themselves available. Your sponsor must appreciate that the sponsor's role is to authorize the project and that your role is to execute it. The sponsor must therefore let the project managers manage the project without getting into the day-to-day particulars themselves.

It is of the utmost importance that you obtain everyone's full commitment up front, because once the project starts; doing so is twice as hard. Typically, executives will say that they support any initiative with a sound return on investment, but then they do not back that up when it comes to allocating the money and resources that are required to make an initiative a success. Obtaining executives' time to resolve problems, for example, can be difficult. We have seen many demoralized, unmotivated project teams result from half-hearted executive support. Often, you start to wonder if your executive sponsor has had a change of heart. We suggest that unless a valid rationale is provided for such behavior, you should stay focused on the project's goals. It is also a good idea to remind the sponsor about the commitment made at the start of the project by making small presentations periodically on the project's achievements and what is left to accomplish.

It is good practice to have the project sponsor begin the kickoff meeting by clearly communicating the business case for the initiative, backed by goals and objectives, benefits, and the vision, so that everyone knows their responsibilities and the kind of contribution expected. Involving the project sponsor in building the project plan will ensure that it is complete and detailed.

Build a business case for positive return on investment

The rationale behind building a business case is to clearly ask for the money and resources required to support a specific business need. Business needs may entail improving system performance; achieving greater customer satisfaction; or increasing profits, lowering costs, or reducing processing time. Benefits can be quantifiable or not. Make sure you have a sound business case that details the background of the project, expected benefits, options available, reasons for short-listing a particular objective, expected costs, risks, and resource requirements. A business case is a collection not only of data, but also of positive and negative opinions and views from relevant stakeholders.

Why do we require building a business case? We do so because a scientific approach to your problem definition always helps. A new SAP TM system provides your organization with fresh opportunities to use and refine new business processes; the business case–building exercise is your first chance to introduce these new areas. Discuss existing processes, business drivers, areas of difficulty, improvement areas, competitors, anticipated impact of changes, and people to be affected. Analyze the historical data to ascertain missed opportunities and wrong assumptions and to suggest a to-be landscape. Assess costs, resources, and time required to realize the ideal scope.

As mentioned earlier, as a CIO, you should help the project sponsor build a sound business case. Comprehensive data collection and analysis together form the first step in planning any initiative of this magnitude. Your team can help educate your organization's business professionals about next-generation technologies that can solve their problems. Organize demonstrations of solution/product vendors if required.

As a transformation leader, you need to work with your sponsor to craft a presentation that gives a complete picture (see Figure 6-3). This should include the scope of the project, potential savings, areas of improvement, possible risks, and challenges (including the support required in terms of time, money, and resources). The presentation should focus on improving the bottom line and on how the initiative can help the organization reach its business objectives, making the benefits clear. Tie benefits to profit, cash flow, and so on. Ideally, you should present a scenario for return on investment. Address executives' concerns, such as whether you can achieve your goal in a reasonable period of time and whether it is even attainable. As the owner of the business case and guardian of the investors' interests, the project sponsor must be the one to secure buy-in from every stakeholder.

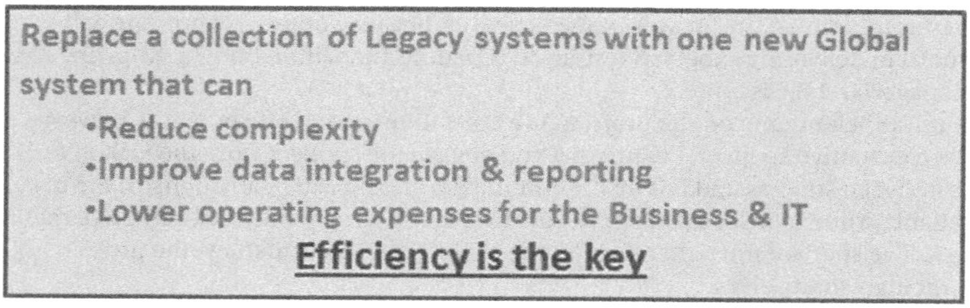

Replace a collection of Legacy systems with one new Global system that can
- Reduce complexity
- Improve data integration & reporting
- Lower operating expenses for the Business & IT
Efficiency is the key

Figure 6-3. *Key drivers for investing in a new, global system*

Set goals, manage by objectives

Before beginning the project, it is important to set goals for each of the following stages of the life cycle:

- Design
- Construction
- Testing
- Deployment

Build the scenario—engage people in your dream

Storytelling is a good way to share messages. Your project sponsor can use this proven tool to share his or her vision and to communicate what you as a team plan on doing, how you are going to accomplish this, what the plan will mean to others, what help you need, who is helping you, how will this affect others in the short and long term, and so on. The project sponsor should conduct workshops, outlining the key individuals involved and inviting people performing different roles to speak. Your project sponsor's aim should be to spread awareness and gain organizational support from every corner of the business in order to minimize internal challenges.

Create a task force—your ambassadors of change

Consider pulling the best talent from various teams to create a task force that will work on accomplishing the common goal. The right mix of talent can give you a quick start and continued success throughout the journey and thereafter. Enlist resources from different levels, making sure to include senior and experienced individuals. Never insist on only the most experienced team members, however. Younger people may provide energy and optimism; veterans may offer insights gained from experience. Often, veterans run the risk of losing touch with what's happening at lower levels of the organization. You will need input as well from those who have a broader view of things.

From this task force, create the following four groups:

- **Steering committee** (two to three members): To facilitate, monitor, and guide the rest of the teams.

- **Change control board** (three to four members): To review and approve changes to the scope.

- **Selection committee** (four to five members): To select the appropriate solution.

- **Project teams and leadership**: Choose a program manager and project leaders for every project team. The project team at the corporate office and the regional project teams should have one subject matter expert (SME) for every process/functional area. We suggest that you colocate (at least initially) the first three groups in order to gain maximum efficiency from them. Periodically relieve the project teams and selection committee of their regular responsibilities. Organize some games and informal workshops for them to build a sense of belonging to a team that is working on a common cause. Workshops conducted by external faculty are a good way to motivate teams and obtain maximum contribution. Monetary incentives are not necessary, but other types of rewards and recognition may have a positive impact.

Train the selection committee

Should the selection committee receive training? The answer is a big yes, as this committee, in the absence of structured training, will be more apt to make bad choices. Many organizations underestimate this important need. Often, choosing a transportation management–centric system is a multimillion-dollar, multiyear decision affecting the entire organization. This certainly demands extensive training in team building, decision-making, assessment, and soft skills. It is advisable that the selection committee undergo training on how to work together, make group decisions, and analyze needs at both the central and local level.

Ensure resource commitment—nothing in life comes for free

Generally, when a corporate initiative launches, people in the branch offices, terminals, and support functions tend to believe that it is the responsibility of the corporate technology team to implement the system and that this team will send someone from the head office to do so. Remember that the success of any initiative is realized when the end organization are brought on board appropriately. Besides the champions in the task force, in which commitment is long-term, you must also have commitment from branch and regional offices and terminals as well as support function teams before you start the project. To get this commitment, you may conduct regional-level workshops, in which you should invite participation from the smallest of your locations and support functions.

Manage change management

Your transformation initiative may have an impact on the way you deal with your customers and vendors. Changes made as a result of the new model, systems, processes, or strategy must be communicated clearly and at an appropriate time and outline how the customers/vendors will be affected in the changed scenario. The group that will be affected the most is your employees. Make sure every employee, irrespective of designation, role, location, seniority, and skill set, is made aware of the changes. Communicate this information to employees up front, and conduct workshops on the transformation initiative. People must gain an understanding of why the change in strategy or in culture is needed and how it will affect them, covering in particular modifications in their roles, responsibilities, location, and teams. Any change is likely to be seen as political, and as employees will be critical in carrying out your firm's initiative, clear communication with them at appropriate times and intervals is suggested. People generally perceive change negatively in the beginning. This is when, besides a central team managing the change, the respective managers must actively contribute toward it. To realize benefits from such a major investment, an integrated technology, process, and awareness of people's needs are of importance.

Do not expect everything will change—set expectations

You have been in the business for some time now. You have been making changes since you started, to comply with regulations, adapt to changing business requirements, or create differentiation. All this is either captured in one of the systems or is part of the manual work being carried out by your teams. The nature of these changes may have been at a global, regional, or branch level. Perhaps some of the changes that evolved over the years are documented, and others are not. A baseline version that captures these changes and decisions and their descriptions should be your starting point. You may also have some other helpful features, such as suggestions from users on adjusting to a new environment. As an unwritten rule, do not expect everything to undergo change in one round—certainly not at the magnitude we are discussing. No one solution can give you everything, and customization (major or minor) may be required. Therefore, internally you need to clearly set expectations in terms of what is achievable and which items are set aside, either for the time being or indefinitely. Acceptance from users will likely be greater if they are aware of what to expect from the transformation.

Manage risk early on

Can you afford to put such a project at risk? Obviously not. But, you cannot have a project without risk, and even a small risk can get out of control and become a major hurdle in optimally delivering the project. Therefore, it is very important to identify potential risks at an early stage, analyze them thoroughly, and initiate appropriate preventive measures to avoid them. Deviations, short supply, idle time, inadequate communication, lack of preparedness, and overruns are some of the risks you should be able to identify easily.

Build a global process repository—include local requirements

Business processes lay the foundation for your business. Organizations that practice standardization of processes across the organization are more successful than their counterparts that do not. For a multinational logistics company, process complexities may increase because

- The organization has its own operations in some countries; agents (some dedicated, some not), or a combination of an agent and a partner, working on behalf of it in other countries; and partners in remaining countries and locations of the network

- The system landscape is not the same at every location

- The processes are different

- The level of automation is different

- Regulatory requirements differ from place to place

- Many processes are not documented, or, if they are documented, they are incomplete or outdated

- No central team has been appointed to control the version or approve changes

As a result of this, process understanding at each location may be different. But, with respect to the transformation initiative, the firm needs to do the following:

- Have a globally standardized process, with localization (permissible only in the case of statutory or compliance requirement) in documented form and controlled at a central location by a central process custodian, the chief process officer (CPO) team

- Ensure that changes have been made to its processes to accommodate what it seeks to accomplish

- Create a site or a link on its knowledge portal, where everyone can easily refer to process documentation (provide read-only access only); right to update should be retained by the central process custodians

- Make the CPO team responsible for retaining version control, with any changes requiring the team's approval

- Capture these processes in a content/document management tool and, if possible, in a business process–mapping tool

- Use the latest version of SAP TM to map processes

- Share any change to processes with the change control board; it should be the board's prerogative to include it at the time of ongoing implementation or to put it aside for the next release

- Engage a third party to study, analyze, and build global processes

- Identify process champions from planning, execution, order management, scheduling, hub, terminal, branches, and all the support functions, if they are not already part of the CPO team; engage these champions early on

- Identify processes that will be affected by implementation of a new solution, and spend extra time standardizing them

It may also be desirable to keep a record of the time taken to perform/complete processes—if not all, at least the key ones, from an operational and customer-facing perspective.

Have clear interface requirements

Now that you know which processes will be affected by implementation of a new solution, we recommend that you identify every single interface requirement of these processes, with respect to give-and-take of data, frequency, use, size, volume, and current mechanism. This will help you in every step of the journey, whether it be selection (if not already made), building a conference room pilot, or testing rollouts. Gathering information on challenges faced during interfacing is also helpful.

Identify events

Event notification is assumed to be part of a main service, and your organization's ability to share events is one of the key criteria on which it is judged. Many of your competitors may be struggling to capture important events and therefore unable to share them. This is a golden opportunity to set things in order for your organization. We suggest that you hold a workshop for departments such as customer service, business development, operations, field, asset management, and accounts receivable to agree on events for which capture and notification of parties are needed. As a rule, information that requires action from someone, closes a loop, or is an intimation to someone needs to be tracked. Make sure to have this information recorded in process documents, in the appropriate locations.

Identify workflow

Workflow plays an important role in informing concerned parties of the need to act. You should have a workflow for time-sensitive tasks to improve your service levels, reduce communication costs, and resolve issues in a timely manner. List all time-sensitive tasks, identifying the people to be notified and the action expected. You may also want to tie this in with your process documents.

Use reports, key performance indicators, dashboards

You may be currently using a tool for your reports. The new system can provide most of them, and more. You need to keep an inventory of reports on your organization's processes as well as the distribution list agreed on. Moreover, you may use this opportunity to look into these reports to see if any can be consolidated or eliminated altogether. You will also want to identify key performance indicators by process, creating a matrix of tasks or activities, by role, for the dashboard.

Clean the master data

Can you guarantee clean master data at any given point in time? You may want to say yes, but you know the real answer. Organizations are spending a lot of time and money to get a single version of master data. A disciplined approach is required to maintain the purity of this data. As a CIO, it is your responsibility to ensure quality master data on people, places, things, and concepts available for implementation. Duplicate records, confusion over what master data are and how they are qualified, and absence of a central team responsible for creation and maintenance of master data can add to the challenge. However, with SAP TM Supply Chain Execution (SCE) platform implementation, master data serve as a key asset. First, they are almost always involved in transactional and analytical operations. Second, users performing different processes across your organization use them. You should clean master data, augmenting and synchronizing them with applications identified for replacement with the new SAP TM–centric solution, respective business processes, and reporting requirements before starting the implementation journey.

Role-based access control (RBAC)—one who creates cannot approve

Identify all roles and responsibilities. Based on roles and responsibilities for a process or part of any process, grant users access to the relevant menu of the new solution. Also, clearly identify rights to create, view, and modify. During data collection, you may come across situations in which your current systems allow users to both create a record and approve it. To avoid this with the new solution, you must clearly document segregation of duties (Doc-RBAC + SOD).

Validate the solution against architecture guiding principles

Your organization may have adopted guiding principles with respect to its architecture and design aspects. The new solution must receive validation against these guiding principles. Any deviation must be understood and its impact, reviewed and agreed on. You should discuss this openly with a solution provider, make him or her aware of any deviation, and find a work-around before moving forward with the new solution.

Decide on an implementation strategy—manageable, in stages

You know your organization well—its program execution strength, challenges, potential internal risks in implementing a new global solution, and support it will receive. Based on all this, you, along with your project sponsor, and the task force or steering committee, must decide on an implementation strategy up front. Having this in place gives confidence to the entire team and to others working on the initiative. More important, you can prioritize, plan ahead, communicate better, and gain the confidence of the business community early on. Following are two strategies:

- Create a global template for accomplishing all your goals at once (big bang adoption).

- Build a global template to be done in stages, aligned to one of the following variables. For example, using the process variable, in the first stage, you may take an order to cash for full container load (FCL) ocean freight or an international air exports business scenario.

- Process

- Functionality

- Mode of transport

- Commodity handled

- Region or cluster

- Stability of legacy systems

- Line of business

- Business volume

For more details on big bang adoption, see the section "Implementation."

Select a product (if you haven't already)

Your selection committee has a tough task in finalizing a product solution. Our product selection framework is an attempt to make your committee's job a bit easier. The committee needs to consider all factors at the time of product selection, including a multimillion dollar, multiyear initiative; a solution to be used for a decade at minimum; evolving technology; ever-demanding customers; increasing cost of maintaining the technology landscape; possessiveness of users toward existing systems; and stiff competition. The committee must also analyze the impact of the new product solution on the remaining technology landscape and ensure that the new product offers all that is best in the old systems, whether it be functionality, ease of navigation, or small utilities.

We suggest that your selection team spend sufficient time on this. With choice of the wrong solution come all the issues thereafter. The selection committee should refer to various research reports and attend product seminars and industry events to collect data on options available in the market. The committee needs to engage very closely with solution providers in order to ascertain their vision, road map, focus on innovation, architecture, domain understanding, commitment, and financial details. Conducting a conference pilot is a good way to assess the solution.

Learn from previous experience

Does your organization have a mechanism for capturing knowledge gained from previous projects or initiatives—what went wrong, and why; how you overcame it; whether you kept it from recurring? If you have captured this information, is it made available for reference? Using such information can help you reduce risks to your new initiative. Organize a workshop to discuss this knowledge to ensure that mistakes from the past are not repeated and that the right actions are built on. If this knowledge is not documented—that is, if you do not have a mechanism for capture in place—your task is a difficult one; you must develop a mechanism for this new initiative.

Inventory systems to be replaced

The new solution will replace one or more of the many current applications. These applications have served your purposes for several years. They have good features that you may want to retain in the new solution. Most valuable are your data. Before you start your new initiative, you must have a clear decommissioning strategy in place, addressing when and how they will be decommissioned. The mapping of features to be retained in the new solution and data migration decisions should be in place. Interfaces both with internal systems and with the outside world should be documented and made available in the new solution as well. Ensure that you have an inventory of every system, application, interface, and database, indicating who is currently managing it, and from where, before you start implementation of a new solution.

Identify SI partners

Your organization may not have the resources and skills required to implement a new solution. With limited resources, implementation will take longer. You therefore need to engage an SI partner to prepare a blueprint; create a global template, with rollouts; and support release management. You may decide to engage more than one SI vendor. Some organizations opt to have one for the global template and initial rollouts and keep a dedicated one for rollouts and perhaps another for release management (this is in addition to the product vendor support you will require for creating a global template). Begin identifying SIs with experience in designing, implementing, and rolling out large solutions. Focus on the transportation industry and SAP TM competency building. You should give preference to SIs with experience implementing SAP TM 9.0, but you do not have many to choose from. You also have the option of engaging the SAP AG transportation business unit and consulting team for building a global template.

Select the implementation team

The team involved in building and implementing the global template must have experienced and knowledgeable consultants. The implementation team may comprise internal consultants, SAP AG, and the SI partner or subcontractors, as SAP TM consultants are in short supply.

Establish project teams

The steering committee identifies project teams, with representatives from sales, customer service, operations, rating, planning, carrier and vendor relations teams, purchasing, billing, pricing, costing, accounting, and technology. Project team members must have a sound understanding of processes, procedures, deviations, exceptions, reporting requirements, and data exchange requirements in their subject area and have been active system users with hands-on experience and knowledge of the current systems' capabilities as well as limitations. Members of the steering committee and the project sponsor communicate the project's goals and objectives to the project teams.

Implementation

Your organization is now ready for SAP TM solution implementation. You have completed most of the preparatory tasks discussed. You have followed a scientific framework to select an SAP TM solution. Remember that implementing an SAP TM solution is not as simple as implementing a module—it is equivalent to replacing most of your landscape. You must therefore stay focused on your organization's goals and objectives throughout. The slightest loss of focus could have an adverse impact on costs, schedule, and benefits as well as invite new risks and challenges to the initiative.

In recent years, SAP TM solution implementations were mainly carried out for a single process, function, or mode of transport. But, with integrated SAP 9.0 (SAP, SAP Event Management [SAP EM], SAP Extended Warehouse Management [SAP EWM], and SAP Global Trade Services [SAP GTS]), easy integration with business intelligence (BI), and ready availability of FICO, we now suggest that you go for big bang adoption. First, take a few representative countries from your network, and implement a global template. Upon successful implementation of the template in these pilot countries, roll it out in the rest of the countries in your network. Decide on a maximum of two countries, chosen by world region, for implementing a global template. We recommend a cap of five countries for pilot global template implementation, with the following attributes:

- High volume
- High complexity of business
- Maximum usage of existing systems
- Superset of functionalities required to run business
- The aim of the pilot is to
- Verify that the solution meets the business requirements, goals, and objectives set at the start of the project
- Generate a yes or no decision on rolling out the solution in other countries

You have decided to go ahead with implementation. Whatever your strategy, implementation consists of these stages:

- Discovery and planning
- Design and configuration
- Development
- Testing
- Deployment
- Functional releases and ongoing support

Let's discuss each of these in detail.

Discovery and Planning

Discovery and planning activities start during sales discussion, directly with SAP AG or SI partner. The program manager is expected to involve all stakeholders (steering committee, project leadership, vendor representatives, architecture and product team from a solution provider), get their views, and take note of the constraints and limitations to building a detailed implementation project plan. The project sponsor should kick off the project. At the kickoff meeting, the sponsor should explain that, as part of the project team, the best resources from every subject area have been identified to determine the optimal way to implement the solution. A practical and achievable project plan will act as a guideline throughout implementation.

This stage may last six to ten weeks for every pilot country (we suggest that you run this in parallel), depending on the scope. During this time, the implementation team should engage in discussion with the project team and project sponsor/steering committee in order to advance understanding of these aspects of the project:

- Business domain, model, and logic; to-be processes, with deviations and exceptions; standard operating procedures and events; entities; actors; roles and responsibilities; reporting requirements; interfacing needs; areas of difficulty with current systems; and so on

- Repository of processes, events, interfaces, workflows and reporting, key performance indicators, and dashboard documents

- Vision, expectations, goals, customer needs, and system capabilities as well as other parallel initiatives, if any

Based on the discussions and knowledge gained, the implementation team should

- Construct a project plan in agreement with the project team

- Document the process understanding

- Formulate a potential solution (out-of-the-box functionalities of SAP TM, customization, adaptation to best practices of SAP TM)

- Underline the gaps between the new system and project scope or areas that will require a work-around

- Identify the risks that could push the implementation date, along with steps to mitigate them

Design and Configuration

In this stage the project team and implementation team translate the requirements into potential configuration options in SAP TM. Working closely with the project team, the implementation team should establish configurations and implementation strategies that will be used in the development stage of the project. The following steps are involved:

- Review the master data.

- Train the project team.

- Demonstrate (and walk through) a possible end-to-end business scenario or process.

- Establish a solution configuration, and create a prototype.

- Validate against (Doc-RBAC, SOD).

- Build help for users by documenting procedures to be followed for each function of the SAP TM solution. Having readily available guidelines will help reduce guesswork. Most large-scale implementations face the challenge of losing members of the initial project team; therefore, you must insist on comprehensive documented procedures from the implementation and project team.

Development

In the development stage, you prepare the system to go live by performing the following activities:

- Document items requiring development, as identified in the discovery stage.

- Plan for development, including environment and testing.

- Migrate data, and validate against requirements.

- Develop a user-training manual.

- Customize for identified gaps to build, deploy, and test features, including new processes, screens, reports, and interfaces.

- Configure the system to go live, and load masters and various setups.

- Run a conference room pilot. The implementation team should run an entire to-be process cycle to validate and confirm the design and behavior of the system and whether it meets the business's requirements.

- Allow the project team to play with the new system. The project team should use its own data to study and train on the system. The team should also test scenarios in order to verify that the system configuration is in accordance with project goals.

- Have the implementation and project teams certify for go-live testing.

- Develop training material for end users.

Testing

The objectives of this stage are to confirm that the new solution is functionally aligned with global template requirements, help the implementation team fine-tune configuration, and gain end users' confidence in the system. Some of the key activities to be performed during this stage are as follows:

- Identify users for user acceptance testing (UAT).

- Prepare the UAT plan.

- Develop test scenarios.

- Load the master and dynamic data.

- Run system testing.

- Through testing, adjust the configuration in test as well as the live system.

- Establish a cutover strategy.

- Run a final conference room pilot.

- Deliver the end-user training material.

Deployment

Based on the results from the testing stage, the project team and implementation team make the final go-no-go decision. Prior to going live, you need to carry out these tasks:

- Train end users, and assess their proficiency.

- Perform final evaluation of the system (project and implementation teams).

- Migrate to the new system.

- Load data, and validate against the old systems.

- Confirm interface functioning.

- Start using the new system from a specific date.

- Close incomplete transactions in the old systems; do not carry them forward in the new system.

- Optimize the new system.

Functional Releases and Ongoing Support

In this stage, you provide support for the global template that has been implemented. If any new functional releases are planned, and the first two stages of global template building have already been carried out, then the remaining stages (development, testing, deployment of new functionalities) are managed by the implementation team, if available, or retrograded by rollout teams. If the duration of implementation is increased, and both the implementation and rollout teams have moved on from the project, support is then best handled by the release management team or an ongoing support team.

Rollout

Having successfully implemented the global template in a handful of pilot countries, in mature markets that carry out the most complex, high-volume business in your network, you should be satisfied with your choice of solution and implementation methodology and your organizational preparedness for such a large transformation. You now want to increase your satisfaction by rolling out this solution in other countries.

Rollout consists of these high-level stages

- Country preparation

- Local adaptation

- Realization

- Final preparation

- Going live

- Hypercare

As you approach the go-live of the global template in pilot countries, you need to start planning for rollouts in the next set of countries identified for rollout. The first step is to create a rollout manual based on your experience in the pilot. It is advisable that you share these guidelines with all the countries so that they have sufficient time for preparation. The manual should include

- Details on activities required during rollout

- An indicative project plan, a cutover plan, and a plan for hypercare

- Project organization, including rollout partners, along with roles and responsibilities

- Checklists for overall readiness assessment of individual countries

Based on your knowledge from the global template implementation, you may want to revisit your rollout strategy. You may want to consider these steps as you formulate your strategy:

Categorize countries in your network based on type of ownership. You may have your own operations in some countries, joint operations in other countries, and agents appointed in still others. You may have dedicated agents or agents that are not exclusive to your organization. In the case of nonexclusive agents, you need not deploy your global template, as they are not obliged to follow your processes or accounting procedures in their totality. Further categorize countries based on their volume (low, medium, high) (see Figure 6-4).

Network Partnership	Volume	Global template
Own	High	Yes
Own	Medium	Yes
Own	Low	Yes
Joint Venture	High	Yes
Joint Venture	Medium	Yes
Joint Venture	Low	Yes
Dedicated agent	Any	Yes
General agent	Any	NA

Figure 6-4. *Categorizing country based on ownership type and volume for global template rollout*

Analyze complexities of doing business in each region. Now, you have a list of countries categorized by region, ownership type, volume, and complexity (see Figures 6-5 and 6-6).

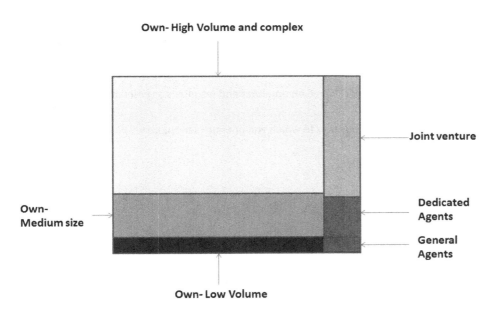

Figure 6-5. *Global rollout template classification based on ownership type, volume and complexity*

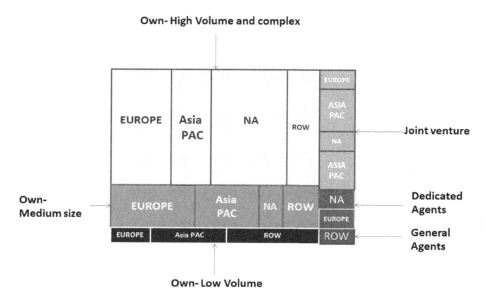

Figure 6-6. *Region-wise global rollout template classification based on ownership type, volume, and complexity*

- In consultation with your rollout partner(s), agree on timelines and resources required for rollout for each country.

- Form clusters based on the number of countries in which you operate (see Figure 6-7).

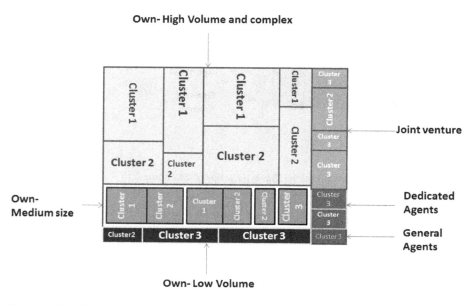

Figure 6-7. *Cluster formation*

- Aim at completing all rollouts in approximately 18 months; do not form more than three clusters.

- Your first cluster should include countries in all the regions with high volume and high complexity.

- You may also consider some medium-size countries with high complexity in cluster 1.

- Your cluster 2 should include countries with medium volume and complexity.

- You may also consider some low-volume countries with medium complexity in cluster 2.

- All other countries should fall under cluster 3.

- Once the clusters are formed, create waves within them.

- Clusters 1 and 2 may have three to four waves each.

- Planning should be managed at each cluster level.

- Waves are formed based on preparedness of countries and on geography, so that the rollout and project teams spend a minimum of time traveling. This will result in multiple go-live dates, with each wave having an individual date.

- Decide on whether the rollout teams will physically travel to the location or carry out the rollout from a central location, to which representatives of small-volume countries and dedicated agents will travel for training and from which they will subsequently receive assistance. Following are the four options for rollout:

- The entire team visits the country for implementation.

- Part of the team visits the country for implementation (team members have multiple skills).

- Members of project teams assemble at a central location, receive training, and subsequently carry out rollout in their country, with support provided from one of the regional locations.

- Rollouts are carried out from a regional/central location.

- In the end, you will have a list of countries by region, volume, complexity, type of ownership, cluster, wave, and type of approach for rollout (see Figure 6-8).

Country	Region	Ownership Type	Volume	Complexity	Cluster No	Wave No	Rollout approach
Country 1							
Country 2							
Country 3							
Country 4							
Country N							

Figure 6-8. *Rollout plan*

- Create a program organization to carry out rollouts. We recommend a three-tier structure under the central leadership, made up of the central leadership, or global team; regional team and cluster; and country teams (see Figure 6-9).

Rollout program organization

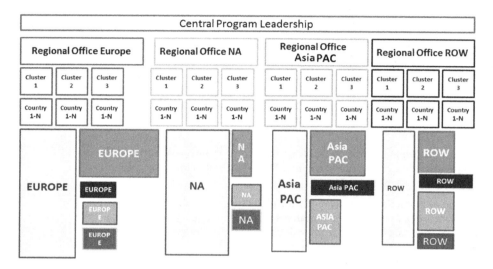

Figure 6-9. *Three-tier program organization structure*

- Every tier should be made responsible for the success of the rollouts, with consistent contribution required. We have seen some small to midsize countries in want of the global or regional team's attention and involvement. You can use the responsibility chart illustrated in Figure 6-10 for planning and charting responsibilities.

Rollout organization responsibility chart				
Tasks	Global team	Regional team	Cluster, country	Remarks
Carry out preparation activities and initiate project	Y			
Setup of the project organization	Y	Y	Y	
Setup of a project plan	Y	Y	Y	
Performing business migration and change management	Y	Y	Y	Supported by regional & cluster, country teams
Consolidation of legal, fiscal and physical necessary localizations	Y	Y	Y	Each at different level
Data loading coordination and coordination of setup of configuration	Y		Y	
Coordination and tracking	Y	Y		
Support of trainers and super-users	Y	Y	Y	
Updating of deliverables	Y	Y		
Prepare country support			Y	
Support of user acceptance testing,			Y	
Support of business adaptation/ standardization			Y	
Cutover planning and local execution	Y	Y	Y	
HyperCare local execution	Y	Y	Y	
Quality, risk management and issue management	Y	Y	Y	
Management reporting	Y	Y	Y	
Collect lessons learned and enhance the rollout approach	Y	Y		
Coordinate rollout new release during global rollout period	Y	Y		
Perform train the trainer		Y	Y	
Coordination with release management team		Y		

Figure 6-10. *Organization-wise responsibility chart*

The responsibilities of key roles are shown in Figure 6-11.

Teams	Key Roles	Responsibilities
Global	Project Sponsor	Demonstrates senior-level commitment through active and visible participation in the program, facilitating timely decisions; supporting the Program Manager to accomplish the project goals
	Process Owners	Ensure that the business targets and objectives are met by the system, take ownership of the business-process area and the system after go-live.
	Program Manager	Overall program ownership, resolving escalated issues, supporting the Vendor's Project Manager to accomplish the project goals
Regional	Rollout Manager	Ownership of rollout at regional level, issue resolution at regional level
	Trainers	Understand the solution, participate in trainings, and ensure achieving required competencies for end-user training
	Data Manager	Ownership of data-cleansing activities, help project team on coordination with data providers and data cleansing
Cluster, Country	Country Manager	Accountable for country rollout, ensure business users' availability as per agreed schedule and rollout, provide necessary approvals and sign off
	Key Users	Participate in solution-understanding workshop, provide local and legal business requirements, perform data cleansing, perform UAT and provide signoff
	BMC Agents	Understand the program objectives, work with Organization Change manager and help implement BMC at site
	End Users	Participate in training and acquire required competencies to work on solution

Figure 6-11. *Key roles responsibility chart*

Following are some other considerations:

- **Localization:** Your rollout teams will come across many local requirements in every country. Here are some suggestions:

- Gather to assess and consolidate local requirements at the rollout site.

- Share local requirements with the cluster, regional, and global teams.

- Obtain approvals from the change management board.

- Implement localizations that are legally, fiscally, and physically required.

- Validate localizations once they are built.

- **Retrograde:** You may have functional releases planned after the first stage of the rollout of the global template. In such cases, retrograde rollouts need to be performed in those countries. In some large-scale implementations, you may have three to four retrogrades in just two to three years.

- **Industrialized approach:** Gone are the days when rollouts went on for many years. In today's world a suggested timeline for completing rollouts after successful implementation of the pilot is no more than one-and-a-half years if your operation is in 180 to 200 countries. How do you deal with this constraint? The answer is to build an industrialized approach. This requires rollout partners with the necessary tools, assets, framework, methodology, resources, and experience.

- **Language strategy:** Language plays an important role in global rollouts. You need to have a clear understanding of the language requirements for every rollout site and communicate these to your rollout partners so that they engage consultants with the requisite language skills. The rollout team should have a minimum of one key consultant for language strategy, which is needed for training and various types of documentation (business, legal, and so on).

- **E-learning:** Even with classroom and on-the-job training in place, it is important to make maximum use of an e-learning platform for competency building. E-learning provides flexibility, offering material that is easy to update, easy to deliver, and cost-effective. We suggest that you have a dedicated team that is responsible for developing an e-learning strategy for building and delivering e-content.

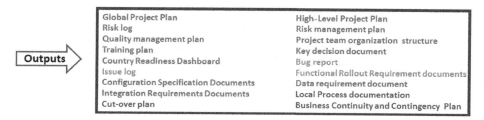

Figure 6-12. *Deliverables from rollout teams*

Release Management

We hope you have partners who can scale as you need on short notice. In this phase, you are responsible for planning, scheduling, and controlling the building, testing, and deployment of releases, including new functionalities required by the business, while protecting the integrity of the global template. Discuss this with your partners, and agree on schedule, deliveries, and expectations.

Figure 6-13 presents a summary of a release management strategy in which release packages are built, installed, tested, and deployed.

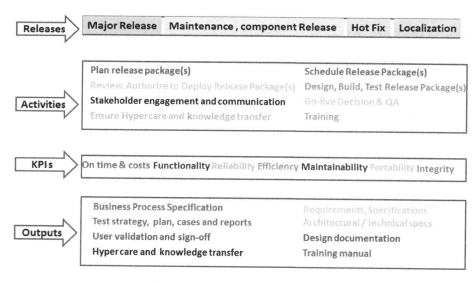

Figure 6-13. *Release management strategy*

These are some of the keys to success in release management:

- Standardize whenever possible.

- Localize when necessary.

- Deploy release packages to minimize impact on IT service in production as well as on operations and support.

- Reference configuration items and release components being maintained.

- Synchronize deployment of the global template and local application of adaptations/deployment.

Figure 6-14 displays the activities carried out in different releases.

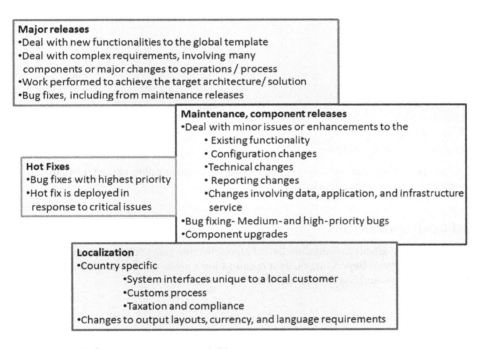

Figure 6-14. *Release management activities*

The following tasks need to be completed jointly with your release management partner:

- Set up an incident/change management process.

- Establish a configuration management process.

- Agree on a list of requirements to be released under the current scope.

- Develop the stages and their schedules.

- Build clear and comprehensive release plans.

- Arrange for or identify resources, and agree on their roles and responsibilities.

- Establish a quality plan and acceptance process.

- Develop the design and testing of localization, along with defect management.

- Set up data loading, testing, and validation for test environment.

- Create a test strategy, test plan, and test cases for the performance unit, system, performance, volume, stress, security, disaster recovery, regression (functional and interfaces), and user acceptance testing to verify functional and nonfunctional requirements.

- Release packages that are deployed to various environments, including development, quality assurance, and preproduction.

- Assess issues and risks related to every release package.

- Agree on and communicate the date and timeline for deployment.

- Execute handover from release to production.

- Update training material for the delta.

- Train end users.

- Go live.

- Provide support for releases.

- Hand over project deliverables.

- Transfer knowledge.

- Communicate with a change management team.

Your partners should keep you updated by sharing weekly status reports on progress made against the plan and any issues that may affect delivery, costs, milestones, and quality.

Project Organization and Locations

Your release management team should be available at minimum 24/6. Essentially, this means that you have teams available in different areas by providing support. Depending on your organization's presence, you may choose to have one team each in Asia Pacific (APAC), Europe, and North America (NA).

Summary

Users of new solutions, such as SAP TM, want to understand both basic features and the more complex capabilities of the system. User proficiency is an important issue that the project sponsor's task force needs to attend to on an ongoing basis. The success or failure of a new solution depends on how quickly and accurately the user community gets to know the system and exploit its potential in their daily use. User turnover should be addressed through regular trainings for new users. In addition, it is advisable to have more users trained than required. In the absence of proper and continual training, users will become frustrated, having to create work-arounds to get their work done.

Your new solution will only be as good as the investment you continue to make in it. We recommend a system review at least once a year to identify areas for improvement through version upgrades, new interfaces, additional modules, more efficient processes, and additional user training. A commitment to this process will enable you to optimize your return on investment, while extending your capabilities to help you achieve even greater success.

CHAPTER 7

Team Composition and Skill Matrix Required for TM Engagement: How to Build Competency in TM

In this chapter, we will consider the following:

- The importance of team composition for SAP TM projects
- Roles and their skill sets
- Team composition for all phases (implementation to support)
- How to ramp up team and build competency
- Ways to retain SAP TM consultants

In Chapter 6, we discussed various approaches to successfully implementing SAP TM. You may choose any of these methods, depending on the size, business needs, challenges, and vision of your organization. Success also depends on commitment from leadership, preparedness, and the systems integrator (SI) partner. Key, however, is the team chosen for implementation. Team composition is therefore very important. You need teams with different skill sets for the different phases: implementation, rollout, and support. Because SAP TM version 9.0 is relatively new to the market, obtaining experienced consultants is a major challenge. Project sponsors are currently struggling to get SAP TM functional and technical consultants on board, but this will change as ongoing implementations bring experienced resources into the market. The team should have a sufficient number of logistics domain consultants with a comprehensive knowledge and understanding of logistic processes and the ability to validate business requirements, exceptions, and deviations—consultants who can not only expedite business process mapping, but also offer error-free deliverables.

Doing everything in-house is not a good idea. You should engage qualified SIs to provide experienced resources for the various roles required. You should also engage SAP AG's transportation business unit while designing the solution and aligning requirements with their future road map. You need to form three teams internally: one to focus on strategy, a second to guide and monitor business and technical architecture, and a third to manage the program. It is advisable that you break the program into several projects of manageable size. Many projects can be undertaken simultaneously or in sequence, depending on the vision and road map decided on. It is also recommended that you retain architecture roles in-house. However, if your firm does not have competent architects, you should never bring in architects from a company/source that you have engaged to carry out implementation. It is always better to have your architecture designed and monitored by you. This will ensure that your architecture best practices are followed. Furthermore, you should keep your business architecture in your custody because your business is yours—you know what makes it different from your competitors, your unique sales proposition (USP), and your company secrets. You best understand what affects your business. To derive maximum benefit from your investment, the business and technology architecture teams must be part of one group.

Your SI partner for the existing SAP landscape may be the best choice in terms of timelines, quality, and cost but may not necessarily be the most appropriate one for implementing SAP TM. Few SI vendors have a track record of implementing SAP TM, including some leading ones. In contrast, a number of boutiques have invested time and energy over the past years, have gained an almost complete understanding of what SAP TM can do, and have built integrations with other systems and assets that can expedite implementation. In fact, these shops can set up a pilot demonstrating your scenario in a few weeks' time. Experience is one of the criteria for selection; other factors that you should consider before engaging an SI vendor are as follows:

- Does the SI vendor have sufficient understanding of a logistics domain?

- How many trained, experienced resources does the SI vendor have?

- Does the SI vendor have a lab or environment where its resources have built or are building scenarios?

- How closely is the SI vendor working with the SAP AG transportation unit? Is the SI vendor building any solutions jointly, or is it part of SAP's custom development initiative?

- Has the SI vendor invested in hosting SAP TM solutions?

The answers to these questions can help you choose the right SI partner.

Team Composition for Implementation

A SAP TM implementation program is different from implementing SAP Enterprise Resource Planning (SAP ERP) modules because SAP TM is not a module, but a complete mini-ERP that addresses the core functions of the logistics business. Migrating to SAP TM as a core system therefore requires the highest level of commitment from leadership and an organizational-level readiness for transformation in both technology and process areas. Process standardization is key to optimizing processes, clarifying roles and responsibilities, and removing personal dependencies; in addition, documented processes act as a reference guide for every individual in the organization. The standardization of processes is the first step in getting ready for such a major initiative. Standardized processes, with due consideration of local needs, such as taxation, border-crossing regulations, and country/product-specific documentation, leads to easy blueprinting for SAP TM. Given these considerations, and the importance attached to such a program, we present here recommendations for roles at the corporate and program level.

Corporate-Level Roles

At the corporate level of the organization implementing SAP TM, the following roles are suggested:

Project Sponsor: The chief operating officer (COO), or head of the business unit, generally sponsors SAP TM implementation programs. A business case detailing vision, goals and objectives, scope, tentative timelines, success criteria, proposed investment, areas of improvement, opportunities for growth, and return on investment are prepared. A detailed study may be undertaken to build a meaningful business case. The project sponsor presents the business case to the board or owners, who must approve it in order for the program to go forward. It is the responsibility of the project sponsor to deliver the value assured the business in the business case. The sponsor resolves issues at the organizational level, as well as any external impacts, to ensure smooth running of the program. The sponsor must also guide the program team. Other duties include monitoring project costs, schedule, and key success factors and participating in pricing and terms negotiations with software, consulting, SI, hardware, communication, and training vendors. Monthly to quarterly reviews of the program by the sponsor are suggested to monitor the health of the program.

Steering Committee: The project sponsor should appoint steering committee members upon receiving approval of the business case. The steering committee comprises identified leaders from various functions, such as process engineering, procurement, risk and compliance, quality control, business development, customer service, strategic planning, budgeting, and technology. The chief information officer (CIO) generally heads the committee, who reports to the project sponsor on a regular basis. The purpose of the committee is to guide program organization and help the program run smoothly by providing resolutions and removing dependencies. The committee is responsible for devising a vendor selection framework, selecting vendors and contracting with them, monitoring the progress of the program, and guiding the program team. The committee is also responsible for the budget and hence must assess spending versus achievement of objectives. It is advisable that the committee meets once a month, at minimum, to take stock of the program.

Enterprise Architect: A group of business and technology architects headed by an enterprise architect plays an important role in a program of this size. Business architects deal with business changes and their impact, areas of improvement, opportunities to automate, and process standardization. Technology architects ensure that principles of design are followed and that architecture guidelines are adhered to. They offer understanding of the existing technology landscape and planned transformation as well as the vision detailed in the business case. Both groups, under the leadership of the enterprise architect, should ensure implementation of enterprise architecture through the life cycle of the SAP TM program. As mentioned earlier, it is in the interest of the organization to have this group staffed internally. In cases in which the group requires external resources, they should be sourced from vendors that are not assigned an implementation or rollout task. It is also advisable that a detailed review of the architecture framework of industry experts be undertaken, as new technology platforms, offerings, and models are evolving rapidly.

Program Manager (owner): The program manager (owner) serves as single point of contact (SPOC) for the program. Preferably, the program manager (owner) should have experience managing large projects in the area of logistics or supply chain management. Experience delivering large SAP programs is a plus. The project sponsor should appoint the program manager (owner) while the steering committee is being formed. The program manager (owner) creates scope documents for appointing vendors, logically breaks scope into manageable projects, identifies the risks associated with the program, and writes a mitigation plan. Other duties include creating change management and critical resource plans; identifying dependencies; and devising a program organization structure, measurement criteria, an induction plan, and a reporting mechanism. It is also the responsibility of the program manager (owner) to sign off on meaningful deliverables received from vendors.

Whether it be a pilot, a partial implementation, or an organizational-level implementation, these roles are necessary at the corporate level to achieve success with your program.

Program-Level Roles

Based on our experience with TM engagement, we suggest the following program-level roles for implementation. Their numbers will depend on the size and scope of implementation.

Program Manager (SI): The program manager (SI) serves as single point of contact (SPOC) for the program from the SI side. Preferably, the program manager (SI) should have experience managing large projects in the area of logistics or supply chain management. Experience delivering large SAP programs is a plus. The project sponsor should appoint the program manager (SI) during the solution-building stage. The program manager (SI) must ensure the delivery of the scope agreed on, as outlined in the statement of work (SOW). The program manager (SI) works closely with the program manager (owner) to stay aligned and resolve issues at the program level. The program manager (SI) reports progress to the program manager (owner), who in turn presents it to management. Other duties include getting the project milestone completion signoff from the program manager (owner) or the steering committee, as stated in the contract.

Project Manager: The project manager develops and monitors the project plan. The project manager is also responsible for status reporting; risk management; escalation of issues that cannot be resolved by his or her team; and generally making sure the project is delivered within the confines of the budget, on schedule, and in accordance with the scope agreed on. You will need project managers for every project identified as part of this large transformation program. You can have a mix of them, staffed in-house and onboarded from SI or other vendors.

Logistics Domain Consultant (SME): This role is vital to the success of SAP TM implementation. A consultant with a few years' experience in the logistics industry appreciates difficult areas and the challenges faced by different roles within a logistics company. He or she can therefore play a large part in putting together the right solutions. A logistics domain consultant with experience implementing SAP TM is preferable; however, a consultant with experience implementing TM products other than SAP TM can also meet your needs. In fact, these types of consultants can be assets, as they know the good and bad sides of implementing other products; this knowledge can be leveraged. The way the industry is organized, it would be difficult to find an individual with a strong understanding of all areas of the business. Some consultants may have excellent knowledge of ocean freight but no experience with airfreight or value-added services. Consultants with a background in road transportation may not have the required understanding of global trade management. Therefore, based on your implementation strategy, you may elect to engage logistics domain consultants by line of business or by business process. You can have a combination of consultants—some from your organization, others from SI or consulting organizations. It is advisable to select, at minimum, 50 percent of the SME team from in-house. Consultants chosen from SI or business-consulting organizations bring varied experience and the best practices followed by competitors/industry leaders. By conducting workshops, a logistics domain consultant can easily connect with business users to capture key performance indicators, success criteria, roles played by actors in the ecosystems, data exchange requirements, cross-border requirements, compliance needs, and volume of transactions. The logistics domain consultant is also expected to provide recommendations for process optimization. Moreover, a logistics domain consultant is a process consultant; therefore, experience working with business process–modeling or -mapping tools is desirable.

SAP TM Functional Consultant: A functional consultant needs to have strong SAP TM knowledge and hands-on experience. The consultant should have a good understanding of Business Rule Framework plus (BRFPlus). It will be advantageous to engage a consultant who has experience with other SAP modules, such as SAP Logistics and Execution (SAP LE), SAP ERP Sales and Distribution (SAP SD), and SAP Material Management (SAP MM). Logistics domain knowledge is desirable as well. The main responsibilities of a SAP TM functional consultant are to map business requirements in SAP TM and to configure systems that meet business requirements.

SAP TM Technical Consultant: The SAP TM technical consultant must have strong knowledge of advanced business application programming (ABAP) and hands-on experience with the SAP TM ecosystem. The technical consultant also needs to have a good understanding of the following areas:

- **Business Object Processing Framework (BOPF):** Used to create a service interface based on a business object structure at design time. BOPF is considered the heart of SAP TM's technical area, and the SAP TM technical consultant should have good knowledge of it.

- **Floor Plan Manager (FPM):** A user interface that interacts with the process control framework and the strategies for adjusting the process step sequence; adds additional, customer-specific steps to support SAP TM business strategies, while creating conditions and decision points to influence business strategies in SAP TM.

- **SAP NetWeaver Business Client (NWBC).**

- **Business Rule Framework plus (BRFPlus).**

SAP Process Integration (PI) Consultant: SAP PI has to connect SAP TM with SAP ERP Central Component (SAP ECC) and other systems and third-party products used in your organization by vendors, customers, and border agencies. The SAP PI consultant builds these interfaces. SAP TM also requires interfacing with SAP Event Management (SAP EM), SAP Global Trade Services (SAP GTS), business intelligence (BI), and warehouse management systems (WMS). A SAP PI consultant with hands-on experience, preferably in supply chain execution and collaboration systems interfacing, should be brought on board.

SAP Basis Consultant: The SAP Basis consultant handles SAP TM system administration, including installation (SAP R/3, SAP NetWeaver and NetWeaver components, SAP Solution Manager [SolMan]), configuration (printers, remote function call [RFC], SAP Transport Management System [SAP STMS]), administration (user, client, backup), and maintenance (monitoring servers, background jobs, and system performance; avoiding bottlenecks). The SAP Basis consultant is responsible for ensuring the smooth running of the system, with high performance.

SAP Finance and Controlling (FICO) Consultant: If you are a SAP shop, and FICO is already implemented, your financial settings may already be configured. The SAP FICO consultant is needed to configure financial settings in the SAP ECC system. SAP TM is integrated with SAP ECC for managing customer receipts and vendor payments through accounts receivable (AR), accounts payable (AP), general ledger (GL), cost center, and profit center.

SAP Material Management (MM) Consultant: The SAP MM consultant creates a service framework for the system, thereby enabling vendor invoice settlement. This consultant is required only if you do not have the necessary configuration in place at the time of SAP TM implementation. Generally, an organization that is already using SAP ECC may have these configurations in place.

SAP Event Management (EM) Consultant: Event management is one of the most desired functionalities. Your customers rate your service based on the maturity of your event management capabilities. Correct settings are a must. Hence, an EM consultant is needed.

Global trade management (GTM) Consultant: It is advisable that you bring on board a GTM consultant who can configure GTM functionalities. Global trade settings must be carried out with the utmost care, because the ramifications of incorrect settings are severe and may mean loss of business or the incurrence of penalties.

Legacy System Expert: The involvement of legacy system experts is vital for decommissioning, as during data migration, you may lose wealth preserved for many years in the form of a special requirement. This role is important in terms of interfacing and data migration as well.

Quality Assurance Consultant: You should staff this position internally, as you know your business better than anyone. Should you decide to engage with an external vendor to run your test factory, make sure you have found a vendor experienced with both the test factory and the logistics domain. Testing and quality control are important not only because SAP TM 9.0 is new, but also because it interfaces with most of your landscape as well as outside it. Ensure that batch processes are running as expected and that all the interfaces, functionalities, and, more important, custom-built functionalities are working.

Some of the resources discussed here may be needed on a part-time basis and when required, as indicated in the program plan. It is recommended that the entire program team be situated at a single site for better collaboration. Depending on the success of Implementation and subsequent support phase, you may want to revisit your rollout plan. The implementation team conducts workshops to share solution details, architecture aspects, environment, configuration, user setup, and documentation with rollout leadership.

Team Composition for Rollout and Release Management

The corporate team continues on throughout the rollouts. It is good practice to retain a few key resources from the implementation team for the initial rollouts. These resources can act as mentors to the rollout teams. The steering committee appoints one or more rollout partners and release management partners, depending on the number of sites and time allotted.

Rollout Team

Rollout partners are best enlisted toward the last phase of implementation of the global template. They should shadow the implementation team during the warranty stage at the first site.

You need all the skills of the implementation team to carry out the rollouts. However, you do not need the same number of resources. Retain consultants with multiple skill sets. Also, the competency level required for implementation is higher than that needed for rollout. Rollout consultants should have knowledge of the implementing country or site-specific localization. Different countries have different legal and statutory requirements; these must be addressed while rolling out the standard template. Forms and documents may also be required in the local language(s) and format.

If you can spare a few members of the implementation team for rollouts, you will soon become self-sufficient. However, it is not always possible to contribute to the rollout teams from corporate or regional teams. From your side, you must arrange for all support at the site to assist the team carrying out the rollout. It is the responsibility of the steering committee to form a local rollout support team, composed of location manager, location Internet technology single point of contact (IT SPOC), local process champions, power users, and key business users as testers.

Rollout team members, with the exception of the project manager, are expected to conduct training in their respective area/domain for power users and key associates identified at the site. The rollout team is responsible for data migration; demonstrating end-to-end scenarios, as indicated in the global template; identifying and documenting new functionalities; configuring localization; and conducting training.

The rollout manager is responsible for rolling out the global template at sites identified by the steering committee. Rollouts at large sites may require a dedicated team; however, a rollout team can also be deployed to work at many small, less complex sites. These teams may perform rollouts simultaneously. The best practice in such a case is to situate key resources from the small sites at a central location, train them, and subsequently guide them remotely while they perform rollout at their respective sites.

Release Management Team

It is good practice to have two different vendors engaged for rollout and release management. The release management team supports the rollout team, which shares new requirements identified and issues faced during rollout. The release team resolves issues, either alone or with the help of the SAP AG development team. The steering committee prioritizes new requirements. The release team carries out those requirements in need of immediate development. A few requirements are considered for rollout at later stage, and the remaining ones are approved or not considered. Newly developed functionalities are retrofitted for sites where the rollout team has acted by the release management team.

The release management team is best enlisted toward the last stage of implementation of the global template. This team should further shadow the implementation team during the warranty stage at the first site. The release management team may start shadowing and subsequently take over as the prime team. In this way, team members can learn the system and how issues are resolved and build understanding of the framework, the product development kit, and documentation.

The release management team should also have all the skills required for implementation of the SAP TM solution. The team can perform most of its tasks from a remote location, except in cases in which certain team members must travel to sites to conduct training on major releases. The release management team is also expected to support multiple rollouts simultaneously. It is advisable to have two or three different release management teams supporting countries in the same region and time zone. You can also achieve optimization by overlapping team availability in different time zones. The release management team is headed by the release manager and supported by a leader for the respective release teams.

Team Composition for Support

The support management team takes over for the release management team. The vendor may be different or the same. It is not recommended that you find support internally, as SI vendors bring to the table best practices, tools, and assets that will help optimize the support resources. Also, these being 24/7 requirements, SI vendors have the advantage of leveraging shared resources and teams from low-cost countries.

It is suggested that the support management team include SAP TM functional and technical consultants, SAP Basis consultants, and SAP PI consultants.

SAP TM Team Ramp-Up and Competency-Building Plan

SAP TM implementation is a major transformational project for 3PLs and requires a great many experienced and trained SAP TM resources to manage implementation and multiple rollouts and provide support. SAP TM 9.0 is the latest and most comprehensive version to date and was released for general availability in the third quarter of 2012. As discussed previously, because SAP TM 9.0 is relatively new, availability of resources with SAP TM 9.0 skills represents a major challenge. This challenge can be addressed by implementing a ramp-up and competency-building plan. We believe that SAP TM consultants must have sound knowledge of freight forwarding and logistics in addition to SAP TM skills. We propose a joint capability development strategy with four levels of maturity, from E1 (beginner) to E4 (expert). Furthermore, it is suggested that these resources be involved in different stages of the project/initiative life cycle, depending on their maturity. These are some ways to build the team:

Category 1: Bring on board internal associates who are working in business areas but who are IT savvy and keen to learn new product technology. Training in technology should be given. Such resources bring domain understanding, an important asset. With this knowledge, they can grasp SAP TM faster and be deployed for process mapping, requirement gathering, and documentation.

Category 2: Identify internal IT resources and competent power users (working with other SAP modules) who are willing to make the move to SAP TM technology, and train them in SAP TM.

Category 3: Engage experienced consultants who are working with SAP TM (and other SAP modules), and train them in SAP TM.

Category 4: Recruit SAP TM resources directly from the market to augment teams. This can meet your immediate requirements. However, using onboard resources from the market can be costly. Consultants may be hired on a contract basis, but this is expensive and a relatively risky proposition. The opportunity to build knowledge is also lost when you hire only contractors.

We recommend following a competency-building plan for associates joining the project. Based on their background and category, individuals would undergo the following training as applicable:

E1-A: SAP technology overview and navigation for category 1 resources.

E1-B: Internal transportation domain training covering specific SAP TM processes (one week) for category 2 resources. Senior members from various functional areas may conduct this training.

E2: SAP TM 9.0 product training conducted internally for categories 1, 2, and 3. Resources trained at the E2 level may be used as shadow resources for support or release management.

E3: SAP TM 9.0 product training conducted by either a SAP AG training center or internal faculty identified as skilled trainers. Training will be three to four weeks in duration, cover all product features, and offer hands-on experience with SAP TM functionality and integration needs. This will necessitate the creation of an internal environment and scenarios for demonstrating and practicing the information. E3-level resources can be engaged in release management.

E4: Consultants with E3-level certification and experience with release management/implementation of a major release (internally or with SI organizations) should be given implementation tasks, such as requirement review, configuration, blueprinting, and realization. Such consultants, after an implementation, can be categorized at the E4 level of competency.

A typical training agenda may cover the following aspects:

Foundation—E1

- Logistics overview (for category 2)
- Logistics processes (for category 2)

- SAP terminology (for category 1)
- SAP overview (for category 1)
- SAP NetWeaver overview (for category 1)

Basic—E2

- SAP TM overview
- TM architecture overview
- SAP TM terminology
- Master data
- Order management, including order-based transportation requirement, delivery-based transportation requirement, and forwarding order
- Charge management
- Transportation planning
- Freight-order management
- Forwarding and freight settlement
- Demonstration of complete end-to-end scenarios

Advanced—E3

- Airfreight processes
- Standard operating procedures
- Cost distribution
- Export/Import handling
- Service products and items

Retention of TM Consultants

Because of strong demand and weak supply, retention of the SAP TM consultant is a major challenge for user organizations. Skilled resources are rare, and implementations that are approved and underway, offering jobs with higher compensation, rewards, and growth opportunities are common. With due consideration of this scenario, an organization needs to develop a comprehensive plan to ensure retention of its skilled SAP TM consultants. Cross-modular exposure to enhance skills is one solution. Nomination to different training programs to update skills and facilitate job rotation and rationalizing compensation are some other ways to retain good SAP TM consultants.

Summary

SAP TM implementation is a major transformational project for 3PLs and requires a great many experienced and trained SAP TM resources to manage implementation and multiple rollouts and provide support. However, because SAP TM 9.0 is relatively new, availability of skilled and experienced resource represents a major challenge. Therefore, for realizing early return on investment and project success, you need to create a comprehensive ramp-up and competency-building plan to address this challenge. You should put together a mix of resources with logistics domain knowledge and SAP TM experience. Also, doing everything in-house is not a good idea. You need to engage qualified SI vendors to provide experienced resources for various roles. Engaging SAP AG's transportation business unit while designing the solution and aligning requirements with their future road map is also suggested.

Your transformation initiative may affect the way you will deal with your customers and vendors going forward. This must be managed with sensitivity. The next chapter deals with how to manage this impact.

CHAPTER 8

███

Transformation Impact of SAP TM Implementation

In this chapter, we will cover the following:

- The role of communication in the journey of transformation

- Who and what are affected, and how and when impact occurs

- How to manage affected processes, people, and systems

- How companies are using SAP TM for transformation

Previously, we discussed using SAP TM as a solution for meeting the growing business needs of 3PLs and approaches to deploying the solution across your organization. SAP TM implementation is a major transformational project that is expected to render the benefits envisioned at the time of its inception. Some of the common benefits, such as cost savings, improved processes, and accurate and timely information may be realized, but it is essential that you evaluate whether the benefits projected while justifying the business case to senior management have been achieved. Therefore, there is first a need to assess how the transformation will affect your organization and key factors for ensuring that the transformation is smooth.

Communication is a key to success. Your transformation initiative may have an impact on the way you will deal with your customers and vendors. Therefore, any changes made as a result of the new model, systems, processes, or strategy must be communicated clearly and at an appropriate time and be in agreement with your views. The other group that is affected the most is your employees. Make certain that every employee to be influenced by such changes, irrespective of designation, role, location, seniority, or skill set, is made aware of the changes, and communicate this information up front. Conduct workshops on the transformation initiative. People must gain some understanding of why the change in strategy or culture is needed and what the impact on them will be, in particular shifts in roles, responsibilities, location, and teams. Any change is bound to be seen as political, and as people will be critical in carrying out your firm's initiative, clear communication with them at appropriate times and intervals is suggested. People will generally perceive changes negatively in the beginning. This is when, besides a central team managing the change, respective managers must actively contribute toward it. To realize benefits from such a major investment, an integrated technology, process and awareness of people's needs are essential. Consistent behavior and willingness to sacrifice uniqueness for gaining standardization also prove helpful.

SAP TM Transformational Impact

The following sections deal with the impact of SAP TM implementation on processes, people, and systems.

Processes

You have now implemented new processes informed by best practices. These processes may differ greatly from your old processes. We hope you have trained your resources on these new processes. Teams that have worked together for years become used to doing things a certain way. They may perform a lot of tasks the way they were performing them before, purely out of habit. This can lead to confusion, delays, issues with reconciliation, missed connections, and incorrect routes and may result in service-level failure or penalties. Newer processes are supposed to ensure that such lapses are identified and corrected; however, inadequate training and lack of audits can result in such errors. One-time training is not going to help. You need to make a provision for a series of trainings and create innovative ways of training. We hope you have an e-learning platform on which these new processes, or any changes to processes, are available. Contents on an e-learning platform should be simple, easy to access, and self-explanatory. Offer a means of accessing e-learning, and conduct audits to assess the effectiveness of these trainings.

Collaborative ways of sharing information can help you achieve success much faster. Make use of some of the collaboration platforms at an organizational level. Use networking tools to chat, share information, and provide online help. Create teams of process consultants or champions at various levels (global, regional, country). These teams should give additional assistance with new processes.

Some of the new or changed processes may require modification in infrastructure, such as scanners, conveyor belts, sorting machines, network, connectivity, and so on. Make certain that the infrastructure needed is in place before announcing go-live dates for new processes. Also, perform testing and training to ensure that the system behaves as desired. Full or partial automation of processes means fewer manual tasks. This may result in fewer resources required and a higher volume of work performed in less time. However, you may not want to let go of the additional resources. They have been your assets up until now. They have an understanding of your business, clients, and processes. We suggest you retrain and absorb them in some other area of the business.

With your changed processes, you need to keep in mind the most important business partners: the customer and the carriers. Your new processes afford improved integration with these partners, giving them visibility of shipments, actionable reports, and improved workflow through load tendering, communication, electronic payment and reconciliation of invoices, and many other new features. To achieve all such benefits, changes have to be made at both your end and theirs. You have carried out the required changes at your end. Now, you must communicate clearly with your partners what they need to change at theirs for mutual benefit. Make sure you are asking for the minimum required, as they are not obliged to make changes. Also, perform comprehensive testing of changes made before starting any new process or exchange of information.

People

People are your biggest asset. They should own this transformation. They have been with your organization and have helped it grow. Your efforts toward the modernization, simplification, and rationalization of systems and processes should be seen by them as their initiative and of great benefit, elevating their career and widening their horizons. This transformation should bring positive change to the work environment. The people aspect of change management is more critical than the strategic or project management aspect.

People in your organization were using different legacy systems for data entry, as no one system was available everything. SAP TM enables multiple functionalities, and data entry is done in one application rather than using multiple applications. SAP TM implementation brings about a radical change in how people operate and in the overall working environment. Implementing change is an uphill battle. Because people are comfortable doing things the old way, they are often resistant to change. They may see change as threatening. It is the responsibility of the transformation sponsor or chief executive officer (CEO) of your organization to be clear and to share information up front about the planned change and its impact. This can shift the perception of change from negative to positive. This transformation should be seen as an organization-wide mission. The backing of executives and management support are thus critical success factors. Executive-level management should come out with a visualization of the project's success that should be cascaded throughout the company.

It is important to understand people's thinking about the change. People using the system and performing relevant processes should own this transformation. They should be involved early on in the process and also be told clearly what role they are going to play and what is expected of them. It is our experience that kickoff is positive when the channel of communication is opened early on. Informing the people about the change as early as possible will give them time to accept it. Communicating change requires expressing briefly and modestly the benefits of the change. Communication should not be a set of one-time messages but rather a series of campaigns that begin early on and that do not stop until implementation is a demonstrable success. Those who will be affected by the change will need evidence that the solution is the right one—that it will solve the problem, that it is feasible, and that it can be implemented. When developing a communication plan, consider all those who will be affected, from the board room and senior executives to the operations manager and dockworker.

You can help people who are going to be affected in several ways. The project sponsor and project leadership must be preemptive regarding worry and destructive energy. Target relevant groups by sending motivational messages, or implement an awareness-building campaign. Furthermore, start discussing with employees the future change on the company's web site. You could include frequently asked questions and provide opportunity for employees to post their queries and worries. This would also give you the chance to learn what are employees' major concerns. You should consider these with an open mind. You may decide to change your approach a bit or convince people with rational facts, to their satisfaction.

Change cannot be achieved without participation from your firm's people. They should be involved and willing and, more important, know how to perform the changed processes and work on the new system. Both process training and system training are a must. Lack of adequate training can result in data errors, wrong operations, incomplete capture of data, incorrect process steps, and so on. Cleaning up the mess means redoing a lot of work and increased costs, in addition to customer and partner dissatisfaction. You need to provide e-learning and classroom and hands-on training on new systems and processes. You can also have "sandbox training," so that employees can try their hand at the system before it goes live, and new associates can play with the system. A good understanding of the basics of SAP TM will help reduce resistance and foster greater acceptance of the new system.

You may have technology loyalists who do not wish to migrate to the new platform. They may have been working with other technology for years. They have a fear of losing their seniority and may also be unwilling to be trained on another platform. In such a case, you may lose these associates and their domain knowledge, but this loss must be minimized.

You have the option of hiring from the job market, training your own associates, or both. When it comes to hiring associates, obtaining experienced resources may be a problem. Also, these new resources bring a different culture and may take time to become productive. It is therefore recommended that you have the right mix of resources for your team. Your firm has the choice of selecting the most qualified vendor to do the job. Not having a sound team on your side can prove to be a major handicap.

Systems

Your organization has been using legacy systems to manage transportation planning, execution, and related activities. You were using multiple systems for different modes of transport, lines of business, and regions/countries, perhaps with different systems specific to a customer or product line. Your new system replaces multiple disparate systems with one integrated solution in which all the functionalities are supported.

Retirement of the legacy application is a major transformational change. Now, you must decide what to retire, what to decommission, what to do with data in the old systems, and how to handle active shipments as well as billing and invoicing. Very few of these questions have a clear and appropriate answer. Users find it convenient to work with old systems and may prolong using them until the new system is available. Reconciliation becomes a major problem. You must have a clear strategy for decommissioning old applications so that they do not interfere with usage of the new solution. Make sure you migrate required data and archive what is needed for reference, as indicated in the guidelines. It makes sense to close the shipments in the systems in which they originated. The few that may have attracted claims and penalties should be dealt with separately; you will require their data for settlement.

With a highly integrated and single solution implemented, you require a team that provides 24/7 support. If you were decentralized earlier, your resources were supporting the old applications during working hours. However, in the new scenario, your team members will need to work around-the-clock, because being a global company, some of or all the countries in your network could be working at any time of the day or night. It is best to use resources from a systems integrator (SI) vendor. If you were managing everything in-house so far, introduction of SI vendors to manage the new environment may also represent yet another challenge.

SAP TM is helping organizations transform. A logistics and transport service provider based out of Europe has implemented the SAP TM solution to transform itself from a regional to a global transportation player. The organization was able to achieve cost reduction and increased operational efficiencies using SAP TM. Major gains were also experienced in decreasing the time required to process pricing and invoicing and in streamlining fleet routing, transportation planning, and distribution. The SAP TM solution is helping organizations differentiate themselves from their competitors.

Morever, one of the world's largest 3PLs, headquartered in Europe, is implementing a transformational program with SAP TM at its center that targets three key improvement areas:

- Increased customer intimacy

- Improved transparency

- Greater productivity

This global business, with its Internet technology (IT) transformation program, is enabling introduction of a new, homogeneous, consistent process landscape and transformation of the current IT landscape to one that is state-of-the-art.

Finally, these are some of the key benefits realized by a leading food service manufacturer headquartered in North America post SAP TM implementation:

- Reduced execution costs by optimizing freight consolidation.

- Improved decision making and exception management by leveraging SAP TM capability to provide visibility throughout the freight life cycle.

- Improved collaboration with carriers/partners; better tendering process, load acceptance, status details, sharing of details of actual performance and areas of improvement/opportunity, and so on.

Summary

Transformation affects processes, people, and systems. All of these play a major role in your business. You must appreciate, assess, and find solutions for the impacts of the change on your organization, or the goals of your transformation journey will not be achieved. It is important to share transformation vision and goals with all the partners in the ecosystem, including your customers and vendors. This transformation should be seen as an organization-wide mission. The backing of executives and management support are thus critical success factors. Executive-level management should come out with a visualization of the project's success that should be cascaded throughout the company. Transformations should be handled in such a way as to miminize negative effects on your organization, so that business can run as usual.

CHAPTER 9

■ ■ ■

New Dimension Products: HANA, Mobility, and Analytics—Their Impact on Transportation Management

In this chapter, we will deal with the following:

- Introduction to the new SAP TM suite of products/solutions

- How these products/solutions can help obtain early return on investment

In the development of trade, and thereby commerce, an efficient transportation and logistics network is essential. In this arena any inefficiency can result in loss. Hence, players in the transportation and logistics industry are under constant pressure with respect to their operations to be more agile, reduce cost and complexity through better forecasting and analysis, improve efficiency by gaining more insight into supply chain execution, and foster sustainability. The complexity associated with managing a global network—changing cross-border and trade rules and regulations, evolving offering models, and increasingly demanding customers—is forcing transportation and logistics industry players to innovate.

We strongly suggest that transportation and logistics players (like you) invest in solutions that can provide these benefits:

1. Access to real-time data; for example, having access to real-time information generated from assets can dynamically determine maintenance needs (predictive maintenance).

2. The ability to analyze large volumes of data to generate meaningful insights; for instance, carriers can use big data analytics to determine potential routes for operations, thereby minimizing overhead costs associated with failed routes.

3. Integrated solutions that present a single view of data throughout the enterprise, thus greatly reducing cost and complexity.

4. The capability to track, analyze, and interpret conversations with customers on the social web.

In sum, you need integrated solutions that can give you access to real-time data, while offering analytical capabilities for structured and unstructured data. Here, we suggest a few solutions from the SAP TM product suite that can meet these challenges. We also believe that once you have implemented SAP, introducing these products/solutions in your landscape can help you obtain early return on investment.

SAP HANA Solutions

SAP HANA is at the center of SAP's technology strategy, and its key applications already support SAP HANA or have SAP HANA support in the road map. A few key SAP HANA–based solutions are available for the transportation and logistics industry. SAP HANA's adoption by this industry has been relatively slow. However, we believe that adoption will soon increase as more logistics organizations implement SAP TM and as predictive technologies gain prevalence and achieve widespread acceptance. SAP HANA enables businesses to access transactional data in real time and to analyze large volumes of data quickly. We are sure your organization can use the capabilities of HANA for ensuring optimization and on-time performance; improving planning, forecasting, and carrier selection; and much more. In the following sections, we examine the key business drivers of a few select subindustries within the transportation and logistics industry to demonstrate how HANA can add value.

Fleet Operators (Surface Transportation)

Trucks form an integral part of surface transportation. The profitability of a fleet operator is dependent on his or her ability to ensure optimal capacity use, on-time performance, and availability and to reduce fuel expenses and maintenance overheads. SAP HANA can help fleet operators in the following ways:

- **Vehicle maintenance:** SAP HANA can help fleet operators better manage vehicle maintenance. Data models can analyze information collected from onboard computers to gauge a vehicle's maintenance needs. Based on this analysis, fleet operators can perform vehicle maintenance proactively.

- **Real-time route management:** Access to real-time information can enable operators to change routes dynamically to prevent inadvertent delays resulting from inclement weather or traffic problems.

- **Capacity and fuel management:** By using sophisticated planning and forecasting models, operators can identify the optimal number of trucks to operate and the shortest possible route for each trip, thereby reducing overhead costs caused by inferior routes and empty trucks.

Rail Operators

Some of the key advantages that SAP HANA offers fleet operators, such as proactive maintenance, optimal route planning, and capacity, are equally applicable to rail operators. In addition, SAP HANA can help rail operators in the areas of asset management and customer management.

- **Asset management:** Information, generated from sensors across the rail network, can be fed into data models to determine disruptions in real time. Insights from this data can help identify network problems proactively, thereby reducing repair overheads and ensuring safety.

- **Customer management:** During rollout of new service product and promotion, rail operators can leverage SAP HANA's ability to process large volumes of data to segment customers, thus helping rail operators better target them.

Airlines (Air Transportation)

The air transportation industry can also benefit substantially from the real-time data management capabilities of SAP HANA. In the case of the airline industry, we recommend use of HANA for all the aforementioned as well as the following areas:

- **Predictive maintenance:** Airlines can best make use of HANA for predicting maintenance of assets, as part of maintenance, repair and overhaul (MRO).

- **Route profitability and fuel management:** HANA can be used for forecasting route potential and profitability.

Along similar lines, firms involved in ocean freight can also benefit from the capabilities of SAP HANA.

SAP TM is gaining acceptability in the transportation and logistics industry as an integrated system used for transactions, planning, and monitoring. Essentially, this means that SAP TM is the source of most of the data generated within any organization that implements it. Therefore, we suggest integration of SAP TM with SAP HANA for analysis of any kind. The next version of SAP TM running SAP HANA will have prebuilt supply chain reporting, which will enhance reporting capabilities and near real-time decision-making. Also, large and global rail freight operators are exploring implementation of a freight management solution leveraging the power of SAP HANA.

Mobility

Your organization manages the "move" function in the supply chain, in which you are responsible for planning, implementing, and controlling forward and reverse flow of goods, services, and related information between point of origin and destination. Freight moves either directly or through one or more transshipment points by one or more modes of transport, and multiple agencies handle the freight at different stages of its life cycle. Also on the move are assets, such as trucks; trailers; trains; vessels; containers; aircraft; material-handling equipment; and people performing pickup, delivery, and sales jobs. With so many actors on the move, it is important to know where they are, what they are engaged with, when they will be available for the next task, what they can perform, whether they faced any difficulties in the field, whether they are performing as expected, and much more; customers expect you to know what is happening to their freight, how far it has traveled, when it will be delivered to them, whether is it intact or damaged, and so on. You need to have visibility of the life cycle of freight, along with asset use and two-way access to people in the field. Mobile technologies integrated with SAP–centric supply chain execution can address most of these challenges. Mobile devices in the field can capture freight-related data and share them with a central server on which a SAP-centric supply chain execution platform is installed. The information can thus be made available ahead of time for freight planning. Information on delivery, delays, and deviations captured in the field can be easily populated in the system and used internally and outputted to customers and vendors. In this way, you can increase productivity, while lowering operational costs and enhancing customer service.

Mobile technologies that can be deployed in the your industry are the Global Positioning System (GPS), for tracking assets and location-based services; radio frequency identification (RFID), for locating freight in warehouses/terminals; RFID readers and scanners, for faster scans, counts, issues, and receipts; and mobile phones with business applications, for inquiries, updates, and two-way communication.

With the help of various mobile technologies, you can

- Streamline load planning, routing, and scheduling to eliminate the costly misrouting of shipments

- Monitor driver and vehicle performance and relay dynamic routing decisions to drivers to help reduce costs

- Ensure on-time delivery of shipment by route optimization, constant connect and communication on real-time basis with drivers, and tracking of last-minute changes

- Eliminate costly paper-based processes by using advanced data capture technologies to scan freight data digitally, transmit them to central/local servers, update delivery information and payment details, and transmit photos of damaged freight to insurance and claims departments

- Get real-time visibility of driver and vehicle performance to identify the location of your drivers, the speed at which they are driving, and their driving patterns

- Track idling beyond normal limits, accurately schedule load pickups, and deploy the most appropriate truck to the customer

- Use smart business applications on mobile devices with reporting dashboards and workflows to improve collaboration between actors in the supply chain execution; as SAP TM sits at the center of the landscape, it can play the role of data hub—all updates to data can go through SAP TM or get updated into SAP

Social Media Integration

Given the increased use of social networks worldwide, social media is opening up new business opportunities by creating two-way communication, enabling customer feedback and response in real time. For the size and scope of the industry, it is imperative to tap the potential of social media to drive efficiencies and connect with customers; business partners; and ecosystems, such as universities, research organizations, and regulatory agencies.

Social media allows the sharing of information relevant to the industry, such as updates on fuel prices, carrier rates, new lanes, industry news, available loads, travel advisories, complaints, feedback, and views. Some of the information provided can be used as is. Modern carriers are proactively handling customer issues and complaints through Facebook and Twitter. Many 3PLs are posting freight details on Twitter to help find carriers to transport it. Trucking companies are sharing the location of equipment, looking for loads to haul. The first thing most shippers using transportation management systems (TMS) do is broadcast load tendering to a relatively small and select group of carriers with which a relationship has already been established while handling other lanes. Shippers and brokers post loads that are visible only to such carriers, which they trust. Carriers post available capacity and regular lanes on their web site, as they are confident that only their trusted shippers or brokers can see them. Videos of your operations and demonstrations illustrating how you are different from others can have a long-lasting impact on customers.

Social media is complementary to and not a replacement of TMS; order execution is managed by TMS after an appropriate match is made. Integration with social media is important for making full use of SAP. Leading 3PLs have portals that provide data access to all partners and customers, while offering access to social discussions to others.

SAP, being the core transaction system, can share its data on social networks, such as availability of freight or assets. You can use cases built on SAP TM to fetch this data using logic; for example, freight that has not found a buyer in six hours can be sent to social media for sharing. A logistics company with a small program using social media to match offers to available freight or to suggest best matches, along with SAP, will have options beyond the limited partner base.

Analytics

The industry is moving beyond just reporting historical data to predictive analysis. The major hurdle, however, is data residing in disparate systems. In the absence of integrated data, actionable intelligence that can lead to gains in efficiency, cost savings, and improved customer service is lost. Organizations implementing SAP TM have this data residing in a single system, saving the time required to mine data. More important, the sanctity of the data is retained, thus supporting fact-based decisions with little expenditure of time.

SAP TM addresses a number of issues, such as the following:

- Amount of weight transported per trade lane, business share, or transportation allocation

- Amount of volume transported per trade lane, business share, or transportation allocation

- Number of containers shipped on a specific relation

- Average transport costs per trade lane, carrier, shipper, or consignee

- Reliability of shipper, carrier, or consignee (based on time data from SAP)

- Percentage of dangerous goods shipments, compared with the overall number of shipments per trade lane

SAP TM also provides many ready-made reports:

- **SAP TM BW 7.3 Enhancement Package 1:** More focused on cost and carrier analysis

- **SAP TM 8.0:** More shipper specific

- **SAP TM 9.0:** Covers revenue-related reports

However, given the wealth of data SAP TM will have after a few months of implementation, organizations should identify key performance indicators for their business; derive definitions (formulas) for them; identify data elements; and build a strategy to move relevant data into the workplace to monitor key performance indicators, build "what if?" scenarios, and create dashboards for decision makers at every level of the organization.

Summary

A SAP TM platform integrated with HANA, a mobility platform, a social media platform, and business intelligence (BI) can give you access to real-time information, while providing you with analytical capabilities from structured and unstructured data. In this chapter, we have highlighted some benefits across the transportation and logistics industry. Knowing the capabilities and features of these products/solutions, we strongly believe that once you have implemented SAP, introducing these products/solutions in your landscape can help you obtain early return on investment.

CHAPTER 10

■ ■ ■

Process Mapping End-to-End Freight Life Cycle Scenarios

In this chapter, we will discuss the following:

- High-level processes that make up the end-to-end life cycle of freight logistics

- Mapping these processes in SAP TM

- The mapping of one end-to-end freight logistics process flow scenario in SAP TM

Having gained an understanding of SAP TM and its architecture, let's take a look at the freight process life cycle as well as its mapping in SAP TM, together with SAP Event Management (SAP EM), SAP Global Trade Services (SAP GTS), and SAP ERP.

Setting Up a Customer Account

Once the customer agrees to the financial and service terms and conditions and the 3PL, the credit department reviews the customer's credit history and establishes credit limits. The finance department sets up a client account in the system, with credit limits and, subsequently, a pricing agreement.

The finance department uses a financial system, such as SAP FICO, to set up the customer account and credit limits. The customer account is then transferred to SAP TM as a business partner or location, or both. The pricing agreement is created in SAP TM as forwarding agreement.

Receiving a Shipment Booking

The 3PL receives the booking request from the customer via phone, fax, e-mail, electronic data display (EDI), or portal. The customer contacts the 3PL's local office, centralized customer service department, or agent/subsidiary.

The customer service agent in the location contacted by the customer gathers more information from the customer with respect to the shipment. Typically, this information includes mode of transportation (air, ocean, or ground [road or rail]), size (full container load [FCL] or less than container load [LCL]), whether the shipment consists of dangerous goods or perishables, when the shipment is available to move or is needed at its destination, the shipment's place of origin and destination, and whether the shipment is be picked up or dropped off by the customer at the location specified by the 3PL—a branch, gateway, port, warehouse, and so on.

Orders from multiple applications, customers, and modes (phone, fax, e-mail, EDI, portal) are received in SAP TM as transportation requirements. Based on the order's requirements and the business rules setup, the system builds freight units (the smallest transportation unit in SAP TM), which are used for consolidation or dividing of transportation requirements, or both, in order to size the shipment properly for transportation resources, such as trailers, containers, vessels, and railcars.

Sending a Notification of a Customer's Order

The customer's order notification is sent via phone, fax, or e-mail to the necessary parties, such as the export agent and the Planning department.

SAP TM offers a personal object work list (POWL) through which the concerned parties (export agent, Planning department, and so on) can access, manage, and track tasks related to the order.

Planning Freight Transportation Route

The Planning department plans the route the freight will travel to its destination. Sometimes, the Planning department may route the freight from customer, to branch, to gateway; other times, the freight may be routed directly from customer to gateway, airport, or port. The main goal is to get the freight from place of origin to destination at the lowest cost possible.

In SAP TM the Planning department has the option of planning the order either manually or automatically. With automatic planning the vehicle-scheduling and -routing engine running in the background plans the order's route. To plan manually, SAP TM offers transportation cockpit, which the Planning department should use. Once supplied with selection and planning profile, the transportation cockpit determines which orders will be listed for planning as well as the resources and schedules available. Furthermore, the Planning department has the following options in cases of manual planning:

- **Interactive planning:** Orders to be planned are selected and then dragged and dropped onto the resource/schedule.

- **One-step planning:** Once orders to be planned are selected, the vehicle-scheduling and -routing engine is called to plan them.

- **Generation of transportation proposal:** This option is used if multiple routing options are to be viewed before making decisions.

Once the route is planned, the carrier can be selected. SAP TM provides manual and automatic options for choosing the carrier. SAP TM also has these tendering options:

- **Peer-to-peer tendering:** The freight request for quotation is sent sequentially to each proposed carrier.

- **Broadcast tendering:** The freight request for quotation is sent to all proposed carriers simultaneously.

The direct tendering process can also be used to send the order directly to a specific carrier without requesting a quotation.

Booking a Carrier

The Planning department arranges for the carrier booking for the main leg. The Planning department communicates with the carrier via phone, fax, e-mail, or, EDI and requests a booking of necessary space. After receiving the booking request, the carrier may decide to accept or reject the request or accept it with modification. In all cases, thecarrier notifies the Planning department of the decision.

To enter the booking information, SAP TM provides a freight-booking user interface. Through this interface, the Planning department can request the booking for space with the carrier. The information can be transferred from SAP TM to carrier via fax, e-mail, EDI, or portal. The interface also allows for capture of carrier response.

Confirming an Order with the Customer

Once the carrier accepts the booking, the customer receives order confirmation via phone, fax, e-mail, or EDI.

The forwarding-order user interface in SAP TM offers the option of confirming the order with the customer.

Arranging for the Pickup of Freight

If freight pickup is required, the branch export agent arranges for it with a local carrier. The pickup request is made to the local carrier via phone, fax, e-mail, or EDI. The pickup request contains information such as where to pick up and deliver the freight, date and time of pickup, and whether any special equipment is required. After receiving confirmation (to carry out the pickup) from the carrier, the necessary documents are provided to the carrier.

The branch export agent can use the freight-order user interface in SAP TM for the pickup request. The interface allows the user to enter the required information, generate the necessary documents, and send the information and documents to the carrier. In addition, acceptance and rejection of the pickup request can be captured.

Picking Up Freight and Delivering It to the Origin Dock

On the prearranged date of freight pickup, the carrier is dispatched, along with documentation, to the location of the shipper/supplier. There, the freight is loaded onto a truck, and shipping documentation, such as commercial invoice (CI), shipper's letter of instruction (SLI), and shipper's export declaration (SED), is collected from the shipper/supplier. Freight and documentation are delivered to a branch or location communicated at the time of the pickup request. A dockworker unloads the freight from the carrier's truck, checks it in, signs the paperwork, stores the freight in the branch warehouse or other storage location, and turns in the paperwork to the export agent.

Freight execution and track and trace are handled in SAP TM through the freight-order user interface. SAP TM offers a standard set of events concerning the cargo, such as "Ready for Loading," "Loaded," "Departed," and "Arrived," for track and trace. SAP TM can also be integrated with SAP EM for better track and trace.

Preparing a Shipment for Movement

The branch export agent receives the paperwork from the dockworker and creates a pick list document for the dockworker so that he or she can pull shipments (whole or partial) for consolidation. Instructions for any special services or handling that may need to be performed are also noted.

The SAP TM freight-order user interface can be used to print various documents.

Performing Export Customs Clearance (if Requested)

Not every customer awards this to the same 3PL. If awarded, however, export compliance checking for a denied party, embargoed countries, known shippers, and denied commodities is performed. Information is supplied to a customs official via fax, e-mail, EDI, or portal; by using a third-party provider; or by submitting hard copy of documents. The customs official processes the shipments and either holds them or gives clearance.

Customs clearance status for the order can be set manually in SAP TM. Depending on the setting, SAP TM may block further order execution if required. If SAP TM is integrated with SAP GTS, the customs status can be set automatically.

Preparing Consolidation and Documentation

Based on the pick list document received from the export agent, a dockworker pulls the freight from the branch warehouse shelves or other storage location and builds consolidation as needed. If any additional services are to be performed, such as packing, shrink-wrapping, or fumigation, these are noted on the pick list document. The dockworker makes note on the pick list document of discrepancies, services performed, and collected paperwork with regard to these services, adding additional comments if necessary.

Shipping instructions can be viewed as well as printed with the SAP TM freight-order user interface.

Handing Over Consolidation to the Line-Haul Carrier

The line-haul carrier arrives, the freight is loaded onto the truck, and the paperwork is signed and turned over to the carrier driver.

SAP TM provides the option to view as well as print the shipping manifest using the freight-order user interface.

Moving Freight to the Gateway

The carrier departs from the branch or other specified location en route to the gateway. The gateway is notified via phone, fax, or e-mail.

SAP TM has a standard set of status events, such as "Departed" and "In Execution," through the freight-order user interface. Based on the status of the freight order, the status of the forwarding order is updated automatically, thereby allowing order tracking. SAP TM can be integrated with SAP EM for more enhanced tracking. Morever, using POWL, personnel can access and track orders that are expected for arrival.

Delivering Freight to the Gateway

The line-haul carrier delivers the freight and documentation to the gateway. A dockworker unloads the freight from the carrier's truck, checks in the freight, signs the paperwork, stores the freight in a gateway warehouse location, and turns in the paperwork to the gateway agent. The carrier invoices the 3PL for services performed.

The SAP TM freight-order user interface can be used to calculate the freight charges the carrier will be invoicing. The interface can also be used to update the status to "Arrived." Based on the status of the freight order, the status of the forwarding order is updated automatically, thereby allowing order tracking. . SAP TM can be integrated with SAP EM for more enhanced tracking.

Planning Outbound Consolidation

The gateway agent views the inbound consolidations and determines the outbound consolidations that need to be planned for, such as necessary equipment (containers, and so on). Outbound consolidation plans are based on when the inbound consolidations will arrive, their destination, the services required for the shipments in those consolidations, the type of commodity, whether the shipment consists of dangerous goods or perishables or is of high value, and whether the shipment is oversized or overweight for its mode of transport.

The gateway agent can use the planning engine to identify the resources available as well as shipments that can be consolidated. With consolidation the planning engine takes into consideration various parameters, such as incompatibilities, capacity, and loading and unloading duration. The planning engine also checks for dangerous goods. Planning can be done automatically or manually.

Assigning a Shipment to Outbound Gateway Consolidation

The gateway agent assigns the shipments (whole or partial) to movements that have been confirmed by the carrier. The agent also creates a pick list document for the dockworker so that he or she can pull the shipments for consolidation. Instructions for any special services or handling that may need to be performed are noted.

The gateway agent can use the freight-booking user interface in SAP TM to generate a shipping document to be given to the dockworker, with instructions for physical/actual consolidation.

Preparing Consolidation

A dockworker receives the pick list document from the gateway agent, pulls the freight on the pick list from the gateway warehouse shelves, and builds consolidation; additional services are performed as requested, such as packing, shrink-wrapping, and fumigation. The dockworker makes note on the pick list document of discrepancies , services performed, and collected paperwork with regard to these services. The dockworker turns in the notated pick list to the gateway agent.

Creating Paperwork for the Main Carriage

The gateway agent creates appropriate transportation paperwork, such as house bill of lading (HBL), master bill of lading (MBL), and forwarder's cargo receipt (FCR)/master bill of detailed manifest. The gateway agent sends the completed paperwork to the appropriate parties, for example, delivering transportation paperwork to the dockworker or providing documents to the carrier (via fax, e-mail, or EDI).

The SAP TM freight-booking user interface offers the option to view as well as print the manifest and other documents.

Creating Paperwork for Cartage and Dispatching it to the Main Carrier

The gateway agent arranges for the movement of consolidations (of cartage) from the gateway to the main carrier. The cartage carrier may pick up and deliver one or more consolidations. The cartage carrier arrives, and the freight is loaded onto the truck. The paperwork is signed and turned over to the cartage carrier driver. The cartage carrier departs and takes the consolidations to the appropriate carriers. The gateway agent may update the movements to"Tendered to Carrier" status. Freight is delivered to the main carrier.

A freight order can be created with the freight-booking user interface in SAP TM. The gateway agent can use the interface to arrange for cartage movement and to generate the necessary documents.

Moving Freight to the Destination Gateway or Branch

After delivery to the main carrier, the freight is loaded onto the means of transport (aircraft, ship, truck, railcar). The transport departs; departure and arrival information can be sent via EDI to the destination gateway, branch, and transshipment gateway as applicable.

The freight-booking user interface in SAP TM provides a standard set of status events, such as "In Execution" and "Uplift Confirmed." SAP TM will automatically create the import freight booking and forwarding order as soon as the status of the freight booking is set to "Uplift Confirmed" (in case of air) or "Shipped on Board" (in case of ocean). SAP TM can be integrated with SAP EM for more enhanced tracking.

Performing Import Customs Clearance

Once the freight is loaded onto aircraft, ship, truck, or railcar, and that vehicle departs for its international destination, the inbound destination branch/gateway is kept informed as well as the customs agency at the destination port/border. The destination branch of the 3PL informs customers about expected shipments. Clearance of the inbound shipment may or may not be carried out by the 3PL responsible for forwarding the shipment, as every customer is free to appoint a customs clearing agent, and this can be the 3PL carrying the shipment or another player. Customs may choose to inspect the cargo using x-ray, physical examination, document inspection, and so on; duties and taxes are paid to customs either by the 3PL or by the customer directly.

SAP TM offers the option to update the customs status of the order manually. Furthermore, SAP TM can be integrated with SAP GTS to enable compliance checking and communication with customs as well as receipt of status updates from customs.

Arranging for Pickup of the Freight from the Carrier

If freight pickup from the main carrier is required, the branch/inbound gateway agent arranges for it with a carrier. A collection order is generated for the cartage carrier for pickup of the freight from the main carrier. The collection order is sent to the cartage carrier, informing it of where to pick up and deliver the cargo as well as of any special equipment needed to move it. At the main carrier's location, the freight is loaded onto the truck. Typically, shipping documentation (sent via fax, e-mail, or mail) is collected from the main carrier. The cartage carrier delivers the freight and documentation to the specified location.

From the main carrier the freight may be moved directly to the destination branch location, or it may stop at a gateway before moving to the branch. The cartage carrier invoices for services performed. A dockworker unloads the freight from the cartage carrier's truck, checks it in, signs the paperwork, stores the freight in the warehouse, and turns in the paperwork to the import agent.

The branch agent can use either the freight-order user interface or freight-booking user interface in SAP TM to create a freight order for picking up the freight from the main carrier and delivering it to the destination branch or gateway.

Arranging for the Delivery of Freight

Once the freight is cleared by customs, clients can pick it up from the branch. If delivery is required, however, a branch agent arranges for it with a local carrier. A request for delivery is made to the carrier via phone, fax, e-mail, or EDI. The carrier confirms the request using one of these same methods. The necessary documents are generated and sent to the carrier, informing it of where to pick up and deliver the freight as well as of any special equipment needed to move it.

The branch agent can use the freight-order user interface in SAP TM to request delivery. Once the order is accepted, the necessary documents can be generated.

Delivering Freight to the Customer

The local carrier arrives at the designated customer location. The freight is unloaded, and the documentation, if any, is handed over to the customer, who in turn gives the proof of delivery to the carrier. The carrier may inform the branch agent of the delivery and give the proof of delivery to him or her. The branch agent then marks the order as delivered. If money has to be collected from the delivery address, the driver delivering the freight collects it and subsequently brings it to the branch or to his or her company.

A standard set of events is provided in SAP TM to track and trace the freight order. In addition, SAP TM can be integrated with SAP EM for better trace and track.

Calculating the Charges on a Shipment

Charges on a shipment may be categorized as follows:

- Origin charges

- Transportation charges (main transportation charge and other charges associated with it, e.g., fuel surcharge, security fee)

- Destination charges

- Duties and taxes (pass-through charges)

Charges may be entered in as one currency and billed in another, in which case the Currency Adjustment Factor (CAF) is charged. Charges may be included in a rate, waived, or rolled up. International Commercial Terms (Incoterms) help in determining which party will pay for what charges.

SAP TM offers the option to store the contractual rates agreed to with the customer. These rates are used to calculate the charges to be levied on the customer.

Invoicing for Services

The billing clerk may manually invoice charges, or charges may be invoiced based on the business rules setup. Moreover, clients may be invoiced at different times:

- Origin clients may be invoiced after a shipment departs from its country of origin.

- Destination clients may be invoiced after delivery to the consignee.

Once the invoice is created, it can be printed at a location designated by the user or at a centralized location and sent to the customer either electronically (via EDI) or in print format. Documents often pulled from imaging may need to be attached to the invoice, such as house bill of lading/(HAWB), master air waybill (MAWB)/MBL, Goods Received Voucher GRV, and FCR.

SAP TM provides options for calculating the charges automatically or manually. After the charges have been calculated, a forwarding settlement document is created in SAP TM. This document is then transferred to a financial system, such as SAP FICO (ERP), where the final invoice is created and posted.

Verifying the Invoice and Executing the Freight Settlement

The carrier whose services were used sends an invoice to the accounts payable department for settlement. The accounts payable clerk checks the invoice submitted for any discrepancies. If no discrepancies are found, the invoice is processed for settlement. In the case of a discrepancy, it is resolved by issuing a debit or credit note.

The freight charges that the carrier invoices can be calculated manually or automatically in SAP TM. The charges are calculated based on the freight agreement in the system. A freight settlement document is created and transferred to a financial system. If the financial system is SAP FICO, then a purchase order and service entry sheet are automatically created based on the freight settlement document. Then, invoice verification can be done, followed by posting and final settlement.

Now that you have had an overview of process mapping, let's look at the process flows and their SAP TM mapping for a door-to-door LTL/parcel air shipment scenario (see Figure 10-1). Assume that the customer account is set up and that the customer has requested a door-to-door international movement of LTL shipment as well as customs clearance service at both export and import side; the main leg is via air, and the other legs, via road.

Figure 10-1. *Door-to-door LTL air shipment scenario*

Figures 10-2–10-8 illustrate the process flows for the shipment scenario.

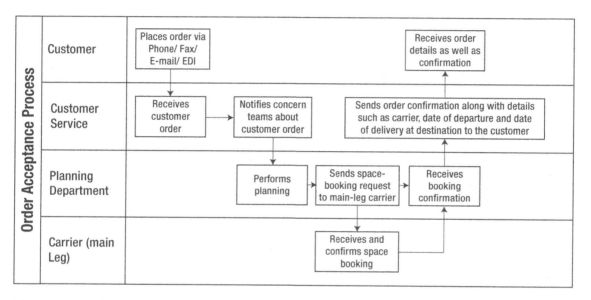

Figure 10-2. *Order acceptance process flow*

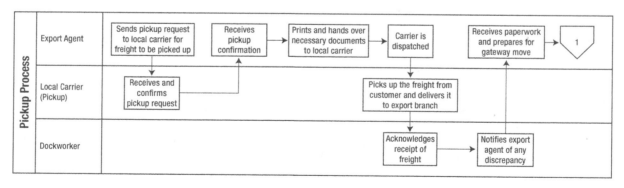

Figure 10-3. *Pickup process flow*

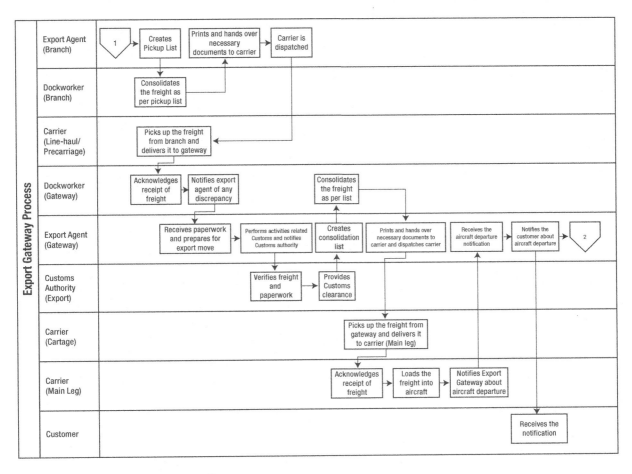

Figure 10-4. *Export gateway process flow*

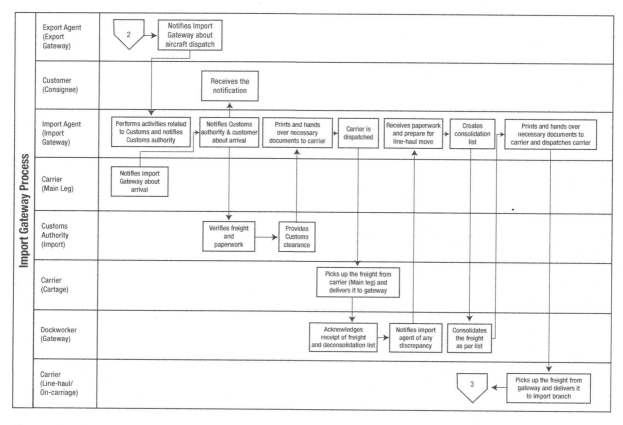

Figure 10-5. *Import gateway process flow*

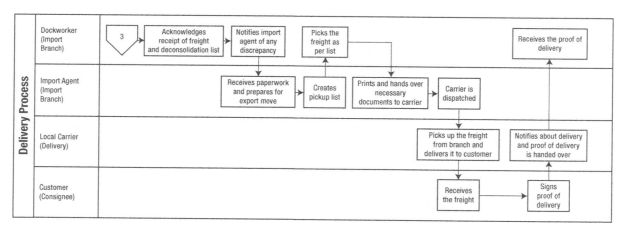

Figure 10-6. *Delivery process flow*

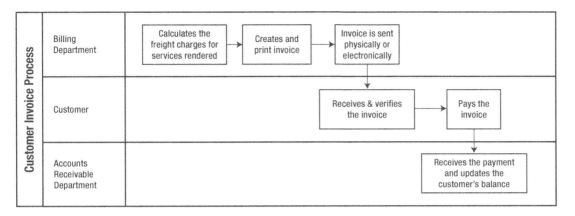

Figure 10-7. *Customer invoice process flow*

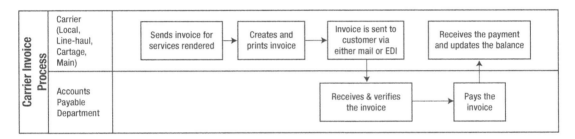

Figure 10-8. *Carrier invoice process flow*

Now, let's look at how these process flows are mapped in SAP TM (see Figures 10-9–10-15).

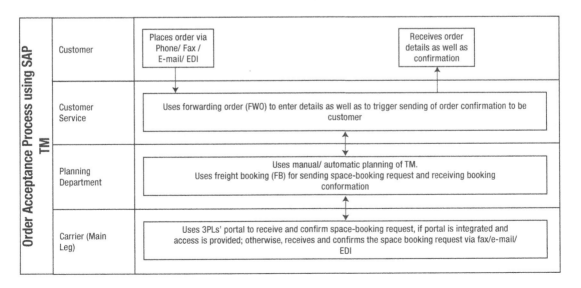

Figure 10-9. *Order acceptance process flow in SAP TM*

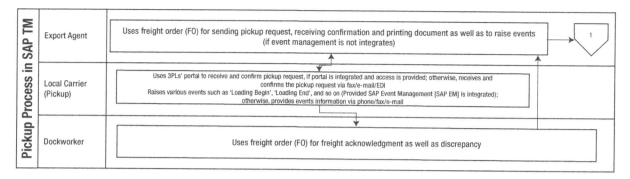

Figure 10-10. *Pickup process flow in SAP TM*

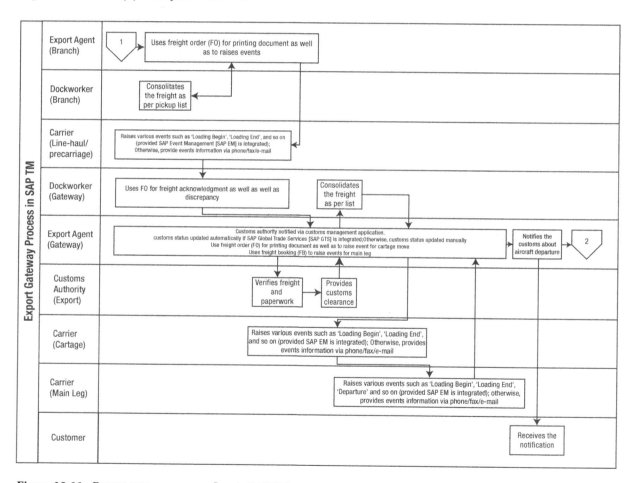

Figure 10-11. *Export gateway process flow in SAP TM*

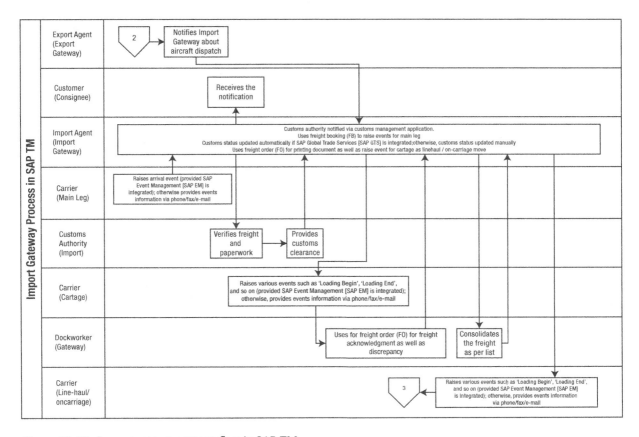

Figure 10-12. *Import gateway process flow in SAP TM*

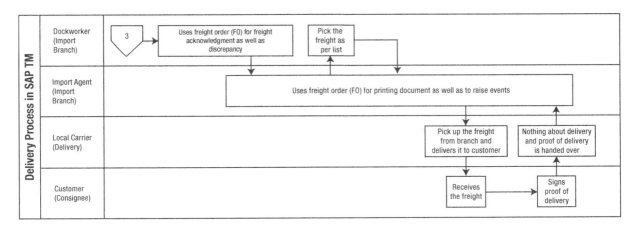

Figure 10-13. *Delivery process flow in SAP TM*

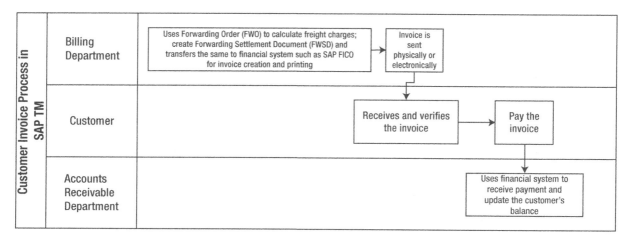

Figure 10-14. *Customer invoice process flow in SAP TM*

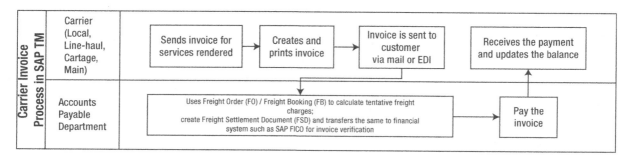

Figure 10-15. *Carrier invoice process flow in SAP TM*

Summary

In this chapter, we gave an overview of the end-to-end freight life cycle, along with its mapping in SAP TM. We also looked at process flow and mapping in SAP TM by taking one scenario as an example. This is further explained in the Appendix.

Step-by-Step Guide to Configuring and Implementing SAP TM 9.0

Given the freight life cycle process mapping discussed in the previous chapter, let us drill down to see the typical configuration and master data in SAP TM.

Before proceeding, let's take a look at some of the terms and abbreviations used in this chapter:

- **Tcode**: Transaction code.

- **Customizing for SAP TM/SAP ERP**: Enter Tcode as SAP project runtime object (SPRO), and click the SAP Reference IMG button.

- **Customizing request**: This is required for any customization so that it can be transported to other systems.

Systems Requirements

The systems required to configure the scenario are

- SAP TM 9.0 service package 5 (SAPK-11005INSAPTM)

- SAP Event Management (SAP EM) 9.0

- SAP ERP 6.0 enhancement pack 6

Assumptions

It is assumed that:

- Basic settings, such as activating queues, creating active versions and models, and activating business functions, have been performed in the SAP TM system

- Basic configuration required to integrate SAP TM and SAP ERP has been performed

- Basic configuration required to integrate SAP TM and SAP EM has been performed

---

■ **Note**   The purpose of this appendix is to provide a glimpse of SAP TM functionalities and should not be seen as standard. Furthermore, SAP TM provides multiple options for performing activities, and this appendix is restricted to illustrating only one of the variety of options available for each.

Scenario

To get a better understanding of SAP TM functionality, let's consider the following scenario:

HEPUSHA Corporation Ltd., a multinational 3PL, has operations in Japan and the United States. Operations in Japan are handled by HEPUSHA Japan. Operations in the United States are handled by HEPUSHA USA.

In Japan, HEPUSHA has many gateways, including one in Narita, as well as many stations catering to different locations in Japan, including Yokohama. Similarly, the company has gateways and stations in a number of locations in the United States, including Los Angeles and San Francisco, respectively.

The Yokohama station receives an order from Shipcam International to move consignment from Yokohama to Coman Ltd., in San Diego.

The Yokohama station in turn hires Vistala Roadways to pick up the consignment from Shipcam International and bring it to the Yokohama station. To move the consignment from the Yokohama station to the Narita gateway, Astala Carriers is used. From the Narita gateway the consignment will be on loaded on a Mistala Airlines plane at Narita International Airport (NRT) and brought to Los Angeles International Airport (LAX) and then on to the Los Angeles gateway. Next, the consignment will be moved to the San Francisco station, using the services of MacMovers Carriers. Finally, it will be delivered to Coman Ltd., using the services of Delta Roadways.

Following are the master data and configurations required for this scenario.

Organizations

The SAP TM organizational model is independent from the SAP ERP organizational model. SAP TM offers these six organizational unit functions:

- **Corporate**: This organizational unit function is the highest; it is optional.

- **Company**: This is similar to ERP company.

- **Forwarding house**: This organizational unit function is used for a single organization that can perform the functions of planning and execution, purchasing, and sales.

- **Planning and execution**: For the organization that is responsible for the planning and execution function.

- **Purchasing**: For the organization that is responsible for the purchasing function.

- **Sales**: For the organization that is responsible for the sales function.

The three SAP TM organizational unit roles are as follows:

- **Organization**: This organizational unit role is the highest that can be assigned to an organization.

- **Office**: The office unit role can be defined only for an organizational unit with a sales function. The role can be assigned to an organizational unit with the organization role.

- **Group**: This role can be defined for an organizational unit with the sales, purchasing, planning and execution, or forwarding house function. The role can be assigned to an organizational unit with the organization or office role.

For the given scenario, you will need to create the organization shown in Table A-1.

Table A-1. *Organizational Data*

Field	Value	Value	Value	Value
Basic Data Tab				
Organization code	HEPUSHA	HEPUSHAJAP	HEJPFHNAR	HEJPFHYOK
Validity	01-01-2013 to 31-12-9999	01-01-2013 to 31-12-9999	01-01-2013 to 31-12-9999	01-01-2013 to 31-12-9999
Description	HEPUSHA Corporation Ltd.	HEPUSHA Ltd.— Japan	HEPUSHA Japan Narita gateway	HEPUSHA Japan Yokohama station
Organizational Data Tab				
Organization function	Corporate	Company	Forwarding house	Forwarding house
Organization role	Organization	Organization	Organization	Organization
Address Tab				
Address	5-28-11 Higashi-ikebukuro, Toshima-ku	2-1-1 Akabane, Kita	2130, Tokko	20-1-3 Minato Mirai
City	Tokyo	Tokyo	Narita	Yokohama
Postal code	3981-9360	115-0046	286-0106	220-8173
Country	JP	JP	JP	JP
Region	13	13	12	14
Basic Data Tab				
Organization code	HEPUSHAUSA	HEUSFHLA	HEUSFHSFR	
Validity	01-01-2013 to 31-12-9999	01-01-2013 to 31-12-9999	01-01-2013 to 31-12-9999	
Description	HEPUSHA Ltd.— USA	HEPUSHA USA Los Angeles gateway	HEPUSHA USA San Francisco station	
Organizational Data Tab				
Organization function	Company	Forwarding house	Forwarding house	
Organization role	Organization	Organization	Organization	
Address Tab				
Address	300 Park Plaza Dr.	739 S. Main St.	435 O'Farrell St.	
City	Secaucus	Los Angeles	San Francisco	
Postal code	07094	90014	94102	
Country	US	US	US	
Region	NJ	CA	CA	

To define an organization, in SAP NetWeaver Business Client, click Master Data ➤ Organization ➤ Create Organization and Staffing, or use the Tcode (PPOCE).

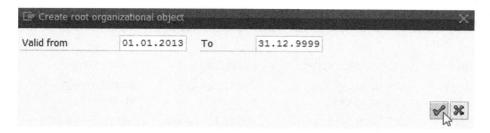

Figure A-1. *Validity dialog box for creating an organization*

Next, click the Continue ✔ button. Enter organization details, such as name, organization data, and address.

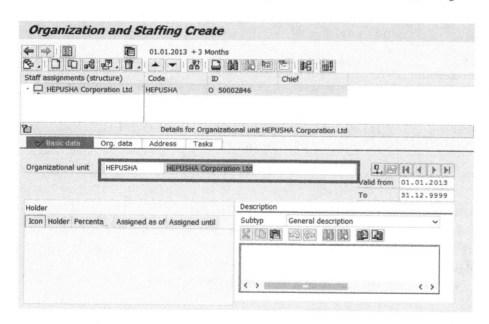

Figure A-2. *Creating an organization: – Basic data tab*

Once the organizational unit's basic data are entered, save the entry by clicking the Save 🖫 button. Then, select the Organizational data tab, and click the Create ☐ button.

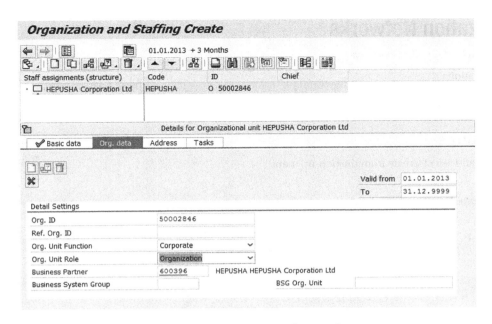

Figure A-3. *Creating an organization: Organizational Data tab*

▪ **Note** Make sure to write down the auto-created organization identification (ID) number and business partner; they will be required later in the scenario.

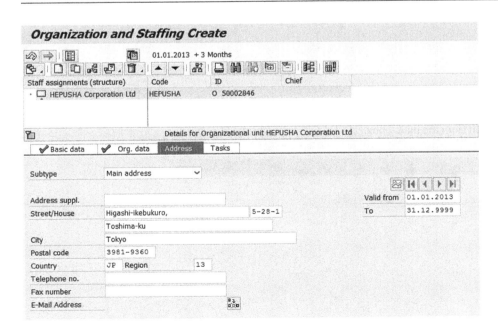

Figure A-4. *Creating an organization: Address tab*

Defining Organization Networks

The organization network can be defined in two ways:

- Creating organizations
- Assigning organizations

Creating Organizations

Right-click the organization, and select Create from the pop-up menu.

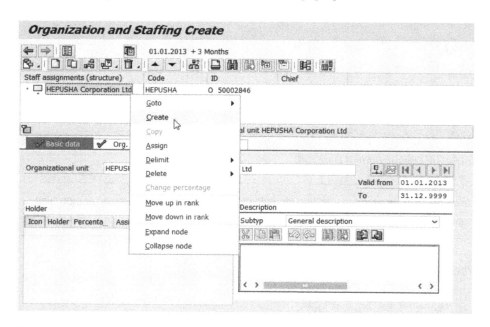

Figure A-5. *Creating organizational hierarchy*

Select Organizational unit from the dialog box.

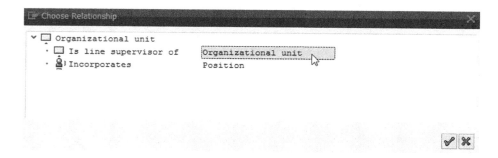

Figure A-6. *Relationship dialog box for creating an organization*

Click the Continue ✔ button, and create the other organizations, using Table A-1.

Assigning Organizations

For assigning one organization to another, both organizations have to have already been created. To assign an organization to another, in SAP NetWeaver Business Client, click Master Data ➤ Organization ➤ Edit Organization and Staffing, or use the Tcode (PPOME).

Now, search for the parent organization, using the search term. Double-click the name to open the organizational hierarchy. Right-click the organization, and select Assign from the pop-up menu.

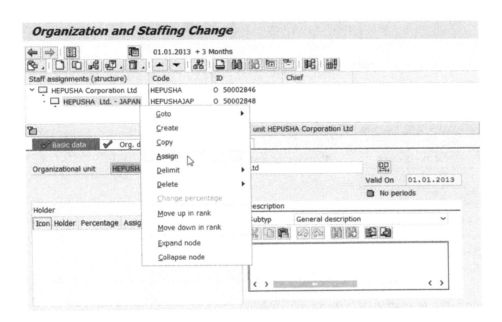

Figure A-7. *Assigning an organization*

Select Is line supervisor of from the dialog box.

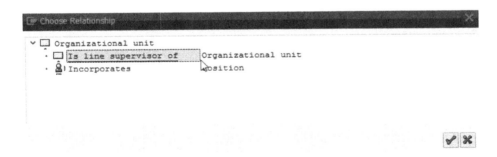

Figure A-8. *Relationship dialog box for assigning an organization*

A search is provided for searching for the child organization (i.e., the organization that is to be assigned).

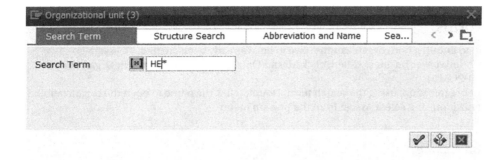

Figure A-9. Search window for searching for an organization

From the search result, select the organization that needs to be assigned.

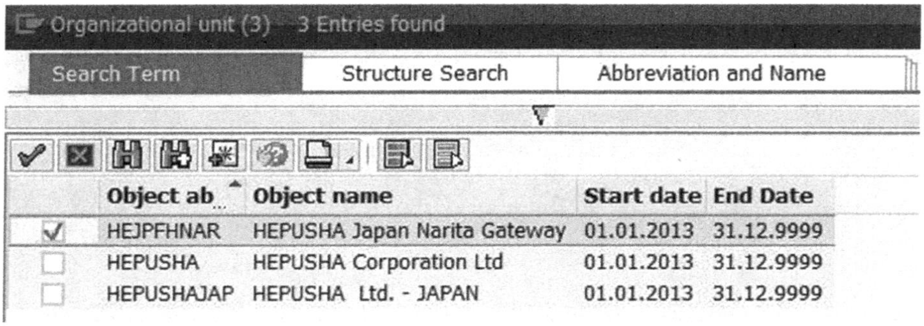

Object ab ▲	Object name	Start date	End Date
☑ HEJPFHNAR	HEPUSHA Japan Narita Gateway	01.01.2013	31.12.9999
☐ HEPUSHA	HEPUSHA Corporation Ltd	01.01.2013	31.12.9999
☐ HEPUSHAJAP	HEPUSHA Ltd. - JAPAN	01.01.2013	31.12.9999

Organizational unit (3)   3 Entries found

Search Term | Structure Search | Abbreviation and Name

Figure A-10. Selecting an organization to be assigned in the Search window

Click the Copy ✔ button to assign the organization.

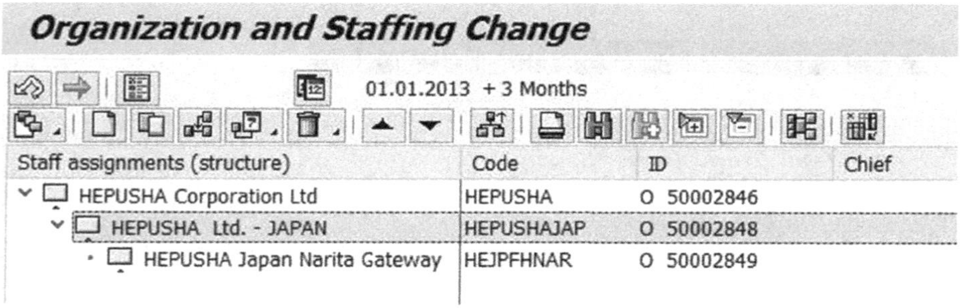

Organization and Staffing Change

01.01.2013 + 3 Months

Staff assignments (structure)	Code	ID	Chief
∨ ▢ HEPUSHA Corporation Ltd	HEPUSHA	O 50002846	
∨ ▢ HEPUSHA Ltd. - JAPAN	HEPUSHAJAP	O 50002848	
• ▢ HEPUSHA Japan Narita Gateway	HEJPFHNAR	O 50002849	

Figure A-11. Organizational hierarchy after assignment

In this way, create the remaining organizations.

Figure A-12. *Complete organizational hierarchy*

Defining Business Partners

A business partner is any person, organization, group of people, or group of organizations with which a company has business interests.

For the business partner of type "organization," SAP TM provides the following roles:

- **General business partner**: This role is automatically assigned to the business partner when the business partner is created. General data related to the business partner, such as name and address (valid for all business roles), are stored in this role.

- **Carrier**: This role is assigned to the business partner that is a carrier. The standard carrier alpha code or airline codes can be defined for this business partner role.

- **Vendor**: Assign this role to the business partner that is a supplier.

- **Ship-to party**: This role is assigned to the business partner that is a customer.

- **Sold-to party**: This role is also assigned to the business partner that is a customer.

- **Organizational unit**: This role represents an organizational unit of a company.

For the business partner of type "person," SAP TM offers these roles:

- **Employee**: This role is assigned to the business partner that is an employee. This business partner can then be assigned to an organizational unit.

- **Internet user**: Assign this role to the business partner that will be taking part in the tendering process.

- **Contact person**: Assign this role also to the business partner that will be taking part in the tendering process.

■ **Note**   If customer and vendor data are already set up in SAP ERP, this data can be transferred to SAP TM.

For the given scenario, you will need to create as business partners the carriers listed in Table A-2.

Table A-2. *Business Partner Data: Carriers*

Field	Value	Value	Value	Value	Value	Value
Business partner code	HE-CR-01	HE-CR-02	HE-CR-03	HE-CR-04	HE-CR-05	HE-CR-06
Grouping	External number assignment	External number assignment	External number assignment	External number assignment	External number assignment	External number assignment
Business partner role	Carrier	Carrier	Carrier	Carrier	Carrier	Carrier
Address Tab						
Name Section						
Name	Vistala Roadways	Astala Carriers	Mistala Airlines	MacMovers Carriers	Delta Roadways	Mistala Airlines—USA
Street Address Section						
Street/House number	10-97-1 Nakamura Ward	1-47-1 Nagono, Nakamura Ward	739 Hanasakicho	9860 Crocker St.	841 Harrison St.	7225 W. Century Blvd.
Postal code	2310063	4640000	2860103	90013	94103	90045
City	Yokohama	Nagoya	Naritia-shi	Los Angeles	San Francisco	Los Angeles
Country	JP	JP	JP	US	US	US
Region	14	13	12	CA	CA	CA
Identification Tab						
Identification Numbers Section						
ID type			TM0001			
Identification number			MA			

For the given scenario, the customers listed in Table A-3 must also be created as business partners.

Table A-3. *Business Partner Data: Shipper and Consignee*

Field	Value	Value
Business partner code	HE-CU-01	HE-CO-01
Grouping	External number assignment	External number assignment
Business partner role	Ship-to party	Sold-to party
Address Tab		
Name Section		
Name	Shipcam International	Coman Ltd.
Street Address Section		
Street/House number	2-2-19 Kanagawa Prefecture	547 Bush St.
Postal code	2200012	92104
City	Yokohama	San Francisco
Country	JP	US
Region	14	CA

▪ **Note**   To set the shipper HE-CU-01 as "Known shipper," assign it the business partner role "vendor," and, in the Vendor Data tab, create the data given in Table A-4.

Table A-4. *Known Shipper Data for HE-CU-01*

Field	Value
Vendor Data Tab	
Air Cargo Security Section	
Shipper security status	Known shipper
Known-from date	<Enter date that is 180 days prior (today's date minus 180 days)>
Expiry date	31-12-2020

To define a business partner, in SAP NetWeaver Business Client, click Master Data ➤ General ➤ Define Business Partner, or use the Tcode (BP).

To create the business partners for this scenario, click the Organization button or Business Partner ➤ Create ➤ Organization (Ctrl+F5).

Then, click the Organization ☐ Organization button, and enter the data from Tables A-2 and A-3 in the Address tab.

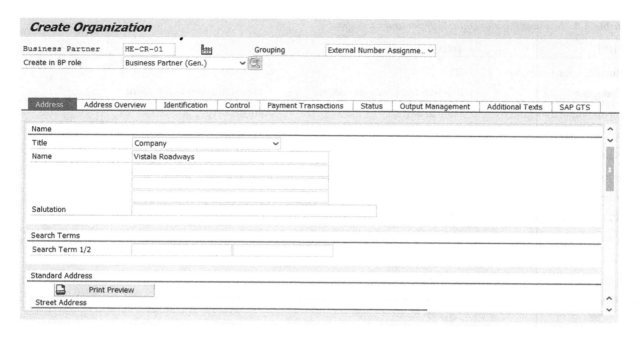

Figure A-13. *Creating a business partner*

First, you create the business partner, which is automatically assigned a general role. Then, add the respective roles to the business partner by clicking the Edit 📝 button.

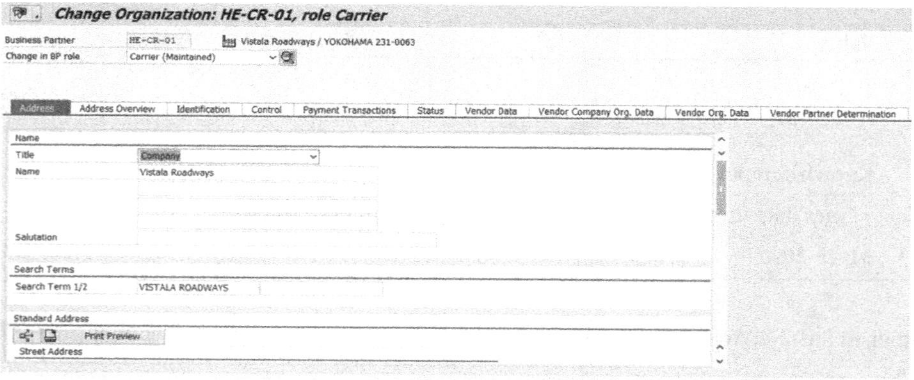

Figure A-14. *Adding a role to a business partner*

In this way, create the remaining business partners, with their respective roles.

■ **Note** To specify that HE-CU-01 is the known shipper, open HE-CU-01 Business Partner in edit mode, and select the vendor role. In the Vendor Data tab, enter the data from Table A-5 in the Air Cargo Security section.

Table A-5. *HE-CU-01 Known Shipper Data*

Field	Value
Shipper security status	Known shipper
Known-from date	<Enter date that is 180 days prior (today's date minus 180 days)>
Expiry date	31-12-2020

Defining Location

A location is a place (source, destination, transshipment) that is used in the transportation process. SAP TM offers a variety of location types for classifying location:

- Production plant

- Distribution center

- Shipping point

- Customer

- Vendor

- Terminal

- Port

- Airport

- Railway station

- Container freight station

- Hub

- Gateway

- Container yard

For the given scenario, you will need to create the locations shown in Tables A-6–A-8.

Table A-6. *Location Data: Customer*

Field	Value	Value
Location code	HE-CO-01	HE-CU-01
Location type	Customer	Customer
Address Tab		
Name Section		
Name	Coman Ltd.	Shipcam International
Street Address Section		
Street/House number	547 Bush St.	2-2-19 Kanagawa Prefecture
Postal code	92104	2200012
City	San Francisco	Yokohama
Country	US	JP
Region	CA	14
General Tab		
Partners Section		
Business partner	HE-CO-01	HE-CU-01

Table A-7. *Location Data: Organization*

Field	Value	Value	Value	Value
Location code	HEGWJPNAR	HESTAJPYOK	HEGWUSLA	HESTAUSSFR
Location type	Gateway	Distribution center	Gateway	Distribution center
Address Tab				
Name Section				
Name	Narita gateway	Yokohama station	Los Angeles gateway	San Francisco station
Street Address Section				
Street/House number	2130, Tokko	20-1-3 Minato Mirai	739 S. Main St.	435 O'Farrell St.
Postal code	2860106	2208173	90014	94102
City	Narita	Yokohama	Los Angeles	San Francisco
Country	JP	JP	US	US
Region	12	14	CA	CA
General Tab				
Partners Section				
Business partner	600399	600400	600402	600403

Table A-8. *Location Data: Airport*

Field	Value	Value
Location code	HEMFNRT	HEMFLA
Location type	Airport	Airport
Address Tab		
Name Section		
Name	Mistala Airlines–NRT	Mistala Airlines–LA
Street Address Section		
Street/House number	1305, Tensai Atamo	Cargo Bldg. 2, Block B, Imperial Hwy., 7201
Postal code	2820007	90045
City	Narita	Los Angeles
Country	JP	US
Region	12	CA
General Tab		
Identifier Section		
International Air Transportation Association (IATA) code	NRT	LAX
Partner Section		
Business partner	HE-CR-03	HE-CR-06

To define a location, in SAP NetWeaver Business Client, click Master Data ➤ Transportation Network ➤ Location ➤ Define Location, or use the Tcode (/SCMTMS/LOC3).

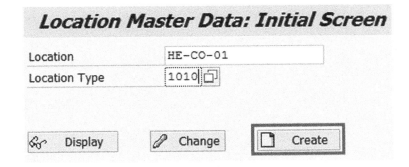

Figure A-15. *Initial screen for location master data*

Next, click the Create button. Enter the name, and select the Address tab to enter the address.

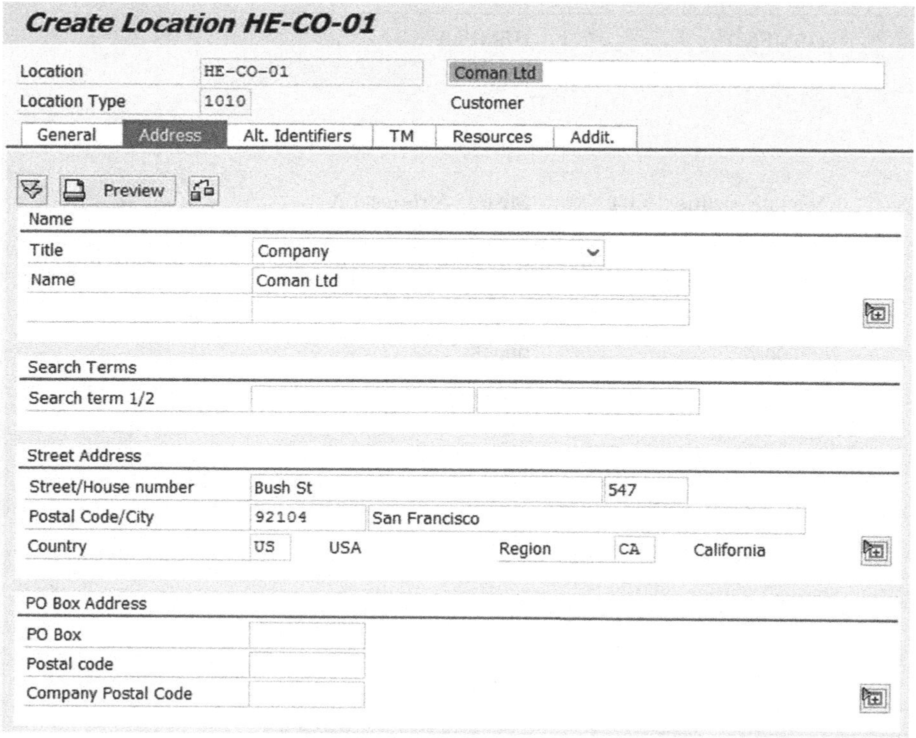

Figure A-16. *Creating location: Address tab*

Attach the business partner to the location in the General tab.

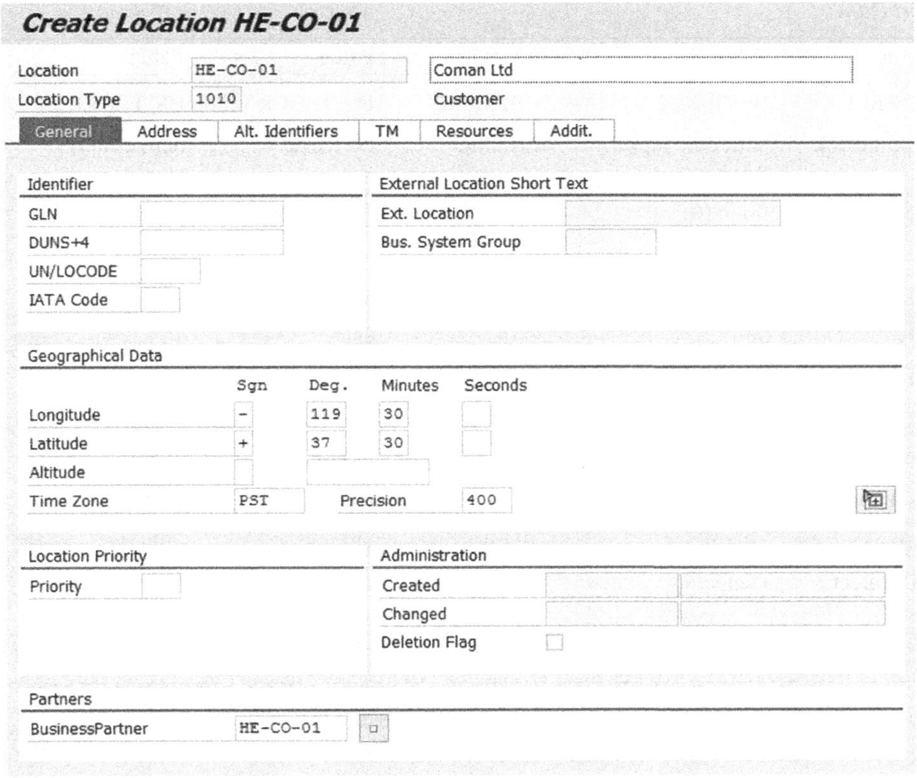

Figure A-17. *Creating location: General tab*

After entering the necessary data, save the data by clicking the Save 🖫 button. In this way, create the remaining locations.

Defining Means of Transport

Vehicle resource classes are defined as means of transport, for example, "cargo ship."

For the given scenario, you must create the means of transport provided in Table A-9.

Table A-9. *Means of Transport Data*

Field	Value	Value	Value	Value	Value
Means of transport	JP_TRUCK	JP_TRUCK_S	AIRPLANE	US_TRUCK	US_TRUCK_S
Means of transport description	Japan truck	Schedule Japan truck	Airplane	US truck	Schedule US truck
Mode of transport	Road (01)	Road (01)	Air (05)	Road (01)	Road (01)
Speed					
Low	40	40	650	45	45
Medium	50	50	750	55	55
High	60	60	850	65	65
Average	50	50	750	55	55
Distance factor	<Blank>	<Blank>	1	<Blank>	<Blank>
Multiresource	<Select>	<Select>	<Select>	<Select>	<Select>
Number of resources	<Blank>	<Blank>	<Blank>	<Blank>	<Blank>
Schedule means of transport	<Deselect>	<Select>	<Select>	<Deselect>	<Select>

■ **Note** If a number of resources are to be entered, then you can do so after the record is saved.

To define a means of transport, go to Customizing for SAP Transportation Management, and click Transportation Management ➤ Master Data ➤ Resource ➤ Define Means of Transport.

Next, click the New Entries New Entries button, and add the data from Table A-9.

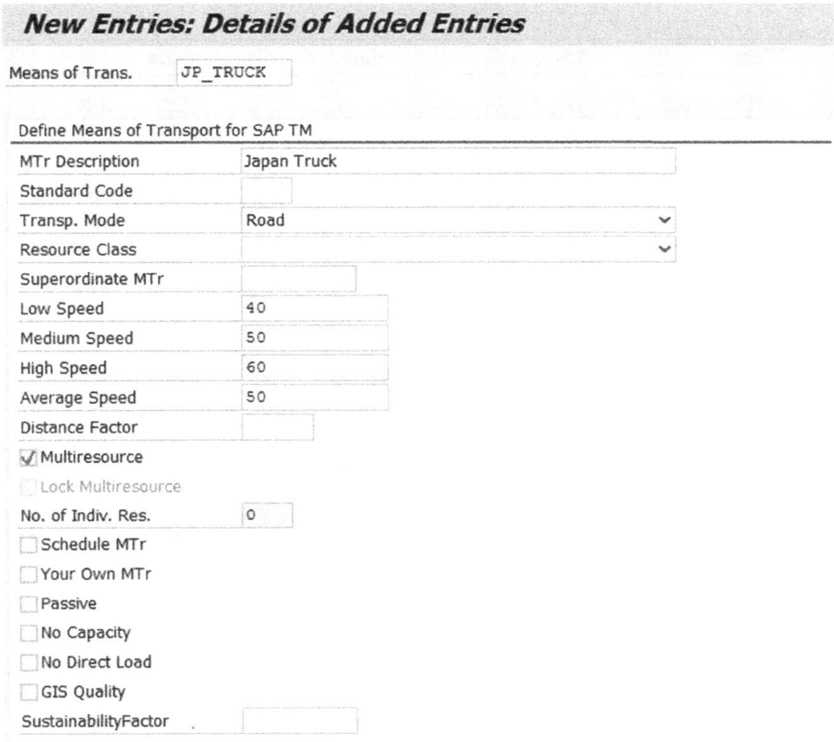

New Entries: Details of Added Entries

Means of Trans.   JP_TRUCK

Define Means of Transport for SAP TM

MTr Description	Japan Truck
Standard Code	
Transp. Mode	Road
Resource Class	
Superordinate MTr	
Low Speed	40
Medium Speed	50
High Speed	60
Average Speed	50
Distance Factor	
✓ Multiresource	
☐ Lock Multiresource	
No. of Indiv. Res.	0
☐ Schedule MTr	
☐ Your Own MTr	
☐ Passive	
☐ No Capacity	
☐ No Direct Load	
☐ GIS Quality	
SustainabilityFactor	

Figure A-18. *Creating means of transport*

After entering the necessary data, save the data by clicking the Save 🖫 button.
In this way, define the remaining means of transport.

Defining Resources

In SAP TM, resources play a vital role in planning and execution. Resource data, such as capacity and working times, serve as valuable input while planning an order.

SAP TM supports three types of resources:

- **Vehicle resource**: A vehicle resource is a means of transport that can provide transportation service. The resource's capacity and availability are defined in vehicle resource.

- **Calendar resource**: This is a resource that can be assigned to a calendar. To schedule the processing time for good receipt and issue, a calendar resource is used.

- **Handling resource**: A handling resource is a device that is used for handling goods at a specific location. The loading and unloading capacities of a resource are defined in handling resource.

For the given scenario, you will need to create the resources listed in Table A-10.

Table A-10. *Resource Data*

Field	Value	Value	Value	Value	Value
Resource	HEJP_TRUCK	HEJP_TRUCK_S	HE_AIRPLAN	HEUS_TRUCK	HEUS_TRUCK_S
Resource type	Vehicle (09)	Vehicle (09)	Vehicle (09)	Vehicle (09)	Vehicle (09)
Vehicle Tab					
Means of transport	JP_TRUCK	JP_TRUCK_S	AIRPLANE	US_TRUCK	US_TRUCK_S
Time zone	Japan	Japan	Japan	UTC-8	UTC-8
Continuous dimension	Mass	Mass	Mass	Mass	Mass
Factory calendar	W8	W8	W8	W8	W8
Capacity	40	40	2,000	40	40
Unit	TO	TO	TO	TO	TO
General Tab of Vehicle Tab					
Passive means of transport	<Deselect>	<Deselect>	<Deselect>	<Deselect>	DeSelect
Number of individual resources	0	0	0	0	0

To define a resource, in SAP NetWeaver Business Client, click Master Data ➤ Resource ➤ Define Resource, or use the Tcode (/SCMTMS/RES01).

Transportation Resource Master

Resource Selection				
Resource	HEJP_TRUCK			⇨
Location		to		⇨
Organization Unit ID		to		⇨
Resource Type	09	to		⇨
Resource Class		to		⇨

Figure A-19. *Initial screen for transportation resource master data*

Once the resource and resource type data are entered, click the Create ▯ button.
Next, in the Vehicle tab, enter the means of transport, time zone, and so on, using Table A-10.

Create Resources: Header Data

| 1 Vehicle | 0 Calendar | 0 TranspUnit | 0 Handling |

Resource	Resource Class	Location	Means of T...	Time Zone	Continuous Dim.	Factory Calendar	Capacity	Unit
HEJP_TRUCK	Truck		JP_TRUCK	JAPAN	Mass	W8	40	TO

Figure A-20. *Creating resources: Vehicle tab*

In the General tab of the Vehicle tab, enter other attributes of the resource, again using Table A-10.

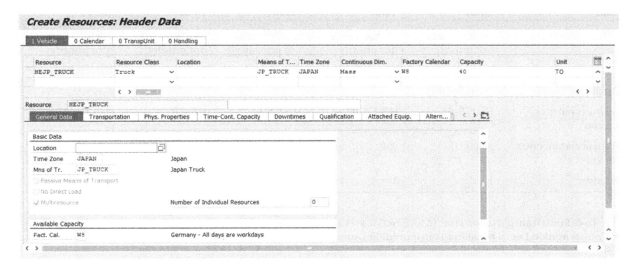

Figure A-21. *Creating resources: General Data tab of the Vehicle tab*

After entering the necessary data, save the data by clicking the Save 🖫 button.
In this way, define the remaining resources.

Defining Transportation Lanes

A transportation lane is used to define the link between two locations or zones or a combination of locations and zones. For each transportation lane, you must attach the means of transport; attaching the carrier assignment is not mandatory, however.

For the given scenario, create the transportation lanes shown in Table A-11.

Table A-11. *Transportation Lane Data*

Field	Value	Value	Value	Value	Value
Start location/zone	HE-CU-01	HESTAJPYOK	HEGWJPNAR	HEGWUSLA	HESTAUSSFR
Destination location/zone	HESTAJPYOK	HEGWJPNAR	HEGWUSLA	HESTAUSSFR	HE-CO-01
Means of Transport Section					
Means of transport	JP_TRUCK	JP_TRUCK_S	AIRPLANE	US_TRUCK_S	US_TRUCK
Start date	01-01-2013	01-01-2013	01-01-2013	01-01-2013	01-01-2013
End date	31-12-9999	31-12-9999	31-12-9999	31-12-9999	31-12-9999
Relevant to carrier Selection	<Select>	<Select>	<Select>	<Select>	<Select>

(continued)

Table A-11. (*continued*)

Field	Value	Value	Value	Value	Value
Priority/Costs	Neither costs nor priority	Neither costs nor priority	Neither costs nor priority	Neither costs nor priority	Neither costs nor priority
Cost origin	Internal costs	Internal costs	Internal costs	Internal costs	Internal costs
Carrier for Means of Transport Section					
Business partner (carrier)	HE-CR-01	HE-CR-02	HE-CR-03	HE-CR-04	HE-CR-05
Transportation costs per km	1,000	950	1,500	900	975
Priority	1	1	1	1	1

To define a transportation lane, in SAP NetWeaver Business Client, click Master Data ➤ Transportation Network ➤ Transportation Lanes ➤ Define Transportation Lanes, or use the Tcode (/SCMTMS/TL5).

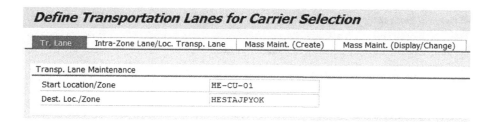

Figure A-22. *Creating a transportation lane*

Once the start location/zone and destination location/zone are entered, click the Create ☐ Create button.

Now, in the Means of Transport section, click the Creation of New Entry ☐ button to add attributes, such as means of transport and validity period, using Table A-11.

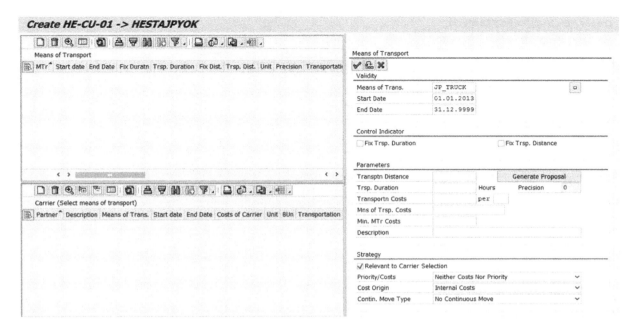

Figure A-23. *Creating a transportation lane: Means of transport*

Once the data related to means of transport are entered, save the data by clicking the Copy and Close button.

▪ **Note**   When the system asks whether you would like to create a transportation proposal, click No.

Next, in the Carrier for Means of Transport section, click the Creation of New Entry button to add the carrier and its attributes, using Table A-11.

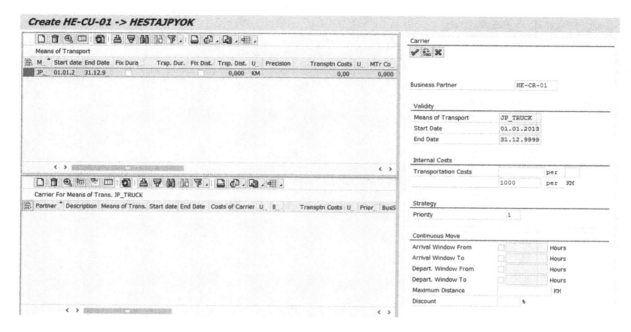

Figure A-24. *Creating a transportation lane: Carrier*

Once the data related to the carrier are entered, save the data by clicking the Copy and Close ✔ button. In this way, define the remaining transportation lanes.

Defining IATA Aircraft Type Codes

International Air Transport Association (IATA) aircraft type codes are used to define aircraft types and to assign an aircraft type, such as freighter or passenger, to the type.

For the given scenario, you must create the IATA aircraft type codes shown in Table A-12.

Table A-12. *IATA Aircraft Type Code Data*

Field	Value	Value
Aircraft type	74T	777
Description	Boeing 747-100 (freighter)	Boeing 777 (passenger)
Category	Freighter	Pax

To define an IATA aircraft type code, go to Customizing for SAP Transportation Management, and click Transportation Management ➤ Master Data ➤ Resource ➤ Define IATA Aircraft Type Codes.

Then, click the New Entries New Entries button, and add the respective aircraft type codes, using Table A-12.

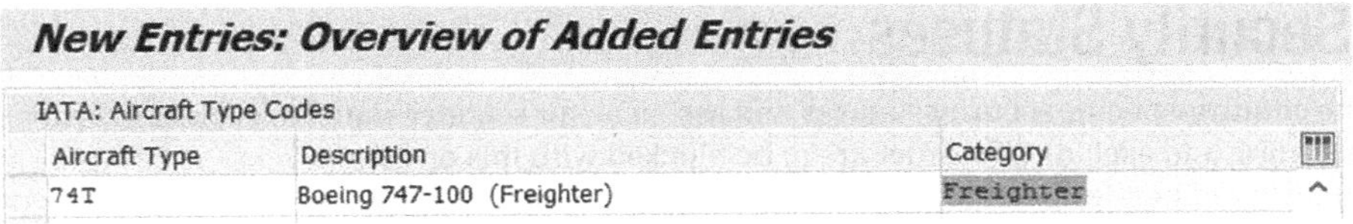

New Entries: Overview of Added Entries

IATA: Aircraft Type Codes

Aircraft Type	Description	Category	
74T	Boeing 747-100 (Freighter)	Freighter	^

Figure A-25. *Creating an IATA aircraft type code*

After entering the necessary data, save the data by clicking the Save 🖫 button.

In this manner, define the remaining IATA aircraft type codes.

Defining IATA Airline Codes

This option is used to define airline codes for each airfreight carrier as well as to assign an air waybill prefix to them. You can also specify whether the carrier is a member of the IATA with this option.

In the user interface of an airfreight document, such as an air forwarding order, there is an option to enter airline code. If airline code is entered, then the system automatically identifies the associated air waybill prefix. Furthermore, if there is a one-to-one relationship between the airline code and the associated carrier, the system can determine the relevant carrier based on the airline code entered.

Table A-13. *IATA Airline Code Data*

Field	Value
Airline	MA
Description	Mistala Airlines
AWB prefix	739
IATA member	<Select>
Check digit	<Select>
Prefix	<Deselect>

For the given scenario, you will need to create the IATA airline codes listed in Table A-13.

To define an IATA airline code, go to Customizing for SAP Transportation Management, and click Transportation Management ➤ Master Data ➤ Business Partner ➤ Define IATA Airline Codes.

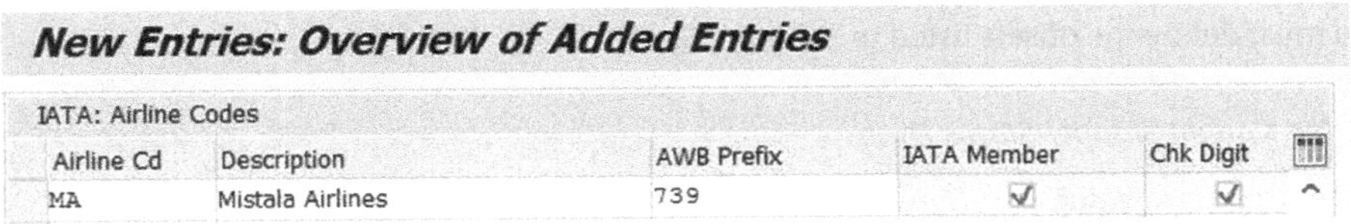

New Entries: Overview of Added Entries

IATA: Airline Codes

Airline Cd	Description	AWB Prefix	IATA Member	Chk Digit	
MA	Mistala Airlines	739	☑	☑	^

Figure A-26. *Creating an IATA airline code*

Now, click the New Entries New Entries button, and add the respective airline codes, using Table A-13.

After entering the necessary data, save the data by clicking the Save 🖫 button.

Define Air Cargo Security Statuses

You can use this option to define country-specific security statuses and assign an air security status to each of them. You can also specify whether planning and execution of order are to be blocked with this option.

For the given scenario, you must define the air cargo security statuses presented in Table A-14.

Table A-14. *Air Cargo Security Status Data*

Field	Value	Value
Country status	JP1	US1
Short description	Known shipper handled by regulated agent	Known shipper handled by regulated agent
Country	JP	US
Screened by large-scale planes (LSP)	<Deselect>	<Deselect>
Block status	<Deselect>	<Deselect>
Air cargo security (ACS) status	Secure for passenger aircraft	Secure for passenger aircraft

To define an Air Cargo Security Status, go to Customizing for SAP Transportation Management, and click Transportation Management ➤ Basic Function ➤ Security ➤ Define Air Cargo Security Statuses.

Then, click the New Entries   New Entries   button, and add the respective data, using Table A-14.

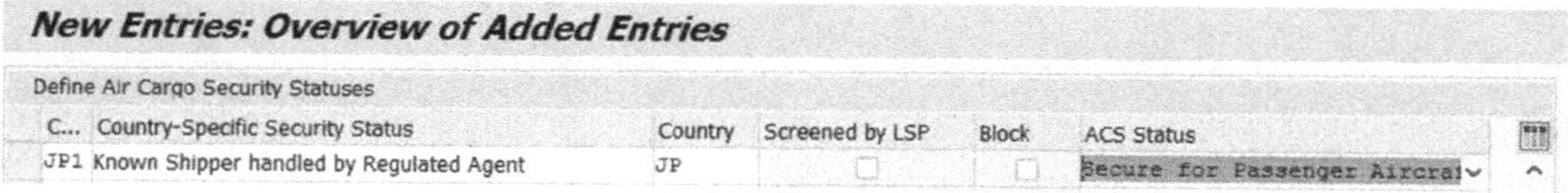

Figure A-27. *Creating an air cargo security status*

After entering the necessary data, save the data by clicking the Save 🖫 button.

In this way, define the remaining air cargo security statuses.

Defining Offsets for Calculating Known Shipper Status

Defining the offsets enables the system to determine whether the shipper has been known long enough to accept the cargo as secured from that shipper. The system allows country-specific offsets to be defined in days.

For the given scenario, you must define the offsets listed in Table A-15.

Table A-15. *Offsets for Calculating Known Shipper Status Data*

Field	Value	Value
Country	Japan	US
Offset in days	180	180

To define an offset for calculating known shipper status, go to Customizing for SAP Transportation Management, and click Transportation Management ➤ Basic Function ➤ Security ➤ Define Offsets for Calculating Known Shipper Status.

Now, click the New Entries New Entries button, and add the respective data, using Table A-15.

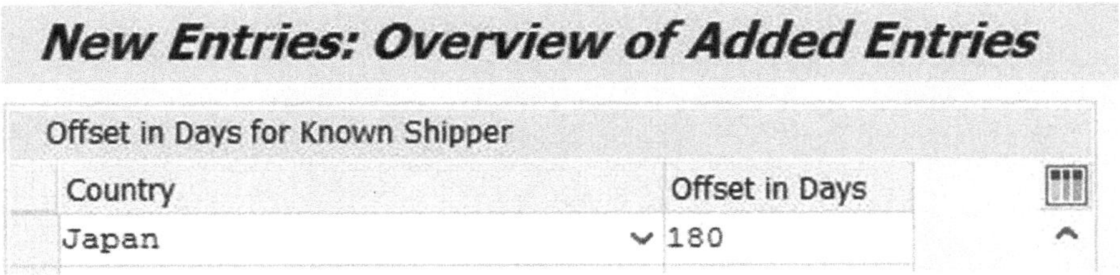

New Entries: Overview of Added Entries

Offset in Days for Known Shipper		
Country	Offset in Days	🎛
Japan ⌄	180	⌃

Figure A-28. *Creating an offset for calculating known shipper status*

After entering the necessary data, save the data by clicking the Save 💾 button.
In this manner, define the remaining offsets for calculating known shipper status.

Defining Waybill Number Stock Types

This option lets you specify the attributes of a waybill, such as the number of digits in a waybill number, check digit, and prefix relevant for the waybill.

For the given scenario, you will need to define the waybill number stock types displayed in Table A-16.

Table A-16. *Waybill Number Stock Type Data*

Field	Value	Value
Stock type	MAWB	HAWB
Description	Master air waybill	House air waybill
Transportation mode code (TrM)	05	05
Organization category	Purchasing	Sale
Number of digits	7	10
Check digits	<Select>	<Select>
Prefix	<Select>	<Select>

To define a waybill number stock type, go to Customizing for SAP Transportation Management, and click Transportation Management ➤ Master ➤ Waybill Stock ➤ Define Waybill Number Stock Types.

Next, click the New Entries New Entries button, and add the respective data, using Table A-16.

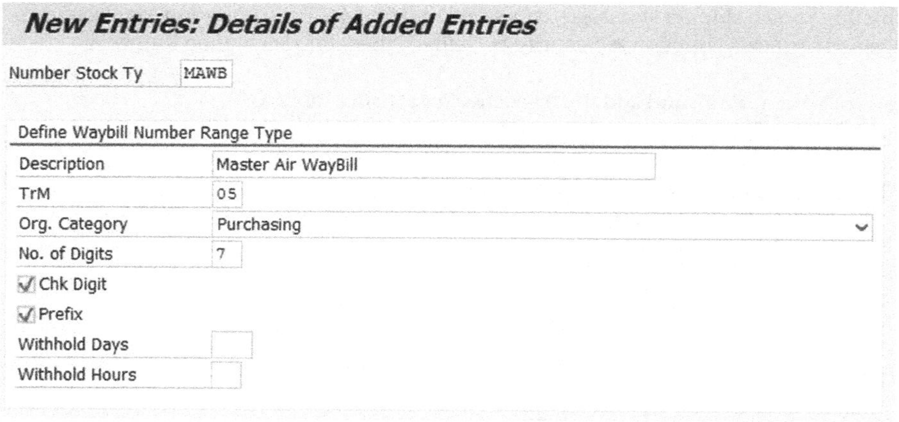

New Entries: Details of Added Entries

Number Stock Ty	MAWB

Define Waybill Number Range Type	
Description	Master Air WayBill
TrM	05
Org. Category	Purchasing ⌄
No. of Digits	7
✓ Chk Digit	
✓ Prefix	
Withhold Days	
Withhold Hours	

Figure A-29. Creating a waybill number stock type

After entering the necessary data, save the data by clicking the Save 🖫 button.
In this way, define the remaining waybill number stock types.

Defining Package Type Codes

This option allows you to specify package codes, thereby standardizing the packages used for transportation.
For the given scenario, you must define the package type codes shown in Table A-17.

Table A-17. Package Type Codes Data

Field	Value
Package types	Box
Description	Box

To define a package type code, go to Customizing for SAP Transportation Management, and click Transportation Management ➤ Forwarding Order Management ➤ Define Package Type Codes.
Then, click the New Entries New Entries button, and add the respective data, using Table A-17.

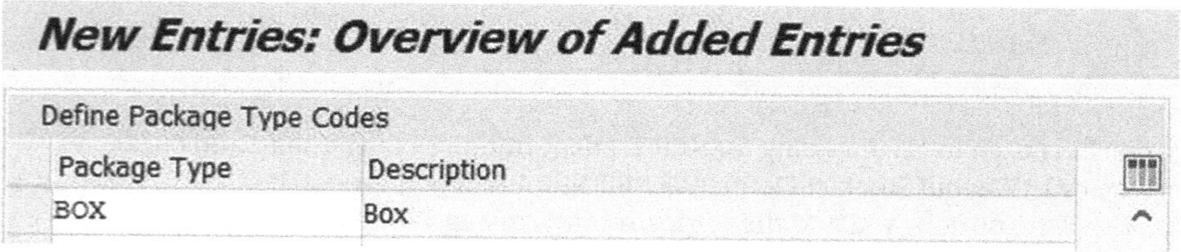

New Entries: Overview of Added Entries

Define Package Type Codes	
Package Type	Description
BOX	Box

Figure A-30. Creating a package type code

After entering the necessary data, save the data by clicking the Save 🖫 button.

Defining Item Types

This option lets you specify parameters for an item, such as the item category, equipment type, and default unit of measure.

For the given scenario, you will have to define the item types provided in Table A-18.

Table A-18. *Item Type Data*

Field	Value	Value
Item type	HEPK	HEPD
Item type description	Packages with specific dimensions	Product
Item category	Package	Product
Package type	Box	Not applicable
Product check	Not applicable	<Deselect>
One piece only	<Deselect>	<Deselect>
Volume summation	<Deselect>	<Deselect>
Default weight unit of measure	kg	kg
Default volume unit of measure	m³	m³
Default pieces unit of measure	ea.	ea.

To define an item type, go to Customizing for SAP Transportation Management, and click Transportation Management ➤ Forwarding Order Management ➤ Define Item Types for Forwarding Order Management. Now, click the New Entries New Entries button, and add the respective data, using Table A-18.

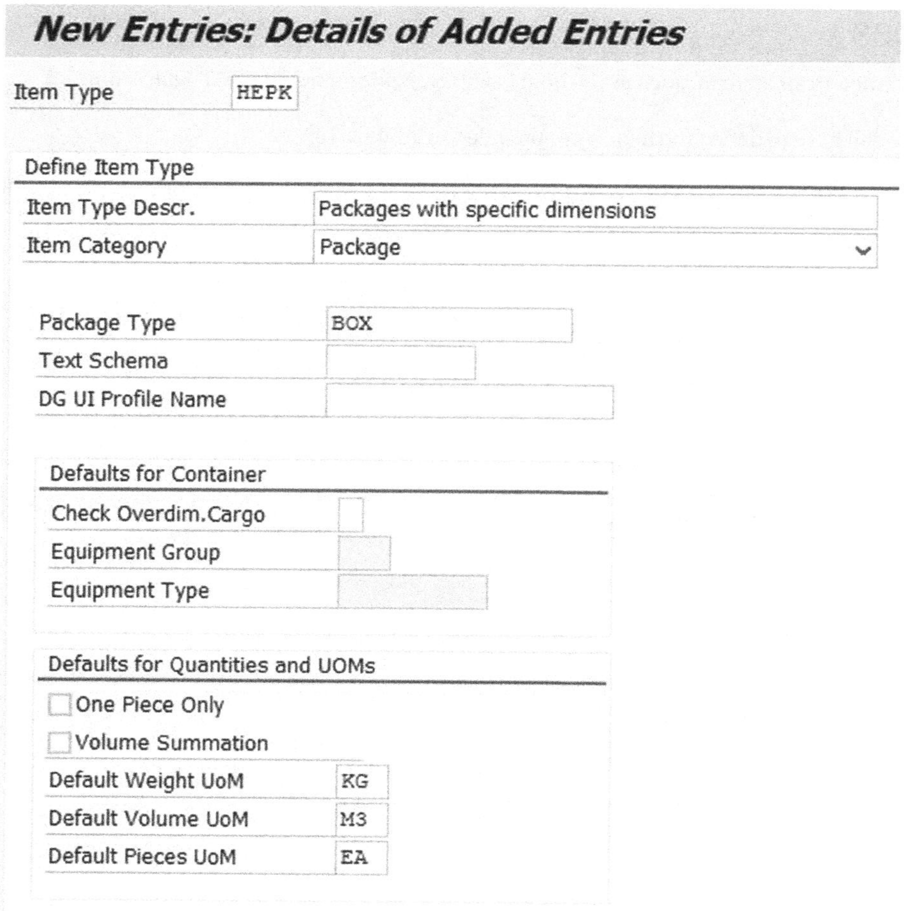

New Entries: Details of Added Entries

Item Type   HEPK

Define Item Type

Item Type Descr.	Packages with specific dimensions
Item Category	Package ⌄

Package Type	BOX
Text Schema	
DG UI Profile Name	

Defaults for Container

Check Overdim.Cargo	
Equipment Group	
Equipment Type	

Defaults for Quantities and UOMs

☐ One Piece Only
☐ Volume Summation

Default Weight UoM	KG
Default Volume UoM	M3
Default Pieces UoM	EA

Figure A-31. Creating an item type

After entering the necessary data, save the data by clicking the Save 💾 button. In this manner, define the remaining item types.

Defining Transportation Groups

This option allows you to specify the transportation groups.

For the given scenario, you will need to define the transportation groups listed in Table A-19.

Table A-19. Transportation Group Data

Field	Value	Value
Transportation Group	0015	0017
Transportation group description	Machinery/Electrical	Miscellaneous

To define a transportation group, go to Customizing for SAP Transportation Management, and click SCM Basis ➤ Master Data ➤ Product ➤ Maintain Transportation Group.

Next, click the New Entries New Entries button, and add the respective data, using Table A-19.

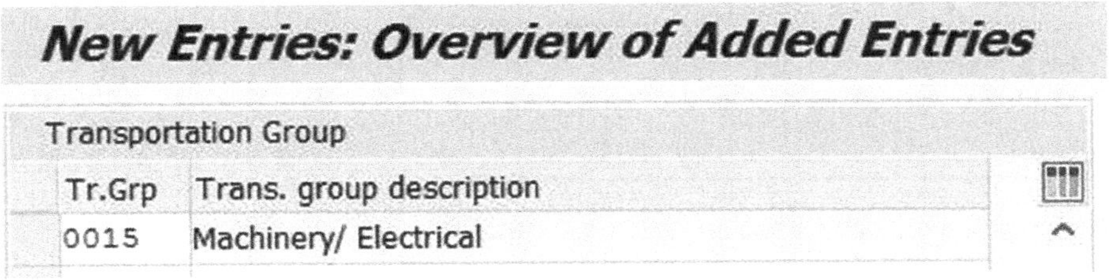

New Entries: Overview of Added Entries

Transportation Group	
Tr.Grp	Trans. group description
0015	Machinery/ Electrical

Figure A-32. *Creating a transportation group*

After entering the necessary data, save the data by clicking the Save 🖫 button.

In this way, define the remaining transportation group.

Defining Products

This option allows you to specify the products that are transportable goods.

For the given scenario, you must define the products presented in Table A-20.

Table A-20. *Product Data*

Field	Value
Product	Auto parts
View Section	
Global	<Select>
General Section	
Base unit of measure	kg
Product Description	Automobile parts
Properties Tab	
Transportation group	0015
Unit of Measure Tab	
Gross weight	50
Net weight	45
Unit of weight	kg
Volume	2
Unit of volume	m^3

123

To define a product, in SAP NetWeaver Business Client, click Master Data ➤ General ➤ Define Product, or use the Tcode (/SAPAPO/MAT1).

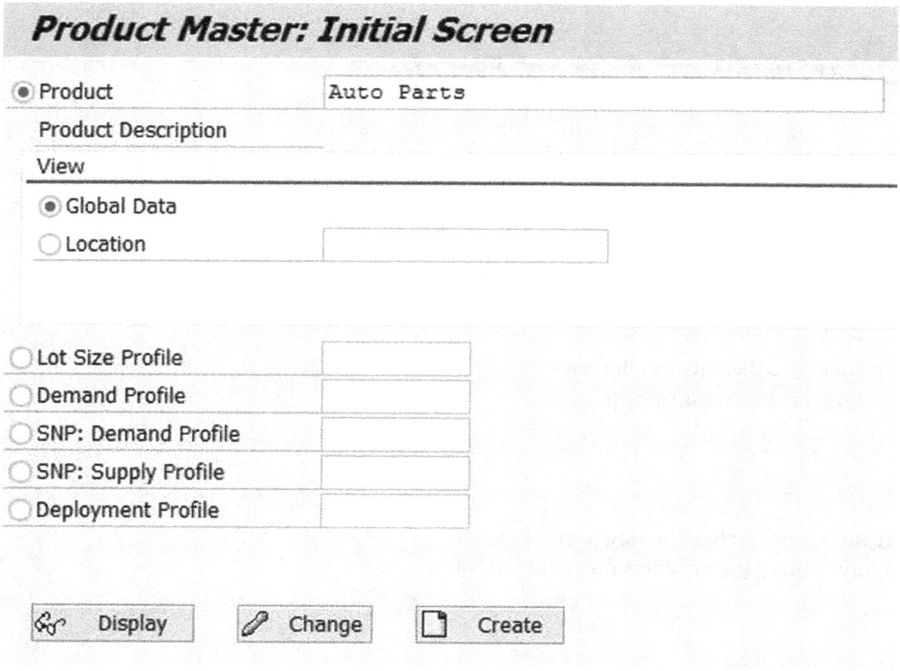

Product Master: Initial Screen

◉ Product   `Auto Parts`

Product Description

View

  ◉ Global Data

  ◯ Location

◯ Lot Size Profile

◯ Demand Profile

◯ SNP: Demand Profile

◯ SNP: Supply Profile

◯ Deployment Profile

  🔍 Display   ✏ Change   🗋 Create

Figure A-33. *Initial screen for product master data*

Once product- and view-related data are entered, click the Create 🗋 Create button.

Then, enter the base unit of measure and product description. In the Properties tab, enter relevant the data from Table A-20.

Create Product AUTO PARTS

Product	AUTO PARTS	Base Unit of Measure	KG
Prod. Descript.	Automobile Parts		

Properties | Properties 2 | Classification | Units of Meas. | ATP Data | SNP 1 | Pkg Data | Storage

External Product Number

AUTO PARTS   Bus. System Grp   TMS100

Created By	Changed By	Checked By
11.09.2013 15:22:37	11.09.2013 15:22:37	

General Data

Material Group	
Product Determ.	
Prod.Hierarchy	
Ctry of Origin	
Transport.Group	0015
☐ Batch Mgmt Reqt	

Measurements and Weights

Gross Weight	0,000
Volume	0,000
Stacking Factor	

Shelf Life

◉ Shelf Life   ☐ Plng with Shelf Life
◯ Min. Shelf Life

Shelf Life		Maturation Time	
Req.Min.Sh.Life		Req.Max.Sh.Life	
Rounding Rule		% Remaining SL	

Other

SDP Relevance

Figure A-34. *Creating a product: Properties tab*

In the Unit of Measure tab, enter the relevant data from Table A-20.

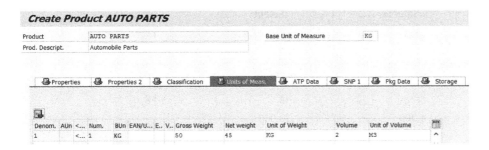

Figure A-35. *Creating a product: Unit of Measure tab*

After entering the necessary data, save the data by clicking the Save 🖫 button.

Defining Equipment Groups and Equipment Types

When a container item category is inserted while creating a forwarding order or forwarding quotation, the equipment types can be used. To group equipment types into categories, use equipment groups.

For the given scenario, you will need to define the equipment groups and equipment types listed in Table A-21, if you have not already done so.

Table A-21. *Equipment Groups and Equipment Types: Transportation Unit Group Data*

Field	Value
Transportation Unit Groups	
Equipment group	ULD
Description	Unit load device

Table A-22. *Equipment Groups and Equipment Types: Mode of Transport Assignment Data*

Field	Value
Mode of Transport Assignment	
Transportation mode category	Air

Table A-23. *Equipment Groups and Equipment Types: Equipment Type Data*

Field	Value	Value	Value
Equipment Types			
Equipment type	AKN	AAP	PAP
Description	Container 79 × 64 × 60 (LD3)	Container 125 × 88 × 64 (LD9)	Flat pallet lower holds and main decks
Airfreight Section			
IATA compliant	<Select>	<Select>	<Select>
Unit load device classification	LD3	LD9	LD7
Physical Properties Section			
Tare weight	82	200	105
Tare weight unit of measure	kg	kg	kg
Tare volume	4,300	10,000	
Tare volume unit of measure	m³	m³	
Capacity Section			
Payload weight	1,506	5,833	4,521
Payload weight unit of measure	kg	kg	kg
Cubic capacity	17,580	10,510	

(continued)

Table A-23. (*continued*)

Field	Value	Value	Value
Cubic capacity unit of measure	m³	m³	
Internal length	200	316	317
Internal width	153	222	223
Internal height	162	161	162
Internal height unit of measure	cm	cm	cm
Temperature Section			
Temperature control	<Deselect>	<Deselect>	<Deselect>
Ventilation	No ventilation	No ventilation	No ventilation

To define equipment groups and equipment types, go to Customizing for SAP Transportation Management, and click Transportation Management ➤ Master Data ➤ Resource ➤ Define Equipment Groups and Equipment Types.

Then, click the New Entries New Entries button, and enter the data related to transportation unit groups from Table A-21.

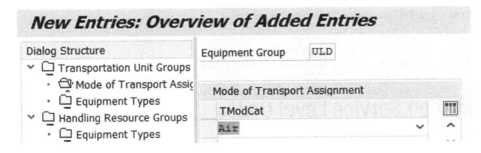

Figure A-36. *Creating equipment group and equipment type: Transportation unit groups*

After entering the necessary data, save the data by clicking the Save 🖫 button.

Next, select the row containing "ULD," and, from the tree structure, select Mode of Transport Assignment. Click the New Entries New Entries button, and enter the data related to mode of transport from Table A-22.

New Entries: Overview of Added Entries

Dialog Structure
- ⌄ ☐ Transportation Unit Groups
  - • ☐ Mode of Transport Assic
  - • ☐ Equipment Types
- ⌄ ☐ Handling Resource Groups
  - • ☐ Equipment Types

Equipment Group   ULD

Mode of Transport Assignment

| TModCat | | |
| Air | ⌄ | ⌃ |

Figure A-37. *Creating equipment group and equipment type: Mode of transport assignment*

After entering the necessary data, save the data by clicking the Save 💾 button.

Return to the Transportation Unit Groups section, select the row containing "ULD," and, from the tree structure, select Equipment Types. Click the New Entries New Entries button, and enter the data related to equipment types from Table A-23.

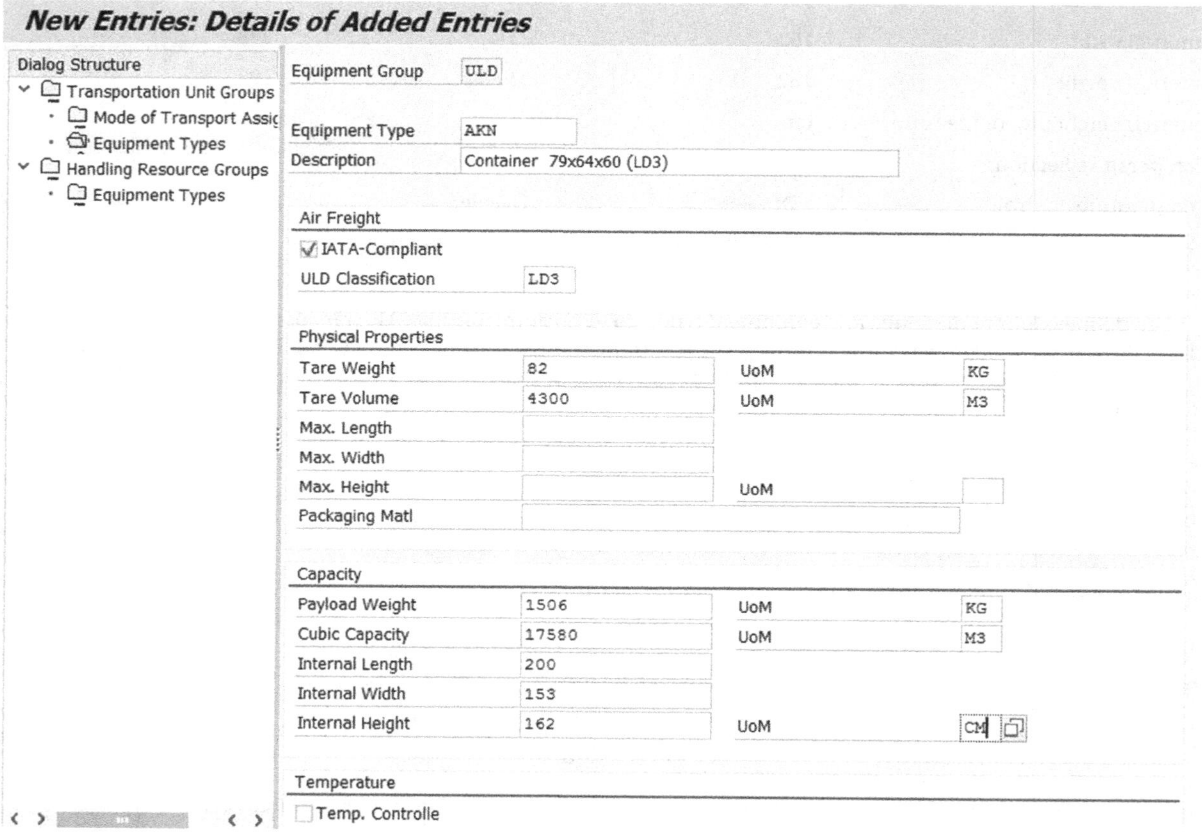

Figure A-38. *Creating equipment group and equipment type: Equipment type*

After entering the necessary data, save the data by clicking the Save 💾 button.

In this manner, define the remaining equipment groups and equipment types.

Defining Transportation Service Level Codes

This option allows you to specify the transportation service level codes.

For the given scenario, you must define the transportation service level codes shown in Table A-24.

Table A-24. *Transportation Service Level Codes Data*

Field	Value	Value
Service level code	01	02
Description	Standard	Express

To define a transportation service level code, go to Customizing for SAP Transportation Management, and click Transportation Management ➤ Forwarding Order Management ➤ Define Transportation Service Level Codes. Next, click the New Entries New Entries button, and enter the data from Table A-24.

Figure A-39. *Creating a transportation service level code*

After entering the necessary data, save the data by clicking the Save 🖫 button. In this way, define the remaining transportation service level codes.

Defining Stage Types

The main carriage, precarriage, on-carriage, and so on are specified by assigning them to a stage type. For the given scenario, you will need to define the stage types provided in Table A-25.

Table A-25. *Stage Type Data*

Field	Value	Value	Value	Value	Value
Stage type	HE1	HE2	HE3	HE4	HE5
Description	Pickup	Precarriage	Main carriage	On-Carriage	Delivery
Stage category	Precarriage	Precarriage	Main carriage	On-Carriage	On-Carriage

To define a stage type, go to Customizing for SAP Transportation Management, and click Transportation Management ➤ Forwarding Order Management ➤ Define Stage Types. Now, click the New Entries New Entries button, and enter the respective data, using Table A-25.

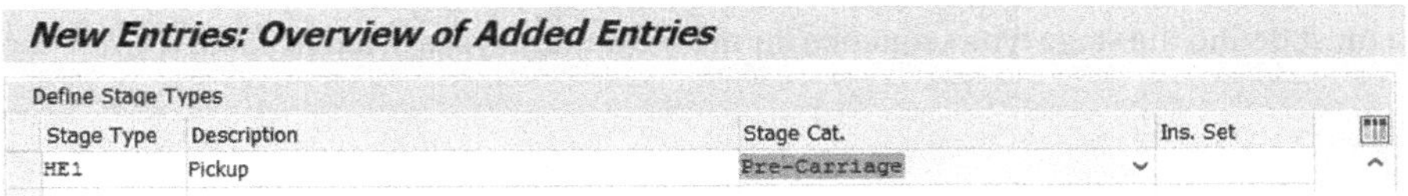

Figure A-40. *Creating a stage type*

After entering the necessary data, save the data by clicking the Save 🖫 button.

In this way, define the remaining stage types.

Defining Movement Types

Movement type is one of the parameters used specify the stages for which logistics service provider is responsible when organizing the transportation.

For the given scenario, you will have to define the movement types displayed in Table A-26.

Table A-26. *Movement Type Data*

Field	Value
Movement type	DD
Description	Door-to-door
Source location	<Deselect>
Destination location	<Deselect>

To define a movement type, go to Customizing for SAP Transportation Management, and click Transportation Management ➤ Forwarding Order Management ➤ Define Movement Types.

Next, click the New Entries New Entries button, and enter the data from Table A-26.

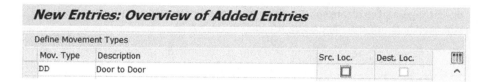

Figure A-41. *Creating a movement type*

After entering the necessary data, save the data by clicking the Save 🖫 button.

Defining Stage Type Sequence for Movement Types

The allowed stage type and sequence for a movement type are specified in this option. This option also lets you specify which stages are relevant for planning.

The system uses the values specified to add automatically the stages in the Actual Route section of the Stages tab of the forwarding quotation or forwarding order when a movement type is entered in the General tab.

For the given scenario, you must define the stage type sequence for the movement types listed in Table A-27.

Table A-27. *Stage Type Sequence for Movement Type Data*

Field	Value	Value	Value	Value	Value
Movement type	DD	DD	DD	DD	DD
Sequence number	10	20	30	40	50
Stage type	HE1	HE2	HE3	HE4	HE5
Stage type occurrence	Stage type must occur at least once	Stage type must occur at least once	Stage type must occur at least once	Stage type must occur at least once	Stage type must occur at least once
Stage proposal	<Select>	<Select>	<Select>	<Select>	<Select>
Determination rule for nonplanning— relevant stages	Not pl – rel. if ex. and sales org. belong to diff. comp. orgs	Not pl – rel. if ex. and sales org. belong to diff. comp. orgs	Not pl – rel. if ex. and sales org. belong to diff. comp. orgs	Not pl – rel. if ex. and sales org. belong to diff. comp. orgs	Not pl – rel. if ex. and sales org. belong to diff. comp. orgs
Internal settlement rule	Not relevant for internal settlement	Not relevant for internal settlement	Not relevant for internal settlement	Not relevant for internal settlement	Not relevant for internal settlement

To define the stage type sequence for a movement type, go to Customizing for SAP Transportation Management, and click Transportation Management ➤ Forwarding Order Management ➤ Define Stage Type Sequence for Movement Type.

Then, click the New Entries New Entries button, and enter the respective data, using Table A-27.

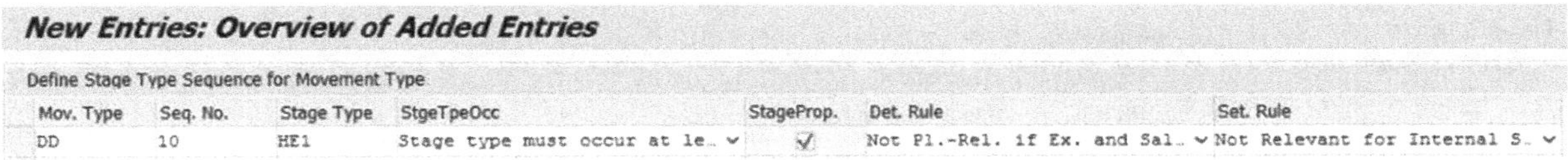

Figure A-42. *Creating the stage type sequence for a movement type*

After entering the necessary data, save the data by clicking the Save 🖫 button.

In this way, define the remaining stage type sequences for movement types.

Defining Stage Profiles

This option lets you specify which stage types are to be created in the forwarding quotation or forwarding order, their sequence, and attributes of the stages.

For the given scenario, you must define the stage profile displayed in Table A-28.

Table A-28. *Stage Profile Data*

Field	Value
Stage profile	HEIM
Description	Import stage profile

In addition, you need to define the stage type sequence shown in Table A-29.

Table A-29. *Stage Profiles: Assigning Stage Type Sequence Data*

Field	Value	Value	Value	Value	Value
Sequence number	10	20	30	40	50
Stage type	HE1	HE2	HE3	HE4	HE5
Stage type occurrence	Stage type must occur at least once	Stage type must occur at least once	Stage type must occur at least once	Stage type must occur at least once	Stage type must occur at least once
Stage proposal	<Select>	<Select>	<Select>	<Select>	<Select>
Determination rule for nonplanning— relevant stages	Never relevant for planning	Never relevant for planning	Never relevant for planning	Always relevant for planning	Always relevant for planning
Internal settlement rule	Not relevant for internal settlement	Not relevant for internal settlement	Not relevant for internal settlement	Not relevant for internal settlement	Not relevant for internal settlement

To define a stage profile, go to Customizing for SAP Transportation Management, and click Transportation Management ➤ Forwarding Order Management ➤ Define Stage Profiles.

Next, click the New Entries New Entries button, and enter the data from Table A-28.

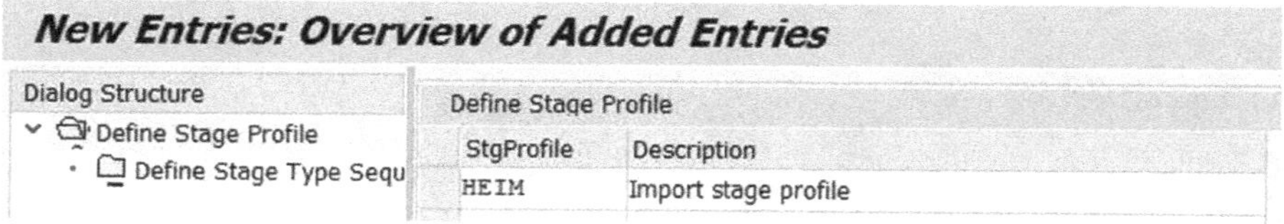

Figure A-43. *Creating a stage profile*

After entering the necessary data, save the data by clicking the Save 🖫 button.

Now, select the stage profile "HEIM", and, from the tree structure, select Define Stage Type Sequence for Stage Profile. Click the New Entries New Entries button, and enter the data related to sequence for stage profile from Table A-29.

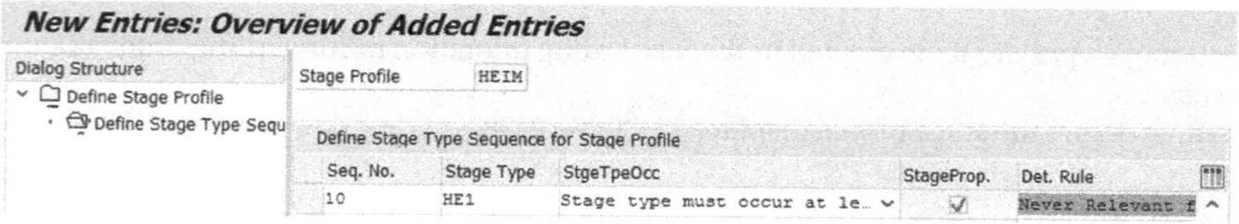

Figure A-44. *Creating a stage profile: Assigning stage type sequence*

In this way, assign the remaining stage type Sequence sequences.

Defining Shipping Types

Specify the shipping type using this option. This option also allows you to specify whether a cargo item, such as a package or product, is to be assigned to equipment items, such as containers or unit load devices (ULDs).

For the given scenario, you will have to define the shipping types shown in Table A-30.

Table A-30. *Shipping Type Data*

Field	Value
Shipping Type Section	
Shipping type	10
Description	Loose
Assignment to equipment item	Cargo items must not be assigned to an equipment item
Transportation Mode Assignments Section	
Transportation mode code	Air (05)

To define a shipping type, go to Customizing for SAP Transportation Management, and click Transportation Management ➤ Forwarding Order Management ➤ Define Shipping Types.

Then, click the New Entries New Entries button, and enter the relevant data from Table A-30.

Figure A-45. *Creating a shipping type*

After entering the necessary data, save the data by clicking the Save 💾 button.

Now, select the shipping type "10," and, from the tree structure, select Transportation Mode Assignments. Click the New Entries New Entries the button, and enter the data related to transportation mode from Table A-30.

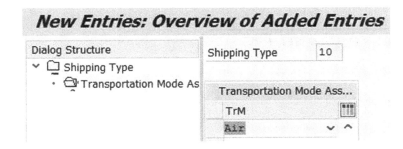

Figure A-46. *Creating a shipping type: Assigning transportation mode*

After entering the necessary data, save the data by clicking the Save 💾 button.

Defining Geographical Selection Attributes

This option lets you specify the source and destination to be taken into consideration while filtering an order for planning.

For the given scenario, you will need to define the geographical selection attributes displayed in Table A-31.

Table A-31. *Geographical Selection Attribute Data*

Field	Value	Value	Value
General Data Section			
Geographical selection attributes	HE-GEO-SEL-PRE	HE-GEO-SEL-MAIN	HE-GEO-SEL-ON
Description	Geographical selection—precarriage	Geographical selection—main carriage	Geographical selection—on-carriage
Both locations	<Select>	<Select>	<Select>
Source Locations Tab			
Sign	Inclusive	Inclusive	Inclusive
Option	=	=	=
Lower value	HESTAJPYOK	HEGWJPNAR	HEGWUSLA
Upper value	<Blank>	<Blank>	<Blank>
Destination Locations Tab			
Sign	Inclusive	Inclusive	Inclusive
Option	=	=	=
Lower value	HEGWJPNAR	HEGWUSLA	HESTAUSSFR
Upper value	<Blank>	<Blank>	<Blank>

To define geographical selection attributes, in SAP NetWeaver Business Client, click Application Administration ➤ Planning ➤ Selection Profile Attributes ➤ Geographical Selection Attributes ➤ Create Geographical Selection Attributes.

Then, in the General Data section, enter the relevant data from Table A-31.

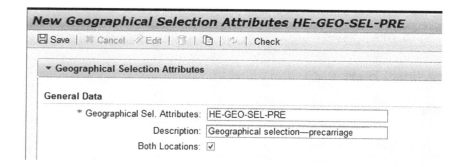

Figure A-47. *Creating geographical selection attributes: General Data section*

In the Source Locations tab, again enter the relevant data from Table A-31.

Figure A-48. *Creating geographical selection attributes: Source Locations tab*

Do the same in the Destination Locations tab.

Figure A-49. *Creating geographical selection attributes: Destination Locations tab*

After entering the necessary data, save the data by clicking the Save 🖫 Save button.
In this way, define the remaining geographical selection attributes.

Defining Time-Related Selection Attributes

This option allows you to specify the demand horizon.

For the given scenario, you must define the time-related selection attributes shown in Table A-32.

Table A-32. *Time-Related Selection Attribute Data*

Field	Value
General Data Section	
Time-related selection attributes	HE-TIME-SEL
Description	Time-related selection
Demand Horizon Section	
Absolute or relative horizon	Use relative horizon
Factory calendar for offset/duration calculation	W8
Other Settings Section	
Use index time for selection	Use index time of stop
Combination of Pickup and Delivery windows	Combination with OR

(*continued*)

135

Table A-32. (*continued*)

Field	Value
Pickup Section	
Pickup in days	30
Offset direction	Future
Delivery Section	
Delivery in days	45
Offset direction	Future

To define time-related selection attributes, in SAP NetWeaver Business Client, click Application Administration ➤ Planning ➤ Selection Profile Attributes ➤ Time-Related Selection Attributes ➤ Create Time-Related Selection Attributes.

In the General Data, Demand Horizon, and Other Settings sections, enter the respective data, using Table A-32.

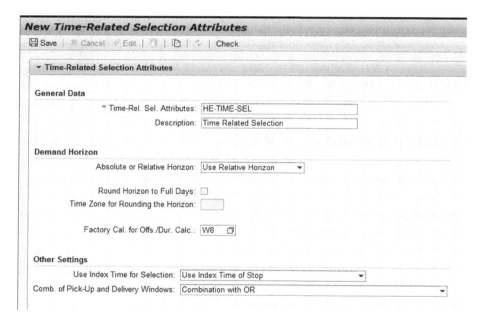

Figure A-50. *Creating time-related selection attributes: General Data, Demand Horizon, Other Settings sections*

In the Pickup and Delivery sections, again enter the respective data, using Table A-32.

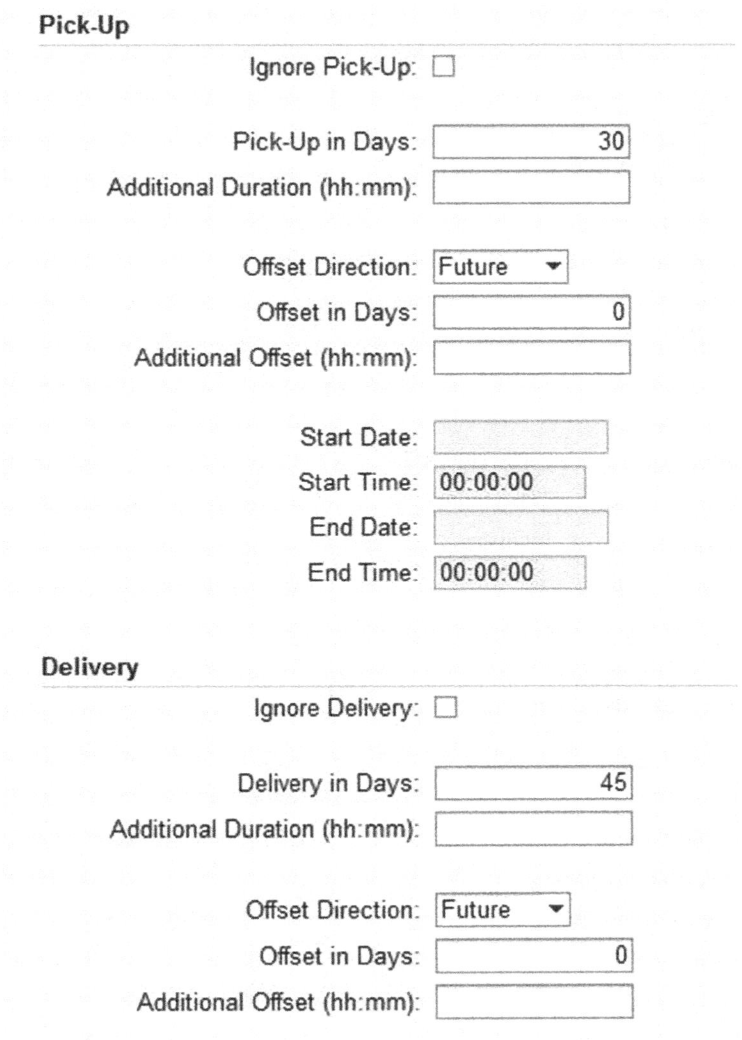

Pick-Up

Ignore Pick-Up: ☐

Pick-Up in Days: 30
Additional Duration (hh:mm):

Offset Direction: Future ▼
Offset in Days: 0
Additional Offset (hh:mm):

Start Date:
Start Time: 00:00:00
End Date:
End Time: 00:00:00

Delivery

Ignore Delivery: ☐

Delivery in Days: 45
Additional Duration (hh:mm):

Offset Direction: Future ▼
Offset in Days: 0
Additional Offset (hh:mm):

Figure A-51. *Creating time-related selection attributes: Pickup and Delivery sections*

After entering the necessary data, save the data by clicking the Save 🖫 Save button.

Defining Additional Selection Attributes

This option is used to specify additional attributes.

For the given scenario, you will have to define the additional selection attributes provided in Tables A-33–A-35.

Table A-33. *Additional Selection Attribute Data: Main Carriage Stage*

Field	Value
General Data Section	
Additional selection attributes	HE-ADD-SEL-BOOK
Description	Additional Selection book
Planned requirements	Include in selection
Blocked documents	Exclude in selection

Table A-34. *Additional Selection Attribute Data: Main Carriage Stage; Selection Values Tab*

Field	Value	Value
Selection Values Tab		
Business object for selection	/SCMTMS/TO	/SCMTMS/TO
Field name	TOR_TYPE	TOR_TYPE
Sign	Inclusive	Inclusive
Option	=	=
Lower limit	FB01	FB02

Table A-35. *Additional Selection Attribute Data: Precarriage Stage*

Field	Value
General Data Section	
Additional election attributes	HE-ADD-SEL-PRE
Description	Additional selection Precarriage
Planned requirements	Include in selection
Blocked documents	Exclude in selection

To define additional selection attributes, in SAP NetWeaver Business Client, click Application Administration ➤ Planning ➤ Selection Profile Attributes ➤ Additional Selection Attributes ➤ Create Additional Selection Attributes. Then, in the General Data section, enter the data from Tables A-33 and A-35.

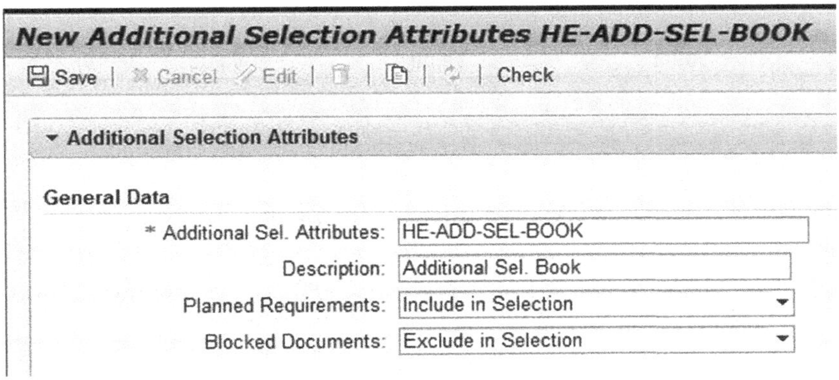

Figure A-52. Creating additional selection attributes: General Data section

In the Selection Values tab, enter the data from Table A-34.

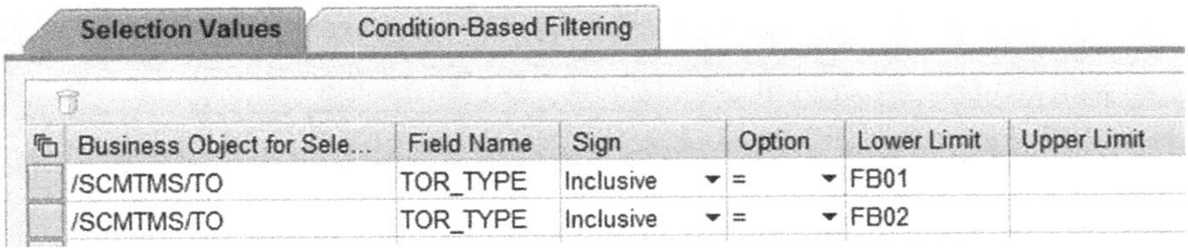

Figure A-53. Creating additional selection attributes: Selection Values tab

After entering the necessary data, save the data by clicking the Save 🖫 Save button.

In this way, define the remaining additional selection attributes.

Defining Selection Profiles

This option allows you to specify which business documents the system is to take into account as well as the maximum number of documents.

For the given scenario, you will need to define the selection profiles presented in Table A-36.

Table A-36. Selection Profile Data

Field	Value	Value	Value	Value
General Data Section				
Selection profile	HE-SEL-PRO-PRE	HE-SEL-PRO-MAIN	HE-SEL-PRO-ON	HE-SEL-PRO-BOOK
Description	Selection profile—precarriage	Selection profile—main carriage	Selection profile—on-carriage	Selection profile—booking
Maximum number of selected objects	75	75	75	250

(continued)

Table A-36. (*continued*)

Field	Value	Value	Value	Value
Profile Assignments Section				
Time-Related selection attributes			HE-TIME-SEL	HE-TIME-SEL
Geographical selection attributes	HE-GEO-SEL-PRE	HE-GEO-SEL-MAIN	HE-GEO-SEL-ON	
Additional selection attributes	HE-ADD-SEL-PRE	HE-ADD-SEL-PRE	HE-ADD-SEL-PRE	HE-ADD-SEL-BOOK

To define a selection profile, in SAP NetWeaver Business Client, click Application Administration ➤ Planning ➤ Selection Profiles ➤ Create Selection Profiles.

In the General Data and Profile Assignments sections, enter the respective data, using Table A-36.

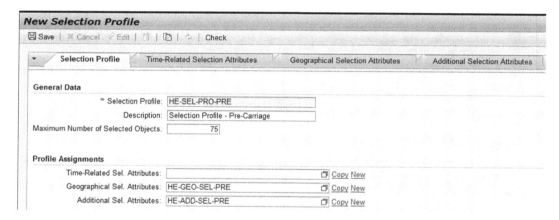

Figure A-54. *Creating a selection profile*

After entering the necessary data, save the data by clicking the Save ⊟ Save button.

In this manner, define the remaining selection profiles.

Define Capacity Selection Settings

This option lets you specify the criteria related to capacity, which are taken into consideration while planning.

For the given scenario, you will need to define the capacity selection settings displayed in Table A-37.

Table A-37. *Capacity Selection Setting Data*

Field	Value	Value	Value
General Data Section			
Capacity selection settings	HE-CAP-SEL-PRE	HE-CAP-SEL-MAIN	HE-CAP-SEL-ON
Description	Capacity settings for precarriage	Capacity settings for main carriage	Capacity settings for on-carriage
Vehicle Resources Tab			
Attributes for vehicle resource selection	VEHICLERES_ID	VEHICLERES_ID	VEHICLERES_ID
Sign	Inclusive	Inclusive	Inclusive
Option	Pattern	=	Pattern
Lower limit	HEJP_TRUCK*	HE_ AIRPLAN	HEUS_TRUCK*
Schedules Tab			
Attribute for schedule selection	SCH_ID	SCH_ID	SCH_ID
Sign	Inclusive	Inclusive	Inclusive
Option	=	Pattern	=
Lower limit	HE-JPTR-SCH-PRE-01	HE-MF-SCH*	HE-USTR-SCH-ON-01

To define capacity selection settings, in SAP NetWeaver Business Client, click Application Administration ➤ Planning ➤ Planning Profile Settings ➤ Capacity Selection Settings ➤ Create Capacity Selection Settings.

Next, in the General Data section, enter the relevant data from Table A-37.

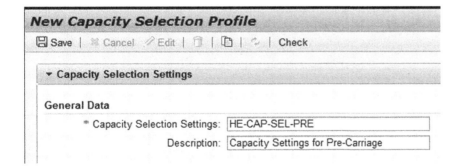

Figure A-55. *Creating capacity selection Settings: General Data section*

In the Vehicle Resources tab, again enter the relevant data from Table A-37.

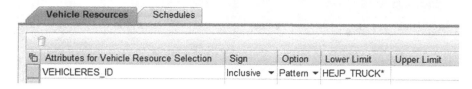

Figure A-56. *Creating capacity selection settings: Vehicle Resources tab*

Do the same in the Schedules tab.

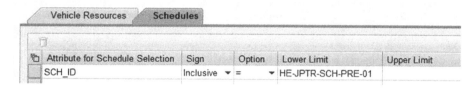

Figure A-57. *Creating capacity selection settings: Schedules tab*

After entering the necessary data, save the data by clicking the Save ⊞ Save button. In this way, define the remaining capacity selection settings.

Define Optimizer Settings

You can use this option to specify settings, such as the optimizer runtime, the maximum number of transshipment locations and processes, and the freight order–building rule.

For the given scenario, you must define the optimizer settings presented in Table A-38.

Table A-38. *Optimizer Setting Data*

Field	Value
General Data Section	
Optimizer settings	HE-OPT-SET
Description	Optimizer settings
Planning strategy	VSR_DEF
Freight order–building rule	New freight order when resource is empty
Transportation Proposal Settings Section	
Accept transport proposal	Save route and freight documents
Planning strategy for transport proposal	VSR_DEF
Maximum number of transport proposals	7

(continued)

Table A-38. (*continued*)

Field	Value
Optimizer Runtime Section	
Maximum Number of parallel processes	9
Maximum runtime (seconds)	60
Automatic runtime regulation	Not used
Rough Planning and Capacity Constraints Section	
Rough planning	Do not use rough planning
Consider capacity during optimization	Yes
Transshipment Locations Section	
Maximum Number of transshipment locations	6

To define optimizer settings, in SAP NetWeaver Business Client, click Application Administration ➤ Planning ➤ Planning Profile Settings ➤ Optimizer Settings ➤ Create Optimizer Settings.

In the General Data and Transportation Proposal Settings sections, enter the respective data, using Table A-38.

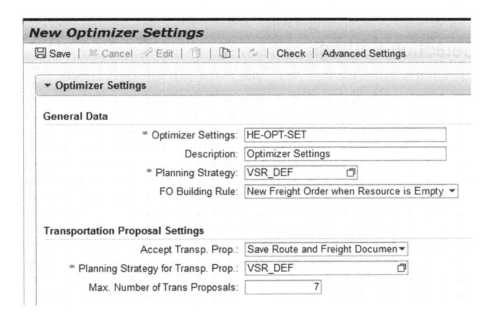

Figure A-58. *Creating optimizer settings: General Data and Transportation Proposal Settings sections*

In the Optimizer Runtime, Rough Planning and Capacity Constraints, and Transshipment Locations sections, again enter the respective data, using Table A-38.

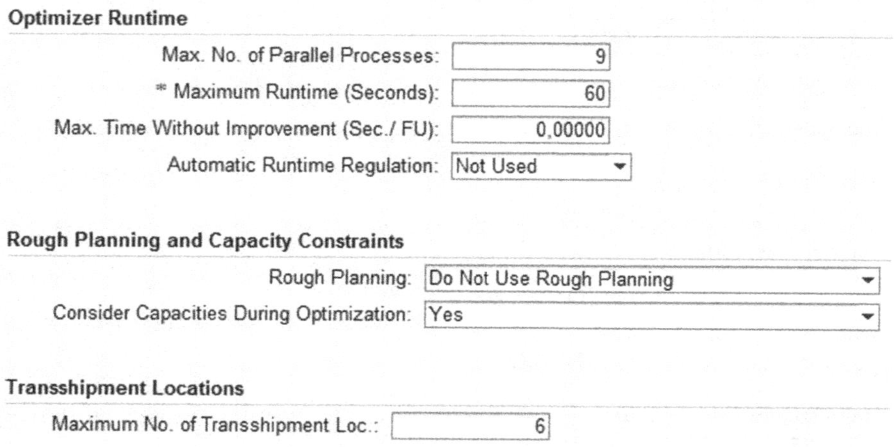

Optimizer Runtime

Max. No. of Parallel Processes: 9

* Maximum Runtime (Seconds): 60

Max. Time Without Improvement (Sec./ FU): 0,00000

Automatic Runtime Regulation: Not Used ▾

Rough Planning and Capacity Constraints

Rough Planning: Do Not Use Rough Planning ▾

Consider Capacities During Optimization: Yes ▾

Transshipment Locations

Maximum No. of Transshipment Loc.: 6

Figure A-59. *Creating optimizer settings: Optimizer Runtime, Rough Planning and Capacity Constraints, and Transshipment Locations sections*

After entering the necessary data, save the data by clicking the Save 🖫 Save button.

Defining Carrier Selection Settings

This option allows you to specify whether the system is to use transportation allocations or business shares while planning.

For the given scenario, you will have to define the carrier selection settings provided in Table A-39.

Table A-39. *Carrier Selection Settings Data*

Field	Value
General Data Section	
Carrier selection settings	HE-CAR-SEL
Description	Carrier selection
Check incompatibilities	< Select>
Parallel processing profile	<Blank>
Type of carrier selection settings	General carrier selection
Other Settings Section	
Allocation usage	Do not use transportation allocations
Business shares usage	Do not use business shares
Strategy	Costs
Carrier cost origin	Use internal costs

(*continued*)

Table A-39. (*continued*)

Field	Value
Advanced Settings Tab	
Planning strategy	TSPS_DEF
Optimizer runtime	6
Action for manual rankings	Remove
Transportation charge interpretation	Accept carrier with charges of zero
Action after carrier selection run	Assign best carrier
Continuous move type	Use transportation lane settings
Continuous move information	<Select>
Check distribution and duration	<Select>
CM cost recalculation of transportation charge management	No recalculation
Use tendered objects for optimization	<Deselect>

To define carrier selection settings, in SAP NetWeaver Business Client, click Application Administration ➤ Planning ➤ Planning Profile Settings ➤ Carrier Selection Settings ➤ Create Carrier Selection Settings.

Then, in the General Data section, enter the relevant data from Table A-39.

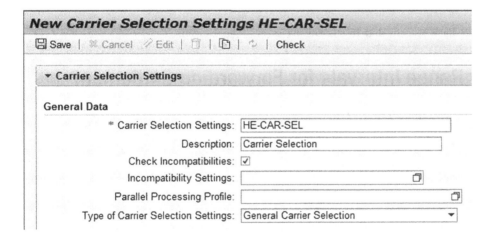

Figure A-60. *Creating carrier selection settings: General Data section*

In the Other Settings section, again enter the relevant data from Table A-39.

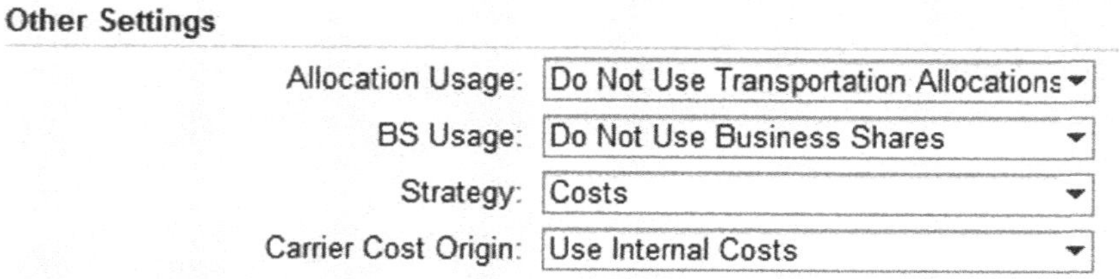

Other Settings

Allocation Usage: [Do Not Use Transportation Allocations ▾]

BS Usage: [Do Not Use Business Shares ▾]

Strategy: [Costs ▾]

Carrier Cost Origin: [Use Internal Costs ▾]

Figure A-61. *Creating carrier selection settings: Other Settings section*

Do the same in the Advanced Settings tab.

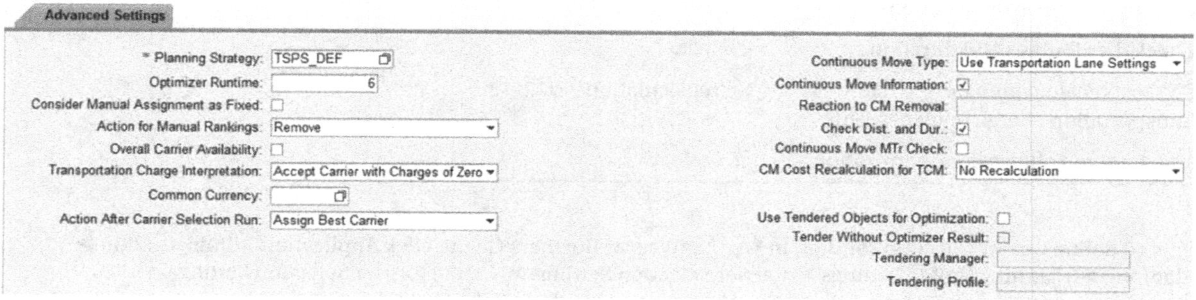

Figure A-62. *Creating carrier selection settings: Advanced Settings tab*

After entering the necessary data, save the data by clicking the Save 🖫 Save button.

Defining Number Range Intervals for Forwarding Settlement Documents

Specify the number range for a forwarding settlement document using this option.

For the given scenario, you must define the number range intervals shown in Table A-40.

Table A-40. *Forwarding Settlement Document Number Range Interval Data*

Field	Value	Value
Number range number	H1	H2
From number	00000000005100000000	00000000006100000000
To number	00000000005199999999	00000000006199999999
External	<Deselect>	<Deselect>

To define a number range, go to Customizing for SAP Transportation Management, and click Transportation Management ➤ Settlement ➤ Forwarding Settlement ➤ Define Number Range Intervals for Forwarding SDs.

To define a number range Interval for a forwarding settlement document, click the Intervals 🖉   Intervals button and then the Insert Line 🗟 button. Enter the number range from Table A-40.

Maintain Intervals: FWSD - Number Range

No	From No.	To Number	NR Status	Ext
H1	0000000000510000000	0000000005199999999		☐

Figure A-63. *Creating a number range interval for a forwarding settlement document*

After entering the necessary data, save the data by clicking the Save 🖫 button.

▪ **Note**   In the Transport number range intervals dialog box, click the Continue ✔ button.

In this way, define the remaining number range intervals.

Defining Forwarding Settlement Document Types

This option lets you specify the various parameters of forwarding settlement documents.

For the given scenario, you will need to define the forwarding settlement document types displayed in Table A-41.

Table A-41. *Forwarding Settlement Document Type Data*

Field	Value	Value
Forwarding settlement document type	FW01	IS01
Description	Forwarding settlement document	Internal settlement document
Forwarding settlement document category	Forwarding settlement document	Internal settlement document
Track changes	<Select>	<Select>
Business warehouse relevance	<Select>	<Select>
Number Range Setting Section		
Number range interval	H1	H2
Output Options Section		
Output profile	/SCMTMS/CFIR	/SCMTMS/CFIR
Additional output profile	/SCMTMS/CFIR_PRINT	/SCMTMS/CFIR_PRINT
Dynamic determination of output profile	<Deselect>	<Deselect>

To define a forwarding settlement document type, go to Customizing for SAP Transportation Management, and click Transportation Management ➤ Settlement ➤ Forwarding Settlement ➤ Define Forwarding Settlement Document Types.

Next, choose the New Entries New Entries button, and enter relevant the data from Table A-41.

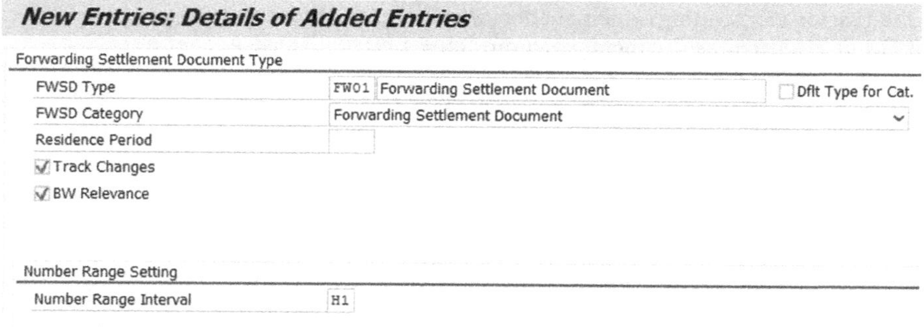

New Entries: Details of Added Entries

Forwarding Settlement Document Type

FWSD Type	FW01 Forwarding Settlement Document	☐ Dflt Type for Cat.
FWSD Category	Forwarding Settlement Document ⌄	
Residence Period		
☑ Track Changes		
☑ BW Relevance		

Number Range Setting

Number Range Interval	H1

Figure A-64. *Creating a forwarding settlement document type*

In the Output Options section, again enter the relevant the data from Table A-41.

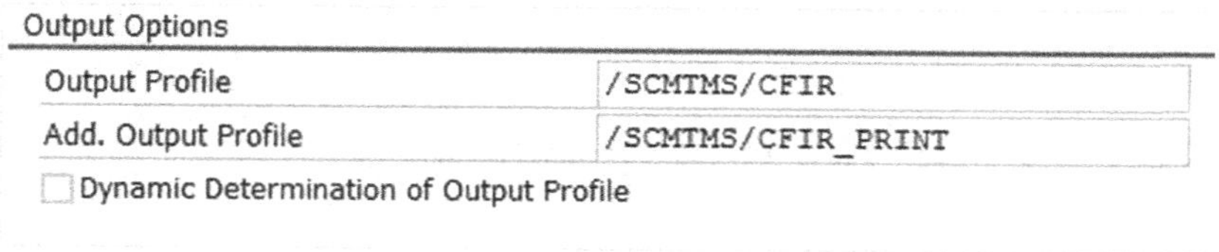

Output Options

Output Profile	/SCMTMS/CFIR
Add. Output Profile	/SCMTMS/CFIR_PRINT

☐ Dynamic Determination of Output Profile

Figure A-65. *Creating a forwarding settlement document type: Output Options section*

After entering the necessary data, save the data by clicking the Save 🖫 button.
In this manner, define the remaining settlement document types.

Defining Number Range Intervals for Freight Settlement Documents

Specify the number range for a freight settlement document using this option.

For the given scenario, you will have to define the number range intervals shown in Table A-42.

Table A-42. *Freight Settlement Document Number Range Interval Data*

Field	Value
Number range number	H1
From number	00000000000400000000
To number	00000000000499999999
External	\<Deselect\>

To define a number range, go to Customizing for SAP Transportation Management, and click Transportation Management ➤ Settlement ➤ Freight Settlement ➤ Define Number Range Intervals for Freight SDs.

To define a number range interval for a Freight settlement document, click the Intervals 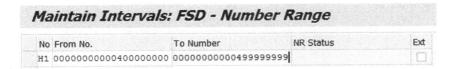 button and then the Insert Line 📑 button. Enter the number range from Table A-42.

Maintain Intervals: FSD - Number Range

No	From No.	To Number	NR Status	Ext
H1	0000000000400000000	0000000000499999999		☐

Figure A-66. *Creating a number range interval for a freight settlement document*

After entering the necessary data, save the data by clicking the Save 💾 button.

■ **Note**   In the Transport number range intervals dialog box, click the Continue ✔ button.

Defining Freight Settlement Document Types

This option lets you specify the various parameters of freight settlement documents.

For the given scenario, you must define the freight settlement document types offered in Table A-43.

Table A-43. *Freight Settlement Document Type Data*

Field	Value
Freight settlement document type	FS01
Description	Carrier settlement document
Freight settlement document category	Freight settlement document
Track changes	<Select>
Business warehouse	<Select>
Enable cost distribution	<Select>
Number Range Setting Section	
Number range interval	H1
Output Options Section	
Output profile	/SCMTMS/TOR_INV_PREP
Additional output profile	/SCMTMS/SFIR_PRINT
Dynamic determination of output profile	<Deselect>

To define a freight settlement document type, go to Customizing for SAP Transportation Management, and click Transportation Management ➤ Settlement ➤ Freight Settlement ➤ Define Freight Settlement Document Types. Then, click the New Entries New Entries button, and enter the relevant data from Table A-43.

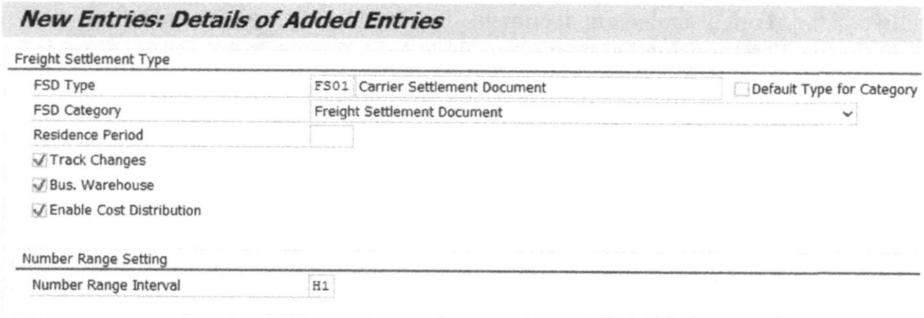

New Entries: Details of Added Entries

Freight Settlement Type

FSD Type	FS01 Carrier Settlement Document	☐ Default Type for Category
FSD Category	Freight Settlement Document	⌄
Residence Period		
☑ Track Changes		
☑ Bus. Warehouse		
☑ Enable Cost Distribution		

Number Range Setting

Number Range Interval	H1

Figure A-67. *Creating a freight settlement document type*

In the Output Options section, again enter the relevant data from Table A-43.

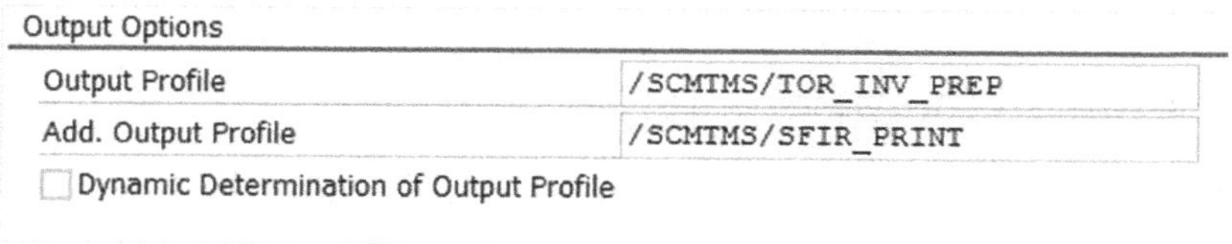

Output Options

Output Profile	/SCMTMS/TOR_INV_PREP
Add. Output Profile	/SCMTMS/SFIR_PRINT

☐ Dynamic Determination of Output Profile

Figure A-68. *Creating a freight settlement document type: Output Options section*

After entering the necessary data, save the data by clicking the Save 🖫 button.

Defining Number Range Intervals for Freight-Order Management

Specify the number range for business documents, such as freight orders, freight bookings, freight units, and transportation units, using this option.

For the given scenario, you will need to define the number range intervals displayed in Table A-44.

Table A-44. *Freight-Order Management Number Range Interval Data*

Field	Value	Value	Value	Value	Value
number range number	H1	H2	H3	H4	H5
From number	0000000000060 0000000	0000000000070 0000000	0000000000080 0000000	0000000000090 0000000	000000000010 00000000
To number	0000000000069 9999999	0000000000079 9999999	0000000000089 9999999	0000000000099 9999999	0000000000199 9999999
External	<Deselect>	<Deselect>	<Deselect>	<Deselect>	<Deselect>

To define a number range, go to Customizing for SAP Transportation Management, and click Transportation Management ▶ Freight Order Management ▶ Define Number Range Intervals for Freight Order Management.

To define a number range interval for freight order management, click the Intervals 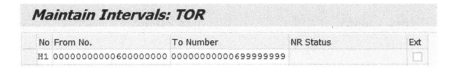 button and then the Insert Line 🖪 button. Enter the number range from Table A-44.

Maintain Intervals: TOR

No	From No.	To Number	NR Status	Ext
H1	0000000000600000000	0000000000699999999		☐

Figure A-69. *Creating a number range interval for freight order management*

After entering the necessary data, save the data by clicking the Save 🖫 button.

■ **Note**   In the Transport number range intervals dialog box, click the Continue ✅ button.

In this manner, define the remaining number range intervals.

Defining Freight-Order Types

This option lets you specify the various parameters that influence the processing of freight orders.

For the given scenario, you must define the freight-order types shown in Table A-45.

Table A-45. *Freight-Order Type Data*

Field	Value	Value
Freight order type	FO01	FO02
Description	Freight order for airfreight pickup/del	Freight order for airfreight pre/on-car
Basic Settings Section		
Freight order can be subcontracted	Relevant for subcontracting	Relevant for subcontracting
Shipper/Consignee determination	Determination based on predecessor documents	Determination based on predecessor documents
Fix document when saving	<Deselect>	<Deselect>
Freight order can be deleted	<Select>	<Select>
Enable settlement	<Select>	<Select>
Enable charge calculation	<Select>	<Select>
Enable internal settlement	<Select>	<Select>
Enable Internal charge calculation	<Select>	<Select>
Enable cost distribution	<Select>	<Select>
Sequence type of tops	Defined and linear	Defined and linear

(*continued*)

Table A-45. (*continued*)

Field	Value	Value
Change Controller Settings Section		
Default change strategy	DEF_CHACO	DEF_CHACO
Execution Settings Section		
Execution tracking relevance	Execution tracking with external event management <(select this option only if integration with SAP EM is configured)>	Execution tracking with external event management <(select this option only if integration with SAP EM is configured)>
Display mode for Execution tab	Actual events from TM and EM, expected events from EM	Actual events from TM and EM, expected events from EM
Propagate execution info	<Select>	<Select>
Event Management Settings Section		
Application object type	ODT30_TO	ODT30_TO
Last expected event	POD	POD
Tendering Settings Section		
Use default settings	<Select>	<Select>
Additional Settings Section		
Default freight settlement document type	Carrier settlement document	Carrier settlement document
Default carrier selection settings	HE-CAR-SEL	HE-CAR-SEL
Business warehouse relevance	<Select>	<Select>
Track changes	<Select>	<Select>
Number Range Settings Section		
Time for drawing	Draw number immediately	Draw number immediately
Number range interval	H1	H2
Additional Strategies Section		
Save strategy	CALC_CHARG	CALC_CHARG
Default Means of Transport Determination Section		
Transportation mode	01	01
Output Options Section		
Output profile	/SCMTMS/TOR_PRINT_ROAD	/SCMTMS/TOR_PRINT_ROAD

To define a freight-order type, *go to* Customizing for SAP Transportation Management, and click Transportation Management ➤ Freight Order Management ➤ Freight Order ➤ Define Freight Order Types.

Next, click the New Entries New Entries button, and enter the freight order type.

Then, in the Basic Settings and Change Controller Settings sections, enter the respective data, using Table A-45.

New Entries: Details of Added Entries

Freight Order Types

Freight Order Type	FO01	Freight Order for Air Freight Pickup/Del

☐ Default Type
☐ Default Type for ERP Shipment Integration

Basic Settings

Freight Order Can Be Subcontracted	R... ⌄
Shipper/Consignee Determination	Determination Based on Predecessor Documents ⌄
☐ Fix Document When Saving	☑ Freight Order Can Be Deleted
☑ Enable Settlement	☑ Enable Charge Calculation
☑ Enable Internal Settlement	☑ Enable Internal Charge Calculation
☑ Enable Cost Distribution	
Sequence Type of Stops	Defined and Linear ⌄
Self-Delivery/Customer Pick-Up	⌄

Change Controller Settings

Default Change Strategy	DEF_CHACO
Change Strategy Determination Cond.	
Quantity Tolerance Condition	
Date Tolerance Condition	

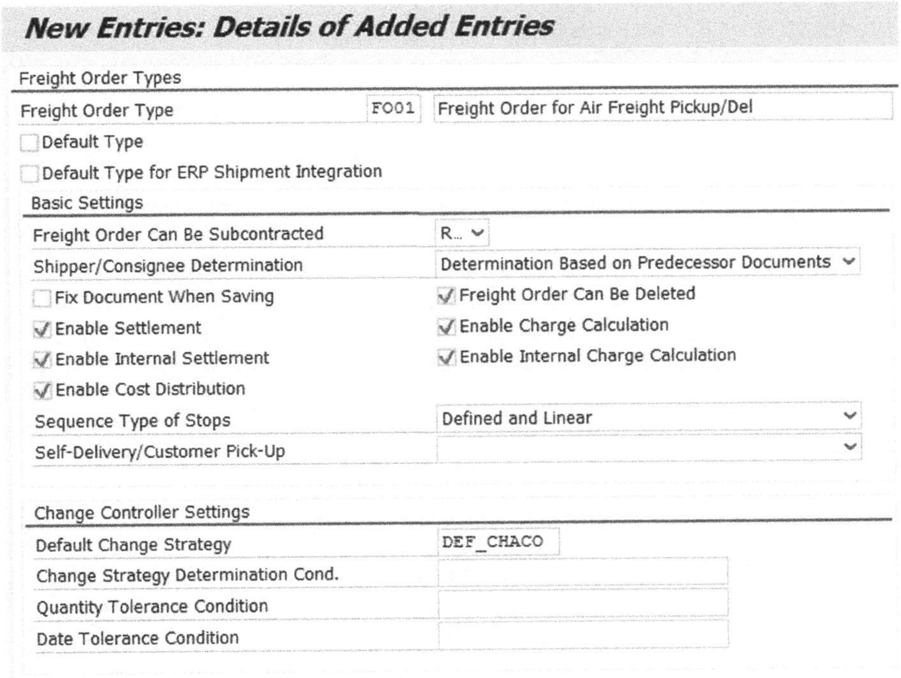

Figure A-70. *Creating a freight-order type: Basic Settings and Change Controller Settings sections*

In the Execution Settings and Tendering Settings sections, enter the respective data, using Table A-45.

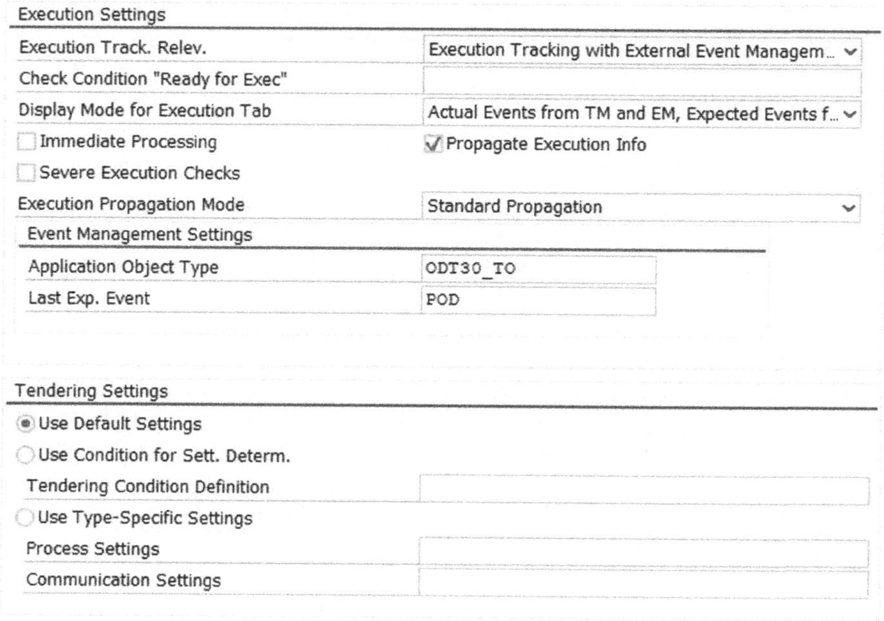

Execution Settings	
Execution Track. Relev.	Execution Tracking with External Event Managem... ⌄
Check Condition "Ready for Exec"	
Display Mode for Execution Tab	Actual Events from TM and EM, Expected Events f... ⌄
☐ Immediate Processing	☑ Propagate Execution Info
☐ Severe Execution Checks	
Execution Propagation Mode	Standard Propagation ⌄
Event Management Settings	
Application Object Type	ODT30_TO
Last Exp. Event	POD

Tendering Settings	
◉ Use Default Settings	
○ Use Condition for Sett. Determ.	
Tendering Condition Definition	
○ Use Type-Specific Settings	
Process Settings	
Communication Settings	

Figure A-71. *Creating a freight-order type: Execution Settings and Tendering Settings sections*

In the Additional Settings section, enter the relevant data from Table A-45.

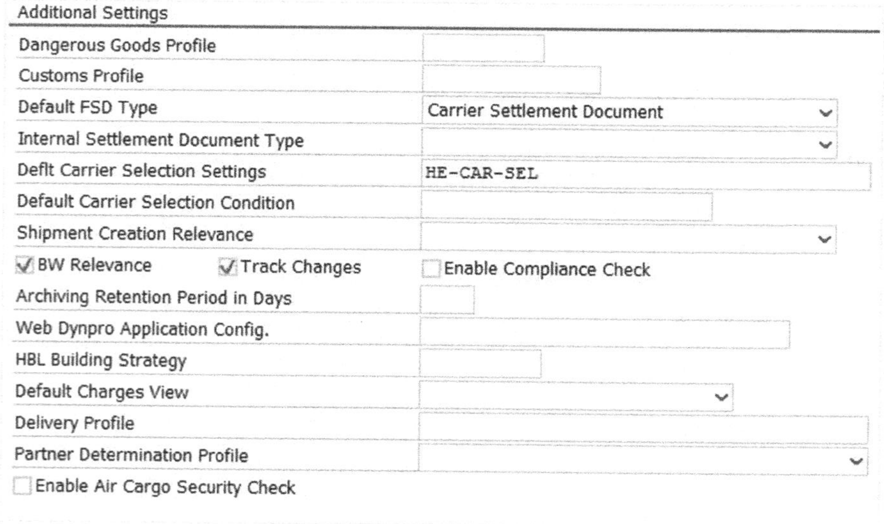

Additional Settings			
Dangerous Goods Profile			
Customs Profile			
Default FSD Type	Carrier Settlement Document ⌄		
Internal Settlement Document Type	⌄		
Deflt Carrier Selection Settings	HE-CAR-SEL		
Default Carrier Selection Condition			
Shipment Creation Relevance	⌄		
☑ BW Relevance	☑ Track Changes	☐ Enable Compliance Check	
Archiving Retention Period in Days			
Web Dynpro Application Config.			
HBL Building Strategy			
Default Charges View	⌄		
Delivery Profile			
Partner Determination Profile	⌄		
☐ Enable Air Cargo Security Check			

Figure A-72. *Creating a freight-order type: Additional Settings section*

In the Number Range Settings and Additional Strategies sections, enter the respective data, using Table A-45.

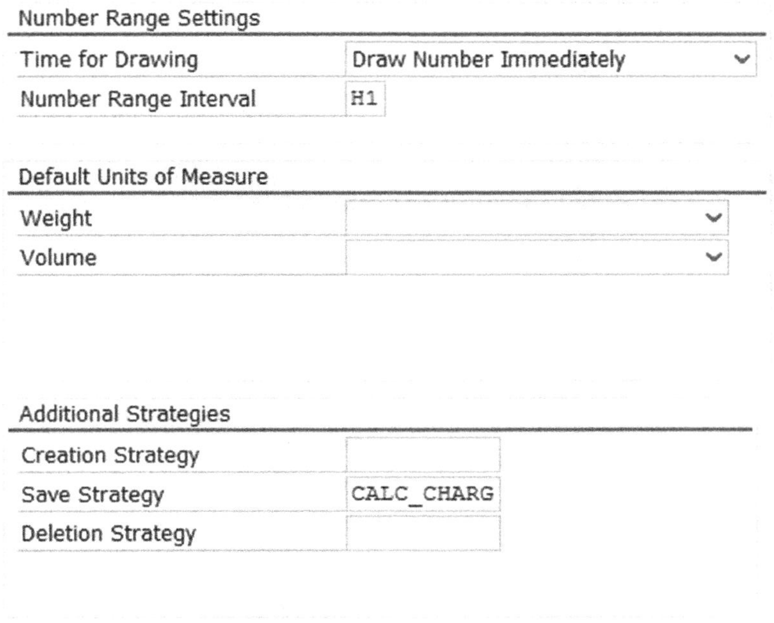

Number Range Settings

Time for Drawing	Draw Number Immediately ⌄
Number Range Interval	H1

Default Units of Measure

Weight	⌄
Volume	⌄

Additional Strategies

Creation Strategy	
Save Strategy	CALC_CHARG
Deletion Strategy	

Figure A-73. *Creating a freight-order type: Number Range Settings and Additional Strategies sections*

In the Default Means of Transport Determination and Output Options sections, enter the respective data, using Table A-45.

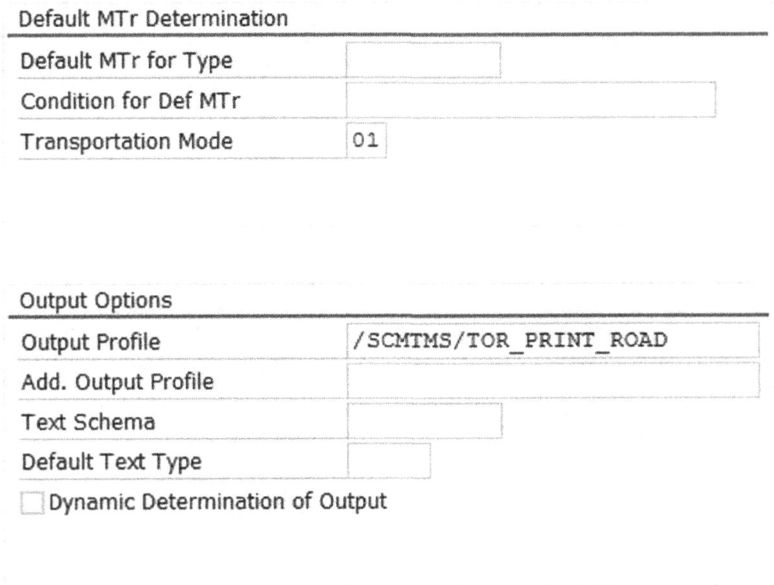

Default MTr Determination

Default MTr for Type	
Condition for Def MTr	
Transportation Mode	01

Output Options

Output Profile	/SCMTMS/TOR_PRINT_ROAD
Add. Output Profile	
Text Schema	
Default Text Type	

☐ Dynamic Determination of Output

Figure A-74. *Creating a freight-order type: Default Means of Transport Determination and Output Options sections*

155

After entering the necessary data, save the data by clicking the Save 🖫 button. In this way, define the remaining freight-order types.

Defining Freight-Booking Types

This option allows you to specify the various parameters that influence the processing of freight booking. For the given scenario, you will have to define the freight-booking types provided in Table A-46.

Table A-46. *Freight-Booking Type Data*

Field	Value	Value
Freight-booking type	FB02	FB01
Description	Import freight booking for airfreight	Export freight booking for airfreight
Transportation mode category	Air	Air
Transportation mode	05	05
Basic Settings Section		
Shipper/Consignee determination	Determination based on predecessor documents	Determination based on predecessor documents
Fix booking	Do not fix	Do not fix
Booking can be deleted	<Select>	<Select>
Enable settlement	<Select>	<Select>
Enable cost distribution	<Select>	<Select>
Enable charge calculation	<Select>	<Select>
Coload	<Deselect>	<Deselect>
Change Controller Settings Section		
Default change strategy	DEF_CHACO	DEF_CHACO
Execution settings		
Carrier confirmation	Carrier confirmation not required	Carrier confirmation not required
Execution tracking relevance	Execution tracking with external event management <(select this option only if integration with SAP EM is configured)>	Execution tracking with external event management <(select this option only if integration with SAP EM is configured)>
Display mode for Execution tab	Actual events from TM and EM, expected events from EM	Actual events from TM and EM, expected events from EM
Immediate processing	Life cycle is not to be set to "In Process" immediately	Life cycle is not to be set to "In Process" immediately
Severe execution checks	<Deselect>	<Deselect>
Propagate execution information	<Select>	<Select>

(continued)

Table A-46. (*continued*)

Field	Value	Value
Event Management Settings Section		
Application object type	ODT30_TO	ODT30_TO
Last expected event	POD	POD
Additional Settings Section		
Default freight settlement document type	Carrier settlement document	Carrier settlement document
Default freight-order type for pickup	FO01	FO01
Default freight-order type for delivery	FO01	FO01
Business warehouse relevance	<Select>	<Select>
Track changes	<Select>	<Select>
Enable compliance check	<Deselect>	<Deselect>
Container item source	Container item is defined in booking	Container item is defined in booking
Web Dynpro application configuration	/SCMTMS/FRE_BOOK_CBAIR	/SCMTMS/FRE_BOOK_CBAIR
Import-Booking type		FB02
Air Cargo Security (ACS) Check	<Deselect>	<Deselect>
Number Range Settings Section		
Time for drawing	Draw numbers immediately	Draw numbers immediately
Number range Interval	H4	H3
Service Definition Section		
Consolidation (source)	With consolidation	With consolidation
Consolidation (destination)	With consolidation	With consolidation
Shipping type	10	10
Traffic direction	Import	Export
Output Options Section		
Output profile	/SCMTMS/TOR	/SCMTMS/TOR
Additional output profile	/SCMTMS/TOR_PRINT_AIR	/SCMTMS/TOR_PRINT_AIR
Predecessor Document Handling Section		
Update from predecessor	Asynchronous update from predecessor allowed	Asynchronous update from predecessor allowed

To define a freight-booking type, go to Customizing for SAP Transportation Management, and click Transportation Management ➤ Freight Order Management ➤ Freight Booking ➤ Define Freight Booking Type.

Next, click the New Entries New Entries button, and enter the booking type.

Now, in the Basic Settings and Change Controller Settings sections, enter the respective data, using Table A-46.

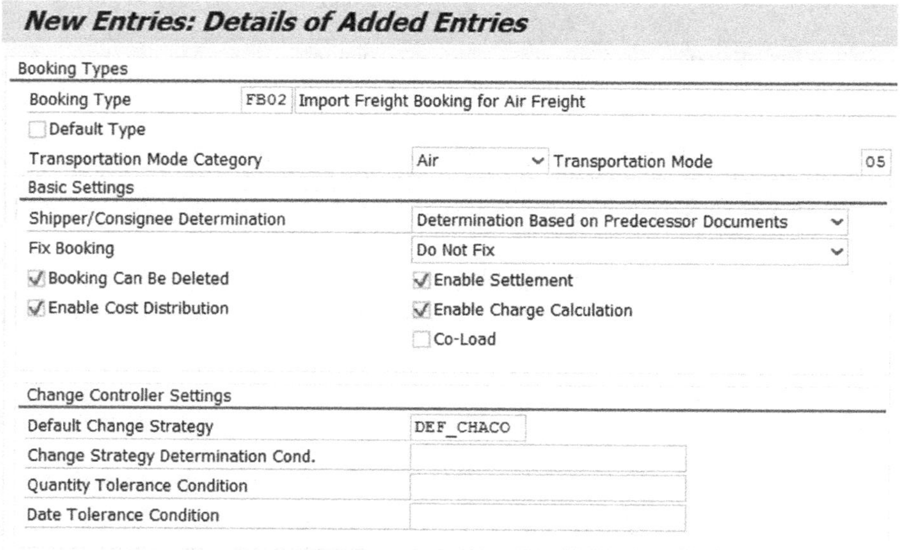

New Entries: Details of Added Entries

Booking Types

Booking Type	FB02	Import Freight Booking for Air Freight
☐ Default Type		
Transportation Mode Category	Air ⌄	Transportation Mode 05

Basic Settings

Shipper/Consignee Determination	Determination Based on Predecessor Documents ⌄
Fix Booking	Do Not Fix ⌄
☑ Booking Can Be Deleted	☑ Enable Settlement
☑ Enable Cost Distribution	☑ Enable Charge Calculation
	☐ Co-Load

Change Controller Settings

Default Change Strategy	DEF_CHACO
Change Strategy Determination Cond.	
Quantity Tolerance Condition	
Date Tolerance Condition	

Figure A-75. *Creating a freight-booking type: Basic Settings and Change Controller Settings sections*

In the Execution Settings section, enter the relevant data from Table A-46.

Execution Settings

Carrier Confirmation	Carrier Confirmation Not Required ⌄
Exec. Track. Relevance	Execution Tracking with External Event Management ⌄
Display Mode for Execution Tab	Actual Events from TM and EM, Expected Events from EM ⌄
Immediate Processing	Life Cycle Is Not to Be Set to "In Process" Immediately ⌄
☐ Severe Execution Checks	☑ Propagate Execution Info
Execution Propagation Mode	Standard Propagation ⌄
Check Condition "Ready for Exec"	

Event Management Settings

Application Object Type	ODT30_TO
Last Exp. Event	POD

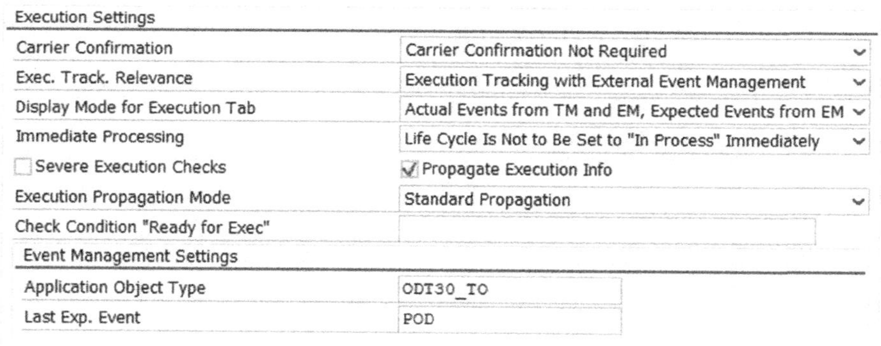

Figure A-76. *Creating a freight-booking type: Execution Settings section*

In the Additional Settings section, again enter the relevant data from Table A-46.

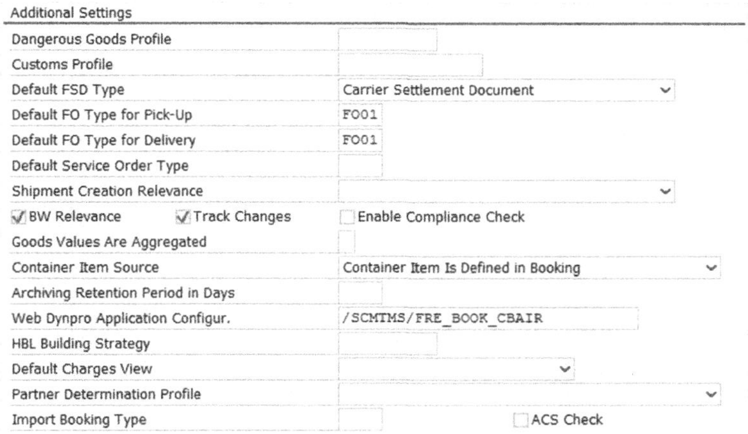

Additional Settings

Dangerous Goods Profile	
Customs Profile	
Default FSD Type	Carrier Settlement Document ⌄
Default FO Type for Pick-Up	FO01
Default FO Type for Delivery	FO01
Default Service Order Type	
Shipment Creation Relevance	⌄
☑ BW Relevance ☑ Track Changes	☐ Enable Compliance Check
Goods Values Are Aggregated	
Container Item Source	Container Item Is Defined in Booking ⌄
Archiving Retention Period in Days	
Web Dynpro Application Configur.	/SCMTMS/FRE_BOOK_CBAIR
HBL Building Strategy	
Default Charges View	⌄
Partner Determination Profile	⌄
Import Booking Type	☐ ACS Check

Figure A-77. *Creating a freight-booking type: Additional Settings section*

In the Number Range Settings, Service Definition, and Output Options sections, enter the respective data, using Table A-46.

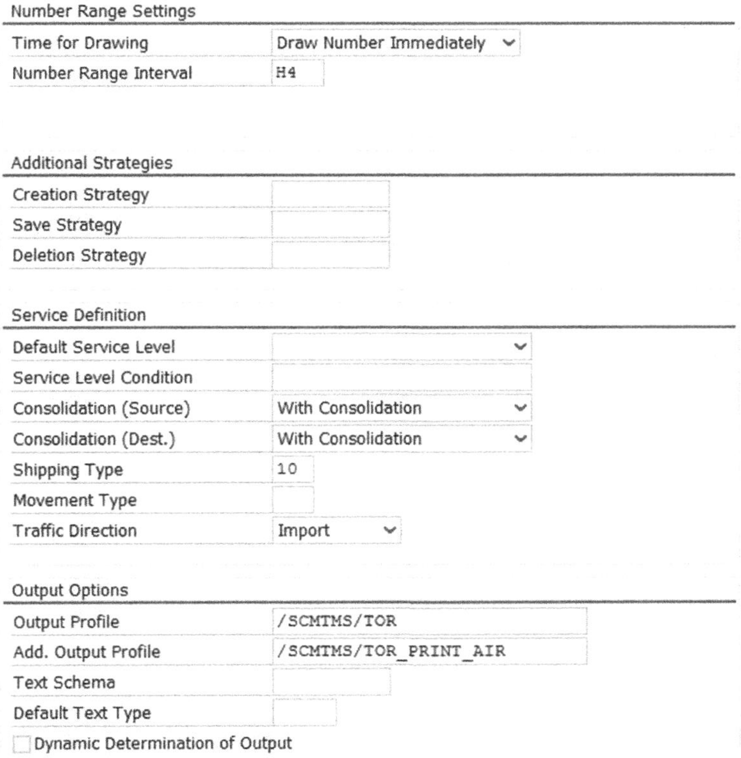

Number Range Settings

Time for Drawing	Draw Number Immediately ⌄
Number Range Interval	H4

Additional Strategies

Creation Strategy	
Save Strategy	
Deletion Strategy	

Service Definition

Default Service Level	⌄
Service Level Condition	
Consolidation (Source)	With Consolidation ⌄
Consolidation (Dest.)	With Consolidation ⌄
Shipping Type	10
Movement Type	
Traffic Direction	Import ⌄

Output Options

Output Profile	/SCMTMS/TOR
Add. Output Profile	/SCMTMS/TOR_PRINT_AIR
Text Schema	
Default Text Type	
☐ Dynamic Determination of Output	

Figure A-78. *Creating a freight-booking type: Number Range Settings, Service Definition, and Output Options sections*

In the Predecessor Document Handling section, enter the relevant data from Table A-46.

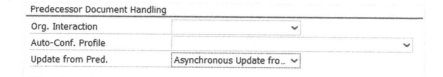

Figure A-79. *Creating a freight-booking type: Predecessor Document Handling section*

After entering the necessary data, save the data by clicking the Save ▣ button.
In this way, define the remaining freight-booking types.

Defining Contract Basis

For freight booking a contractual commitment is made to the carrier. This option lets you define the basis of the contract.

For the given scenario, you must define the contract basis.

Table A-47. *Contract Basis Data*

Field	Value	Value
Contract basis	01	02
Description	Allotment	Blocked space

To define a contract basis, go to Customizing for SAP Transportation Management, and click Transportation Management ➤ Freight Order Management ➤ Freight Booking ➤ Define Contract Basis.
Then, click the New Entries button, and enter the data from Table A-47.

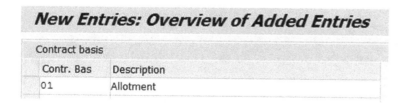

Figure A-80. *Creating a contract basis*

After entering the necessary data, save the data by clicking the Save ▣ button.
In this way, define the remaining contract bases.

Defining Freight Unit Types

This option lets you specify the various parameters that influence the processing of freight units.
For the given scenario, you will need to define the freight unit types displayed in Table A-48

Table A-48. *Freight Unit Type Data*

Field	Value
Freight unit type	FU01
Description	Freight unit for airfreight
Default type	<Deselect>
Basic Settings Section	
Freight unit can be deleted	<Select>
Change Controller Settings Section	
Default change strategy	DEF_CHACO
Execution Settings Section	
Execution tracking relevance	Execution tracking with external event management <(select this option only if integration with SAP EM is configured)>
Display mode for Execution tab	Actual events from TM and EM, expected events from EM
Immediate processing	<Select>
Event Management Settings Section	
Application object type	ODT30_FU
Last expected event	POD
Additional Settings Section	
Rule for Pickup/Delivery window	Pickup and delivery, as defined in forwarding order, FWO, FWQ, OTR or DTR
Business warehouse relevance	<Select>
Track changes	<Select>
Number Range Settings Section	
Time for drawing	Draw number when saving document
Number range interval	H5
Freight-Order Determination Section	
Freight-Order type	FO01

To define a freight unit type, go to Customizing for SAP Transportation Management, and click Transportation Management ➤ Planning ➤ Freight Unit ➤ Define Freight Unit Types.

Now, click the New Entries New Entries button, and enter the unit type.

In the Basic Settings, Change Controller Settings, and Execution Settings sections, enter the respective data, using Table A-48.

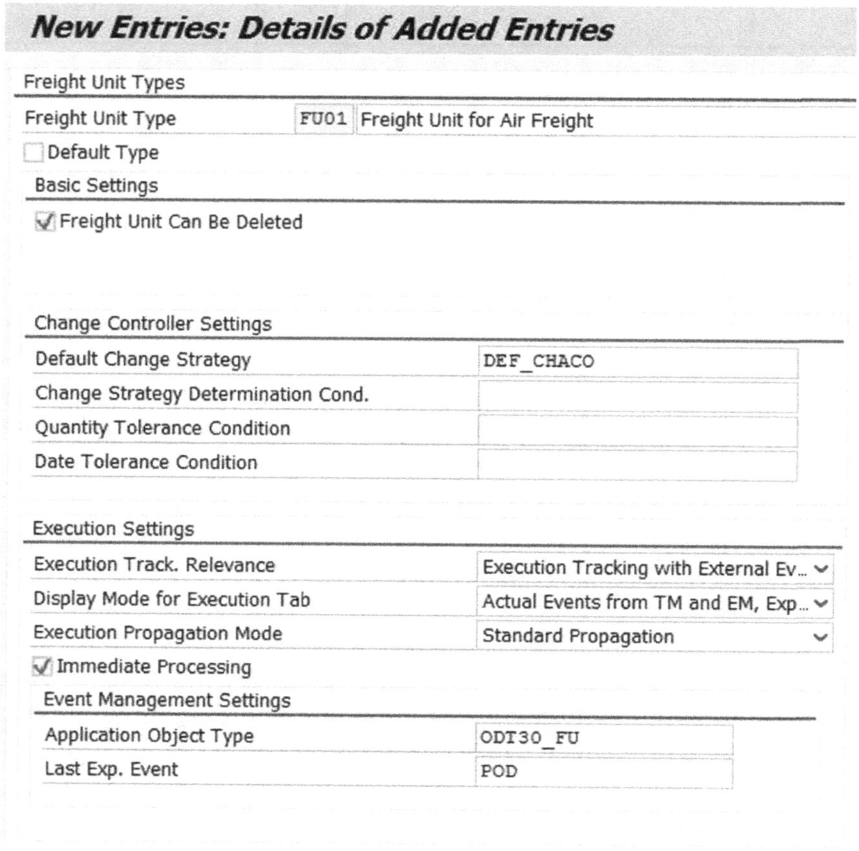

New Entries: Details of Added Entries

Freight Unit Types

| Freight Unit Type | FU01 | Freight Unit for Air Freight |

☐ Default Type

Basic Settings

☑ Freight Unit Can Be Deleted

Change Controller Settings

Default Change Strategy	DEF_CHACO
Change Strategy Determination Cond.	
Quantity Tolerance Condition	
Date Tolerance Condition	

Execution Settings

Execution Track. Relevance	Execution Tracking with External Ev... ⌄
Display Mode for Execution Tab	Actual Events from TM and EM, Exp... ⌄
Execution Propagation Mode	Standard Propagation ⌄

☑ Immediate Processing

Event Management Settings

| Application Object Type | ODT30_FU |
| Last Exp. Event | POD |

Figure A-81. Creating a freight unit type: Basic Settings, Change Controller Settings, and Execution Settings sections

In the Additional Settings section, enter the relevant data from Table A-48.

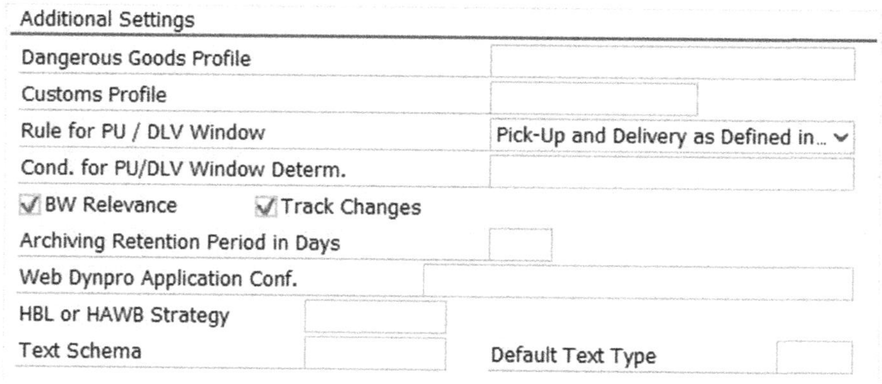

Additional Settings

Dangerous Goods Profile	
Customs Profile	
Rule for PU / DLV Window	Pick-Up and Delivery as Defined in... ⌄
Cond. for PU/DLV Window Determ.	

☑ BW Relevance   ☑ Track Changes

Archiving Retention Period in Days	
Web Dynpro Application Conf.	
HBL or HAWB Strategy	
Text Schema		Default Text Type	

Figure A-82. Creating a freight unit type: Additional Settings section

In the Number Range Settings and Freight-Order Determination sections, enter the respective data, using Table A-48.

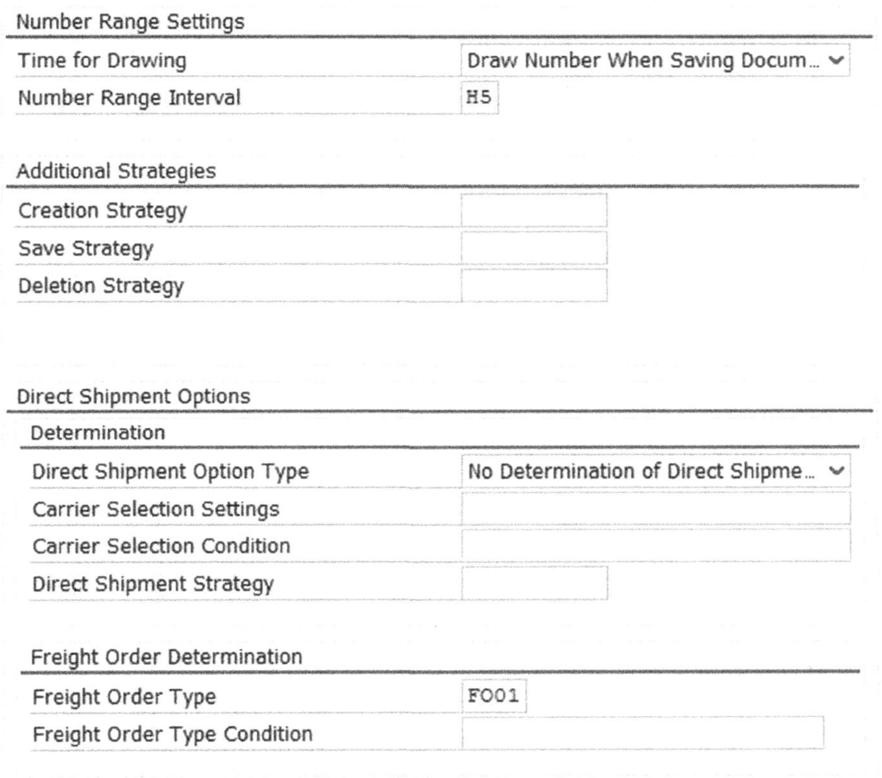

Number Range Settings	
Time for Drawing	Draw Number When Saving Docum... ⌄
Number Range Interval	H5

Additional Strategies	
Creation Strategy	
Save Strategy	
Deletion Strategy	

Direct Shipment Options	
Determination	
Direct Shipment Option Type	No Determination of Direct Shipme... ⌄
Carrier Selection Settings	
Carrier Selection Condition	
Direct Shipment Strategy	

Freight Order Determination	
Freight Order Type	FO01
Freight Order Type Condition	

Figure A-83. *Creating a freight unit type: Number Range Settings and Freight-Order Determination sections*

After entering the necessary data, save the data by clicking the Save 🖫 button.

Creating Freight Unit–Building Rules

Based on the forwarding order, how the system should create a freight unit is defined as a rule in the system. For planning this rule also lets you specify the dimensions, which are transferred from the forwarding order to the freight unit as capacity requirements.

For the given scenario, you will need to create the freight unit–building rule.

Table A-49. *Freight Unit–Building Rule Data*

Field	Value
General Data Section	
Freight unit–building rule	HE-FUBR-01
Description	Freight unit rule for Airfreight
Other Settings Section	
Document type	FU01
Control Section	
Freight unit–building strategy	Consolidate per item
Critical quantity	Gross weight
Item split allowed	<Select>
Advanced Settings Tab	
Document type Det. Cnd	<Blank>
Process controller strategy	FUB_AUTO

Table A-50. *Freight Unit–Building Rule: Planning Quantities Table Data*

Field	Value	Value
Planning Quantities Tab		
Planning quantity for freight unit building	Gross weight	Gross volume
Unit of measure of split quantity	kg	m^3
Split quantity	4,000	7
Rounding quantity	<Blank>	<Blank>

To create a freight unit–building rule, in SAP NetWeaver Business Client, click Application Administration ➤ Planning ➤ General Settings ➤ Freight Unit Building Rule ➤ Create Freight Unit Building Rule.

Next, in the General Data and Other Settings sections of the General Data tab, enter the respective data, using Table A-49.

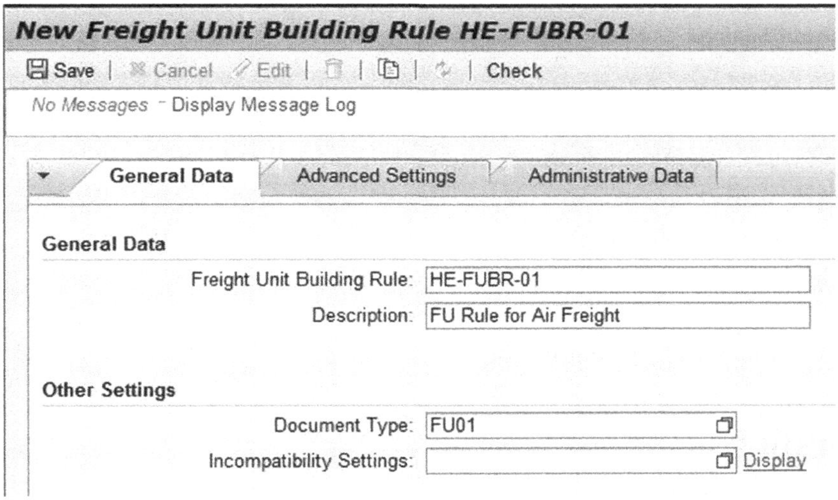

New Freight Unit Building Rule HE-FUBR-01

🖫 Save | ✖ Cancel | ✎ Edit | 🗑 | 🗅 | ↻ | Check

No Messages ˜ Display Message Log

▾ | **General Data** | **Advanced Settings** | **Administrative Data**

General Data

Freight Unit Building Rule:	HE-FUBR-01
Description:	FU Rule for Air Freight

Other Settings

Document Type:	FU01 🗗
Incompatibility Settings:	🗗 Display

Figure A-84. *Creating a freight unit–building rule: General Data and Other Settings sections of the General Data tab*

In the Control section of the General Data tab, enter the relevant data from Table A-49.

Control

Freight Unit Building Strategy:	Consolidate per Item ▾
Critical Quantity:	Gross Weight ▾
Item Split Allowed:	☑
Apply Default Route:	☐

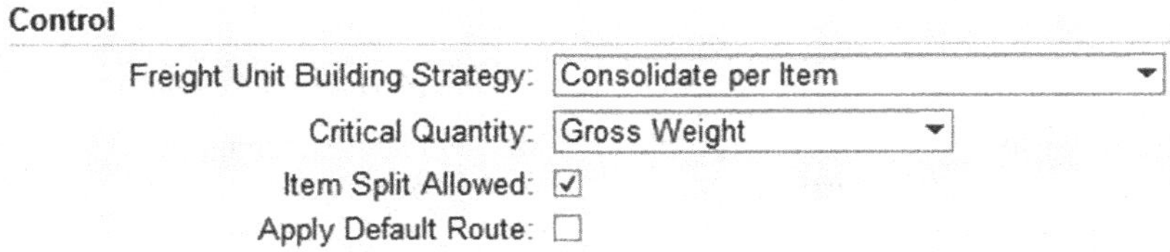

Figure A-85. *Creating a freight unit–building rule: Control section of the General Data tab*

In the Planning Quantities tab, enter the relevant data from Table A-50.

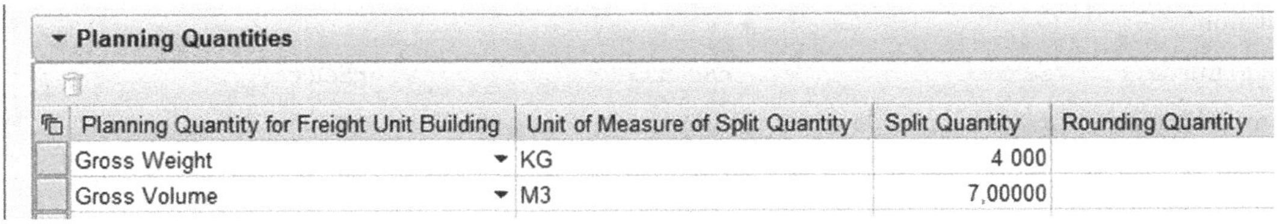

▾ **Planning Quantities**

🗑

Planning Quantity for Freight Unit Building	Unit of Measure of Split Quantity	Split Quantity	Rounding Quantity
Gross Weight ▾	KG	4 000	
Gross Volume ▾	M3	7,00000	

Figure A-86. *Creating a freight unit–building rule: Planning Quantities tab*

In the Advanced Settings section of the Advanced Settings tab, again enter the relevant data from Table A-49.

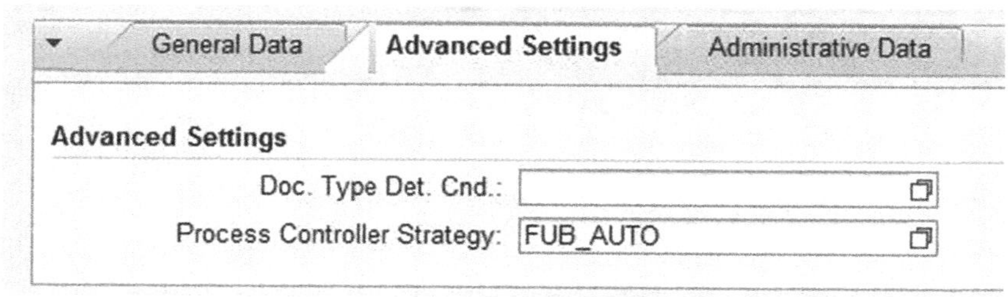

Figure A-87. Creating a freight unit–building rule: Advanced Settings tab

After entering the necessary data, save the data by clicking the Save 💾 Save button.

Defining Planning Profiles

This option allows you to specify the various parameters that are taken into consideration while performing planning. For the given scenario, you must define the planning profiles shown in Table A-51.

Table A-51. Planning Profiles Data

Field	Value	Value	Value
General Data Section			
Planning profile	HE-PLAN-PRO-PRE	HE-PLAN-PRO-MAIN	HE-PLAN-PRO-ON
Description	Planning profile for precarriage	Planning profile for main carriage	Planning profile for on-carriage
Planning Horizon Section			
Duration in days	100	75	100
Offset direction	Future	Future	Future
Offset in days	0	0	0
Factory calendar for offset/ duration calculation	W8	W8	W8
Round horizon to full days	<Select>	<Select>	<Select>
Time zone for rounding the horizon	CET	CET	CET
Profile Assignments Section			
Selection profile for freight bookings		HE-SEL-PRO-BOOK	
Capacity selection settings	HE-CAP-SEL-PRE	HE-CAP-SEL-MAIN	HE-CAP-SEL-ON
Optimizer settings	HE-OPT-SET	HE-OPT-SET	HE-OPT-SET
Carrier selection settings	HE-CAR-SEL	HE-CAR-SEL	HE-CAR-SEL

(continued)

Table A-51. (*continued*)

Field	Value	Value	Value
Business Document Type Section			
Type determination rule	Defined per category in planning profile	Defined per category in planning profile	Defined per category in planning profile
Default type for vehicle resources	FO02	FO02	FO02
Default type for bookings (air)	FB01	FB01	FB01
Manual Planning Section			
Manual planning strategy	VSRI_DEF	VSRI_DEF	VSRI_DEF
Consider fixing status	Error when changing fixed document	Error when changing fixed document	Error when changing fixed document
Scheduling Section			
Scheduling strategy	VSS_DEF	VSS_DEF	VSS_DEF
Consider freight unit dates	Consider freight unit dates as soft constraints only	Do not consider freight unit dates	Do not consider freight unit dates
Scheduling direction	Backward	Backward	Backward
Check Section			
Check strategy	VSR_CHECK	VSR_CHECK	VSR_CHECK
Take capacities into account	Warning	Warning	Warning
Loading and Unloading Duration Section			
Dependence	Freight unit and MTr independent	Freight unit and MTr independent	Freight unit and MTr independent
Loading/Unloading duration	00:00:00	00:00:00	00:00:00

To define a planning profile, in SAP NetWeaver Business Client choose Application Administration ➤ Planning ➤ Planning Profiles ➤ Create Planning Profiles.

Then, in the General Data, Planning Horizon, and Profile Assignments sections, enter the respective data from Table A-51.

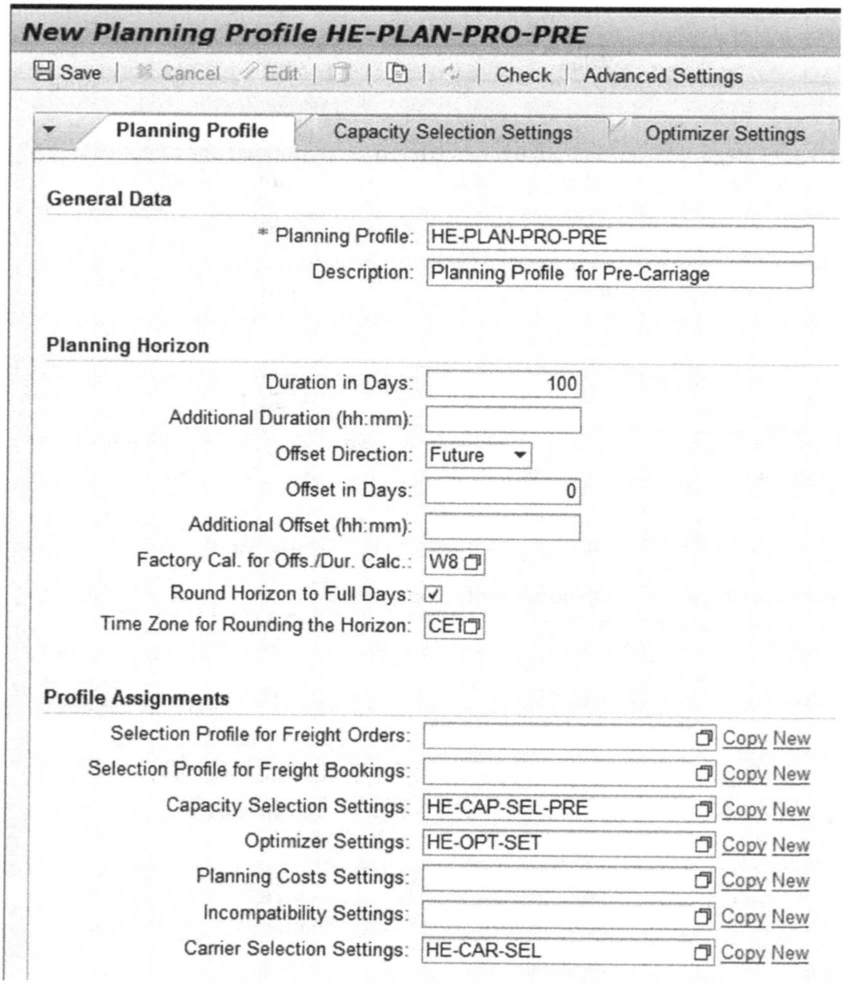

Figure A-88. *Creating a planning profile: General Data, Planning Horizon, and Profile Assignments sections of the Planning Profile tab*

In the Business Document Type, Manual Planning, Scheduling, Check, and Loading and Unloading Duration sections of the Planning Profile tab, enter the respective data from Table A-51.

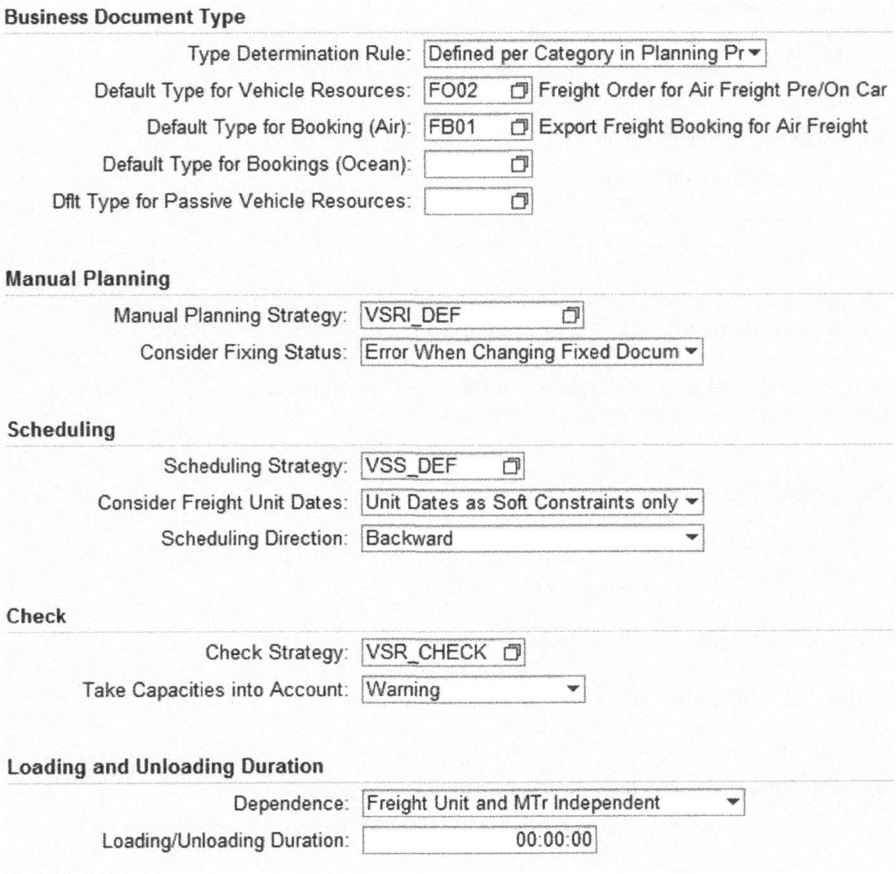

Business Document Type

Type Determination Rule:	Defined per Category in Planning Pr ▼
Default Type for Vehicle Resources:	FO02 ▢ Freight Order for Air Freight Pre/On Car
Default Type for Booking (Air):	FB01 ▢ Export Freight Booking for Air Freight
Default Type for Bookings (Ocean):	▢
Dflt Type for Passive Vehicle Resources:	▢

Manual Planning

Manual Planning Strategy:	VSRI_DEF ▢
Consider Fixing Status:	Error When Changing Fixed Docum ▼

Scheduling

Scheduling Strategy:	VSS_DEF ▢
Consider Freight Unit Dates:	Unit Dates as Soft Constraints only ▼
Scheduling Direction:	Backward ▼

Check

Check Strategy:	VSR_CHECK ▢
Take Capacities into Account:	Warning ▼

Loading and Unloading Duration

Dependence:	Freight Unit and MTr Independent ▼
Loading/Unloading Duration:	00:00:00

Figure A-89. *Creating a planning profile: Business Document Type, Manual Planning, Scheduling, Check, and Loading and Unloading Duration sections of the Planning Profile tab*

After entering the necessary data, save the data by clicking the Save ⊞ Save button.

In this manner, define the remaining planning profiles.

Defining Number Range Intervals for Forwarding-Order Management

Specify the number range for a forwarding order using this option.

For the given scenario, you will have to define the number range intervals presented in Table A-52.

Table A-52. *Forwarding-Order Management Number Range Interval Data*

Field	Value
Number range number	H1
From number	00000000001000000000
To number	00000000001099999999
External	<Deselect>

To define a number range, go to Customizing for SAP Transportation Management, and click Transportation Management ➤ Forwarding Order Management ➤ Define Number Range Intervals for Forwarding Order Management.

To define a number range interval for forwarding-order management, click the Intervals 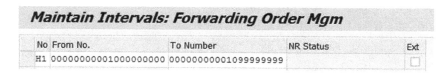 and then the Insert Line ▣ button. Enter the number range from Table A-52.

Figure A-90. *Creating a number range interval for forwarding-order management*

After entering the necessary data, save the data by clicking the Save 🖫 button.

■ **Note** In the Transport number range intervals dialog box, click the Continue ✅ button.

Defining Forwarding-Order Types

This option allows you to specify the various parameters, such as freight unit creation and planning profile, which influence the processing of forwarding orders.

For the given scenario, you must define the forwarding-order types shown in Table A-53.

Table A-53. *Forwarding-Order Type Data*

Field	Value	Value
Forwarding-order type	FW02	FW01
Description	Import forwarding order	Export forwarding order
Number Range Settings Section		
Number range interval	H1	H1
Template number range interval	H1	H1

(continued)

Table A-53. (*continued*)

Field	Value	Value
Process Control/Business Object Mode Section		
Same locations and business partners	<Deselect>	<Deselect>
Automatic block	<Deselect>	<Deselect>
Business warehouse relevance	<Select>	<Select>
Automatic freight unit building	<Select>	<Select>
Enable approval workflow	<Deselect>	<Deselect>
Track document changes	<Select>	<Select>
Enable charge calculation	<Select>	<Select>
Automatic charge calculation	<Deselect>	<Deselect>
Enable internal charge calculation	<Select>	<Select>
Automatic internal charge calculation	<Deselect>	<Deselect>
Transportation mode	05	05
Shipping type	10	10
Traffic direction	2	1
Air Cargo Settings Section		
Air waybill type	04	04
Enable air cargo security check	<Select>	<Select>
Copy air cargo security data	<Select>	<Select>
Stage determination	Stage determination by stage profile	Stage determination by movement type
Stage profile	HEIM	
Enable forwarding settlement	<Select>	<Select>
Default forwarding settlement document type	FW01	FW01
Enable internal settlement	<Select>	<Select>
Default internal settlement document type	IS01	IS01
Automatic confirmation	<Deselect>	<Deselect>
Default confirmation type	O	O
EM integration active	<Select (select this option only if integration with SAP EM is configured)>	<Select (select this option only if integration with SAP EM is configured)>
Event manager	<Specify the name of event management client (select this option only if integration with SAP EM is configured)>	<Specify the name of event management client (select this option only if integration with SAP EM is configured)>

(*continued*)

Table A-53. (*continued*)

Field	Value	Value
Output profile	/SCMTMS/TRQ_FWO	/SCMTMS/TRQ_FWO
Additional output profile	/SCMTMS/TRQ_FWO_PRINT	/SCMTMS/TRQ_FWO_PRINT
Accept transport proposal	Save route only	Save route only
Propagate changes	Synchronous propagation of changes, fall back to asynchronous	Synchronous propagation of changes, fall back to asynchronous
Customs handling	Automatic	Manual
Import forwarding-order type		FW02
Default Values Section		
Default weight unit of measure	kg	kg
Default volume unit of measure	m³	m³
Default pieces unit of measure	PC	PC
Freight unit building–rule	HE-FUBR-01	HE-FUBR-01
Planning profile		HE-PLAN-PRO-MAIN
Organizational Unit Determination Section		
Consider user assignment	<Deselect>	<Deselect>
Sales organization	<Blank>	<Blank>

To define a forwarding-order type, go to Customizing for SAP Transportation Management, and click Transportation Management ➤ Forwarding Order Management ➤ Forwarding Order ➤ Define Forwarding Order Types.

Then, click the New Entries New Entries button, and enter the order type.

In the Number Range Settings, Process Control/Business Object Mode, and Air Cargo Settings sections, enter the respective data, using Table A-53.

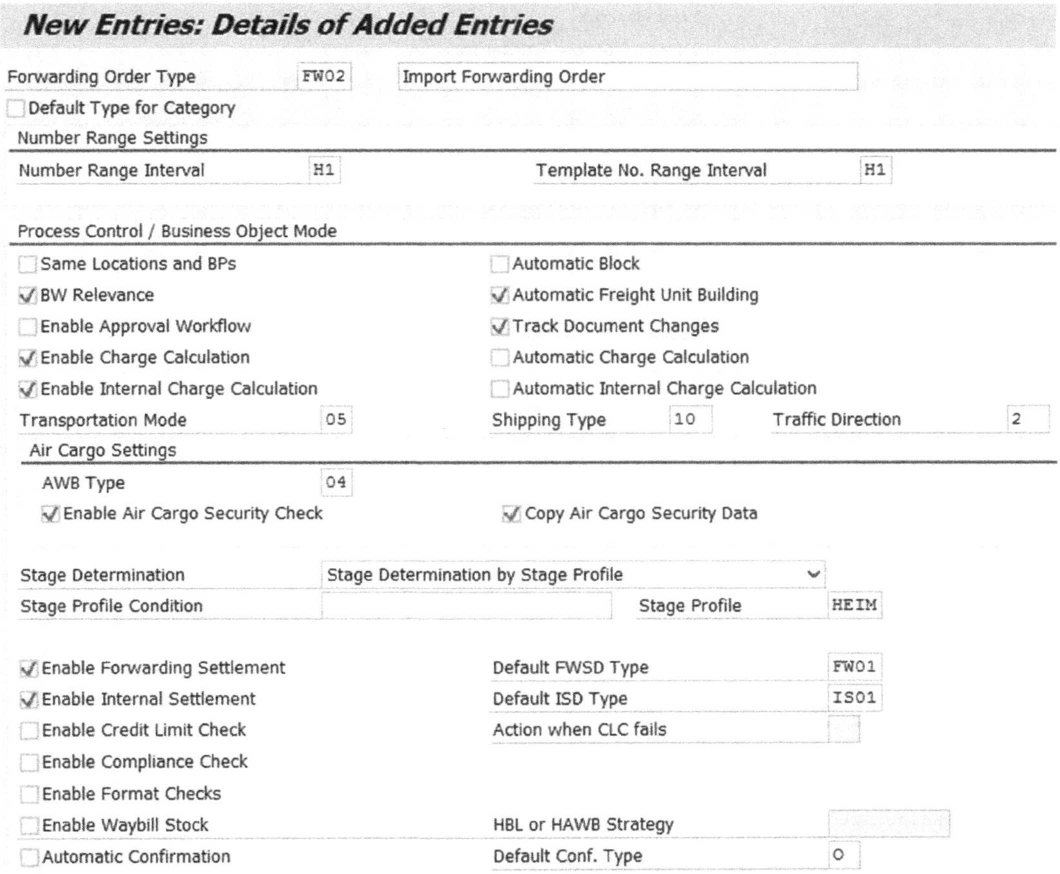

New Entries: Details of Added Entries

Forwarding Order Type	FW02	Import Forwarding Order
☐ Default Type for Category		

Number Range Settings

Number Range Interval	H1	Template No. Range Interval	H1

Process Control / Business Object Mode

☐ Same Locations and BPs	☐ Automatic Block
☑ BW Relevance	☑ Automatic Freight Unit Building
☐ Enable Approval Workflow	☑ Track Document Changes
☑ Enable Charge Calculation	☐ Automatic Charge Calculation
☑ Enable Internal Charge Calculation	☐ Automatic Internal Charge Calculation

Transportation Mode	05	Shipping Type	10	Traffic Direction	2

Air Cargo Settings

AWB Type	04

☑ Enable Air Cargo Security Check	☑ Copy Air Cargo Security Data

Stage Determination	Stage Determination by Stage Profile ⌄		
Stage Profile Condition		Stage Profile	HEIM

☑ Enable Forwarding Settlement	Default FWSD Type	FW01
☑ Enable Internal Settlement	Default ISD Type	IS01
☐ Enable Credit Limit Check	Action when CLC fails	
☐ Enable Compliance Check		
☐ Enable Format Checks		
☐ Enable Waybill Stock	HBL or HAWB Strategy	
☐ Automatic Confirmation	Default Conf. Type	O

Figure A-91. *Creating a forwarding-order type: Number Range Settings, Process Control/Business Object Mode, and Air Cargo Settings (first half) sections*

In the Default Values and Organizational Unit Determination sections, again enter the respective data, using Table A-53.

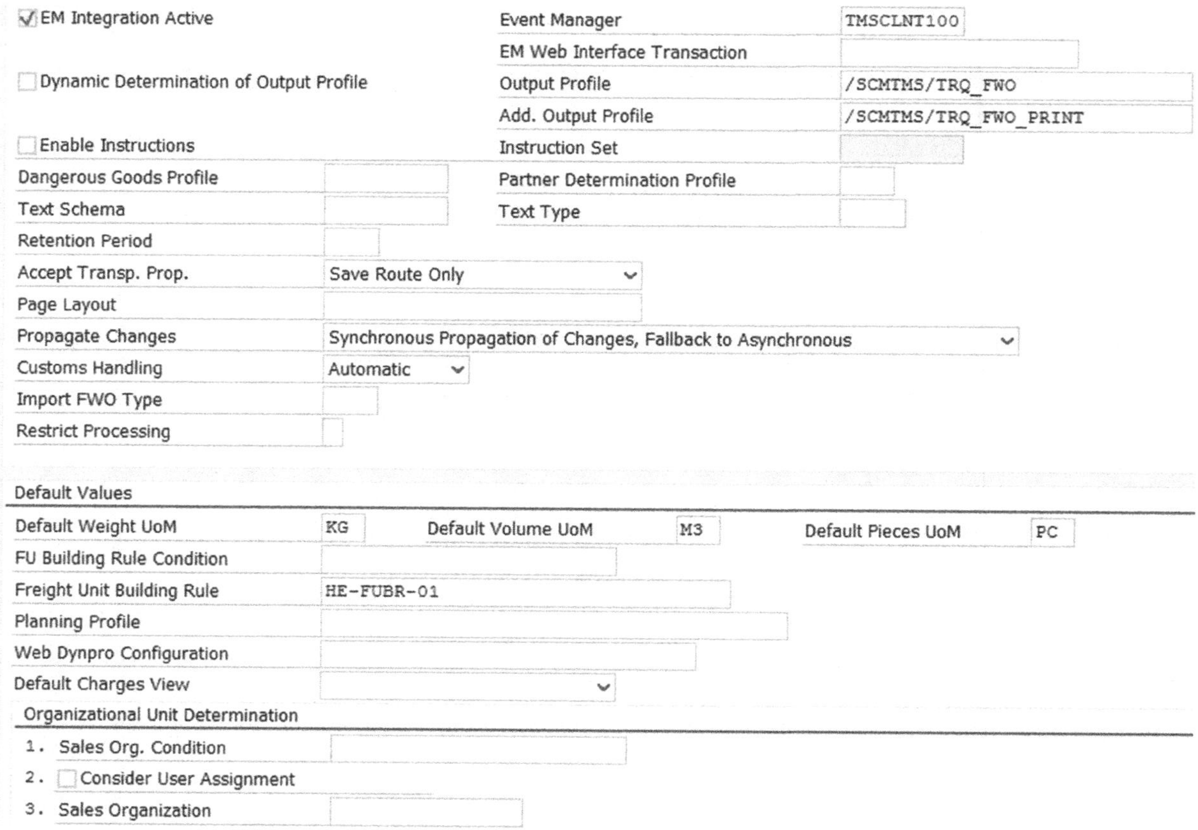

☑ EM Integration Active   Event Manager   `TMSCLNT100`

     EM Web Interface Transaction

☐ Dynamic Determination of Output Profile   Output Profile   `/SCMTMS/TRQ_FWO`

     Add. Output Profile   `/SCMTMS/TRQ_FWO_PRINT`

☐ Enable Instructions   Instruction Set

Dangerous Goods Profile   Partner Determination Profile

Text Schema   Text Type

Retention Period

Accept Transp. Prop.   Save Route Only ⌄

Page Layout

Propagate Changes   Synchronous Propagation of Changes, Fallback to Asynchronous ⌄

Customs Handling   Automatic ⌄

Import FWO Type

Restrict Processing

Default Values

Default Weight UoM	KG	Default Volume UoM	M3	Default Pieces UoM	PC

FU Building Rule Condition

Freight Unit Building Rule   `HE-FUBR-01`

Planning Profile

Web Dynpro Configuration

Default Charges View ⌄

Organizational Unit Determination

1. Sales Org. Condition

2. ☐ Consider User Assignment

3. Sales Organization

Figure A-92. *Creating a forwarding-order type: Air Cargo Settings (second half), Default Values, and Organizational Unit Determination sections*

After entering the necessary data, save the data by clicking the Save 💾 button.
In this way, define the remaining forwarding-order types.

■ **Note** If you find that certain fields are not enabled, press the Enter key.

Assigning Item Type to Forwarding-Order Types

This option lets you specify a valid item type and item category for a forwarding-order type. The purpose of this option is to restrict the type and category of items of a particular forwarding-order type.

For the given scenario, you will need to define the assignments displayed in Table A-54.

Table A-54. *Assigning Item Type to Forwarding-Order Type Data*

Field	Value	Value	Value	Value
Forwarding-Order type	FW01	FW01	FW02	FW02
Item type	HEPK	HEPD	HEPK	HEPD
Default item type	<Select>	<Select>	<Select>	<Select>
Item category	Package	Product	Package	Product

To assign an item type to a forwarding-order type, go to Customizing for SAP Transportation Management, and click Transportation Management ➤ Forwarding Order Management ➤ Forwarding Order ➤ Assign Item Types to Forwarding Order Types.

Now, click the New Entries New Entries button, and enter the data from Table A-54.

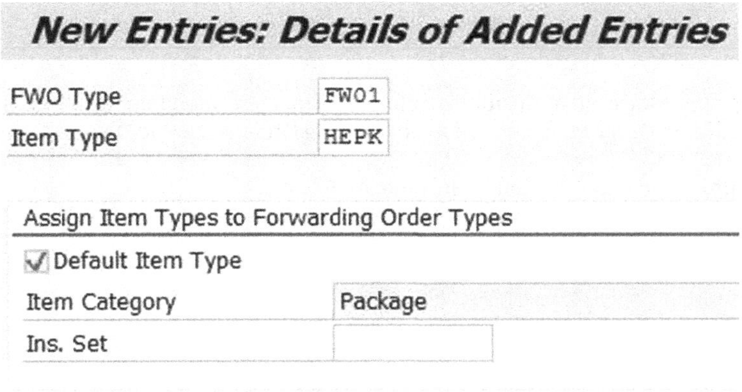

Figure A-93. *Assigning an item type to a forwarding-order type*

After entering the necessary data, save the data by clicking the Save 🖫 button.

In this manner, assign the remaining item types to forwarding-order types.

Defining Default Freight Document Types for Stages

When freight documents are created for a stage, the type of freight order or freight booking to be created is determined through the user interface of the forwarding order, using the values specified in this option.

For the given scenario, you will have to define the default freight document types for the stages provided in Table A-55.

Table A-55. *Default Freight Document Type for Stage Data*

Field	Value	Value	Value	Value	Value
Sequence Number	1	2	3	4	5
Forwarding-Order type	FW01	FW01	FW01	FW02	FW02
Shipping type	Loose	Loose	Loose	Loose	Loose
Stage type	HE1	HE2	HE3	HE4	HE5
Transportation mode	01	01	05	01	01
Sales organization	<Blank>	<Blank>	<Blank>	<Blank>	<Blank>
Document type	FO01	FO02	FB01	FO02	FO01
Create freight document	<Select>	<Select>	<Select>	<Select>	<Select>
Select freight document	<Select>	<Select>	<Select>	<Select>	<Select>
Select schedule	<Select>	<Select>	<Select>	<Select>	<Select>

To define the default freight document type for a stage, go to Customizing for SAP Transportation Management, and click Transportation Management ➤ Forwarding Order Management ➤ Forwarding Order ➤ Define Default Freight Document Types for Stages.

Then, click the New Entries New Entries button, and enter the data from Table A-55.

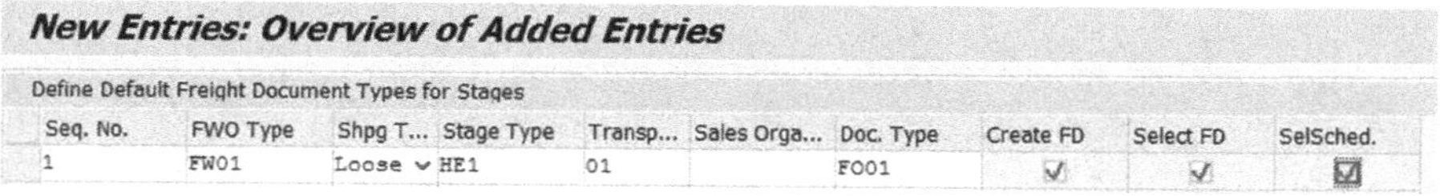
New Entries: Overview of Added Entries

Define Default Freight Document Types for Stages

Seq. No.	FWO Type	Shpg T...	Stage Type	Transp...	Sales Orga...	Doc. Type	Create FD	Select FD	SelSched.
1	FW01	Loose	HE1	01		FO01	✓	✓	☑

Figure A-94. *Creating a default freight document type for a stage*

After entering the necessary data, save the data by clicking the Save button.

In this way, define the remaining default freight document types for stages.

Defining Number Range Intervals for Schedules

Specify the number range for a schedule using this option.

For the given scenario, you will need to define the number range intervals presented in Table A-56.

Table A-56. *Schedule Number Range Interval Data*

Field	Value
Number range number	H1
From number	AAAAAAAAAAAAAAAAAAAA
To number	ZZZZZZZZZZZZZZZZZZZZ
External	<Select>

To define a number range, go to Customizing for SAP Transportation Management, and click Transportation Management ➤ Master Data ➤ Transportation Network ➤ Schedule ➤ Define Number Range Intervals for Schedules.

To define a number range interval for a schedule, click the Intervals [🖉 Intervals] button and then the Insert Line 📑 button. Enter the number range from Table A-56.

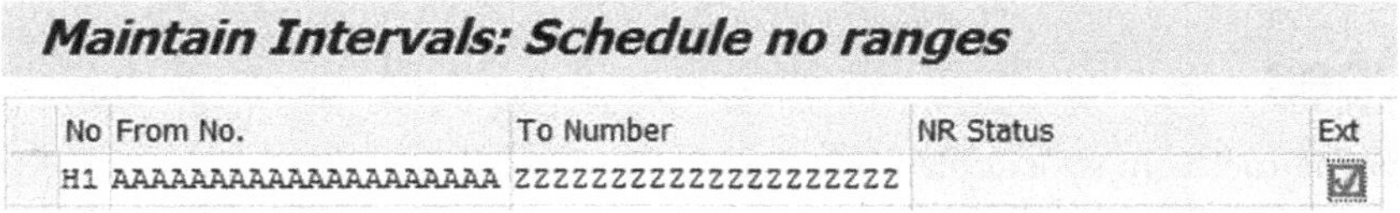

Maintain Intervals: Schedule no ranges

No	From No.	To Number	NR Status	Ext
H1	AAAAAAAAAAAAAAAAAAAA	ZZZZZZZZZZZZZZZZZZZZ		☑

Figure A-95. *Creating a number range interval for a schedule*

After entering the necessary data, save the data by clicking the Save 🖫 button.

■ **Note** In the Transport number range intervals dialog box, click the Continue ✅ button.

Defining Number Range Intervals for Departures

Specify the number range for a departure using this option.

For the given scenario, you must define the number range intervals displayed in Table A-57.

Table A-57. *Departure Number Range Interval Data*

Field	Value
Number range number	H1
From number	0030000000
To number	0039999999
External	<Deselect>

To define a number range, go to Customizing for SAP Transportation Management, and click Transportation Management ➤ Master Data ➤Transportation Network ➤ Schedule ➤ Define Number Range Intervals for Departures.

To define a number range interval for a departure, click the Intervals [🖉 Intervals] button and then the Insert Line 📑 button. Enter the number range from Table A-57.

Maintain Intervals: /SCMTMS/VO

No	From No.	To Number	NR Status	Ext
H1	0030000000	0039999999		☐

Figure A-96. *Creating a number range interval for a departure*

After entering the necessary data, save the data by clicking the Save 🖫 button.

■ **Note** In the Transport number range intervals dialog box, click the Continue ✅ button.

Defining Schedule Types

Use this option to define the movement of trucks, ships, or airplanes that is valid for a specific period of time within the sequence of transportation stops, such as ports, airports, or gateways.

SAP TM allows you to define the following schedules:

- **Flight/Carrier/Road**: This schedule lets you define the sequence of transportation stops served by airplanes, ships, and trucks, respectively. The schedule is used when the origin and destination stops are not gateway. The system also allows you to define departure rules, which in turn create flight/voyage/departure.

- **Master flight/Sailing/Road gateway**: This schedule is used when the origin and destination stops are gateway. With this schedule, reference to flight/carrier/road schedule can be provided. Copying of departure rules and flight/voyage/departure is also possible.

By specifying schedule types, schedules are defined in system.

For the given scenario, you will need to define the schedule types shown in Table A-58.

Table A-58. *Schedule Type Data*

Field	Value	Value	Value
Schedule type	HS01	HS02	HS03
Description	Trucking schedule	Flight schedule	Master flight schedule
Default type	<Deselect>	<Deselect>	<Deselect>
Basic Settings Section			
Transportation mode	01	05	05
Gateway	<Select>	<Deselect>	<Select>
Direct	<Select>	<Deselect>	<Deselect>
Reference	<Deselect>	<Deselect>	<Select>
Document type	FO02	FB01	FB01
Number Range Settings Section			
Header number range	H1	H1	H1
Voyage number range	H1	H1	H1
Additional Settings Section			
Offset time type	Absolute	Relative	Relative
One order	<Deselect>	<Deselect>	<Deselect>
Use capacities	<Deselect>	<Deselect>	<Select>
Use transport costs	<Deselect>	<Deselect>	<Deselect>

To define a schedule type, go to Customizing for SAP Transportation Management, and click Transportation Management ➤ Master Data ➤ Transportation Network ➤ Schedule ➤ Define Schedule Types.

Now, click the New Entries   New Entries   button, and enter the data from Table A-58.

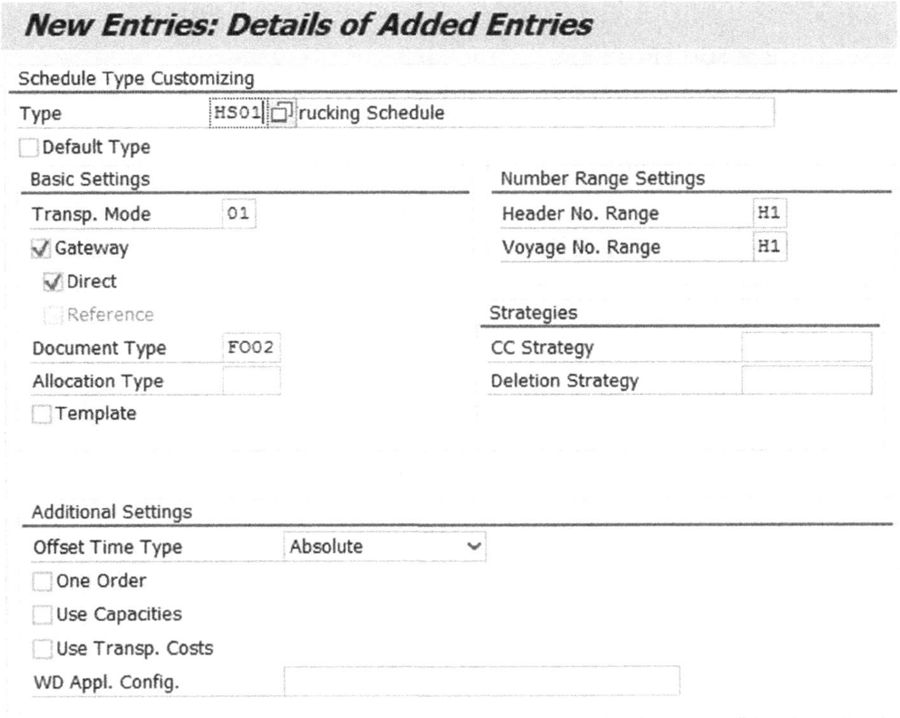

Figure A-97. *Creating a schedule types*

After entering the necessary data, save the data by clicking the Save 🖫 button.

In this way, define the remaining schedule types.

Creating Schedules

After the schedule types have been defined, you can create different schedules using those schedule types.

Precarriage and On-Carriage Schedules

For the given scenario, you must create the precarriage and on-carriage schedules displayed in Table A-59.

Table A-59. *Schedule (Precarriage and On-Carriage) Data*

Field	Value	Value
Schedule type	HS01	HS01
General Data Tab		
Schedule	HE-JPTR-SCH-PRE-01	HE-USTR-SCH-ON-01
Schedule description	Truck schedule—Yokohama to Narita	Truck schedule—Los Angeles to San Francisco
Valid from	01-01-<current year>-	01-01-<current year>
Valid to	31-12-<next year>	31-12-<next year>
Means of transport	JP_TRUCK_S	US_TRUCK_S
Carrier Data Section		
Carrier	HE-CR-02	HE-CR-04
Standard Gateways Section/Tab		
Source Gateway Section		
Location	HESTAJPYOK	HEGWUSLA
Pickup transit duration (hours)	4	5
Cargo cutoff time	13:00:00	06:00:00
Time zone	Japan	UTC-8
Destination Gateway Section		
Location	HEGWJPNAR	HESTAUSSFR
Availability time	19:00:00	13:00:00
Time zone	Japan	UTC-8
Departures Section/Tab		
Departure Rules Tab		
First day of validity	01-01-<current year>	01-01-<current year>
Last day of validity	31-12-<current year>	31-12-<current year>
Monday	<Select>	<Select>
Tuesday	<Select>	<Select>
Wednesday	<Select>	<Select>
Thursday	<Select>	<Select>
Friday	<Select>	<Select>
Saturday	<Select>	<Select>
Sunday	<Select>	<Select>
Factory calendar	W8	W8
Departure time	14:00:00	07:00:00
Time zone	Japan	UTC-8

To create precarriage and on-carriage schedules, in SAP NetWeaver Business Client, click Master Data ➤ Transportation Network ➤ Schedule ➤ Create Schedule.

Enter the schedule type from Table A-59, and click the Continue ⊘ Continue button.

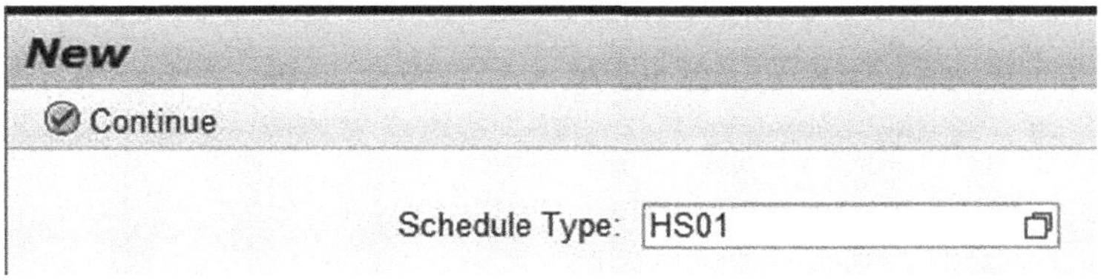

Figure A-98. *Initial screen for creating a schedule (precarriage)*

In the Schedule Data and Carrier Data sections of the General Data tab, enter the respective data, using Table A-59.

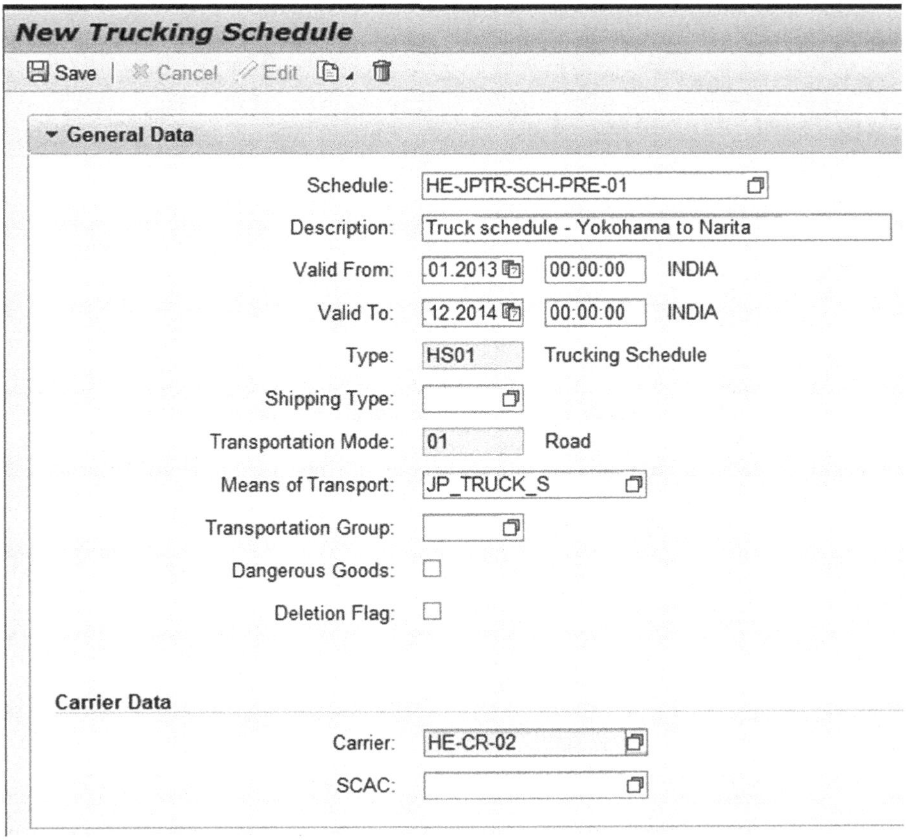

Figure A-99. *Creating a schedule (precarriage): Schedule Data and Carrier Data sections of the General Data tab*

In the Source Gateway section of the Standard Gateways tab, enter the relevant data from Table A-59.

▼ Standard Gateways

Source Gateway

Location:	HESTAJPYOK

Pick-Up Transit Duration (Days):	0
Pick-Up Transit Duration (Hours):	4
Transit Duration (Minutes):	0
Distance:	0,000 KM
Precision :	Straight Line
Cargo Cut-Off (Offset in Days):	0
Cargo Cut-Off Time:	13:00:00
Document Cut-Off (Offset in Days):	0
Document Cut-Off Time:	00:00:00
DG Document Cut-Off (Offset in Days):	0
DG Document Cut-Off Time:	00:00:00
Time Zone:	JAPAN

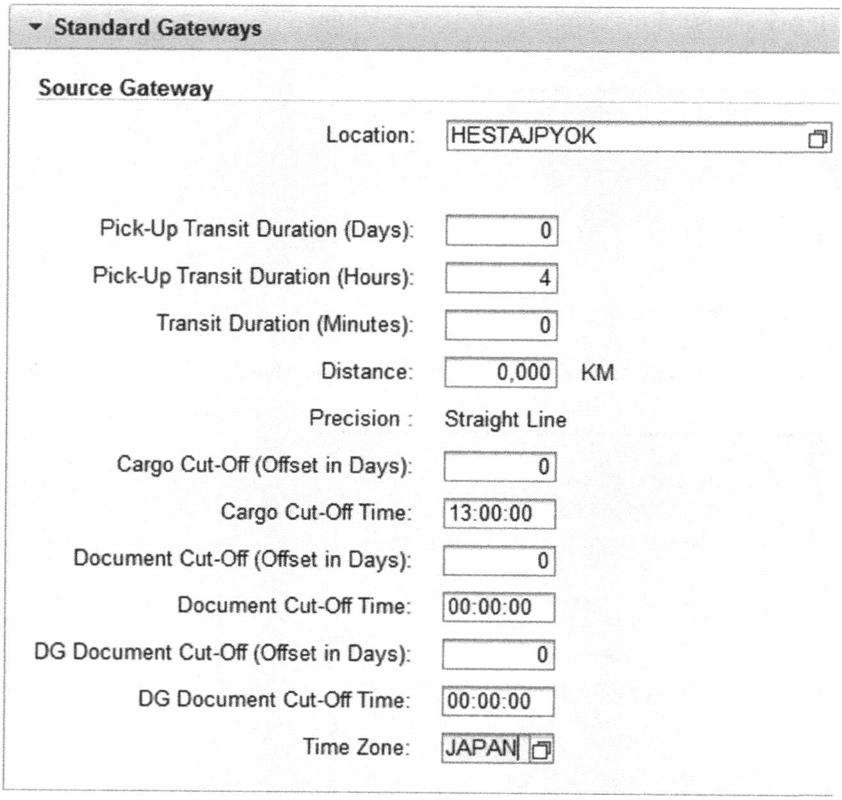

Figure A-100. *Creating a schedule (precarriage): Source Gateway section of the Standard Gateways tab*

In the Destination Gateway section of the Standard Gateways tab, again enter the relevant data from Table A-59.

Destination Gateway

Location:	HEGWJPNAR

Days to Availability:	0
Availability Time:	19:00:00
Time Zone:	JAPAN

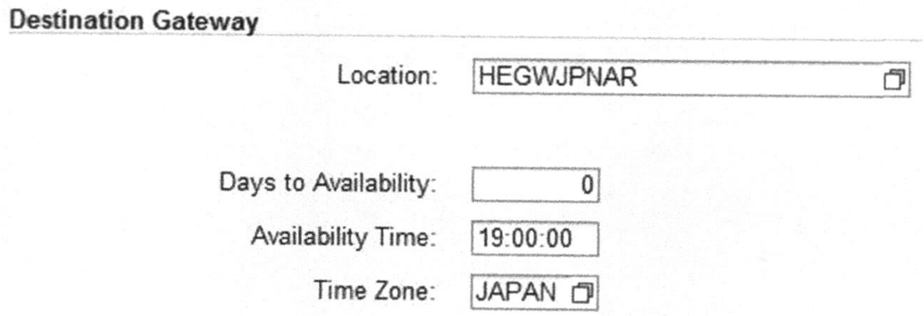

Figure A-101. *Creating a schedule (precarriage): Destination Gateway section of the Standard Gateways tab*

To create the departure rule from Table A-59, in the Departure Rules tab of the Departures tab, click the Create Create button.

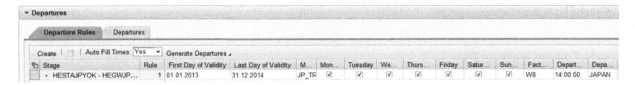

Figure A-102. *Creating a schedule (precarriage): Departure Rules tab of the Departures tab*

To generate the departure data based on the departure rule, select the departure rule row, and then select For Validity Period from the Generate Departures menu.

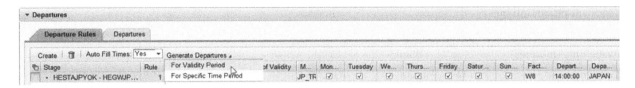

Figure A-103. *Creating a schedule (precarriage): Generating Departures*

After entering the necessary data, save the data by clicking the Save 🖫 Save button.
In this manner, create the remaining precarriage and on-carriage schedules.

Flight Schedule

For the given scenario, you will also need to create the flight schedule displayed in Tables A-60–A-62.

Table A-60. *Schedule (Flight) Data*

Field	Value
Schedule type	HS02
General Data Tab	
Schedule Data Section	
Schedule	HE-FS-SCH-01
Schedule description	Flight schedule—Narita to Los Angeles
Valid from	01-01-<current year>
Valid to	31-12-<next year>
Carrier Data Section	
Airline code	MF
Flight number	739
Aircraft type	777
Carrier	HE-CR-03

Table A-61. *Schedule (Flight): Standard Airport Sequence Data*

Field	Value	Value
Standard Airport Sequence Tab		
Sequence	10	20
Location	HEMFNRT	HEMFLA
IATA code	NRT	LAX
Cargo cutoff (minutes)	55	<Blank>
Transit duration (hours)	9	<Blank>
Transit duration (minutes)	50	<Blank>
Availability (hours)	<Blank>	2
Availability (minutes)	<Blank>	15
Time zone	Japan	UTC-8

Table A-62. *Schedule (Flight): Departure Data*

Field	Value
Flights Tab	
Departure Rules Tab	
First day of validity	01-01-<current year>
Last day of validity	31-12-<current year>
Monday	<Select>
Tuesday	<Select>
Wednesday	<Select>
Thursday	<Select>
Friday	<Select>
Saturday	<Select>
Sunday	<Select>
Aircraft type	777
Departure time	23:55:00
Time zone	Japan

To create a flight schedule, in SAP NetWeaver Business Client, click Master Data ➤ Transportation Network ➤ Schedule ➤ Create Schedule.

Enter the schedule type from Table A-60, and click the Continue ⊘ Continue button.

New
Continue
Schedule Type:
HS02

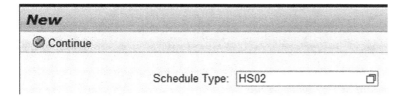

Figure A-104. *Initial screen for creating a schedule (flight)*

In the Schedule Data and Carrier Data sections of the General Data tab, enter the respective data, using Table A-60.

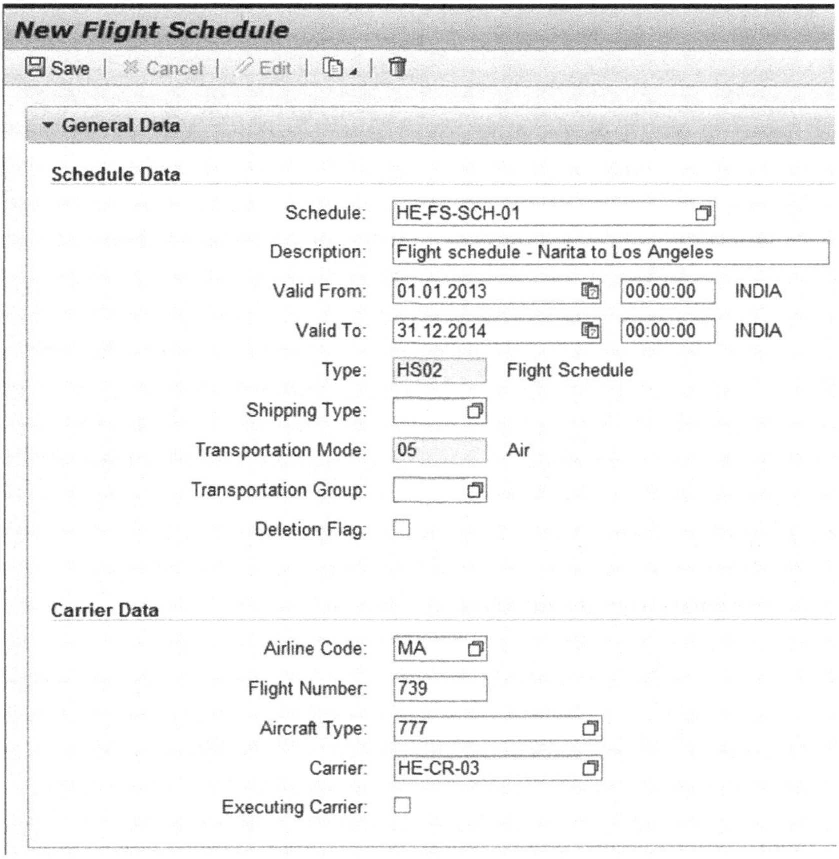

New Flight Schedule
Save
Cancel
Edit
General Data
Schedule Data
Schedule:
HE-FS-SCH-01
Description:
Flight schedule - Narita to Los Angeles
Valid From:
01.01.2013
00:00:00
INDIA
Valid To:
31.12.2014
00:00:00
INDIA
Type:
HS02
Flight Schedule
Shipping Type:
Transportation Mode:
05
Air
Transportation Group:
Deletion Flag:
Carrier Data
Airline Code:
MA
Flight Number:
739
Aircraft Type:
777
Carrier:
HE-CR-03
Executing Carrier:

Figure A-105. *Creating a schedule (flight): Schedule and Carrier Data sections of the General Data tab*

To create the airport sequence, in the Standard Airport Sequence tab, click the Create button, and enter the data from Table A-61.

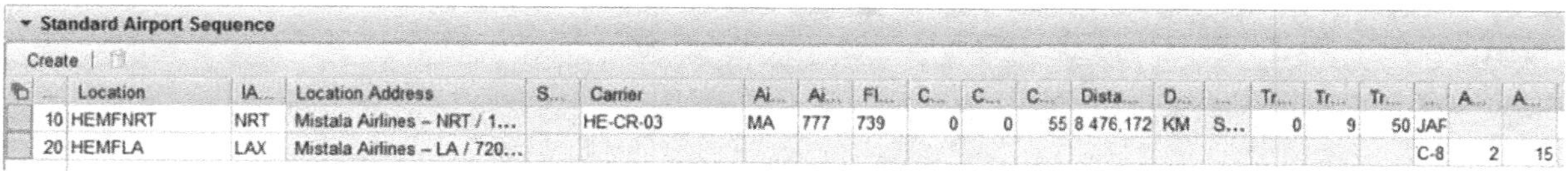

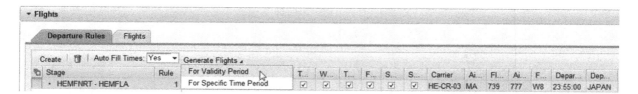

Standard Airport Sequence

	Location	IA...	Location Address	S...	Carrier	Ai...	Ai...	Fl...	C...	C...	C...	Dista...	D...	...	Tr...	Tr...	Tr...	...	A...	A...
10	HEMFNRT	NRT	Mistala Airlines – NRT / 1...		HE-CR-03	MA	777	739	0	0	55	8 476.172	KM	S...	0	9	50	JAF		
20	HEMFLA	LAX	Mistala Airlines – LA / 720...																C-8	2	15

Figure A-106. *Creating a schedule (flight): Standard Airport Sequence tab*

To create the departure rule from Table A-62, in the Flights section of Departures tab, click the Create Create button.

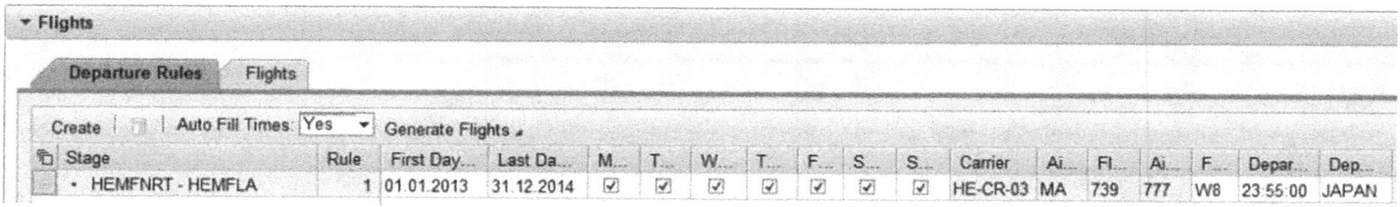

Flights

| Departure Rules | Flights |

Create | Auto Fill Times: Yes | Generate Flights

Stage	Rule	First Day...	Last Da...	M...	T...	W...	T...	F...	S...	S...	Carrier	Ai...	Fl...	Ai...	F...	Depar...	Dep...
• HEMFNRT - HEMFLA	1	01.01.2013	31.12.2014	☑	☑	☑	☑	☑	☑	☑	HE-CR-03	MA	739	777	W8	23:55:00	JAPAN

Figure A-107. *Creating a schedule (flight): Departure Rules tab of the Flights tab*

To generate the flight data based on the departure rule, select the departure rule row, and then select For Validity Period from the General Flights menu.

Flights

| Departure Rules | Flights |

Create | Auto Fill Times: Yes | Generate Flights

Stage	Rule	For Validity Period	T...	W...	T...	F...	S...	S...	Carrier	Ai...	Fl...	Ai...	F...	Depar...	Dep...
• HEMFNRT - HEMFLA	1	For Specific Time Period	☑	☑	☑	☑	☑	☑	HE-CR-03	MA	739	777	W8	23:55:00	JAPAN

Figure A-108. *Creating a schedule (flight): Generating flights*

After entering the necessary data, save the data by clicking the Save Save button.

Master Flight Schedule

For the given scenario, you will have to create as well the master flight schedule displayed in Tables A-63–A-65.

Table A-63. *Schedule (Master Flight) Data*

Field	Value
Schedule type	HS03
General Data Tab	
Schedule Data Section	
Schedule	HE-MF-SCH-01
Schedule description	Master flight sch—Narita to Los Angeles
Valid from	01-01-<current year>
Valid to	31-12-<next year>
Shipping type	10
Carrier Data Section	
Carrier	HE-CR-03
Capacity Section	
Weight	8,000 kg
Volume	25 m^3

Table A-64. *Schedule (Master Flight): Standard Gateway Data*

Field	Value
Standard Gateways Tab	
Source Gateway Section	
Location	HEGWJPNAR
Pickup transit duration (hours)	1
Cargo cutoff (hours)	1
Time zone	Japan
Destination Gateway Section	
Location	HEGWUSLA
Delivery transit duration (hours)	1
Time zone	UTC-8
Availability (hours)	8

Table A-65. *Schedule (Master Flight): Standard Airport Data*

Field	Value
Standard Airports Tab	
Airport of Departure Section	
Location	HEMFNRT
Airport of Destination Section	
Location	HEMFLA

In the Departure Rules tab, enter the data from Table A-66, if the fields are not auto-populated.

Table A-66. *Schedule (Master Flight): Departure Data*

Field	Value
Departure Rules Tab	
First day of validity	01-01-<current year>
Last day of validity	31-12-<current year>
Factory calendar	W8

To create a master flight schedule, in SAP NetWeaver Business Client, click Master Data ➤ Transportation Network ➤ Schedule ➤ Create Schedule.

Enter the schedule type from Table A-63, and click the Continue ⊘ Continue button.

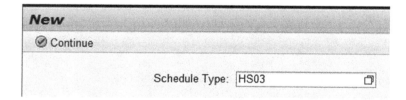

Figure A-109. *Initial screen for creating a schedule (master flight)*

In the Schedule Data and Carrier Data sections of the General Data tab, enter the respective data, using Table A-63.

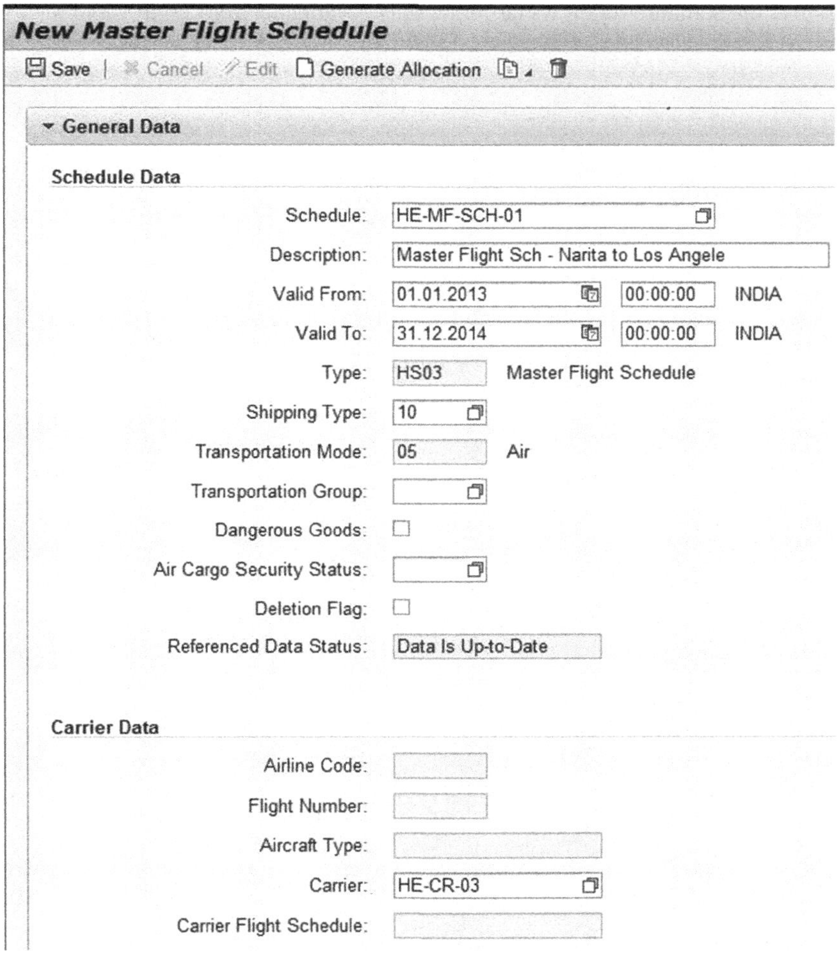

New Master Flight Schedule

🖫 Save | ✖ Cancel | ✎ Edit | ☐ Generate Allocation | ⬚ ⬛ 🗑

▼ General Data

Schedule Data

Schedule:	HE-MF-SCH-01
Description:	Master Flight Sch - Narita to Los Angele
Valid From:	01.01.2013 00:00:00 INDIA
Valid To:	31.12.2014 00:00:00 INDIA
Type:	HS03 Master Flight Schedule
Shipping Type:	10
Transportation Mode:	05 Air
Transportation Group:	
Dangerous Goods:	☐
Air Cargo Security Status:	
Deletion Flag:	☐
Referenced Data Status:	Data Is Up-to-Date

Carrier Data

Airline Code:	
Flight Number:	
Aircraft Type:	
Carrier:	HE-CR-03
Carrier Flight Schedule:	

Figure A-110. *Creating a schedule (master flight): Schedule Data and Carrier Data sections of the General Data tab*

In the capacity section of the General Data tab, enter the relevant data from Table A-63.

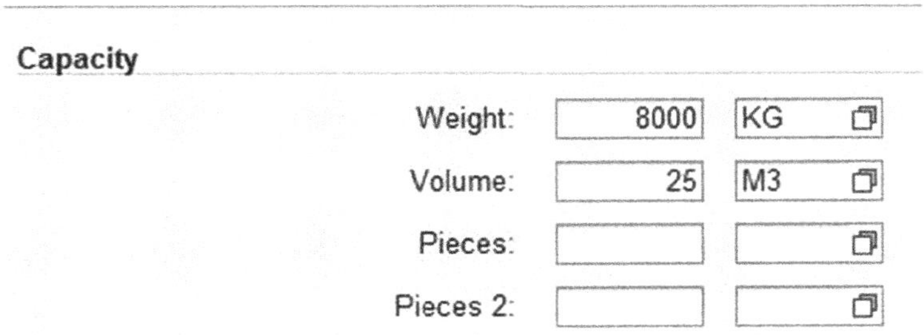

Capacity

Weight:	8000	KG
Volume:	25	M3
Pieces:		
Pieces 2:		

Figure A-111. *Creating a schedule (master flight): Capacity section of the General Data tab*

Next, in the Source Gateway section of the Standard Gateways tab, enter the relevant data from Table A-64.

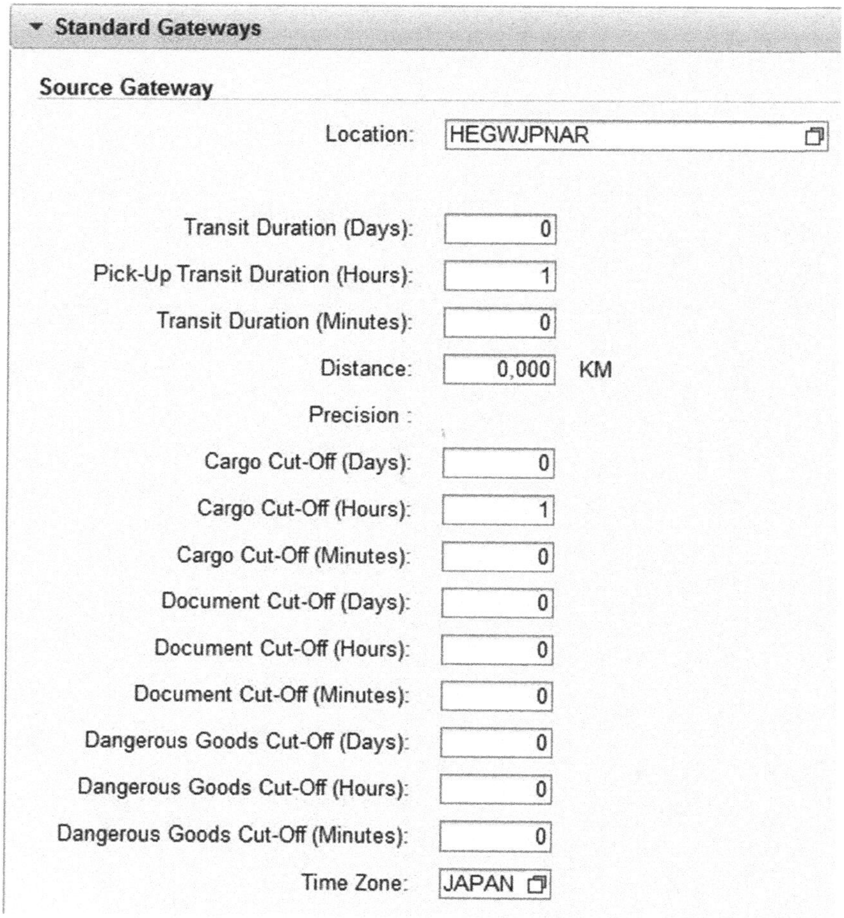

Figure A-112. *Creating a schedule (master flight): Source Gateway section of the Standard Gateways tab*

In the Destination Gateway section of the Standard Gateways tab, again enter the relevant data from Table A-64

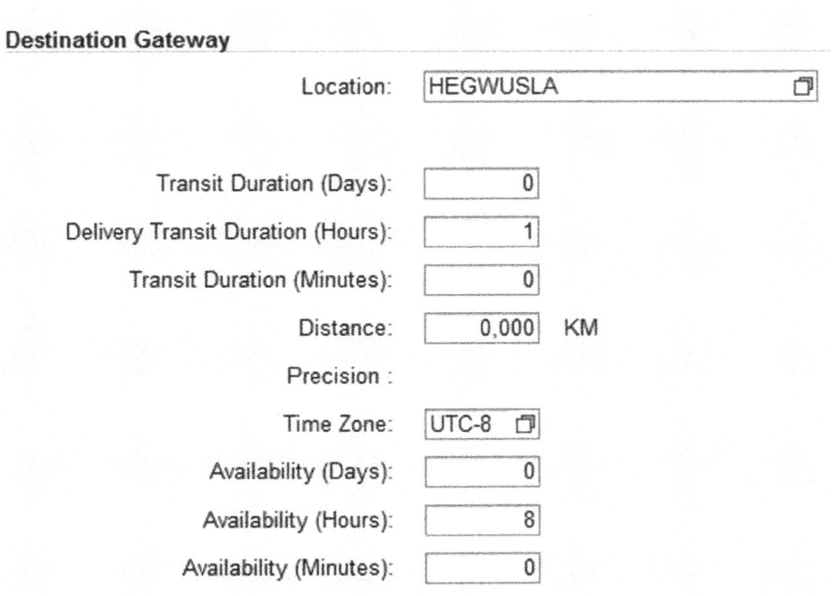

Destination Gateway

Location:	HEGWUSLA
Transit Duration (Days):	0
Delivery Transit Duration (Hours):	1
Transit Duration (Minutes):	0
Distance:	0,000 KM
Precision :	
Time Zone:	UTC-8
Availability (Days):	0
Availability (Hours):	8
Availability (Minutes):	0

Figure A-113. *Creating a schedule (master flight): Destination Gateway section of the Standard Gateways tab*

Now, in the Airport of Departure section of the Standard Airports tab, enter the relevant data from Table A-65.

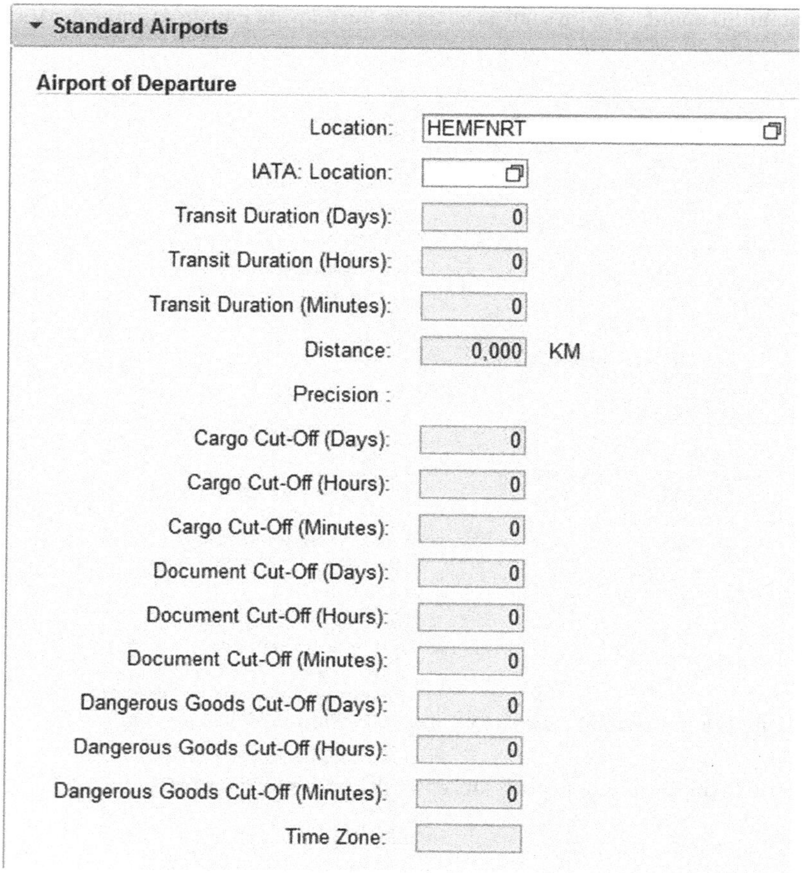

Figure A-114. *Creating a schedule (master flight): Airport of Departure section of the Standard Airports tab*

In the Airport of Destination section of the Standard Airports tab, again enter the relevant data from Table A-65

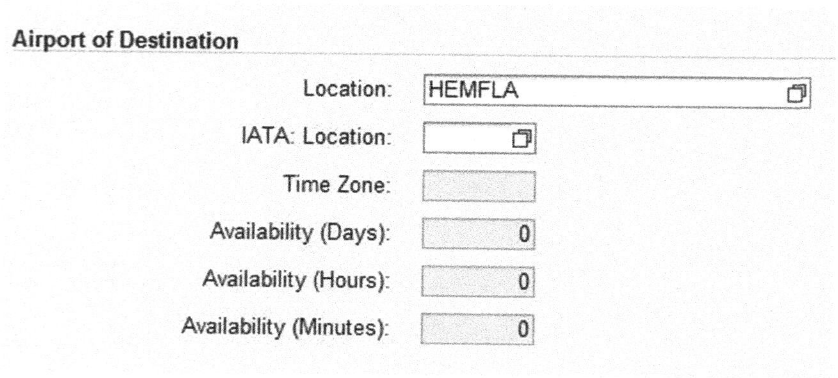

Figure A-115. *Creating a schedule (master flight): Airport of Destination section of the Standard Airports tab*

To create the airport sequence, in the Standard Airport Sequence section/tab, click the Create Create button. Select sequence 10, go to the Schedule menu, and select Assign.

Figure A-116. *Creating a schedule (master flight): Standard Airport Sequence tab*

In the Assign Schedule window, select any one flight schedule from those available, and then click the OK OK button.

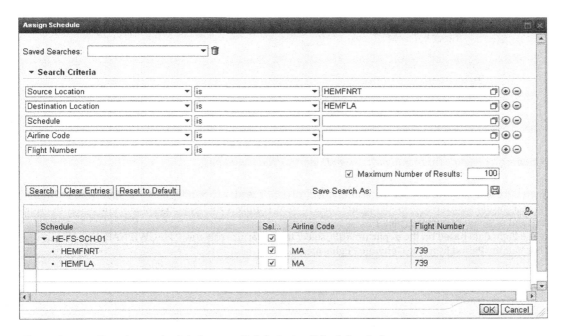

Figure A-117. *Creating a schedule (master flight): Assign Schedule window*

To create the departure rule, in the Flights section of the Departures tab, click the Create Create button.

In the departure rule created, select the row containing the airport sequence ("HEMFNRT–HEMFLA"), and select Assign from the Departure Rule menu.

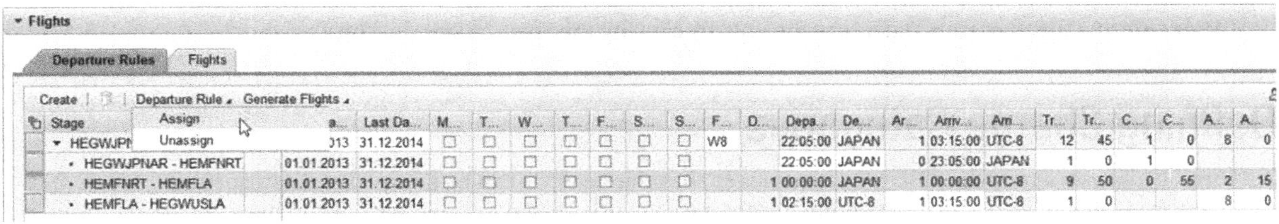

Figure A-118. *Creating a schedule (master flight): Departure Rules tab of the Flights tab*

In the Assign Departure Rule window, select the departure rule containing departure day as Monday, and click the OK $\boxed{OK}$ button.

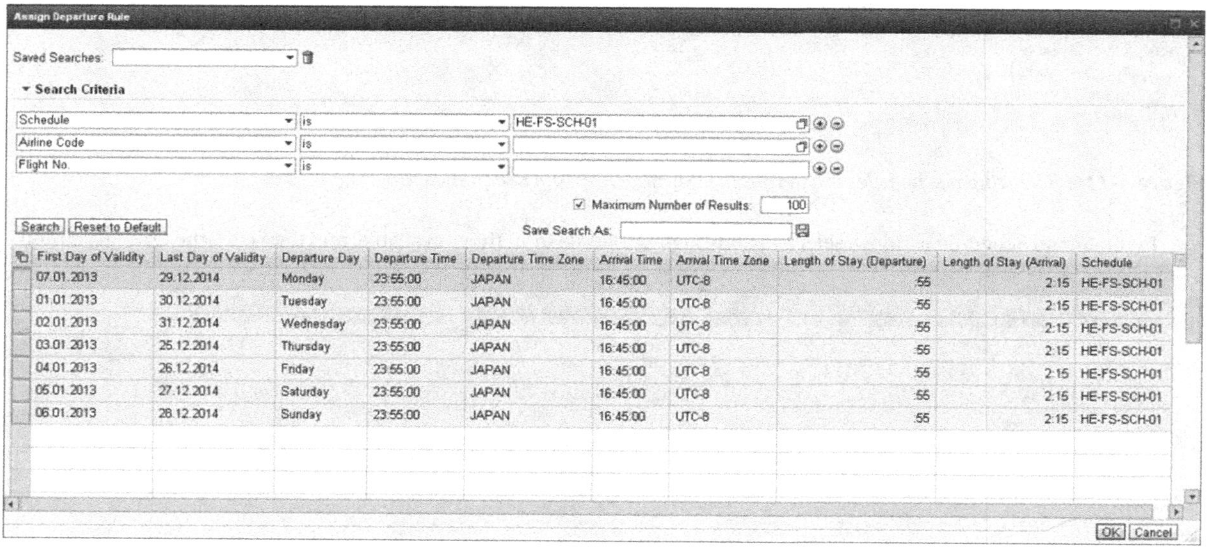

Figure A-119. *Creating a schedule (master flight): Assign Departure Rule window*

In this way, create the departure rule for the remaining days (i.e., Tuesday to Sunday), and assign the departure rule accordingly. You should now have seven departure rules in total. (Apply Note 1843455 to create one departure rule for seven days instead of seven departure rules.)

To generate the flight data based on the departure rule, select the departure rule row ("HEGWJPNAR–HEGWUSLA"), and then select For Validity Period from the Generate Flights menu.

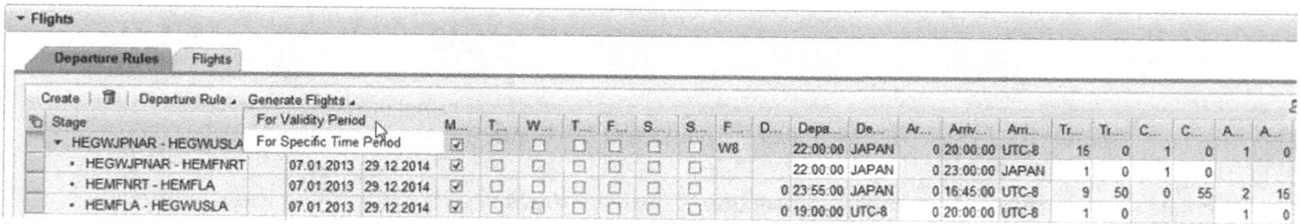

Figure A-120. *Creating a schedule (master flight): Generating flights*

After entering the necessary data, save the data by clicking the Save $\boxed{\text{Save}}$ button.

Defining Charge Categories

This option allows you to define charge categories so that charge types can be grouped and categorized.

For the given scenario, you must define the charge categories listed in Table A-67, if you have not already done so.

Table A-67. *Charge Category Data*

Field	Value	Value
Charge category	003	004
Description	Transport charge and additional charges	Basic freight

To define a charge category, go to Customizing for SAP Transportation Management, and click Transportation Management ➤ Basic Functions ➤ Charge Calculation ➤ Basic Settings for Charge Calculation ➤ Define Charge Categories.

Then, click the New Entries New Entries button, and enter the data from Table A-67.

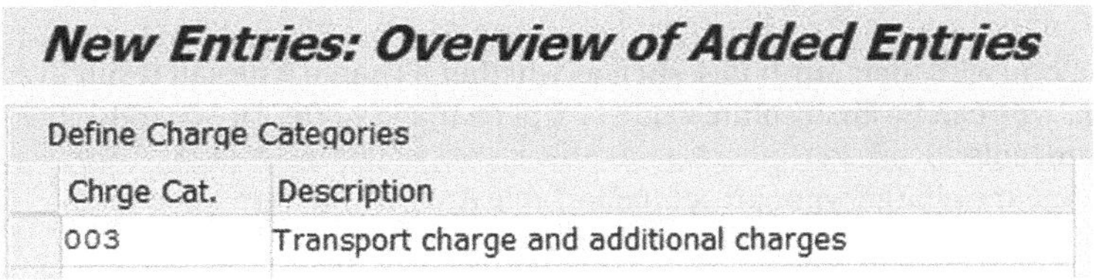

New Entries: Overview of Added Entries

Define Charge Categories	
Chrge Cat.	**Description**
003	Transport charge and additional charges

Figure A-121. *Creating a charge category*

After entering the necessary data, save the data by clicking the Save 🖫 button.

In this manner, define the remaining charge categories.

Defining Charge Subcategories

This option lets you define charge subcategories so that charge types can be grouped and categorized in a more granular way than with charge categories.

For the given scenario, you will need to define the charge subcategories provided in Table A-68, if you have not already done so.

Table A-68. *Charge Subcategory Data*

Field	Value	Value
Charge subcategory	100000	103008
Description	Freight charges	Fuel surcharge
Charge category	004	003

To define a charge subcategory, go to Customizing for SAP Transportation Management, and click Transportation Management ➤ Basic Functions ➤ Charge Calculation ➤ Basic Settings for Charge Calculation ➤ Define Charge Subcategories.

Next, click the New Entries New Entries button, and enter the data from Table A-68.

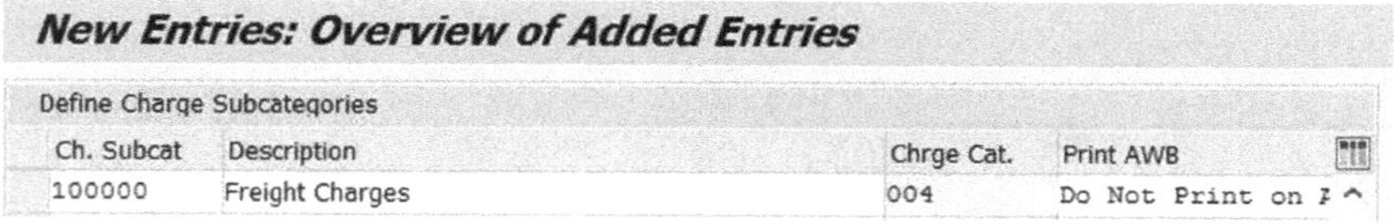

New Entries: Overview of Added Entries

Define Charge Subcategories

Ch. Subcat	Description	Chrge Cat.	Print AWB	
100000	Freight Charges	004	Do Not Print on F	

Figure A-122. *Creating a charge subcategory*

After entering the necessary data, save the data by clicking the Save 💾 button. In this way, define the remaining charge subcategories.

Defining Charge Types

This option allows you to define charge types, along with their attributes, such as whether a charge type can result in a positive or negative value and whether a charge type can be an absolute value or a percentage value. The charge types are further assigned to a calculation sheet or rate table.

For the given scenario, you will have to define the charge types presented in Table A-69, if you have not already done so.

Table A-69. *Charge Type Data*

Field	Value	Value	Value	Value	Value
Charge type	BASE_FA	FB00	FUEL	PU_FEE	COO
Charge category	004	004	003	004	004
Charge subcategory	100000	100000	103008	100000	100000
Positive/Negative	Positive or negative value	Positive or negative value	Positive or negative value	Positive or negative value	Positive or negative value
Value type	Absolute value	Absolute value	Percentage value	Absolute or percentage value	Absolute value
Description	Base airfreight	Basic rate	Fuel surcharge	Pickup fee	Certificate of origin

To define a charge type, go to Customizing for SAP Transportation Management, and click Transportation Management ➤ Basic Functions ➤ Charge Calculation ➤ Basic Settings for Charge Calculation ➤ Define Charge Types.

Now, click the New Entries New Entries button, and enter the data from Table A-69.

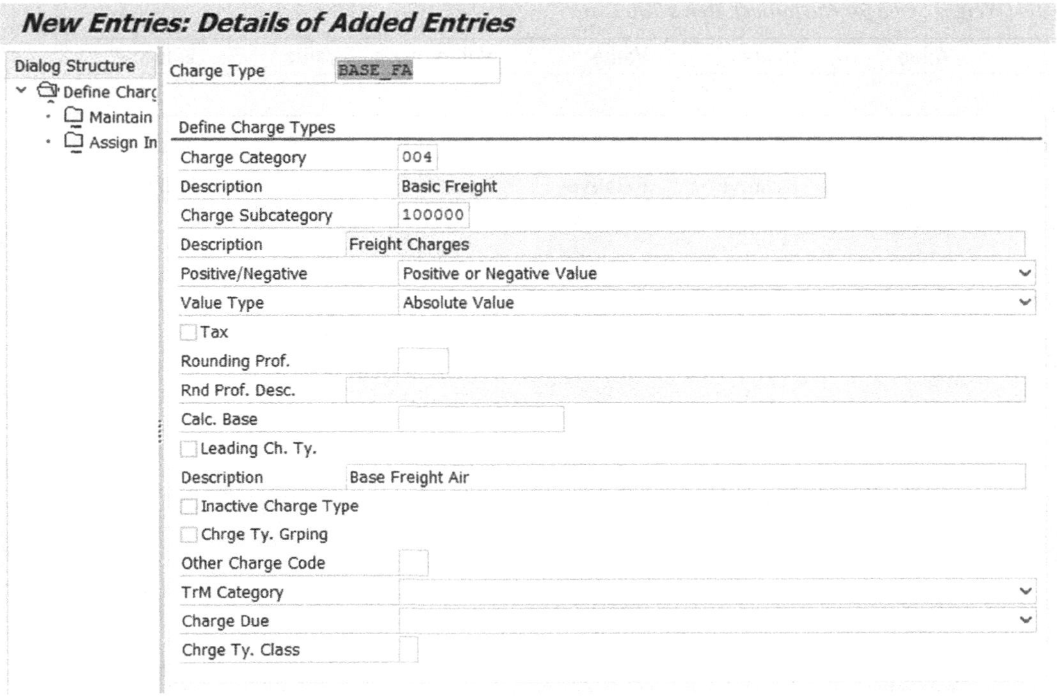

New Entries: Details of Added Entries

Dialog Structure	Charge Type	BASE_FA
∨ ⬡ Define Charg		
• ▢ Maintain	Define Charge Types	
• ▢ Assign In		

Charge Category	004
Description	Basic Freight
Charge Subcategory	100000
Description	Freight Charges
Positive/Negative	Positive or Negative Value ∨
Value Type	Absolute Value ∨
☐ Tax	
Rounding Prof.	
Rnd Prof. Desc.	
Calc. Base	
☐ Leading Ch. Ty.	
Description	Base Freight Air
☐ Inactive Charge Type	
☐ Chrge Ty. Grping	
Other Charge Code	
TrM Category	∨
Charge Due	∨
Chrge Ty. Class	

Figure A-123. *Creating a charge type*

After entering the necessary data, save the data by clicking the Save 🖫 button.
In this manner, define the remaining charge types.

Defining Scales

You can use this option to define scale, which is a dimension of a rate.

For the given scenario, you will need to define the scales displayed in Tables A-70–A-79.

Table A-70. *Scale (Weight Scale for Customer) Data*

Field	Value
General Data Tab	
Basic Data Section	
Scale	HE-SC-WEIGHT
Description	Weight scale for customer
Scale base	Weight
Scale type	Base scale (>=)
Scale unit of measure	kg

Table A-71. *Scale (Weight Scale for Customer): Items Tab Data*

Field	Value	Value	Value	Value	Value	Value
Items Tab						
Scale value—weight	100	300	500	1,000	3,000	5,000
Calculation type	Relative	Relative	Relative	Relative	Relative	Relative

Table A-72. *Scale (Weight Scale for Pickup/Delivery) Data*

Field	Value
General Data Tab	
Basic Data Section	
Scale	HE-SC-WEIGHT-PD
Description	Weight scale–Pickup/Delivery
Scale base	Weight
Scale type	Base scale (>=)
Scale unit of measure	kg

Table A-73. *Scale (Weight Scale for Pickup/Delivery): Items Tab Data*

Field	Value	Value	Value	Value	Value
Items Tab					
Scale value—weight	50	100	250	450	750
Calculation type	Relative	Relative	Relative	Relative	Relative

Table A-74. *Scale (Weight Scale for Main Stage) Data*

Field	Value
General Data Tab	
Basic Data Section	
Scale	HE-SC-WEIGHT-MAIN
Description	Weight scale for main stage
Scale base	Weight
Scale type	Base scale (>=)
Scale unit of measure	kg

Table A-75. *Scale (Weight Scale for Main Stage): Items Tab Data*

Field	Value	Value	Value	Value	Value	Value
Items Tab						
Scale value—weight	500	750	1,000	3,000	5,000	10,000
Calculation type	Relative	Relative	Relative	Relative	Relative	Relative

Table A-76. *Scale (Source Location Scale) Data*

Field	Value
General Data Tab	
Basic Data Section	
Scale	HE-SC-SOC-LOC
Description	Source location scale
Scale base	LOC

Table A-77. *Scale (Source Location Scale): Items Tab Data*

Field	Value	Value	Value	Value
Items Tab				
Internal location	HESTAJPYOK	HEGWJPNAR	HEMFLA	HEGWUSLA
Calculation type	Absolute	Absolute	Absolute	Absolute

Table A-78. *Scale (Destination Location Scale) Data*

Field	Value
General Data Tab	
Basic Data Section	
Scale	HE-SC-DES-LOC
Description	Destination location scale
Scale base	LOC

Table A-79. *Scale (Destination Location Scale): Items Tab Data*

Field	Value	Value	Value	Value
Items Tab				
Internal location	HEGWJPNAR	HEMFNRT	HEGWUSLA	HESTAUSSFR
Calculation type	Absolute	Absolute	Absolute	Absolute

To define a scale, in SAP NetWeaver Business Client, click Master Data ➤ Charge Management and Service Product Catalogs ➤ Scales ➤ Create Scale.

In the in the Basic Data section and Items tab of the General Data tab, enter the respective data, using Tables A-70–A-79.

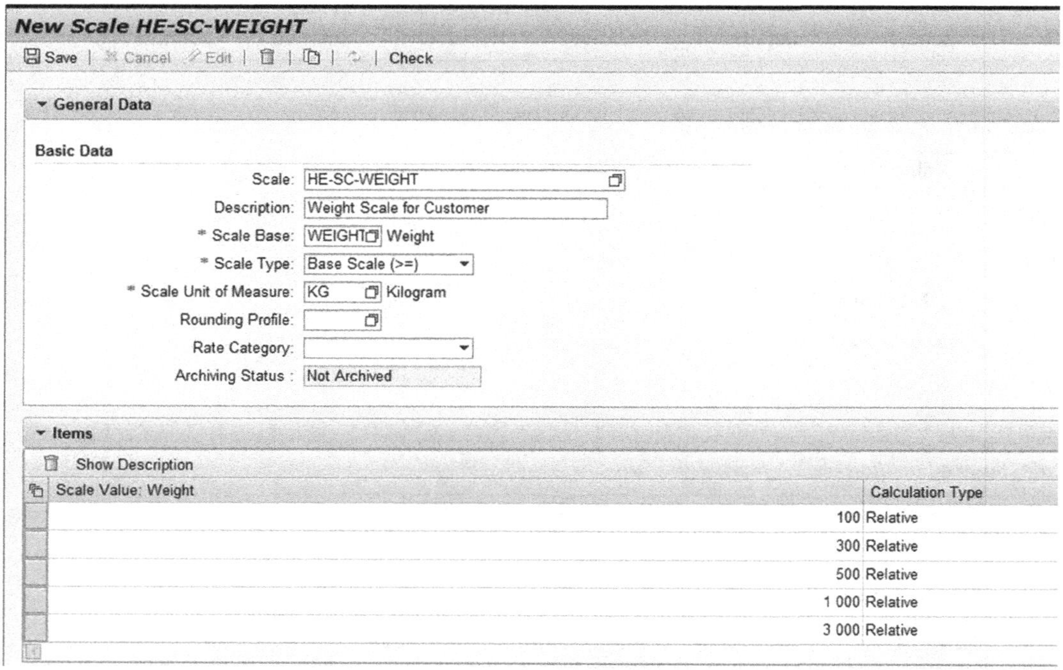

Figure A-124. *Creating a scale*

After entering the necessary data, save the data by clicking the Save 🖫 Save button.
In this way, define the remaining scales.

Defining Rate Tables

This option lets you specify rates for the transportation service as well as the validity of those rates.

For the given scenario, you must define the rate tables provided in Tables A-80–A-109.

Table A-80. *Rate Table (Base Freight for Customer) Data*

Field	Value
General Data Tab	
Basic Data Section	
Rate table	HE-RT-CU-01
Description	Base freight—HE-CU-01
Charge usage	Customer
Charge Type Settings Section	
Charge type	BASE_FA
Value type	Absolute value
Scale Table Section	
Reference scale	HE-SC-WEIGHT
Calculation base	CHRG_WEIGHT
Minimum value	<Select>
Maximum value	<Deselect>
Dates and Values Section	
Valid from	01-01-<current year>
Valid to	31-12-<current year>
Currency	JPY

Table A-81. *Rate Table (Base Freight for Customer): Rates Tab Data*

Field	Value	Value	Value	Value	Value	Value	Value
Dates and Values Section							
Rates Tab							
Weight (values will be displayed)	Minimum	100	300	500	1,000	3,000	5,000
Rate	5,000	1,000	900	800	700	500	300

Table A-82. *Rate Table (Base Freight for Customer): Calculation Rules Tab Data*

Field	Value
Dates and Values Section	
Calculation Rules Tab	
Calculation base	CHRG_WEIGHT
Application level of calculation rule	Rate table
Price unit	1
Unit of measure	kg

Table A-83. *Rate Table (Base Freight for Consignee) Data*

Field	Value
General Data Tab	
Basic Data Section	
Rate table	HE-RT-CO-01
Description	Base freight—HE-CO-01
Charge usage	Customer
Charge Type Settings Section	
Charge type	BASE_FA
Value type	Absolute value
Scale Table Section	
Reference scale	HE-SC-WEIGHT
Calculation base	CHRG_WEIGHT
Minimum value	<Select>
Maximum value	<Deselect>
Dates and Values Section	
Valid from	01-01-<current year>
Valid to	31-12-<current year>
Currency	USD

Table A-84. *Rate Table (Base Freight for Consignee): Rates Tab Data*

Field	Value	Value	Value	Value	Value	Value	Value
Dates and Values Section							
Rates Tab							
Weight (values will be displayed)	Minimum	100	300	500	1,000	3,000	5,000
Rate	6,000	1,500	1,400	1,300	1,200	1,000	800

Table A-85. *Rate Table (Base Freight for Consignee): Calculation Rules Tab Data*

Field	Value
Dates and Values Section	
Calculation Rules Tab	
Calculation base	CHRG_WEIGHT
Application level of calculation rule	Rate table
Price unit	1
Unit of measure	kg

Table A-86. *Rate Table (Base Freight for Pickup) Data*

Field	Value
General Data Tab	
Basic Data Section	
Rate table	HE-RT-PICKUP
Description	Base freight—pickup
Charge usage	Service provider
Charge Type Settings Section	
Charge type	FB00
Value type	Absolute value
Scale Table Section	
Reference scale	HE-SC-WEIGHT-PD
Calculation base	GROSS_WEIGHT
Minimum value	<Deselect>
Maximum value	<Deselect>
Dates and Values Section	
Valid from	01-01-<current year>
Valid to	31-12-<current year>
Currency	JPY

Table A-87. *Rate Table (Base Freight for Pickup): Rates Tab Data*

Field	Value	Value	Value	Value	Value
Dates and Values Section					
Rates Tab					
Weight (values will be displayed)	50	100	250	450	750
Rate	200	150	100	75	50

Table A-88. *Rate Table (Base Freight for Pickup): Calculation Rules Tab Data*

Field	Value
Dates and Values Section	
Calculation Rules Tab	
Calculation base	GROSS_WEIGHT
Application level of calculation rule	Rate table
Price unit	1
Unit of measure	kg

Table A-89. *Rate Table (Base Freight for Precarriage) Data*

Field	Value	
General Data Tab		
Basic Data Section		
Rate table	HE-RT-PRECARRIAGE	
Description	Base freight—precarriage	
Charge usage	Service provider	
Charge Type Settings Section		
Charge type	FB00	
Value type	Absolute value	
Scale Table Section		
Reference scale	HE-SC-SOC-LOC	HE-SC-DES-LOC
Calculation base	SOURCELOC	DESTLOC
Scale type	Same scale (=)	Same scale (=)
Minimum value	<Deselect>	<Deselect>
Maximum value	<Deselect>	Deselect>
Dates and Values Section		
Valid from	01-01-<current year>	
Valid to	31-12-<current year>	
Currency	JPY	

Table A-90. *Rate Table (Base Freight for Precarriage): Rates Tab Data*

Field	Value	Value
Dates and Values Section		
Rates Tab		
Source location	HESTAJPYOK	HEGWJPNAR
Destination location	HEGWJPNAR	HEMFNRT
Rate	50	10

Table A-91. *Rate Table (Base Freight for Precarriage): Calculation Rules Tab Data*

Field	Value
Dates and Values Section	
Calculation Rules Tab	
Calculation base	GROSS_WEIGHT
Application level of calculation rule	Rate table
Price unit	1
Unit of measure	kg

Table A-92. *Rate Table (Base Freight for Main Carriage) Data*

Field	Value
General Data Tab	
Basic Data Section	
Rate table	HE-RT-MAIN
Description	Base freight—main carriage
Charge usage	Service provider
Charge Type Settings Section	
Charge type	FB00
Value type	Absolute value
Scale Table Section	
Reference scale	HE-SC-WEIGHT-MAIN
Calculation base	GROSS_WEIGHT
Minimum value	<Deselect>
Maximum value	<Deselect>
Dates and Values Section	
Valid from	01-01-<current year>
Valid to	31-12-<current year>
Currency	JPY

Table A-93. *Rate Table (Base Freight for Main Carriage): Rates Tab Data*

Field	Value	Value	Value	Value	Value	Value
Dates and Values Section						
Rates Tab						
Weight (values will be displayed)	500	750	1,000	3,000	5,000	10,000
Rate	400	350	300	275	250	225

Table A-94. *Rate Table (Base Freight for Main Carriage): Calculation Rules Tab Data*

Field	Value
Dates and Values Section	
Calculation Rules Tab	
Calculation base	GROSS_WEIGHT
Application level of calculation rule	Rate table
Price unit	1
Unit of measure	kg

Table A-95. *Rate Table (Base Freight for On-Carriage) Data*

Field	Value	
General Data Tab		
Basic Data Section		
Rate table	HE-RT-ONCARRIAGE	
Description	Base freight—on-carriage	
Charge usage	Service provider	
Charge Type Settings Section		
Charge type	FB00	
Value type	Absolute value	
Scale Table Section		
Reference scale	HE-SC-SOC-LOC	HE-SC-DES-LOC
Calculation base	SOURCELOC	DESTLOC
Scale type	Same scale (=)	Same scale (=)
Minimum value	<Deselect>	<Deselect>
Maximum value	<Deselect>	<Deselect>
Dates and Values Section		
Valid from	01-01-<current year>	
Valid to	31-12-<current year>	
Currency	USD	

Table A-96. *Rate Table (Base Freight for On-Carriage): Rates Tab Data*

Field	Value	Value
Dates and Values Section		
Rates Tab		
Source location	HEGWUSLA	HEMFLA
Destination location	HESTAUSSFR	HEGWUSLA
Rate	40	5

Table A-97. *Rate Table (Base Freight for On-Carriage): Calculation Rules Tab Data*

Field	Value
Dates and Values Section	
Calculation Rules Tab	
Calculation base	GROSS_WEIGHT
Application level of calculation rule	Rate table
Price unit	1
Unit of measure	kg

Table A-98. *Rate Table (Base Freight for Delivery) Data*

Field	Value
General Data Tab	
Basic Data Section	
Rate table	HE-RT-DEL
Description	Base freight—delivery
Charge usage	Service provider
Charge Type Settings Section	
Charge type	FB00
Value type	Absolute value
Scale Table Section	
Reference scale	HE-SC-WEIGHT-PD
Calculation base	GROSS_WEIGHT
Minimum value	<Deselect>
Maximum value	<Deselect>
Dates and Values Section	
Valid from	01-01-<current year>
Valid to	31-12-<current year>
Currency	USD

Table A-99. *Rate Table (Base Freight for Delivery): Rates Tab Data*

Field	Value	Value	Value	Value	Value
Dates and Values Section					
Rates Tab					
Weight (values will be displayed)	50	100	250	450	750
Rate	150	125	100	75	50

Table A-100. *Rate Table (Base Freight for Delivery): Calculation Rules Tab Data*

Field	Value
Dates and Values Section	
Calculation Rules Tab	
Calculation base	GROSS_WEIGHT
Application level of calculation rule	Rate table
Price unit	1
Unit of measure	kg

Table A-101. *Rate Table (Internal—Export to Import) Data*

Field	Value
General Data Tab	
Basic Data Section	
Rate table	HE-RT-EXP-IMP
Description	Base freight—export to import
Charge usage	Customer
Charge Type Settings Section	
Charge type	BASE_FA
Value type	Absolute value
Scale Table Section	
Reference scale	HE-SC-WEIGHT
Calculation base	CHRG_WEIGHT
Minimum value	<Select>
Maximum value	<Deselect>
Dates and Values Section	
Valid from	01-01-<current year>
Valid to	31-12-<current year>
Currency	JPY

Table A-102. *Rate Table (Internal—Export to Import): Rates Tab Data*

Field	Value	Value	Value	Value	Value	Value	Value
Dates and Values Section							
Rates Tab							
Weight (values will be displayed)	Minimum	100	300	500	1,000	3,000	5,000
Rate	2,000	500	450	400	350	250	150

Table A-103. *Rate Table (Internal—Export to Import): Calculation Rules Tab Data*

Field	Value
Dates and Values Section	
Calculation Rules Tab	
Calculation base	CHRG_WEIGHT
Application level of calculation rule	Rate table
Price unit	1
Unit of measure	kg

Table A-104. *Rate Table (Internal Precarriage) Data*

Field	Value	
General Data Tab		
Basic Data Section		
Rate table	HE-RT-INT-PRE	
Description	Base freight—internal precarriage	
Charge usage	Internal	
Charge Type Settings Section		
Charge type	FB00	
Value type	Absolute value	
Scale Table Section		
Reference scale	HE-SC-SOC-LOC	HE-SC-DES-LOC
Calculation base	SOURCELOC	DESTLOC
Scale type	Same scale (=)	Same scale (=)
Minimum value	<Deselect>	<Deselect>
Maximum value	<Deselect>	<Deselect>
Dates and Values Section		
Valid from	01-01-current year>	
Valid to	31-12-<current year>	
Currency	JPY	

Table A-105. *Rate Table (Internal Precarriage): Rates Tab Data*

Field	Value
Dates and Values Section	
Rates Tab	
Source location	HESTAJPYOK
Destination location	HEGWJPNAR
Rate	2

Table A-106. *Rate Table (Internal Precarriage): Calculation Rules Tab Data*

Field	Value
Dates and Values Section	
Calculation Rules Tab	
Calculation base	ACTUAL_DIST
Application level of calculation rule	Rate table
Price unit	1
Unit of measure	km

Table A-107. *Rate Table (Internal On-Carriage) Data*

Field	Value	
General Data Section		
Basic Data Section		
Rate table	HE-RT-INT-ON	
Description	Base freight—internal on-carriage	
Charge usage	Internal	
Charge Type Settings Section		
Charge type	FB00	
Value type	Absolute value	
Scale Table Section		
Reference scale	HE-SC-SOC-LOC	HE-SC-DES-LOC
Calculation base	SOURCELOC	DESTLOC
Scale type	Same scale (=)	Same scale (=)
Minimum value	<Deselect>	<Deselect>
Maximum value	<Deselect>	<Deselect>
Dates and Values Section		
Valid from	01-01-<current year>	
Valid to	31-12-<current year>	
Currency	USD	

Table A-108. *Rate Table (Internal On-Carriage) Rates Tab Data*

Field	Value
Dates and Values Section	
Rates Tab	
Source location	HEGWUSLA
Destination location	HESTAUSSFR
Rate	2

Table A-109. *Rate Table (Internal On-Carriage): Calculation Rules Tab Data*

Field	Value
Dates and Values Section	
Calculation Rules Tab	
Calculation base	ACTUAL_DIST
Application level of calculation rule	Rate table
Price unit	1
Unit of measure	km

To define a rate table, in SAP NetWeaver Business Client, click Master Data ➤ Charge Management and Service Product Catalogs ➤ Rate Tables ➤ Create Rate Tables Definition.

Click the Continue ⊘ Continue button without entering the rate table template. In the Basic Data section of the General Data tab, enter the relevant data from the tables.

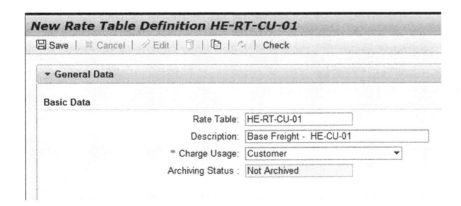

Figure A-125. *Creating a rate table: Basic Data section of the General Data tab*

In the Charge Type Settings section of the General Data tab, again enter the relevant data.

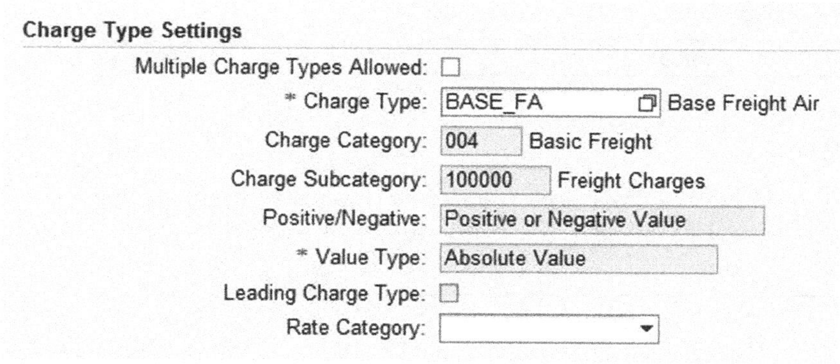

Charge Type Settings

Multiple Charge Types Allowed: ☐

* Charge Type: `BASE_FA` Base Freight Air

Charge Category: `004` Basic Freight

Charge Subcategory: `100000` Freight Charges

Positive/Negative: `Positive or Negative Value`

* Value Type: `Absolute Value`

Leading Charge Type: ☐

Rate Category: ▼

Figure A-126. *Creating a rate table: Charge Type Settings section of the General Data tab*

Now, insert a row in the Scale table by clicking the Insert button, and, in the Scale Table section, enter the data.

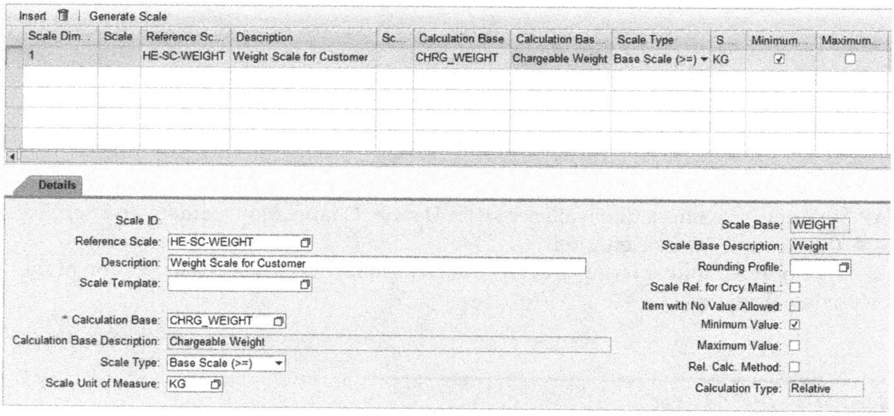

Figure A-127. *Creating a rate table - Scale Table section*

After entering the necessary scale data, select the scale row, and click the Generate Scale `Generate Scale` button. Then, save the data by clicking the Save `💾 Save` button.

Next, click the Edit `🖉 Edit` button, and, in the Dates and Values section, click the Insert `Insert` button to enter the validity data.

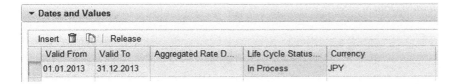

Figure A-128. *Creating a rate table: Dates and Values section*

In the Rates tab of the Dates and Values section, select a new row, and enter the relevant data.

Figure A-129. *Creating a rate table: Rates tab*

In the Calculation Rules tab of the Dates and Values section, again select a new row, and enter the data.

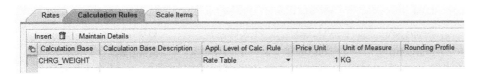

Figure A-130. *Creating a rate table: Calculation Rules tab*

Now, click the Release Release button to release the rate table.
After entering the necessary data, save the data by clicking the Save 🖫 Save button.
In this way, define the remaining rate tables.

Defining Calculation Sheets

To calculate the charges that are incurred for a freight order/booking or forwarding order, calculation sheets are defined in the system.

For the given scenario, you will need to define the calculation sheets offered in Tables A-110–A-129.

Table A-110. *Calculation Sheet (Customer) Data*

Field	Value
General Data Tab	
Basic Data Section	
Calculation sheet	HE-CS-CU-01
Description	Calculation sheet—HE-CU-01
Charge usage	Customer

Table A-111. *Calculation Sheet (Customer): Items Section Data*

Field	Value	Value	Value	Value
Items Tab				
Basic Data Tab				
General Data section				
Line number	20	30	40	50
Instruction type	Standard	Standard	Standard	Standard
Description	Base airfreight	Pickup fees	Base freight	Fuel surcharge
Charge type	BASE_FA	PU_FEE	COO	FUEL
Calculation Method Section	Standard	Standard	Standard	Standard
Rate Tab				
General Data Section				
Rate Table determination rule	HE-RT-CU-01			
Amount	<Blank>	5,000	4,000	20
Currency/ Percentage		JPY	JPY	%
Reference—from line number				20
Reference—to line number				0

Table A-112. *Calculation Sheet (Consignee) Data*

Field	Value
General Data Tab	
Basic Data Section	
Calculation sheet	HE-CS-CO-01
Description	Calculation sheet—HE-CO-01
Charge usage	Customer

Table A-113. *Calculation Sheet (Consignee): Items Section Data*

Field	Value	Value	Value
Basic Data Tab			
General Data Section			
Line number	20	30	40
Instruction type	Standard	Standard	Standard
Description	Base airfreight	Base freight	Fuel surcharge
Charge type	BASE_FA	COO	FUEL
Calculation Method Section	Standard	Standard	Standard
Rate Tab			
General Data Section			
Rate table determination rule	HE-RT-CO-01		
Amount	<Blank>	4,000	20
Currency/Percentage		USD	%
Reference—from line number			20
Reference—to line number			0

Table A-114. *Calculation Sheet (Pickup) Data*

Field	Value
General Data Tab	
Basic Data Section	
Calculation sheet	HE-CS-PICKUP
Description	Calculation sheet—pickup
Charge usage	Service provider

Table A-115. *Calculation Sheet (Pickup): Items Section Data*

Field	Value	Value	Value
Basic Data Tab			
General Data Section			
Line number	20	30	40
Instruction type	Standard	Standard	Standard
Description	Base freight	Pickup fees	Fuel surcharge
Charge type	FB00	PU_FEE	FUEL
Calculation Method Section	Standard	Standard	Standard
Rate Tab			
General Data Section			
Rate table determination rule	HE-RT-PICKUP		
Amount	<Blank>	200	10
Currency/Percentage		JPY	%
Reference—from line number			20
Reference—to line number			0

Table A-116. *Calculation Sheet (Precarriage) Data*

Field	Value
General Data Tab	
Basic Data Section	
Calculation sheet	HE-CS-PRECARRIAGE
Description	Calculation sheet—precarriage
Charge usage	Service provider

Table A-117. *Calculation Sheet (Precarriage): Items Section Data*

Field	Value	Value
Basic Data Tab		
General Data Section		
Line number	20	30
Instruction type	Standard	Standard
Description	Base freight	Fuel surcharge
Charge type	FB00	FUEL
Calculation Method Section	Standard	Standard

(*continued*)

Table A-117. (*continued*)

Field	Value	Value
Rate Tab		
General Data Section		
Rate table determination rule	HE-RT-PRECARRIAGE	
Amount	<Blank>	5
Currency/Percentage		%
Reference—from line number		20
Reference—to line number		0

Table A-118. *Calculation Sheet (Main Carriage) Data*

Field	Value
General Data Tab	
Basic Data Section	
Calculation sheet	HE-CS-MAIN
Description	Calculation sheet—main carriage
Charge usage	Service provider

Table A-119. *Calculation Sheet (Main Carriage): Items Section Data*

Field	Value	Value	Value
Basic Data Tab			
General Data Section			
Line number	20	30	40
Instruction type	Standard	Standard	Standard
Description	Base freight	Base freight	Fuel surcharge
Charge type	FB00	COO	FUEL
Calculation Method Section	Standard	Standard	Standard
Rate Tab			
General Data Section			
Rate table determination rule	HE-RT-MAIN		
Amount	<Blank>	2,000	10
Currency/Percentage		JPY	%
Reference—from line number			20
Reference—to line number			0

Table A-120. *Calculation Sheet (On-Carriage) Data*

Field	Value
General Data Tab	
Basic Data Section	
Calculation sheet	HE-CS-ONCARRIAGE
Description	Calculation sheet—on-carriage
Charge usage	Service provider

Table A-121. *Calculation Sheet (On-Carriage): Items Section Data*

Field	Value	Value
Basic Data Tab		
General Data Section		
Line number	20	30
Instruction type	Standard	Standard
Description	Base freight	Fuel surcharge
Charge type	FB00	FUEL
Calculation Method Section	Standard	Standard
Rate Tab		
General Data Section		
Rate table determination rule	HE-RT-ONCARRIAGE	
Amount	<Blank>	10
Currency/Percentage		%
Reference—from line number		20
Reference—to line number		0

Table A-122. *Calculation Sheet (Delivery) Data*

Field	Value
General Data Tab	
Basic Data Section	
Calculation sheet	HE-CS-DELIVERY
Description	Calculation sheet—delivery
Charge usage	Service provider

Table A-123. *Calculation Sheet (Delivery): Items Section Data*

Field	Value	Value
Basic Data Tab		
General Data Section		
Line number	20	30
Instruction type	Standard	Standard
Description	Base freight	Fuel surcharge
Charge type	FB00	FUEL
Calculation Method Section	Standard	Standard
Rate Tab		
General Data Section		
Rate table determination rule	HE-RT-DEL	
Amount	<Blank>	10
Currency/ Percentage		%
Reference—from line number		20
Reference—to line number		0

Table A-124. *Calculation Sheet (Export to Import) Data*

Field	Value
General Data Tab	
Basic Data Section	
Calculation sheet	HE-CS-EXP-IMP
Description	Calculation sheet—export to import
Charge usage	Customer

Table A-125. *Calculation Sheet (Export to Import): Items Section Data*

Field	Value	Value
Basic Data Tab		
General Data Section		
Line number	20	30
Instruction type	Standard	Standard
Description	Base freight	Fuel surcharge
Charge type	BASE_FA	FUEL
Calculation Method Section	Standard	Standard

(*continued*)

Table A-125. (*continued*)

Field	Value	Value
Rate Tab		
General Data Section		
Rate table determination rule	HE-RT-EXP-IMP	
Amount	<Blank>	5
Currency/Percentage		%
Reference—from line number		20
Reference—to line number		0

Table A-126. *Calculation Sheet (Export Gateway to Station) Data*

Field	Value
General Data Tab	
Basic Data Section	
Calculation sheet	HE-CS-EXP-GW-ST
Description	Calculation sheet—export gateway to station
Charge usage	Internal

Table A-127. *Calculation Sheet (Export Gateway to Station): Items Section Data*

Field	Value	Value
Basic Data Tab		
General Data Section		
Line number	20	30
Instruction type	Standard	Standard
Description	Base freight	Drayage
Charge type	FB00	FB00
Calculation Method Section	Standard	Standard
Rate Tab		
General Data Section		
Rate table determination rule	HE-RT-INT-PRE	<Blank>
Amount	<Blank>	1,500
Currency/Percentage		JPY

Table A-128. *Calculation Sheet (Import Gateway to Station) Data*

Field	Value
General Data Tab	
Basic Data Section	
Calculation sheet	HE-CS-IMP-GW-ST
Description	Calculation sheet—import gateway to station
Charge usage	Internal

Table A-129. *Calculation Sheet (Import Gateway to Station): Items Section Data*

Field	Value	Value
Basic Data Tab		
General Data Section		
Line number	20	30
Instruction type	Standard	Standard
Description	Base freight	Drayage
Charge type	FB00	FB00
Calculation Method Section	Standard	Standard
Rate Tab		
General Data Section		
Rate table determination rule	HE-RT-INT-ON	<Blank>
Amount		1,000
Currency/Percentage		USD

To define a calculation sheet, in SAP NetWeaver Business Client, click Master Data ➤ Charge Management and Service Product Catalogs ➤ Calculation Sheets ➤ Create Calculation Sheet.

Click the Continue ⊘ Continue button without entering the calculation sheet template. In the Basic Data section of the General Data tab, enter the relevant data from the Tables.

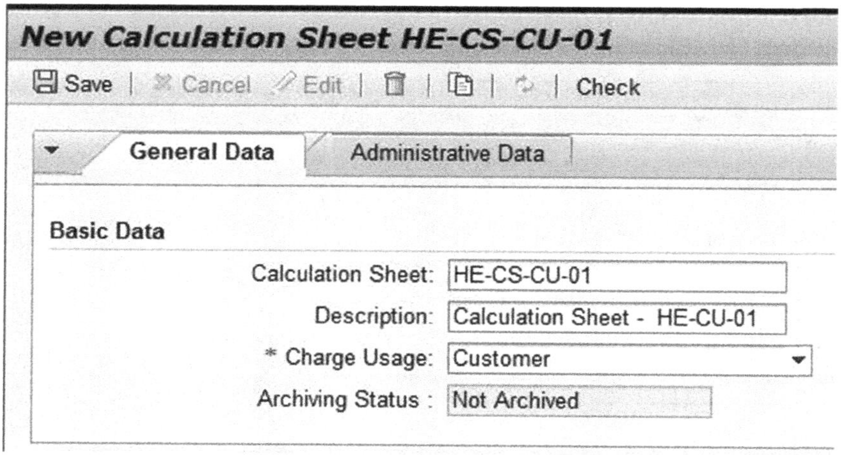

New Calculation Sheet HE-CS-CU-01

🖫 Save | ✖ Cancel | ✒ Edit | 🗑 | 🗐 | ⟳ | Check

▾ | **General Data** | Administrative Data

Basic Data

Calculation Sheet: HE-CS-CU-01

Description: Calculation Sheet - HE-CU-01

* Charge Usage: Customer ▾

Archiving Status : Not Archived

Figure A-131. *Creating a calculation sheet: Basic Data section of the General Data tab*

Next, in the Items section of the Items tab, add a new item line by clicking Insert ➤ Single Item.

▾ Items

▶↓ ▶↑ | Insert ▴ 🗐 🗐 | Add Rate Table | Delete Rate Table | Rate Table Details

🗐 Item Hie | Single Item | ...ucti... | Charge Type | Charge Type Class. | IATA Charge D... | IATA Other Charge Code |
▶ Sum | Multiple Items

Figure A-132. *Creating a calculation sheet: Items Section of the Items tab*

Select the new item line, and, in the General Data and Calculation Method sections of the Basic Data tab, enter the respective data.

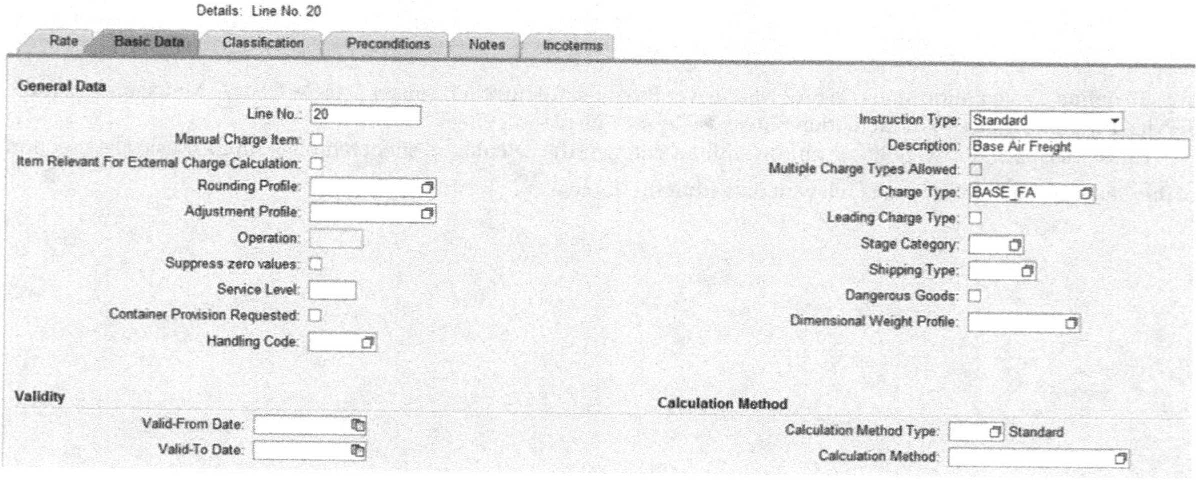

Details: Line No. 20

Rate | **Basic Data** | Classification | Preconditions | Notes | Incoterms

General Data

Line No.: 20 | Instruction Type: Standard ▾
Manual Charge Item: ☐ | Description: Base Air Freight
Item Relevant For External Charge Calculation: ☐ | Multiple Charge Types Allowed: ☐
Rounding Profile: | Charge Type: BASE_FA 🗐
Adjustment Profile: | Leading Charge Type: ☐
Operation: | Stage Category: 🗐
Suppress zero values: ☐ | Shipping Type: 🗐
Service Level: | Dangerous Goods: ☐
Container Provision Requested: ☐ | Dimensional Weight Profile: 🗐
Handling Code: 🗐

Validity

Valid-From Date: 🗐
Valid-To Date: 🗐

Calculation Method

Calculation Method Type: 🗐 Standard
Calculation Method: 🗐

Figure A-133. *Creating a calculation sheet: General Data and Calculation Method sections of the Basic Data tab*

In the General Data section of the Rate tab, enter the relevant data.

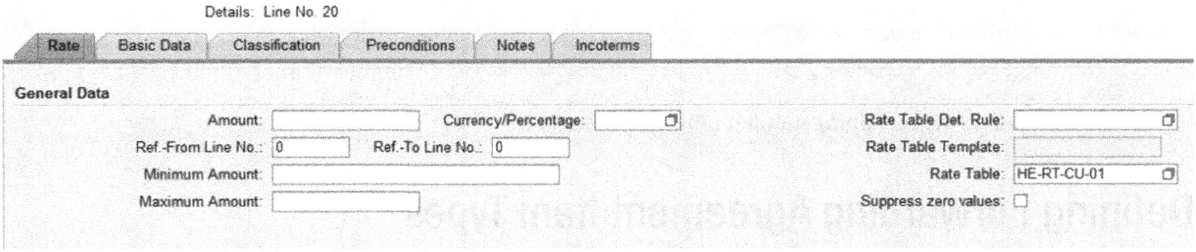

Figure A-134. *Creating a calculation sheet: General Data section of the Rate tab*

In this way, create the remaining items, and define the remaining calculation sheets. After entering the necessary data, save the data by clicking the Save 💾 Save button.

Defining Number Range Intervals for Agreements

Specify the number range for forwarding, freight, and internal agreement documents using this option.
For the given scenario, you will have to define the number range intervals listed in Table A-130.

Table A-130. *Agreement Number Range Interval Data*

Field	Value	Value	Value
number range number	H1	H2	H3
From number	00000000004100000000	00000000005100000000	00000000006100000000
To number	00000000004199999999	00000000005199999999	00000000006199999999
External	<Deselect>	<Deselect>	Deselect>

To define a number range, go to Customizing for SAP Transportation Management, and click Transportation Management ➤ Master Data ➤ Agreements and Service Products ➤ Define Number Range Intervals for Agreements.
To define a number range interval for an agreement, click the Intervals 🖊 Intervals button and then the Insert Line 🗒 button. Enter the number range from Table A-130.

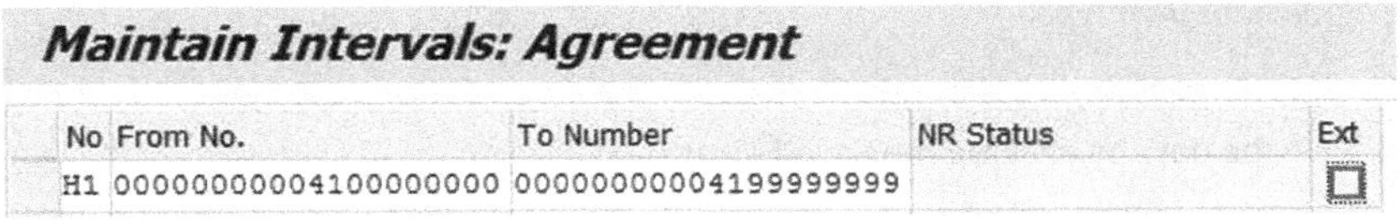

Figure A-135. *Creating a number range interval for an agreement*

After entering the necessary data, save the data by clicking the Save 🖫 button.

▪ **Note** In the Transport number range intervals dialog box, click the Continue ✅ button.

In this way, define the remaining number range intervals.

Defining Forwarding Agreement Item Types

This option allows you to specify the attributes of the items that you add to a forwarding agreement.

For the given scenario, you must define the forwarding agreement item types provided in Table A-131.

Table A-131. *Forwarding Agreement Item Type Data*

Field	Value
Item type	HEFI
Description	Forwarding agreement item
Calculation sheet	Allowed
Add services	<Deselect>

To define a forwarding agreement item type, go to Customizing for SAP Transportation Management, and click Transportation Management ➤ Master Data ➤ Agreements and Service Products ➤ Define FWA and Service Product Item Types.

Then, click the New Entries New Entries button, and enter the data from Table A-131.

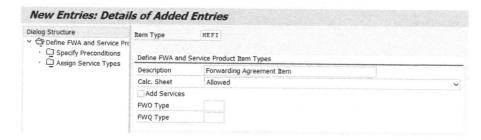

Figure A-136. *Creating a forwarding agreement item type*

After entering the necessary data, save the data by clicking the Save 🖫 button.

Defining Forwarding Agreement Types

This option lets you specify the various attributes related to forwarding agreements.

For the given scenario, you will need to define the forwarding agreement types presented in Table A-132.

Table A-132. *Forwarding Agreement Type Data*

Field	Value
Agreement type	HEFW
Description	Forwarding agreement
Track changes	<Select>
Multiple parties	<Deselect>
Agreement number range	H1

To define a forwarding agreement type, go to Customizing for SAP Transportation Management, and click Transportation Management ➤ Master Data ➤ Agreements and Service Products ➤ Define FWA and Service Product Catalog Types.

Then, click the New Entries ʀɴew ᴇɴtries button, and enter the data from Table A-132.

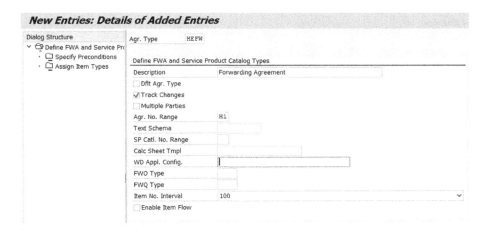

Figure A-137. *Creating a forwarding agreement type*

After entering the necessary data, save the data by clicking the Save 🖫 button.

Defining Freight Agreement Types

This option allows you to specify the various attributes related to freight agreements.

For the given scenario, you will have to define the freight agreement types displayed in Table A-133.

Table A-133. *Freight Agreement Type Data*

Field	Value
Agreement type	HEFA
Description	Freight agreement
Track changes	<Select>
Multiple parties	<Select>
Agreement number range	H2

To define a freight agreement type, go to Customizing for SAP Transportation Management, and click Transportation Management ➤ Master Data ➤ Agreements and Service Products ➤ Define Freight Agreement Types. Now, click the New Entries New Entries button, and enter the data from Table A-133.

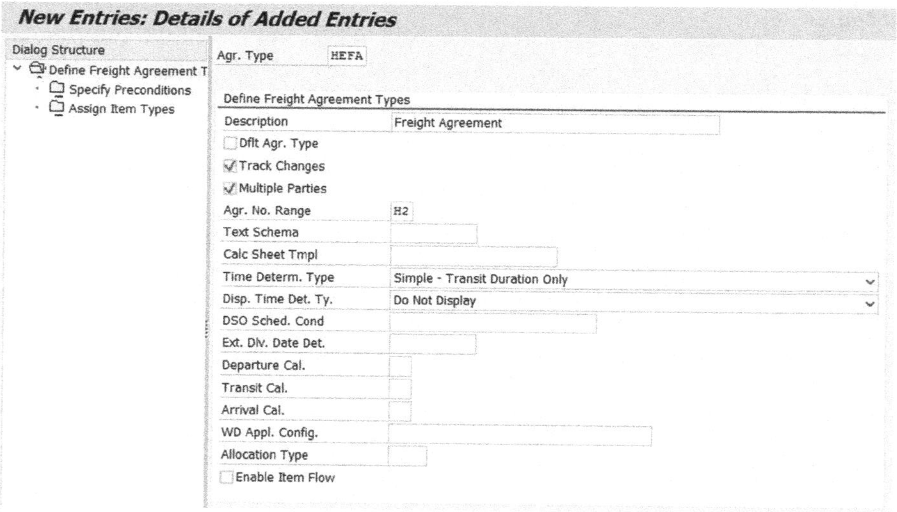

Figure A-138. *Creating a freight agreement type*

After entering the necessary data, save the data by clicking the Save 🖫 button.

Defining Internal Agreement Types

This option is used to specify the various attributes related to internal agreements.

For the given scenario, you will need to define the internal agreement types presented in Table 1-134.

Table A-134. *Internal Agreement Type Data*

Field	Value
Agreement type	HEIA
Description	Internal agreement
Track changes	<Select>
Agreement number range	H3

To define an internal agreement type, go to Customizing for SAP Transportation Management, and click Transportation Management ➤ Master Data ➤ Agreements and Service Products ➤ Define Internal Agreement Types.

Next, click the New Entries New Entries button, and enter the data from Table 1-134.

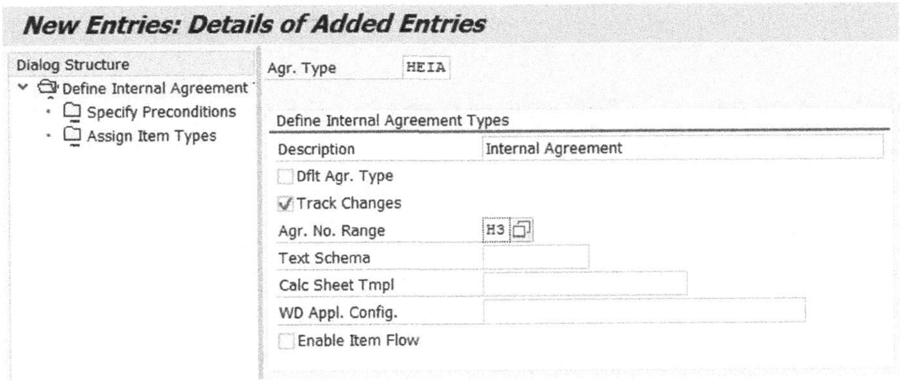

Figure A-139. *Creating an internal agreement type*

After entering the necessary data, save the data by clicking the Save 🖫 button.

Defining Forwarding Agreements

The forwarding agreement is used to define transportation charges billable to the customer.

For the given scenario, you must define the forwarding agreements listed in Table A-135.

Table A-135. *Forwarding Agreement Data*

Field	Value	Value	Value
Agreement type	HEFW	HEFW	HEFW
General Data Tab			
Basic Data Section			
Agreement	HE-FWA-CU-01	HE-FWA-CO-01	HE-FWA-EXP-IMP
Description	Forwarding agreement for HE-CU-01	Forwarding agreement for HE-CO-01	Forwarding agreement—export to import
Involved Parties Section			
Sales organization	<Enter the organization ID of HEJPFHYOK >	<Enter the organization ID of HEUSFHSFR>	<Enter the organization ID of HEJPFHYOK>
Ordering party	HE-CU-01	HE-CO-01	<Enter the business partner ID of HEUSFHSFR>
Details Section			
Valid from	01-01-<current year>	01-01-<current year>	01-01-<current year>
Valid to	31-12-<current year>	31-12-<current year>	31-12-<current year>
Document currency	JPY	USD	JPY
Items Tab/Section			
Item number	100	100	100
Item type	HEFI	HEFI	HEFI
Description	Transportation charges	Transportation charges	Transportation charges
Calculation sheet	HE-CS-CU-01	HE-CS-CO-01	HE-CS-EXP-IMP

To define a forwarding agreement, in SAP NetWeaver Business Client, click Master Data ➤ Charge Management and Service Product Catalogs ➤ Forwarding Agreements ➤ Create Forwarding Agreement.

Enter the forwarding agreement type from Table A-135, and click the Continue ⊘ Continue button.

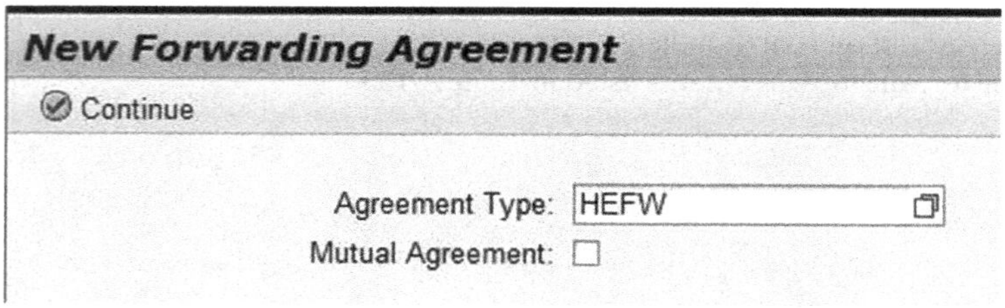

Figure A-140. *Initial screen for creating a forwarding agreement*

In the Basic Data and Involved Parties sections of the General Data tab, enter the respective data, using Table A-135.

Figure A-141. *Creating a forwarding agreement: Basic Data and Involved Parties sections of the General Data tab*

In the Details section of the General Data tab, enter the relevant data from Table A-135.

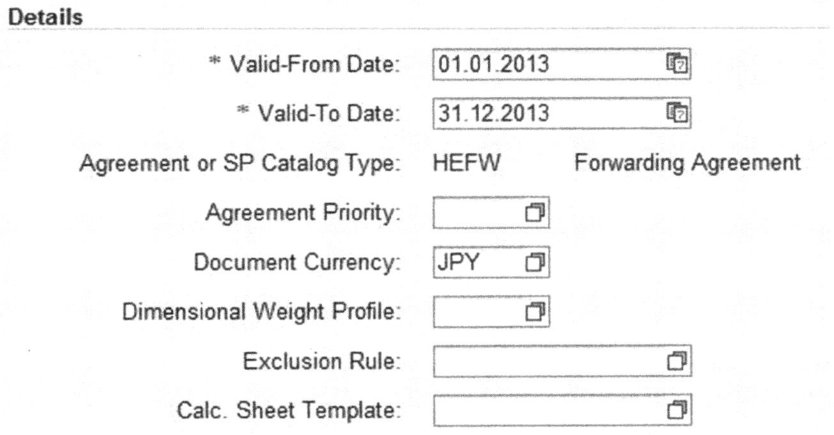

Figure A-142. *Creating a Forwarding Agreement: Details section of the General Data tab*

Next, in the Items tab, go to the Insert menu, and select Item.

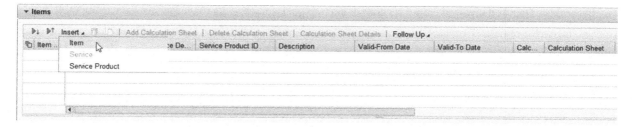

Figure A-143. Creating a forwarding agreement: Items tab

In the items section of the Items tab, enter the data from Table A-135.

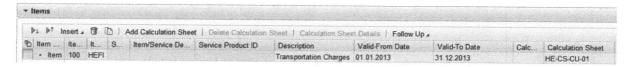

Figure A-144. Creating a forwarding agreement: Items section of the Items tab

After entering the necessary data, release the agreement by selecting Released from the Set Status menu.

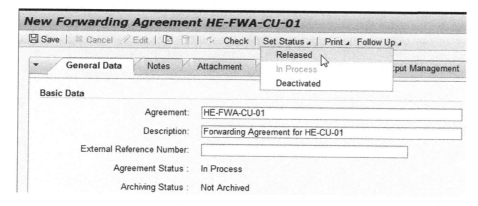

Figure A-145. Creating a forwarding agreement: Releasing the agreement

After releasing the agreement, save the data by clicking the Save ⊟ Save button.
In this way, define the remaining forwarding agreements.

Defining Freight Agreements

A freight agreement is used to define transportation charges billable by the carriers.
For the given scenario, you will have to define the freight agreements shown in Tables A-136–A-139.

Table A-136. *Freight agreement (Pickup, Precarriage, and Main Carriage) Data*

Field	Value
Agreement type	HEFA
General Data Tab	
Basic Data Section	
Agreement	HE-FA-JP-CR
Description	Freight agreement for Japanese carriers
Details Section	
Valid from	01-01-<current year>
Valid to	31-12-<current year>
Document currency	JPY
Involved Parties Section	
Organizational unit	<Enter the organization ID of *HEJPFHYOK, HEJPFHNAR*>
Business partner	HE-CR-01 HE-CR-02 HE-CR-03

Table A-137. *Freight Agreement (Pickup, Precarriage, and Main Carriage): Items Section Data*

Field	Value	Value	Value
Items Tab/Section			
Item number	100	200	300
Calculation sheet	HE-CS-PICKUP	HE-CS-PRECARRIAGE	HE-CS-MAIN
Precondition Tab			
Partners Tab			
Business partner	HE-CR-01	HE-CR-02	HE-CR-03
Party role	12 (carrier)	12 (carrier)	12 (carrier)

Table A-138. *Freight Agreement (On-Carriage and Delivery) Data*

Field	Value
Agreement type	HEFA
General Data Tab	
Basic Data Section	
Agreement	HE-FA-US-CR
Description	Freight agreement for US carriers
Details Section	
Valid from	01-01-<current year>
Valid to	31-12-<current year>
Document currency	USD
Involved Parties Section	
Organizational unit	<Enter the organization ID of *HEUSFHLA, HEUSFHSFR*>
Business partner	HE-CR-04 HE-CR-05

Table A-139. *Freight Agreement (On-Carriage and Delivery): Items Section Data*

Field	Value	Value
Items Tab/Section		
Item number	100	200
Calculation sheet	HE-CS-ONCARRIAGE	HE-CS-DELIVERY
Precondition Tab		
Partners Tab		
Business partner	HE-CR-04	HE-CR-05
Party role	12 (carrier)	12 (carrier)

To define a freight agreement, in SAP NetWeaver Business Client, click Master Data ➤ Charge Management and Service Product Catalogs ➤ Freight Agreements ➤ Create Freight Agreement.

Enter the freight agreement type from Tables A-136 and A-138, and click the Continue ⊘ Continue button.

New Freight Agreement

⊘ Continue

Agreement Type: HEFA

Mutual Agreement: ☐

Figure A-146. Initial screen for creating a freight agreement

In the Basic Data section of the General Data tab, enter the relevant data from Tables A-136 and A-138.

New Freight Agreement

💾 Save | ✕ Cancel | ✎ Edit | 🗐 🗑 | ↻ Check | Set Status ▴ | Print ▴

| ▾ | **General Data** | Notes | Attachment | Administrative Data | Output Management |

Basic Data

Agreement: HE-FA-JP-CR

Description: Freight agreement for Japanese carriers

External Reference Number:

Agreement Status : In Process

Archiving Status : Not Archived

Figure A-147. Creating a freight agreement: Basic Data section of the General Data tab

In the Details section of the General Data tab, again enter the relevant data from Tables A-136 and 138.

Details

* Valid-From Date: 01.01.2013

* Valid-To Date: 31.12.2013

Agreement Type: HEFA   Freight Agreement

Agreement Priority:

Document Currency: JPY

Dimensional Weight Profile:

Exclusion Rule:

Calc. Sheet Template:

Figure A-148. Creating a freight agreement: Details section of the General Data tab

Do the same in the Involved Parties section of the General Data tab.

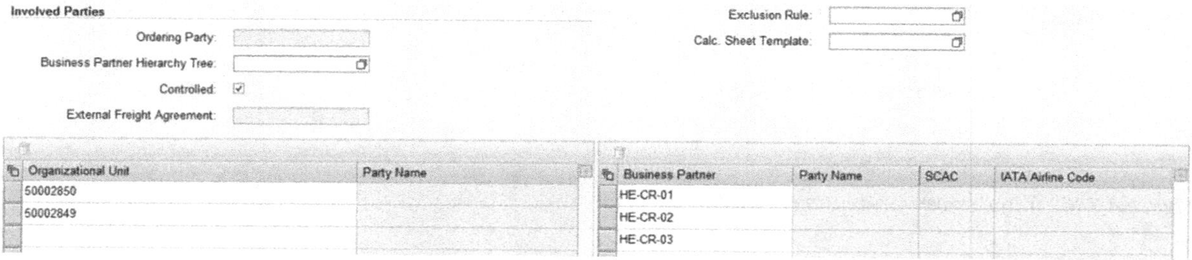

Figure A-149. *Creating a freight agreement: Involved Parties section of the General Data tab*

In the Items tab, click the Insert Insert button to insert a new item line. Now, in the Items section, enter the relevant data from Tables A-137 and A-139.

Figure A-150. *Creating a freight agreement: Items section of the Items tab*

Select the new item line, and, in the Precondition tab, enter the relevant data from Table A-137.

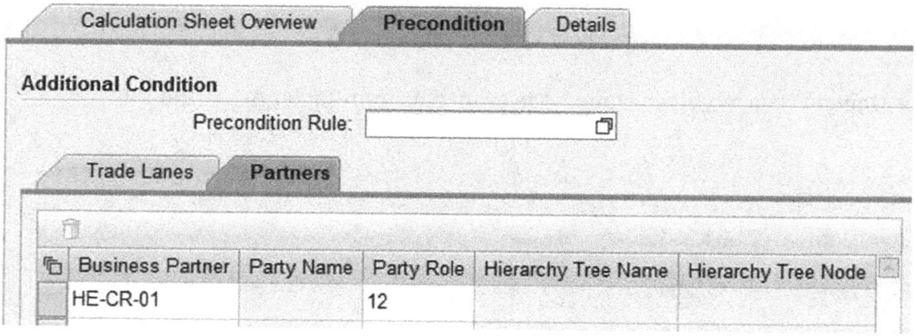

Figure A-151. *Creating a freight agreement: Precondition tab of the Items tab*

In this manner, create other items, along with the precondition.
After entering the necessary data, release the agreement by selecting Released from the Set Status menu.

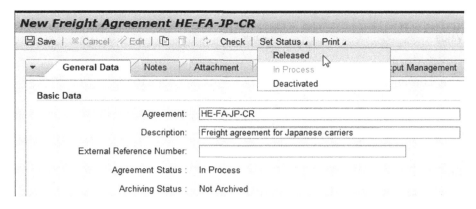

Figure A-152. *Creating a freight agreement: Releasing the agreement*

After releasing the agreement, save the data by clicking the Save ![Save] button. In this manner, define the remaining freight agreements.

Defining Internal Agreements

An internal agreement is used to define transportation charges between organizations of the same company code and between organizations of different company codes in the same company. Internal agreements are also used for distributing costs from export/import gateway to export/import station, including the charges agreed to for drayage.

For the given scenario, you will need to define the internal agreements displayed in Table A-140.

Table A-140. *Internal Agreement Data*

Field	Value	Value
Agreement type	HEIA	HEIA
General Data Tab		
Basic Data Section		
Agreement	HE-IA-EXP-GW-ST	HE-IA-IMP-GW-ST
Description	Internal agreement (export)—gateway to station	Internal agreement (import)—gateway to station
Details Section		
Valid from	01-01-<current year>	01-01-<current year>
Valid to	31-12-<current year>	31-12-<current year>
Document currency	JPY	USD

(*continued*)

235

Table A-140. (*continued*)

Field	Value	Value
Involved Parties Section		
Organizational unit	<Enter the organization ID of HEJPFHNAR	<Enter the organization ID of HEUSFHLA>
Business partner	<Enter the business partner ID of HEJPFHYOK>	<Enter the business partner ID of HEUSFHSFR>
Items Tab/Section		
Item number	100	100
Calculation sheet	HE-CS-EXP-GW-ST	HE-CS-IMP-GW-ST

To define an internal agreement, in SAP NetWeaver Business Client, click Master Data ➤ Charge Management and Service Product Catalogs ➤ Internal Agreements ➤ Create Internal Agreement.

Enter the internal agreement type from Table A-140, and click the Continue ⊘ Continue button.

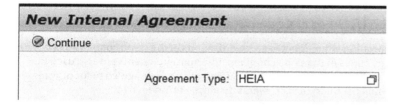

Figure A-153. *Initial screen for creating an internal agreement*

In the Basic Data section of the General Data tab, enter the relevant data from Table A-140.

Figure A-154. *Creating an internal agreement: Basic Data section of the General Data tab*

In the Details section of the General Data tab, again enter the relevant data from Table A-140.

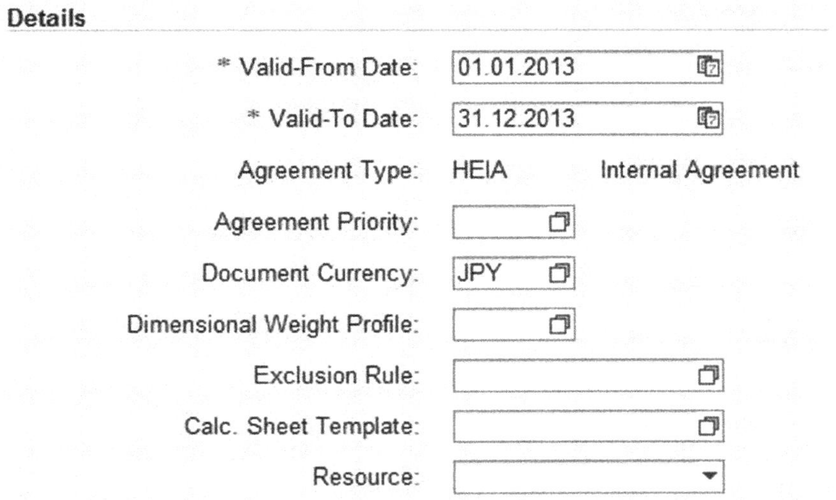

Figure A-155. Creating an internal agreement: Details section of the General Data tab

Do the same in the Involved Parties section of the General Data tab.

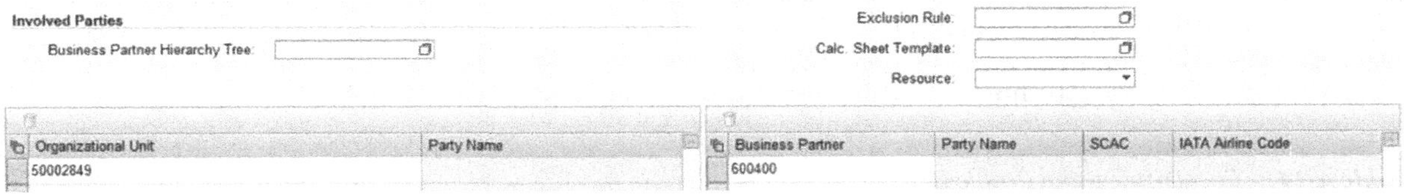

Figure A-156. Creating an internal agreement: Involved Parties section of the General Data tab

In the Items tab, click the Insert Insert button to insert a new item line. Then, in the Items section, enter the relevant data from Table A-140.

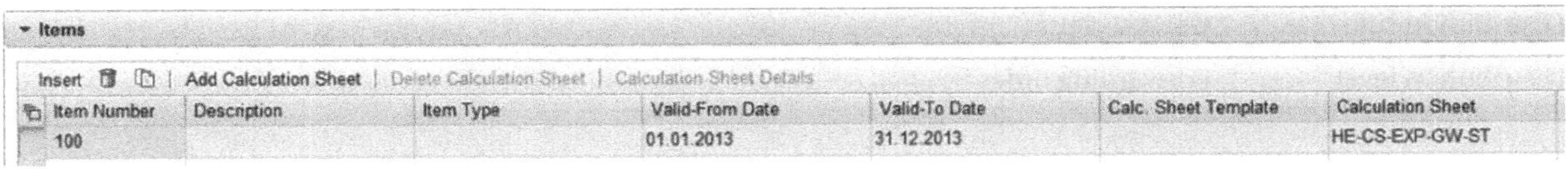

Figure A-157. Creating an internal agreement: Items section of the Items tab

After entering the necessary data, release the agreement by selecting Released from the Set Status menu.

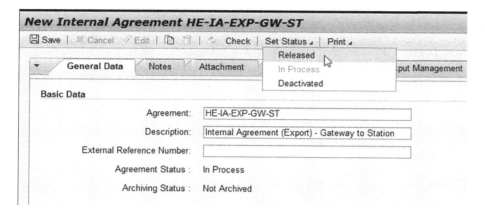

Figure A-158. *Creating an internal agreement: Releasing the agreement*

After releasing the agreement, save the data by clicking the Save 🖫 Save button.
In this manner, define the remaining internal agreements.

Defining Cost Distribution Profiles

This option allows you to specify how internal costs are to be distributed. You can also define other attributes, such as distribution method (direct, hierarchical based), and specify distribution parameters (net weight, gross weight, volume, distance).

For the given scenario, you must define the cost distribution profiles presented in Table A-141.

Table A-141. *Cost Distribution Profile Data*

Field	Value
Distr. Profile	HE-DP-GR_W
Description	Distribution based on forwarding-order item gross weight
Distribution method	Direct
Distribution rule	Gross weight
Distribution level	Forwarding order

To define a cost distribution profile, go to Customizing for SAP Transportation Management, and click Transportation Management ➤ Basic Function ➤ Cost Distribution ➤ Define Cost Distribution Profiles. Next, click the New Entries New Entries button, and enter the data from Table A-141.

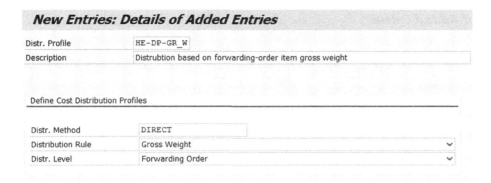

Figure A-159. *Creating a cost distribution profile*

After entering the necessary data, save the data by clicking the Save 🖫 button.

Defining Calculation Profiles

This option lets you specify the settings that the system should use when calculating transportation charges.

For the given scenario, you will need to define the calculation profiles shown in Table A-142.

Table A-142. *Calculation Profile Data*

Field	Value	Value
Calculation profile	HE-CP-01	HE-CP-02
Description	Calculation profile—stagewise	Calculation profile—itemwise
Calculation date type	Expected start date of main carriage	Expected start date of main carriage
Calculation level	Calculation at stage level	Calculation at item level
Through Rates	<Deselect>	<Select>
Dimensional weight profile	I166	I166
Data source	Actual route	Actual route

To define a calculation profile, go to Customizing for SAP Transportation Management, and click Transportation Management ➤ Basic Function ➤ Charge Calculation ➤ Basic Settings for Charge Calculation ➤ Define Calculation Profile.

Now, click the New Entries New Entries button, and enter the data from Table A-142.

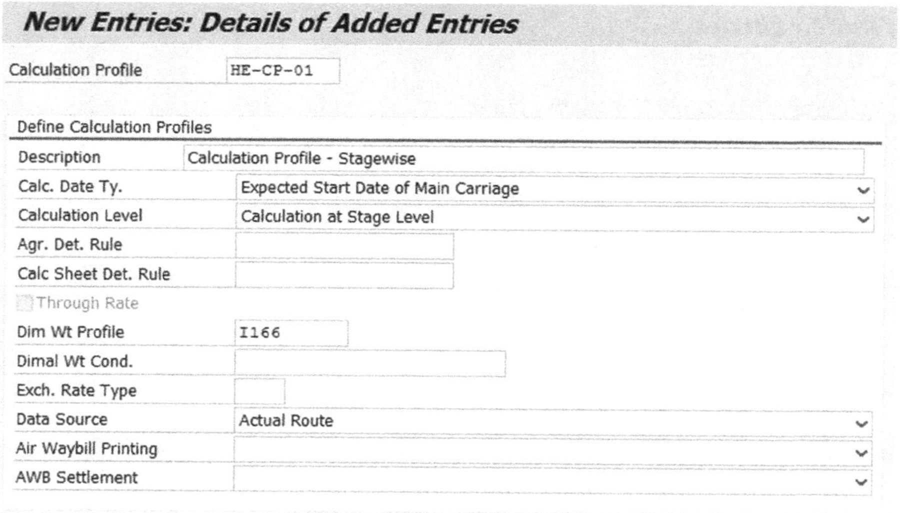

New Entries: Details of Added Entries

Calculation Profile	HE-CP-01

Define Calculation Profiles

Description	Calculation Profile - Stagewise
Calc. Date Ty.	Expected Start Date of Main Carriage ⌄
Calculation Level	Calculation at Stage Level ⌄
Agr. Det. Rule	
Calc Sheet Det. Rule	
☐ Through Rate	
Dim Wt Profile	I166
Dimal Wt Cond.	
Exch. Rate Type	
Data Source	Actual Route ⌄
Air Waybill Printing	⌄
AWB Settlement	⌄

Figure A-160. *Creating a calculation profile*

After entering the necessary data, save the data by clicking the Save 🖫 button.
In this way, define the remaining calculation profiles.

Defining Settlement Profiles

This option lets you specify the set of parameters that control how the system creates invoices.
For the given scenario, you must define the settlement profiles shown in Table A-143.

Table A-143. *Settlement Profile Data*

Field	Value
Settlement profile	HE-SP-01
Description	Settlement profile
Profile category	Forwarding and freight settlement
Data source	Planned data
Split/Cons	<Blank>
Calculation option	Copy all charges
Collective invoice	<Deselect>
Stage split	<Deselect>

To define a settlement profile, go to Customizing for SAP Transportation Management, and click Transportation Management ➤ Settlement ➤ Define Settlement Profile.
Then, click the New Entries New Entries button, and enter the data from Table A-143.

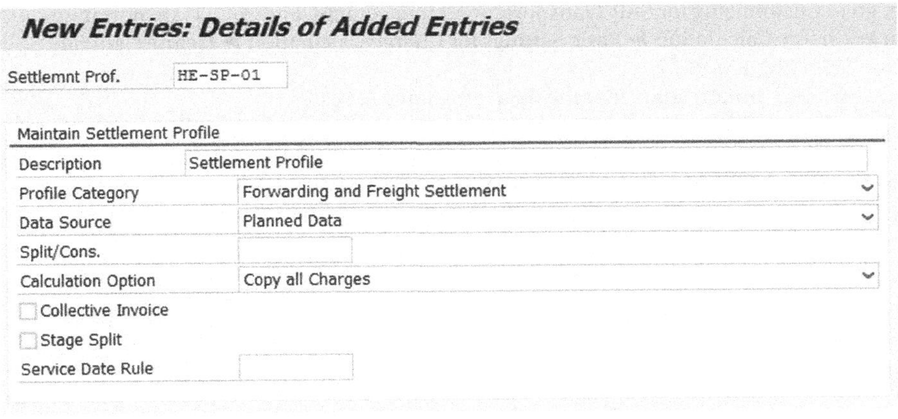

New Entries: Details of Added Entries

Settlemnt Prof. `HE-SP-01`

Maintain Settlement Profile

Description	Settlement Profile
Profile Category	Forwarding and Freight Settlement ⌄
Data Source	Planned Data ⌄
Split/Cons.	
Calculation Option	Copy all Charges ⌄
☐ Collective Invoice	
☐ Stage Split	
Service Date Rule	

Figure A-161. *Creating a settlement profile*

After entering the necessary data, save the data by clicking the Save 💾 button.

Defining General Settings

This option allows you to assign the calculation profile, settlement profile, and distribution profile to an organizational unit.

For the given scenario, you will need to define the general settings displayed in Table A-144.

Table A-144. *General Setting Data*

Field	Value	Value	Value	Value
Organizational unit	\<Enter the organization ID of HEJPFHYOK>	\<Enter the organization ID of HEJPFHNAR>	\<Enter the organization ID of HEUSFHLA>	\<Enter the organization ID of HEUSFHSFR>
Default purchasing organization	\<Enter the organization ID of HEJPFHYOK>	\<Enter the organization ID of HEJPFHNAR>	\<Enter the organization ID of HEUSFHLA>	\<Enter the organization ID of HEUSFHSFR>
Default carrier	\<Blank>	\<Blank>	\<Blank>	\<Blank>
Settlement profile	HE-SP-01	HE-SP-01	HE-SP-01	HE-SP-01
Calculation profile	HE-CP-01	HE-CP-01	HE-CP-01	HE-CP-01
Purchasing calculation profile	HE-CP-02	HE-CP-02	HE-CP-02	HE-CP-02
Local currency	JPY	JPY	USD	USD
Distribution profile	HE-DP-GR_W	HE-DP-GR_W	HE-DP-GR_W	HE-DP-GR_W

To define a general setting, go to Customizing for SAP Transportation Management, and click Transportation Management ➤ Basic Function ➤ Charge Calculation ➤ Basic Settings for Charge Calculation ➤ Define General Settings, or use the Tcode (/SCMTMS/TCM_FASET).

Next, click the New Entries New Entries button, and enter the data from Table A-144.

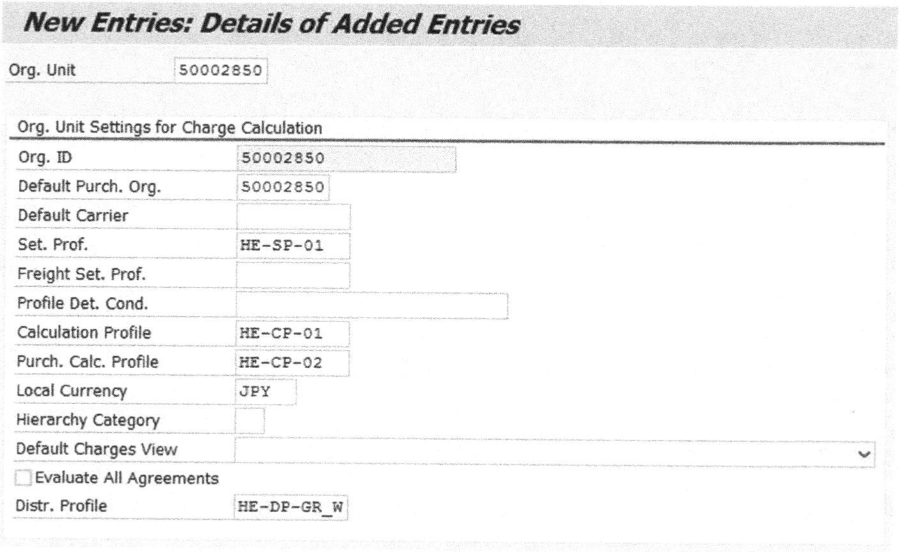

Figure A-162. *Creating a general setting*

After entering the necessary data, save the data by clicking the Save 🖫 button.

In this way, define the remaining general settings.

Defining Default Agreement Party Roles for Stages

This option can be used to specify the agreement party role for a stage type–International Commercial Terms (–Incoterms) combination. When an Incoterms rule is specified in a forwarding order, the system uses the agreement party role to identify the default agreement party for a stage. The system displays the relevant agreement party in the Stages tab of the forwarding-order user interface. The system also uses the agreement party to determine the contract during the charge calculation.

For the given scenario, you will have to define the default agreement party roles for stages provided in Table A-145.

Table A-145. *Default Agreement Party Role for Stage Data*

Field	Value	Value	Value	Value	Value
Incoterms rule	FOB	FOB	FOB	FOB	FOB
Agreement role	Prepaid agreement party	Prepaid agreement party	Collect agreement party	Collect agreement party	Collect agreement party

> ■ **Note**   It is assumed that the Incoterms rule is already defined. If it is not defined, then go to Customizing for SAP Transportation Management, and click Transportation Management ➤ SMC Basis ➤ Master Data ➤ Define Incoterms to define it.

To define a default agreement party role for a stage, go to Customizing for SAP Transportation Management, and click Transportation Management ➤ Forwarding Order Management ➤ Define Default Agreement Party Roles for Stages.

Then, click the New Entries New Entries button, and enter the data from Table A-145.

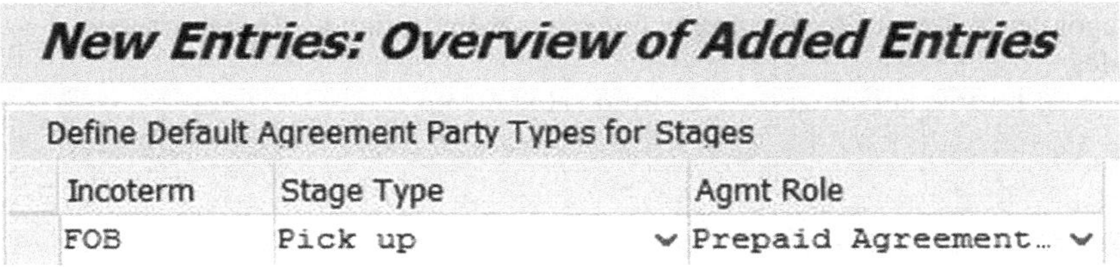

New Entries: Overview of Added Entries

Define Default Agreement Party Types for Stages

Incoterm	Stage Type	Agmt Role
FOB	Pick up	⌄ Prepaid Agreement… ⌄

Figure A-163. *Creating a default agreement party role for a stage*

After entering the necessary data, save the data by clicking the Save 🖫 button.

In this way, define the remaining default agreement party roles.

SAP ERP Customization Settings for Billing and Invoicing (Settlement Document)

Let's look at the SAP ERP customization settings required for billing (forwarding settlement—customer invoice) and invoicing (freight settlement—carrier invoice).

> ■ **Note**   It is assumed that the SAP ERP system is already configured for SAP Sales and Distribution (SAP SD), SAP Material Management (SAP MM) (procure to payment), and SAP Finance and Controlling (SAP FICO). In the SAP ERP system the user profile TM_INVOICE_CLERK is also configured/assigned. Moreover, the relevant customer master, vendor's master (carrier), and organizational structure are defined.

Defining Category Codes

This option allows you to define category codes for transportation charge items.

For the given scenario, you must define the category codes displayed in Table A-146, if you have not already done so.

Table A-146. *Category Code Data*

Field	Value	Value
Category code	003	004
Short description	Transport charge and additional charges	Basic freight

These category codes will have to be defined for billing as well as invoicing.

To define a category code for billing, go to Customizing for SAP ERP, and click Integration with Other SAP Components ➤ Transportation Management ➤ Invoice Integration ➤ Billing ➤ Definition for Transportation Charge Types ➤ Define Category Codes.

To define a category code for invoicing, go to Customizing for SAP ERP, and click Integration with Other SAP Components ➤ Transportation Management ➤ Invoice Integration ➤ Invoicing ➤ Definition for Transportation Charge Types ➤ Define Category Codes.

Next, click the New Entries New Entries button, and enter the data from Table A-146.

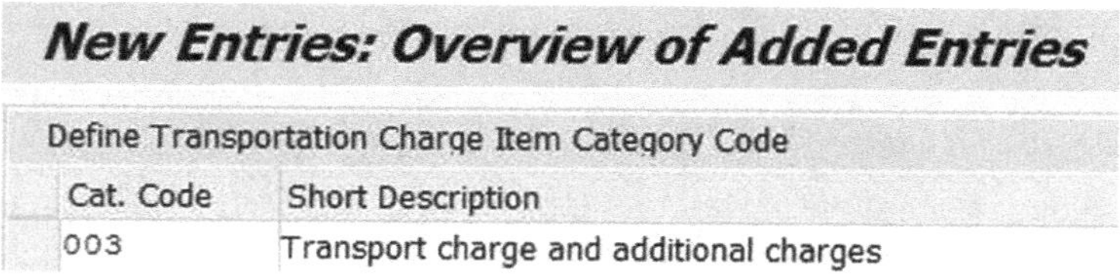

New Entries: Overview of Added Entries

Define Transportation Charge Item Category Code	
Cat. Code	Short Description
003	Transport charge and additional charges

Figure A-164. *Creating a category code*

After entering the necessary data, save the data by clicking the Save 🖫 button.

In this manner, define the remaining category codes.

Defining Subcategory Codes

This option lets you define subcategory codes for transportation charge items.

For the given scenario, you must define the subcategory codes in Table A-147, if you have not already done so.

Table A-147. *Subcategory Code Data*

Field	Value	Value
Subcategory code	100000	103008
Short description	Freight charges	Fuel surcharge

These subcategory codes will have to be defined for billing as well as invoicing.

To define a subcategory code for billing, go to Customizing for SAP ERP, and click Integration with Other SAP Components ➤ Transportation Management ➤ Invoice Integration ➤ Billing ➤ Definition for Transportation Charge Types ➤ Define Subcategory Codes.

To define a subcategory code for invoicing, go to Customizing for SAP ERP, and click Integration with Other SAP Components ➤ Transportation Management ➤ Invoice Integration ➤ Invoicing ➤ Definition for Transportation Charge Types ➤ Define Subcategory Codes.

Now, click the New Entries New Entries button, and enter the data from Table A-147.

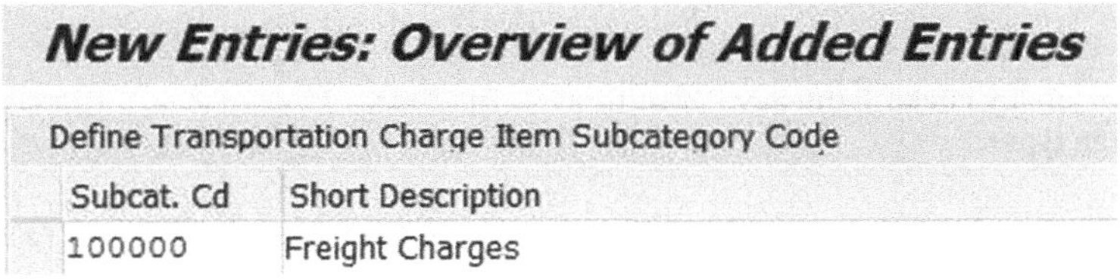

New Entries: Overview of Added Entries

Define Transportation Charge Item Subcategory Code	
Subcat. Cd	Short Description
100000	Freight Charges

Figure A-165. *Creating a subcategory code*

After entering the necessary data, save the data by clicking the Save 🖫 button.

In this way, define the remaining subcategory codes.

Defining Charge Type

This option can be used to define codes for transportation charge types.

For the given scenario, you will need to define the charge types shown in Table A-148, if you have not already done so.

Table A-148. *Charge Type Data*

Field	Value	Value	Value	Value	Value
Charge type	BASE_FA	FB00	FUEL	PU_FEE	COO
Charge type description	Base airfreight	Basic rate	Fuel surcharge	Pickup fee	Certificate of origin
Category code	004	004	003	004	004
Subcategory code	100000	100000	103008	100000	100000

These charge types will have to be defined for billing as well as invoicing.

To define a charge type for billing, go to Customizing for SAP ERP, and click Integration with Other SAP Components ➤ Transportation Management ➤ Invoice Integration ➤ Billing ➤ Definition for Transportation Charge Types ➤ Define Charge Types.

To define a subcategory code for invoicing, go to Customizing for SAP ERP, and click Integration with Other SAP Components ➤ Transportation Management ➤ Invoice Integration ➤ Invoicing ➤ Definition for Transportation Charge Types ➤ Define Charge Types.

Then, click the New Entries New Entries button, and enter the data from Table A-148.

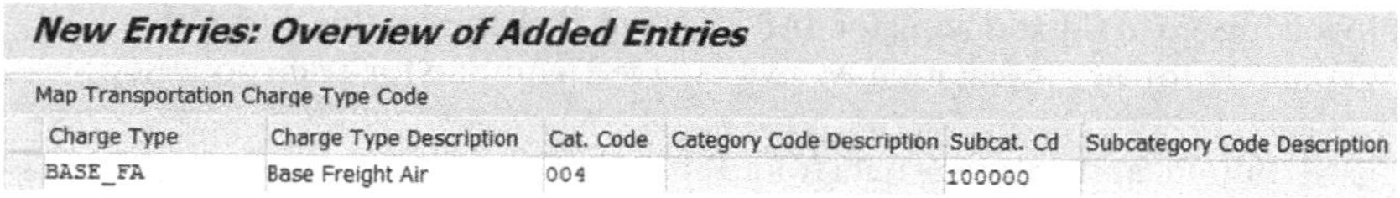

New Entries: Overview of Added Entries

Map Transportation Charge Type Code

Charge Type	Charge Type Description	Cat. Code	Category Code Description	Subcat. Cd	Subcategory Code Description
BASE_FA	Base Freight Air	004		100000	

Figure A-166. *Creating a charge type*

After entering the necessary data, save the data by clicking the Save 💾 button. In this manner, define the remaining charge types.

Assigning Condition Types

This option lets you specify transportation charge type categories, transportation charge type subcategories, and transportation charge types to condition types.

For the given scenario, you will have to define the assignments offered in Table A-149, if you have not already done so.

Table A-149. *Assigning Condition Type Data*

Field	Value	Value	Value	Value	Value
Category code	004	004	003	004	004
Subcategory code	100000	100000	103008	100000	100000
Charge type	BASE_FA	FB00	FUEL	PU_FEE	COO
Condition type (CTyp)	<Enter the condition type that suits your business requirements>	<Enter the condition type that suits your business requirements>	<Enter the condition type that suits your business requirements>	<Enter the condition type that suits your business requirements>	<Enter the condition type that suits your business requirements>

▪ **Note**   It is assumed that the condition type is already defined and is available in the settlement document pricing procedure.

To assign a condition type for billing, go to Customizing for SAP ERP, and click Integration with Other SAP Components ➤ Transportation Management ➤ Invoice Integration ➤ Billing ➤ Assignment of Transportation Charge Types ➤ Assign Condition Types.

Next, click the New Entries New Entries button, and enter the data from Table A-149.

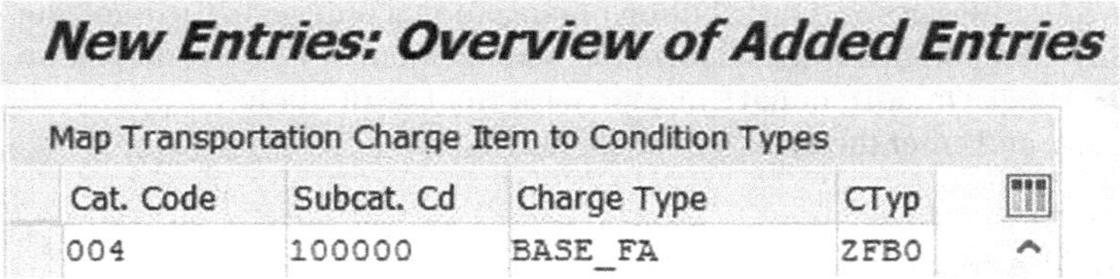

New Entries: Overview of Added Entries

Map Transportation Charge Item to Condition Types

Cat. Code	Subcat. Cd	Charge Type	CTyp	
004	100000	BASE_FA	ZFB0	^

Figure A-167. *Assigning a condition type*

After entering the necessary data, save the data by clicking the Save 🔳 button.
In this way, assign the remaining condition types.

Assigning Organizational Units for Sales and Distribution

This option allows you to assign/map SAP TM sales organizations to SAP ERP sales and distribution organizational units.

For the given scenario, you must define the assignments listed in Table A-150, if you have not already done so.

Table A-150. *Assigning Organizational Units for Sales and Distribution Data*

Field	Value	Value
Logical system	\<Specify the name of the SAP TM client>	\<Specify the name of the SAP TM client>
SAP TM sales organization	\<Enter the organization ID of HEJPFHYOK defined in SAP TM>	\<Enter the organization ID of HEJPFHSFR defined in SAP TM>
SAP TM sales office	\<Blank>	\<Blank>
SAP TM sales group	\<Blank>	\<Blank>
Settlement type	FW01	FW01
Forwarding settlement document category code	\<Enter the forwarding settlement document category code from SAP TM>	\<Enter the forwarding settlement document category code from SAP TM>
Map SAP TM Organizational Unit to Sales Organization Section		
Sales organization	\<Enter the sales organization ID defined in SAP ERP>	\<Enter the sales organization ID defined in SAP ERP>
Distribution channel	\<Enter the distribution channel defined in SAP ERP>	\<Enter the distribution channel defined in SAP ERP>
Division	\<Enter the division defined in SAP ERP>	\<Enter the division defined in SAP ERP>
Procedure	\<Enter the procedure defined in SAP ERP>	\<Enter the procedure defined in SAP ERP>
Billing type	\<Enter the billing type defined in SAP ERP>	\<Enter the billing type defined in SAP ERP>
Sales document type	\<Enter the sales document type defined in SAP ERP>	\<Enter the sales document type defined in SAP ERP>
Item category	\<Blank>	\<Blank>
Number range interval assignment	\<Enter the number range defined in SAP ERP>	\<Enter the number range defined in SAP ERP>

To assign a SAP TM sales organization to a SAP ERP sales and distribution organizational unit, go to Customizing for SAP ERP, and click Integration with Other SAP Components ➤ Transportation Management ➤ Invoice Integration ➤ Billing ➤ Mapping of Organizational Units ➤ Assign Organizational Units for Sales and Distribution.

Now, click the New Entries   New Entries   button, and enter the data from Table A-150.

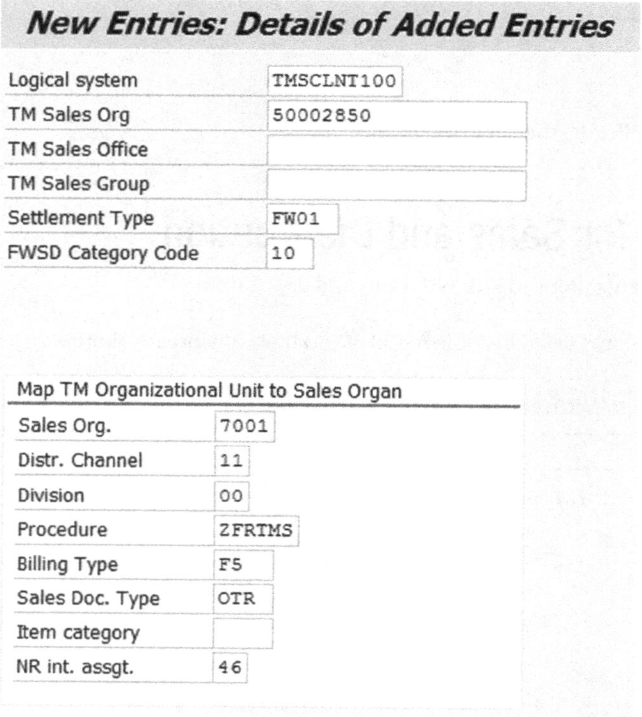

New Entries: Details of Added Entries

Logical system	TMSCLNT100
TM Sales Org	50002850
TM Sales Office	
TM Sales Group	
Settlement Type	FW01
FWSD Category Code	10

Map TM Organizational Unit to Sales Organ

Sales Org.	7001
Distr. Channel	11
Division	00
Procedure	ZFRTMS
Billing Type	F5
Sales Doc. Type	OTR
Item category	
NR int. assgt.	46

Figure A-168. *Assigning an organizational unit for sales and distribution*

After entering the necessary data, save the data by clicking the Save 💾 button.

In this way, assign the remaining SAP TM sales organizations to SAP ERP sales and distribution organizational units.

Assigning Service Master Record and Account Assignment Category

This option can be used to specify transportation charge item categories, transportation charge item subcategories, and transportation charge items for particular service master data records and account assignment categories.

For the given scenario, you must define the assignments presented in Table A-151, if you have not already done so.

Table A-151. *Assigning Service Master Record and Account Assignment Category*

Field	Value	Value	Value	Value	Value
Category code	004	004	003	004	004
Subcategory code	100000	100000	103008	100000	100000
Charge type	BASE_FA	FB00	FUEL	PU_FEE	COO
A	\<Enter the account assignment category that suits your business requirements>	\<Enter the account assignment category that suits your business requirements>	\<Enter the account assignment category that suits your business requirements>	\<Enter the account assignment category that suits your business requirements>	\<Enter the account assignment category that suits your business requirements>
Activity number	\<Enter the number of the service master record defined in SAP ERP>	\<Enter the number of the service master record defined in SAP ERP>	\<Enter the number of the service master record defined in SAP ERP>	\<Enter the number of the service master record defined in SAP ERP>	\<Enter the number of the service master record defined in SAP ERP>
Service short text	Base airfreight	Basic rate	Fuel surcharge	Pickup fee	Certificate of origin

▪ **Note**   It is assumed that the service master records are already defined in SAP ERP.

To assign the service master record and account assignment category for freight settlement, go to Customizing for SAP ERP, and click Integration with Other SAP Components ➤ Transportation Management ➤ Invoice Integration ➤ Invoicing ➤ Assignment of Transportation Charge Types ➤ Assign Service Master Record and Account Assignment Category.

Then, click the New Entries New Entries button, and enter the data from Table A-151.

New Entries: Overview of Added Entries

Map Transportation Charge Item to Service Master Record					
Cat. Code	Subcat. Cd	Charge Type	A	Activity Number	Service Short Text
004	100000	BASE_FA	K	TM_FB00	Base Freight Air

Figure A-169. *Assigning service master record and account assignment category*

After entering the necessary data, save the data by clicking the Save 🖫 button.

In this manner, assign the remaining service master records and account assignment categories.

Assigning Organizational Units for Purchasing

This option allows you to assign/map SAP TM purchasing organizations to SAP ERP purchasing organizational units. For the given scenario, you must define the assignments displayed in Table A-152, if you have not already done so.

Table A-152. *Assigning Organizational Units for Purchasing*

Field	Value	Value	Value	Value
Logical system	\<Specify the name of the SAP TM client\>	\<Specify the name of the SAP TM client\>	\<Specify the name of the SAP TM client\>	\<Specify the name of the SAP TM client\>
SAP TM purchasing organization	\<Enter the organization ID of HEJPFHYOK defined in SAP TM\>	\<Enter the organization ID of HEJPFHNAR defined in SAP TM\>	\<Enter the organization ID of HEUSFHLA defined in SAP TM\>	\<Enter the organization ID of HEUSFHSFR defined in SAP TM\>
SAP TM purchasing group	\<Blank\>	\<Blank\>	\<Blank\>	\<Blank\>
Settlement type	FS01	FS01	FS01	FS01
Map SAP TM Organizational Unit to Purchasing Section				
Purchasing organization	\<Enter the purchasing organization ID defined in SAP ERP\>	\<Enter the purchasing organization ID defined in SAP ERP\>	\<Enter the purchasing organization ID defined in SAP ERP\>	\<Enter the purchasing organization ID defined in SAP ERP\>
Purchasing group	\<Enter the purchasing group defined in SAP ERP\>	\<Enter the purchasing group defined in SAP ERP\>	\<Enter the purchasing group defined in SAP ERP\>	\<Enter the purchasing group defined in SAP ERP\>
Plant	\<Enter the plant defined in SAP ERP\>	\<Enter the plant defined in SAP ERP\>	\<Enter the plant defined in SAP ERP\>	\<Enter the plant defined in SAP ERP\>
Company code	\<Enter the company code defined in SAP ERP\>	\<Enter the company code defined in SAP ERP\>	\<Enter the company code defined in SAP ERP\>	\<Enter the company code defined in SAP ERP\>
Document type	\<Enter the document type defined in SAP ERP\>	\<Enter the document type defined in SAP ERP\>	\<Enter the document type defined in SAP ERP\>	\<Enter the document type defined in SAP ERP\>
Material group	\<Enter the material group defined in SAP ERP\>	\<Enter the material group defined in SAP ERP\>	\<Enter the material group defined in SAP ERP\>	\<Enter the material group defined in SAP ERP\>

To assign a SAP TM purchasing organization to a SAP ERP purchasing organizational unit, go to Customizing for SAP ERP, and click Integration with Other SAP Components ➤ Transportation Management ➤ Invoice Integration ➤ Invoicing ➤ Mapping of Organizational Units ➤ Assign Organizational Units for Purchasing.

Now, click the New Entries New Entries button, and enter the data from Table A-152.

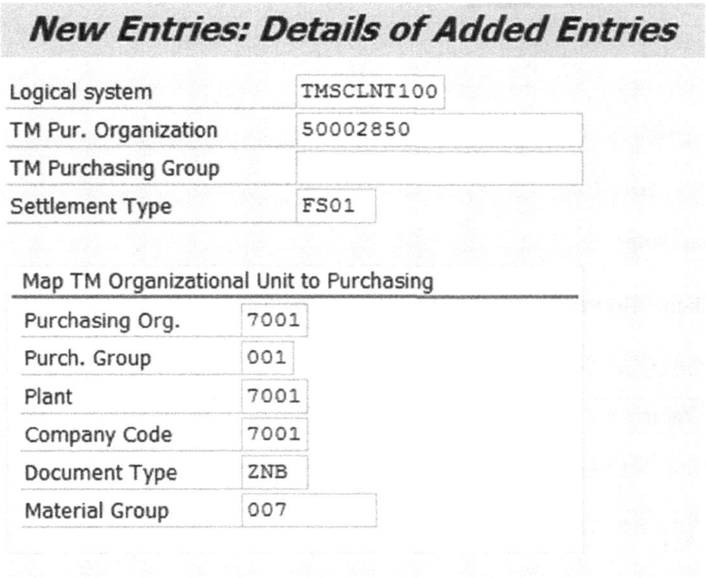

New Entries: Details of Added Entries

Logical system	TMSCLNT100
TM Pur. Organization	50002850
TM Purchasing Group	
Settlement Type	FS01

Map TM Organizational Unit to Purchasing

Purchasing Org.	7001
Purch. Group	001
Plant	7001
Company Code	7001
Document Type	ZNB
Material Group	007

Figure A-170. *Assigning an organizational unit for purchasing*

After entering the necessary data, save the data by clicking the Save 🖫 button.

In this manner, assign the remaining SAP TM purchasing organizations to the SAP ERP purchasing organizational units.

Here, we come to the end of the master data and configurations. Now, let's see how these data and configurations will be used in the end-to-end transportation management process.

The process can be further divided into the following stages:

- Capacity procurement

- Order management

- Planning and subcontracting

- Freight execution and monitoring

- Customer billing and freight settlement

Capacity Procurement: Freight Booking

In this process the procurement department books the capacity with the carriers. The capacity booking is made available to various organizational units only after the carrier has confirmed the booking. The freight-booking user interface is one of the interfaces provided in SAP TM to perform this process.

To create an airfreight booking, in SAP NetWeaver Business Client, click Freight Order Management ➤ Air ➤ Create Air Freight Booking.

For the given scenario, create a freight booking (export) as shown in Figures 171–180.

Enter the freight-booking type as "FB01," and click the Continue ⊘ Continue button.

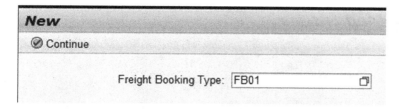

Figure A-171. *Initial screen for creating a freight booking*

Select the Comprehensive View page view. Then, select the Booking tab, and enter the data from Table A-153.

Table A-153. *Freight Booking (Export): Booking Tab Data*

Field	Value
Booking Tab	
Freight-Booking Data Section	
Issuing carrier airline code/Local carrier	MA
Organizational Data Section	
Origin organization	\<Enter the business partner ID of HEJPFHNAR\>
Destination organization	\<Enter the business partner ID of HEUSFHLA\>

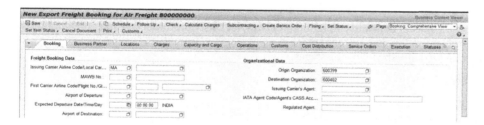

Figure A-172. *Creating a freight booking (export): Freight-Booking Data and Organizational Data sections of the Booking tab*

Assign the schedule to the booking by selecting Assign from the Schedule menu.

Figure A-173. *Creating a freight booking (export): Assigning a schedule*

In the Select Schedule Departure window, do a search of the schedules. From the list, choose one, and click the OK OK button.

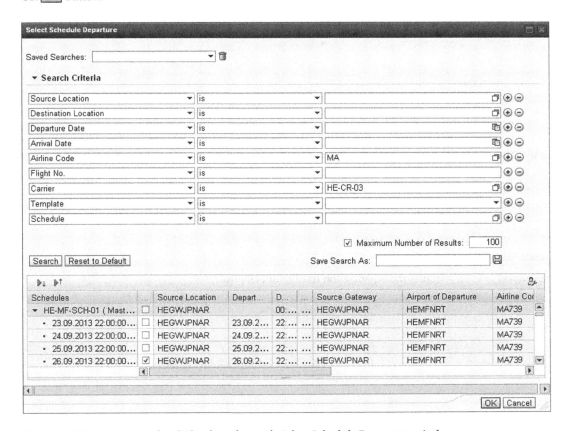

Figure A-174. *Creating a freight booking (export): Select Schedule Departure window*

The data from the schedule are included in the freight booking and are available in the Booking tab.

Figure A-175. *Creating a freight booking (export): Link to assigned schedule in the Booking tab*

Next, select the Operations tab, and enter the data from Table A-154.

Table A-154. *Freight Booking (Export): Operations Tab Data*

Field	Value
Operation Tab	
Organizational Data Section	
Purchasing organization	<Enter the organization ID of HEJPFHNAR>

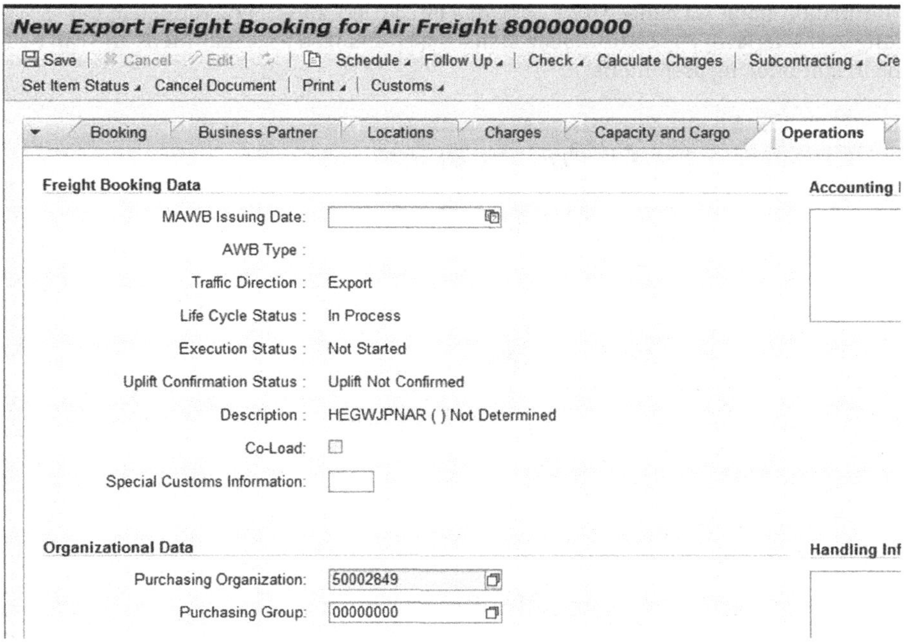

Figure A-176. *Creating a freight booking (export): Organizational data section of the Operations tab*

Save the freight booking (export) by clicking the Save ![Save] button.

To send the booking information to the carrier, edit the freight booking (export) by clicking the Edit ![Edit] button, and then select Send Booking from the Subcontracting menu.

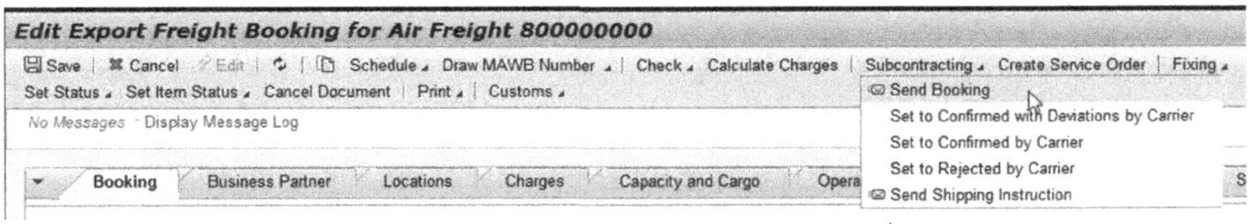

Figure A-177. *Freight booking (export): Sending booking information to the carrier*

Let's assume that the booking is accepted by the carrier and needs to be reported in the system. To do this, edit the freight booking (export) by clicking the Edit ![Edit] button, and then select Set to Confirmed by Carrier from the subcontracting menu.

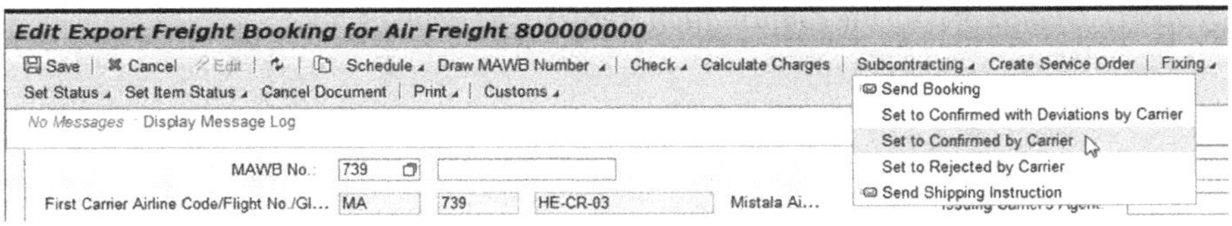

Figure A-178. *Freight booking (export): Confirming the carrier's acceptance*

As a result, the booking confirmation status is changed to "Confirmed by Carrier" and can be verified in the Booking tab of the freight-booking user interface. The confirmation status is also changed to "Confirmed" and can be verified in the Statuses tab of the freight-booking user interface.

Figure A-179. Freight booking (export): Update of booking confirmation status in the Booking tab

Figure A-180. *Freight booking (export): Update of confirmation status in the Statuses tab*

Order Management: Forwarding Order

In this process the customer service agent captures the necessary data communicated by the customer via phone, fax, or e-mail and creates a transportation order. The forwarding-order user interface is one of the interfaces offered in SAP TM to perform this process.

To create a forwarding order, in SAP NetWeaver Business Client, click Forwarding Order Management ➤ Forwarding Order ➤ Create Forwarding Order.

For the given scenario, create a forwarding order (export) as shown in Figures 181–191.

Enter the forwarding order as "FW01," and click the Continue ⊘ Continue button.

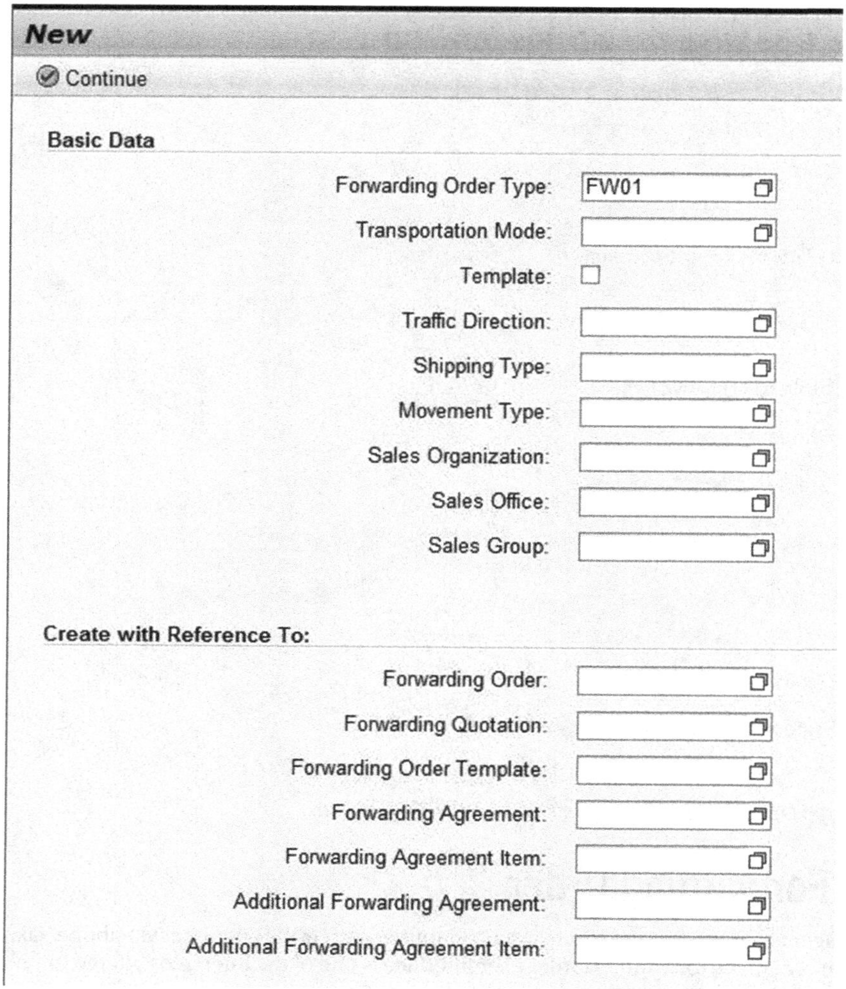

New

◉ Continue

Basic Data

Forwarding Order Type:	FW01
Transportation Mode:	
Template:	☐
Traffic Direction:	
Shipping Type:	
Movement Type:	
Sales Organization:	
Sales Office:	
Sales Group:	

Create with Reference To:

Forwarding Order:	
Forwarding Quotation:	
Forwarding Order Template:	
Forwarding Agreement:	
Forwarding Agreement Item:	
Additional Forwarding Agreement:	
Additional Forwarding Agreement Item:	

Figure A-181. Initial screen for creating a forwarding order

Select the General tab, and enter the data from Table A-155.

Table A-155. Forwarding Order (Export): General Data Tab Data

Field	Value
General Tab	
Organizational Data Section	
Sales organization	<Enter the organization ID of HEJPFHYOK>

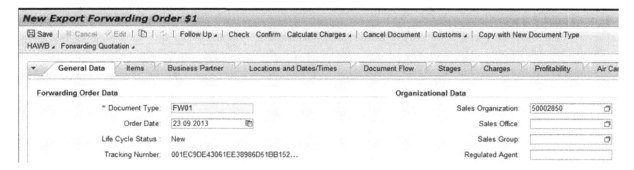

Figure A-182. *Creating a forwarding order (export): Organizational Data section of the General Data tab*

Now, select the Items tab, and insert a new item line by selecting Product from the Insert menu.

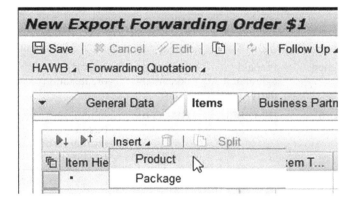

Figure A-183. *Creating a forwarding order (export): Items tab*

In the new item line, enter the data from Table A-156.

Table A-156. *Forwarding Order (Export): Items Tab Data*

Field	Value
Items Tab	
Item	10
Item type	HEPD
Product	Auto parts
Pieces	150
Pieces unit of measure	ea.
Gross weight	3,500
Gross weight unit of measure	kg
Gross volume	6
Gross volume unit of measure	m^3

New Export Forwarding Order $1

🖫 Save | ✖ Cancel | ✐ Edit | 🗋 | ↻ | Follow Up ▴ | Check Confirm Calculate Charges ▴ | Cancel Document | Customs ▴ | Copy with New Doc

HAWB ▴ Forwarding Quotation ▴

General Data	**Items**	Business Partner	Locations and Dates/Times	Document Flow	Stages	Charges	P

▸↓ ▸↑ | Insert ▴ | 🗑 | 🗋 Split

	Item Hierarchy	Item	Item T...	Package	Package...	Product	Pieces	Pi...	Gross W...	G...	Gross V...	G...
	• 🛒 Product	10	HEPD			AUTO PARTS	150	EA	3 500	KG	6	M3

Figure A-184. *Creating a forwarding order (export): Item data in the Items tab*

Select the Business Partner tab, and enter the data from Table A-157.

Table A-157. *Forwarding Order (Export): Business Partner Tab Data*

Field	Value	Value	Value	Value	Value	Value
Business Partner Tab						
Party role	Ordering party	Shipper	Consignee	Prepaid agreement party	Collect agreement Party	Import organization
Business partner	HE-CU-01	HE-CU-01	HE-CO-01	HE-CU-01	HE-CO-01	\<Enter the business partner ID of HEUSFHSFR\>

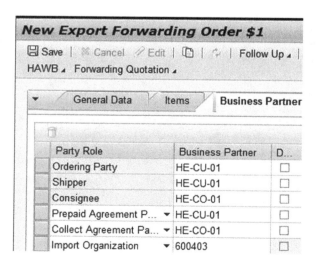

Figure A-185. *Creating a forwarding order (export): Business Partner tab*

Select the Locations and Dates/Times tab, and enter the data from Table A-158.

Table A-158. *Forwarding Order (Export): Locations and Dates/Times Tab Data*

Field	Value
Locations and Dates/Times Tab	
Source Section	
Location	HE-CU-01
Pickup date	<Enter a date>
Destination Section	
Destination	HE-CO-01
Delivery date	<Enter a date past the pickup date>

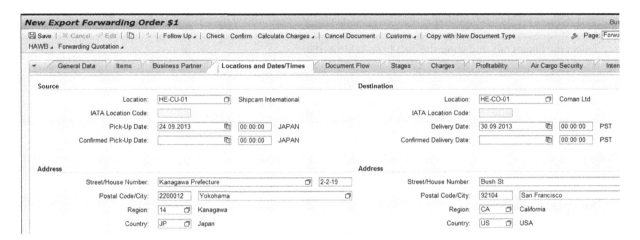

Figure A-186. *Creating a forwarding order (export): Source and Destination sections of the Locations and Dates/Times tab*

Select the General Data tab, and enter the data from Table A-159.

Table A-159. *Forwarding Order (Export): Incoterms and General Terms Sections Data*

Field	Value
General Data Tab	
Incoterms Section	
Incoterms rule	FOB
General Terms Section	
Movement type	DD

Incoterms

Incoterm: FOB

Figure A-187. *Creating a forwarding order (export): Incoterms section of the General Data tab*

General Terms

Service Level:		
Transportation Mode:	05	Air
Traffic Direction:	1	Export
Shipping Type:	10	Loose
Movement Type:	DD	

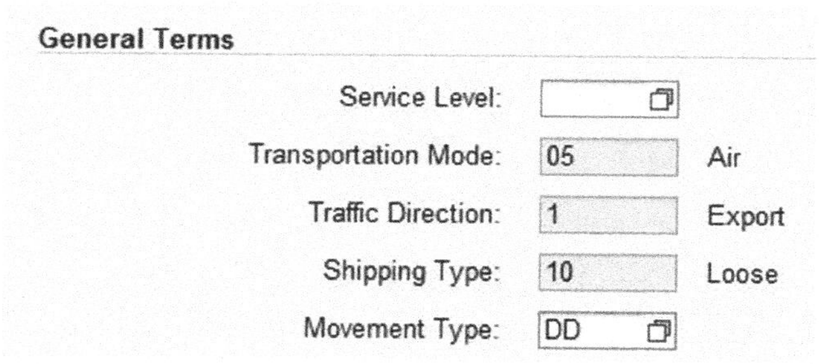

Figure A-188. *Creating a forwarding order (export): General Terms section of the General Data tab*

Select the Stages tab, and enter the data from Table A-160.

Table A-160. *Forwarding Order (Export): Stages Tab Data*

Field	Value	Value	Value	Value	Value
Stages Tab					
Actual route					
Stage type <(if not autopopulated)>	HE1	HE2	HE3	HE4	HE5
Transportation mode <(if not autopopulated)>	01	01	05	01	01
Destination location	HESTAJPYOK	HEGWJPNAR	HEGWUSLA	HESTAUSSFR	HE-CO-01
Planning and execution organization <(if not autopopulated)>	<Enter the organization ID of HEJPFHYOK>	<Enter the organization ID of HEJPFHYOK>	<Enter the organization ID of HEJPFHYOK>	<Enter the organization ID of HEUSFHLA>	<Enter the organization ID of HEUSFHSFR>
Agreement party role <(if not autopopulated)>	Prepaid agreement party	Prepaid agreement party	Collect agreement party	Collect agreement party	Collect agreement Party

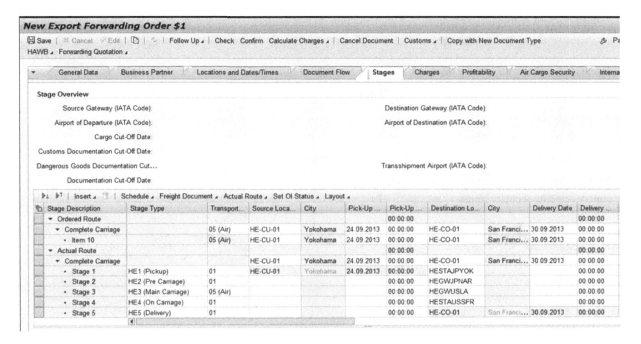

Figure A-189. *Creating a forwarding order (export): Stages tab*

■ **Note** All five stages should have been populated by default.

Save the forwarding order (export) by clicking the Save ⊟ Save button.

When the forwarding order is saved, the system also creates the freight unit based on the freight unit–building rule. The freight unit can be viewed in the Document Flow tab of the forwarding-order user interface.

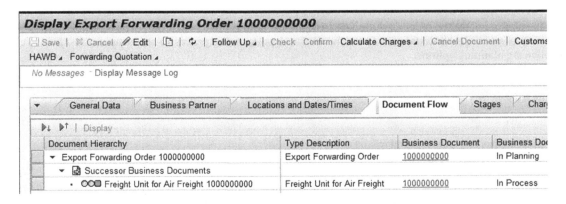

Figure A-190. *Forwarding order (export): Display of freight unit in the Document Flow tab*

Edit the forwarding order (export), and click the Edit ✎ Edit button.
Next, select the Air Cargo Security tab, and enter the data from Table A-161.

Table A-161. *Forwarding Order (Export): Air Cargo Security Tab Data*

Field	Value
Air Cargo Security Tab	
Cargo Handover Party Section	
Security status	Known shipper
Air Cargo Security Status Section	
Country-Specific security status	JP1

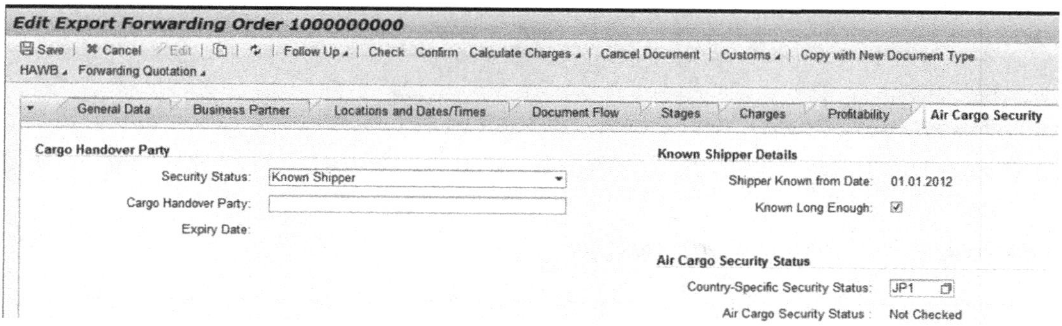

Figure A-191. *Editing a forwarding order (export): Air Cargo Security tab*

Save the forwarding order (export) by clicking the Save 🖫 Save button.

Planning and Subcontracting

In this process the planner plans the order execution and assigns the various orders to carriers. The transportation cockpit user interface is one of the interfaces included in SAP TM to perform this process. Furthermore, SAP TM provides the following planning options:

- Manual

- One- step

- Interactive

For the given scenario, manual planning will be used.

To open the transportation cockpit, in SAP NetWeaver Business Client, click Planning ➤ Manual Planning ➤ Transportation Cockpit.

In the transportation cockpit profile and layout sets user interface, click the New ⬚ New button to enter the selection and planning profiles from Table A-162.

Table A-162. *Transportation Cockpit Data*

Field	Value	Value	Value
Selection profile (freight units)	HE-SEL-PRO-PRE	HE-SEL-PRO-MAIN	HE-SEL-PRO-ON
Planning profile	HE-PLAN-PRO-PRE	HE-PLAN-PRO-MAIN	HE-PLAN-PRO-ON
Transportation cockpit layout	Standard layout	Standard layout	Standard layout
Layout for Planning Result screen	Standard layout	Standard layout	Standard layout

Figure A-192. *Transportation cockpit*

Save the profile and layout by clicking the Save ⊟ Save button.

In this manner, specify the remaining profiles and layouts.

Assigning the Forwarding Order to Freight Booking (Capacity Assignment)

To assign a forwarding order to a freight booking, open the transportation cockpit, and select the row containing the selection profile "HE-SEL-PRO-MAIN" and the planning profile "HE-PLAN-PRO-MAIN", and click the Continue ⊘ Continue button.

In the Transportation Cockpit screen, in the Freight Unit Stages section, select the freight unit that is to be assigned to freight booking, and drag and drop it on the freight booking available in the Freight Orders/Freight Bookings section.

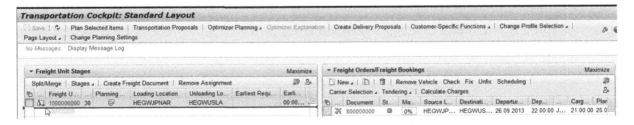

Figure A-193. *Transportation cockpit: Dragging freight unit for assignment to freight booking (export)*

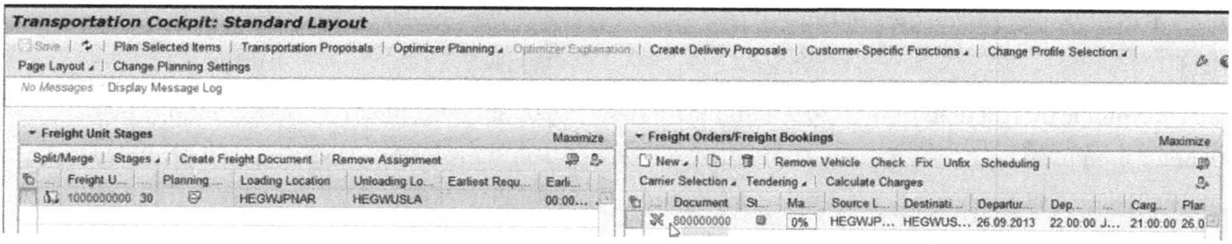

Figure A-194. *Transportation cockpit: Dropping freight unit for assignment to freight booking (export)*

Save the assignment by clicking the Save 🖫 Save button.

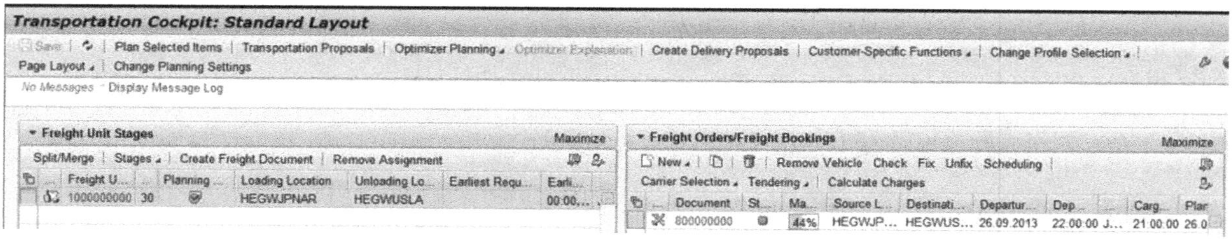

Figure A-195. *Transportation cockpit: Freight unit assigned to freight booking (export)*

The assignment is visible in the Stages tab of the forwarding-order user interface, in stage 3. The freight-booking document number, carrier, and airline code are shown. Also, the status is changed to Planned.

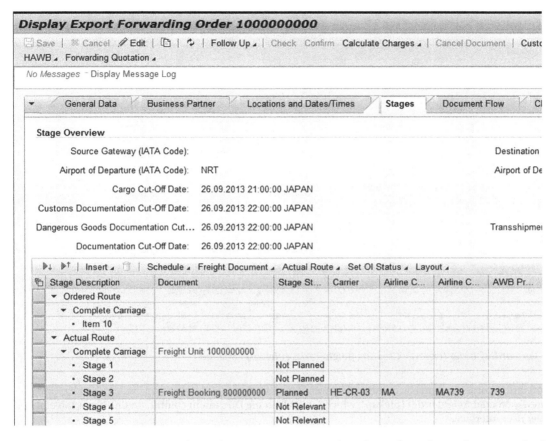

Figure A-196. *Forwarding order (export): Display of freight-booking (export) number in the Stages tab after assignment*

Planning for Pickup

To plan the pickup of the consignment, edit the forwarding order (export) by clicking the Edit ✎ Edit button.

Now, in the Stages tab, select stage 1. Then, select Create from the Freight Document menu.

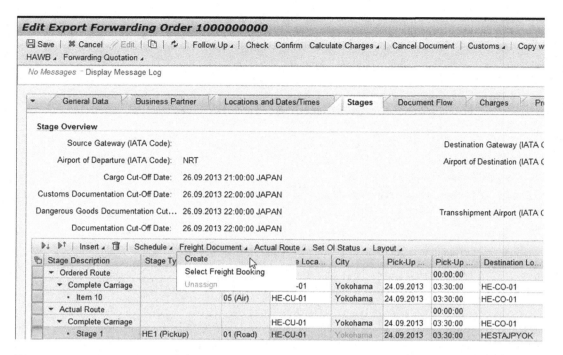

Figure A-197. *Forwarding order (export): Creating freight-order (pickup) for stage 1*

Save the forwarding order (export) by clicking the Save ⊞ Save button.

Click the newly created freight order (pickup), which is visible in the Document column, in the Stages tab of the forwarding-order user interface.

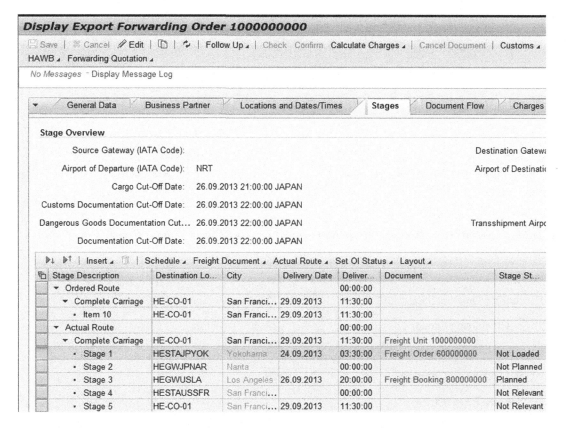

Figure A-198. *Forwarding order (export): Display of freight-order number in the Stages tab*

This will open the Freight-Order window. Edit the freight order by clicking the Edit ✎ Edit button. Then, select the General Data tab, and enter the data from Table A-163.

Table A-163. *Freight Order (Pickup): General Data Tab Data*

Field	Value
General Data Tab	
Transportation Section	
Carrier	HE-CR-01
Resource Capacity Section	
Vehicle	HEJP_TRUCK
Organizational Data Section	
Purchasing organization	<Enter the organization ID of HEJPFHYOK>
Planning and execution organization	<Enter the organization ID of HEJPFHYOK>

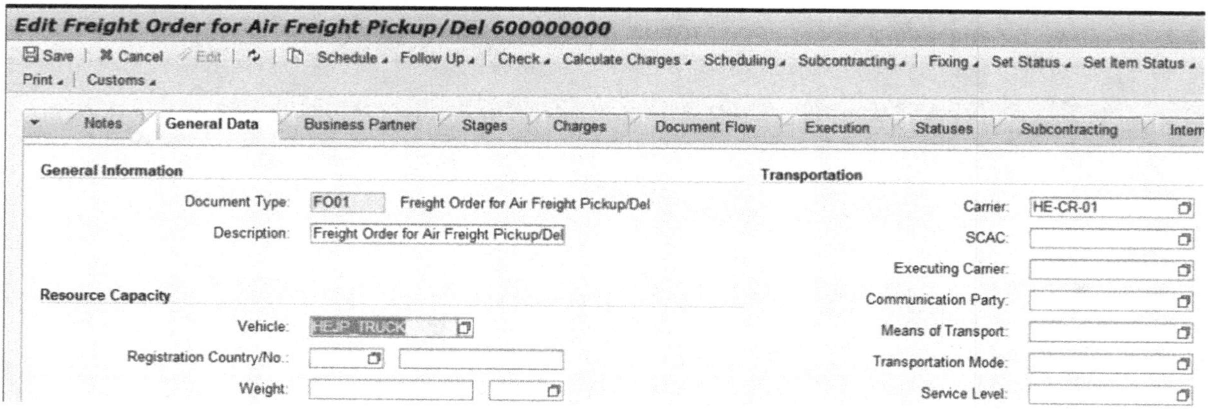

Figure A-199. *Editing a freight order (pickup): Transportation and Resource Capacity sections of the General Data Tab*

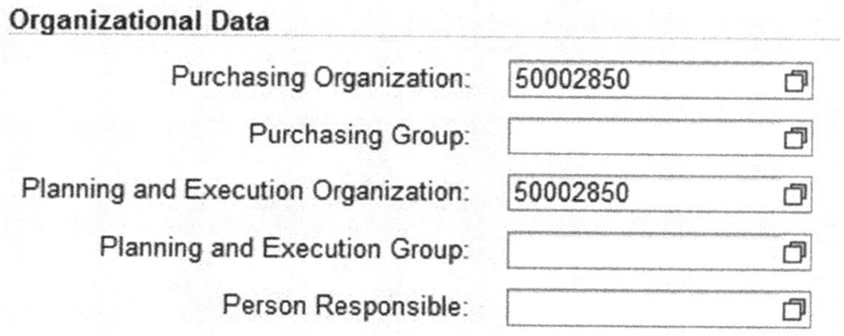

Organizational Data

Purchasing Organization:	50002850
Purchasing Group:	
Planning and Execution Organization:	50002850
Planning and Execution Group:	
Person Responsible:	

Figure A-200. *Editing a freight order (pickup): Organizational Data section of the General Data Tab*

Save the freight order (pickup) by clicking the Save 🖫 Save button.

Planning for Precarriage

To plan for precarriage, open the transportation cockpit, and select the row containing the selection profile "HE-SEL-PRO-PRE" and planning profile "HE-PLAN-PRO-PRE", and click the Continue ⊘ Continue button.

Then, in the Freight Unit Stages section of the Transportation Cockpit screen, select the freight unit whose precarriage is to be planned. In the Schedules tab, select the schedule that meets the requirements, and click the Plan Selected Items Plan Selected Items button. As a result, a new freight order is created for precarriage.

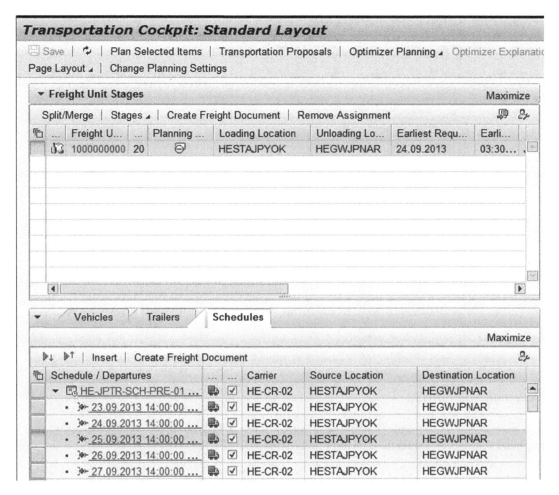

Figure A-201. *Transportation cockpit: Planning for precarriage*

Save the plan by clicking the Save 🖫 Save button.

Click the newly created freight order, which is visible in the Document column, in the Freight Orders/Freight Bookings section of the transportation cockpit.

Figure A-202. *Transportation cockpit: Freight order (precarriage) created through planning*

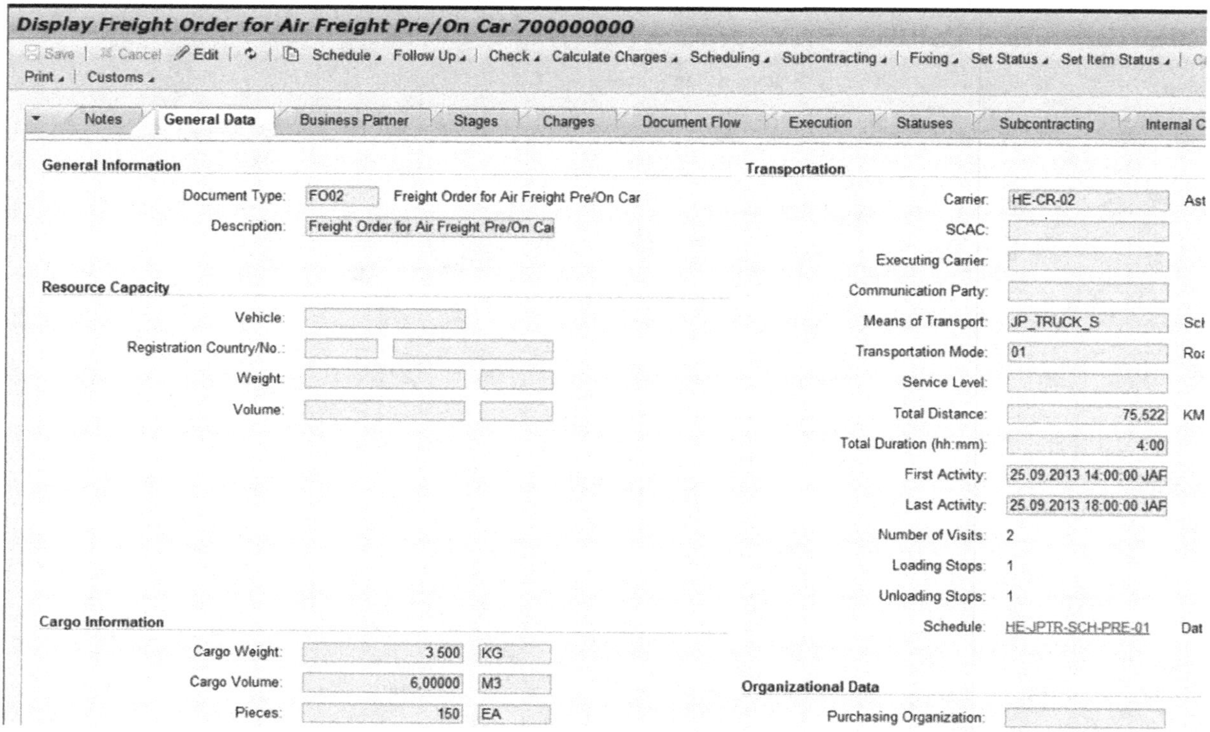

Figure A-203. *Freight order (precarriage)*

This will open the Freight-Order window. Edit the freight order (pre-Carriage) by clicking the Edit ✎ Edit button. Next, select the General Data tab, and enter the data from Table A-164.

Table A-164. *Freight Order (Precarriage): General Data Tab Data*

Field	Value
General Data Tab	
Organizational Data Section	
Purchasing organization	<Enter the organization ID of HEJPFHNAR>
Planning and execution organization	<Enter the organization ID of HEJPFHNAR>

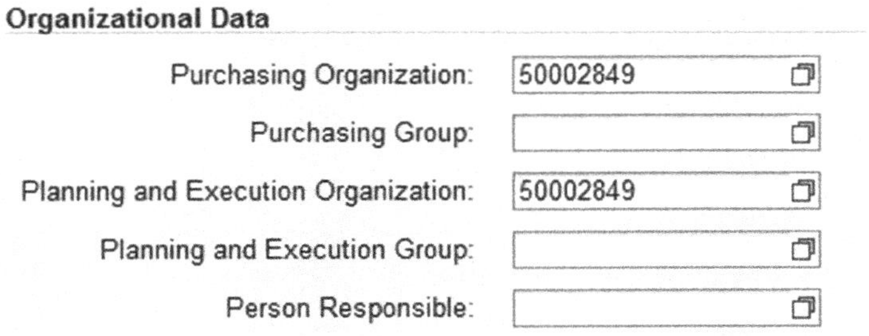

Organizational Data

Purchasing Organization:	50002849
Purchasing Group:	
Planning and Execution Organization:	50002849
Planning and Execution Group:	
Person Responsible:	

Figure A-204. *Freight order (precarriage): Organizational Data section of the General Data tab*

Save the freight order (precarriage) by clicking the Save 🖫 Save button.

Now that all the export stages are planned, confirmation can be sent to the ordering party, using the forwarding-order user interface.

To edit the forwarding order, in SAP NetWeaver Business Client, click Forwarding Order Management ➤ Forwarding Order ➤ Edit Forwarding Order.

Enter the forwarding order (export) number, and click the Continue ⊘ Continue button.

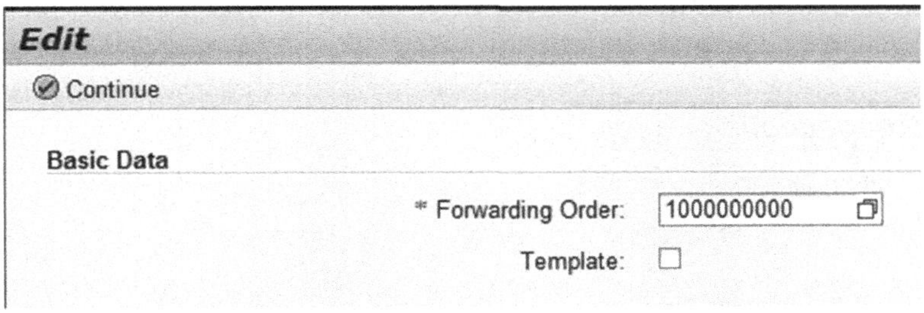

Edit

⊘ Continue

Basic Data

* Forwarding Order:	1000000000
Template:	☐

Figure A-205. *Initial screen for editing a forwarding order*

Now, confirm the order by clicking the Confirm Confirm button.

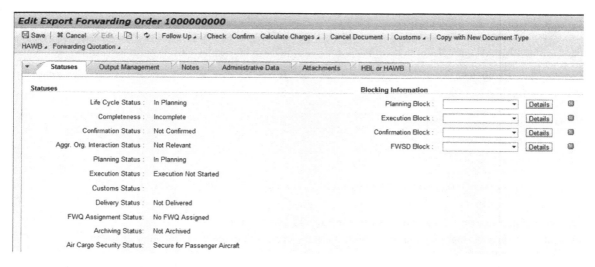

Figure A-206. *Forwarding order (export): Confirming the order*

Save the forwarding order (export) by clicking the Save 🖫 Save button.

Once the order is confirmed, the confirmation status is changed to "Confirmed" and is visible in the Statuses tab of the forwarding-order user interface.

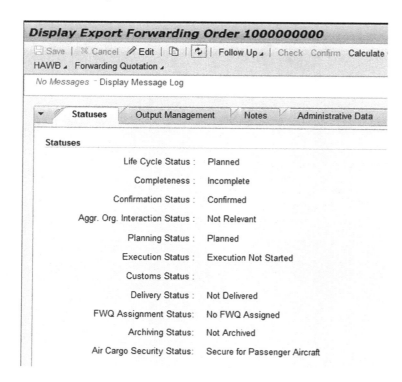

Figure A-207. *Forwarding order (export): Update of confirmation status*

Freight Execution and Monitoring

In this process the dispatcher and the document-processing agent execute orders, handle discrepancies, and document and monitor orders. The freight-order/freight-booking-user interface is one of the interfaces provided in SAP TM to perform these tasks. Also, if SAP EM is available as part of the landscape and is integrated with SAP TM, then raising various transportation events and monitoring can be done using the SAP EM user interface.

Let's see how the execution and monitoring of orders are performed for the given scenario.

Pickup Execution

To start the execution of the freight order (pickup), in SAP NetWeaver Business Client, click Forwarding Order Management ➤ Forwarding Order ➤ Display Forwarding Order.

Enter the forwarding-order number, and click the Continue ⊘ Continue button.

Display

⊘ Continue

Basic Data

* Forwarding Order: `1000000000` ▢

Template: ☐

Figure A-208. *Initial screen for displaying a forwarding order*

Next, select the Stages tab, and click the freight order, which is visible in the Document column (stage 1).

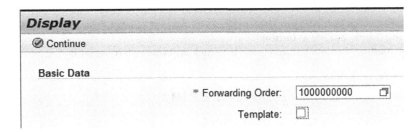

Figure A-209. *Display of forwarding order (export): Stages tab*

This will open the Freight-Order window. Click the Edit ✎ Edit button to edit the freight order (pickup), and then select Set to Ready for Transportation Execution from the Set Status menu.

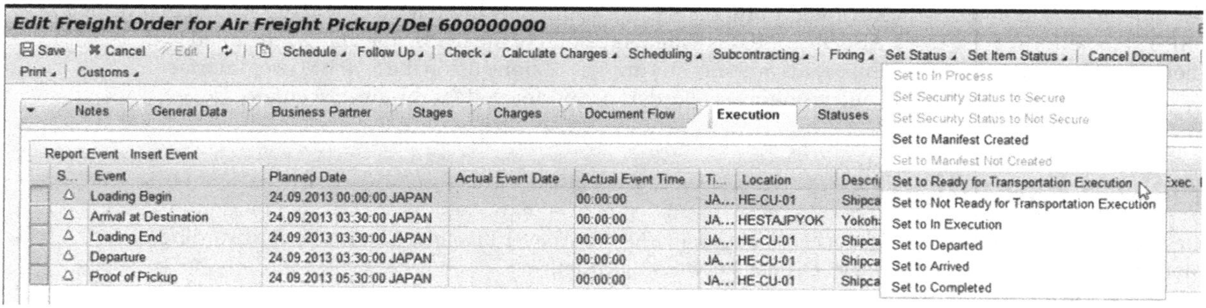

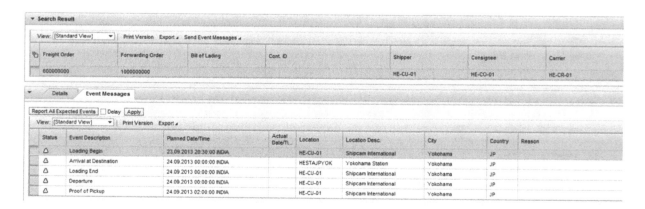

Figure A-210. Freight order (pickup): Setting status as "Ready for Transportation Execution"

Save the freight order (pickup) by clicking the Save 🖫 Save button.
Let's assume that the carrier has started loading the consignment onto the truck and wants to report this.

■ **Note** It is assumed that SAP EM is part of the landscape and is integrated with SAP TM.

To do this, in the event management web user interface (to call the event management web user interface in SAP NetWeaver Business Client, click Event Management ➤ Web Interface ➤ Search, or use the Tcode /SAPTRX/ EM_Start), or, using the result from a portal search for the freight order (pickup), click the freight order (pickup), and select the Event Messages tab, where various events that can be raised are available.

Figure A-211. Event management: Search Result window

Select the Loading Begin event, and click the Report All Expected Events Report All Expected Events button.
Then, in the Report All Expected Events window, click the Loading Begin event, and click the Send Send button.

Other events can also be raised through SAP EM. If SAP EM is not available, then events can be raised directly in SAP TM.

When the consignment arrives at the Yokohama Station, the Arrival event is raised. Let's see how this can be documented using the freight-order user interface.

Open the freight order (pickup) in edit mode, and select the Execution tab.

■ **Note**   If SAP EM is integrated with SAP TM, then various events will be populated by default.

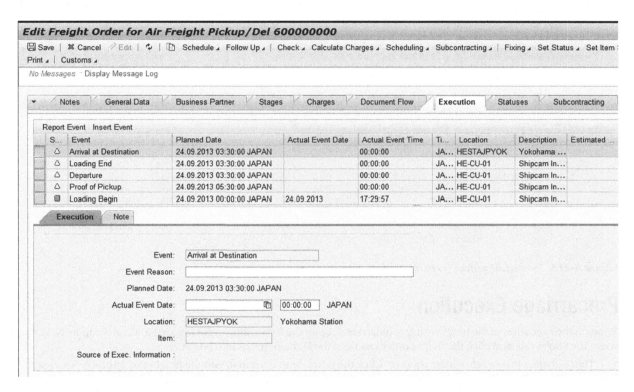

Figure A-212. *Freight order (pickup): Reporting the Arrival at Destination event in the Execution tab*

Now, select the row containing "Arrival at Destination," and click the Report Event Report Event button.

Save the freight order (pickup) by clicking the Save ⊟ Save button.

In this way, other events, such as Unloading Begin and Unloading End, can be raised.

The arrival status is also updated in the forwarding order (export) and is visible in the Stages tab, in the Stage Status column (stage 1).

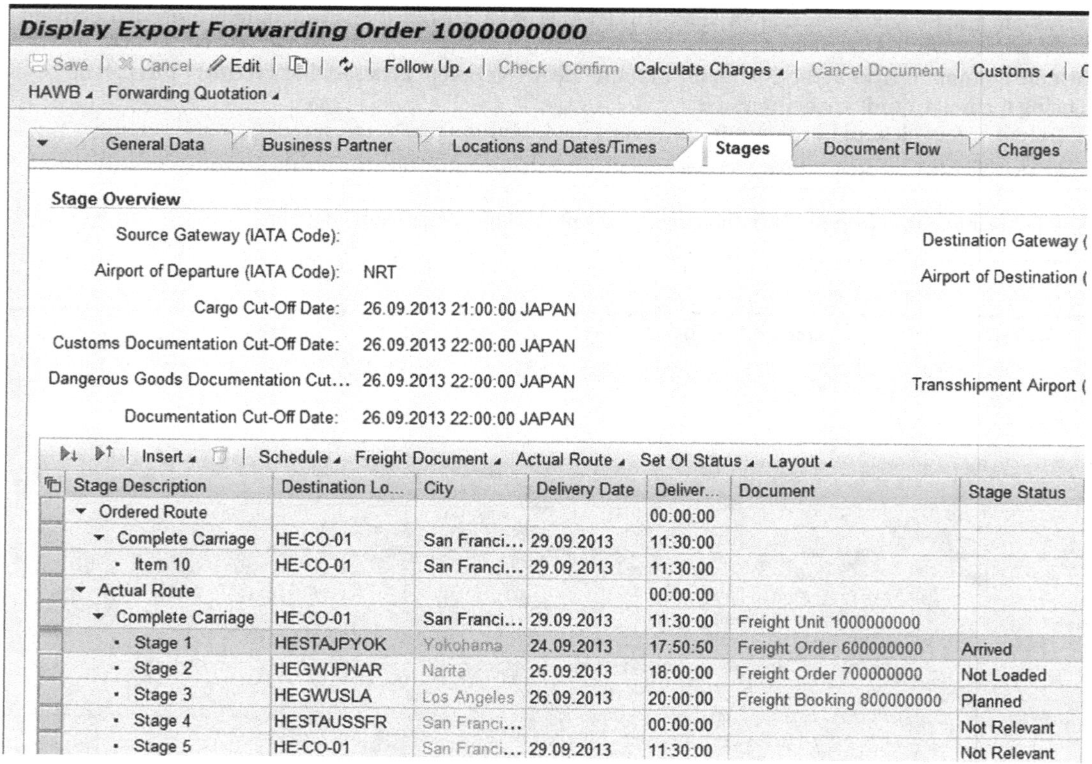

Figure A-213. Forwarding order (export): Update of status (stage 1) to "Arrived"

Precarriage Execution

To begin the execution of the freight order (precarriage), open the forwarding order (export) in display mode. Next, select the Stages tab, and click the freight order visible in the Document column (stage 2).

This will open the Freight-Order window. Click the Edit ✎ Edit button to edit the freight order (precarriage) and then select Set to Ready for Transportation Execution from the Set Status menu.

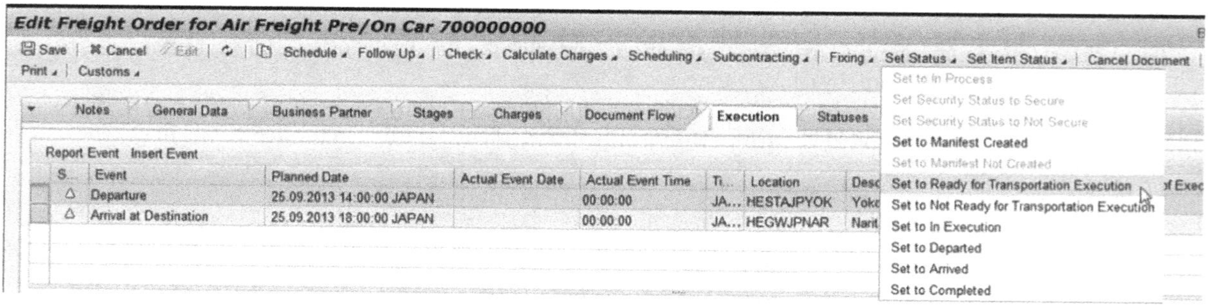

Figure A-214. Freight order (precarriage): Setting status as "Ready for Transportation Execution"

Save the freight order (precarriage) by clicking the Save ⊞ Save button.

To raise the departure event, edit the freight order (precarriage) by clicking the Edit ✎ Edit button, and then select the Execution tab.

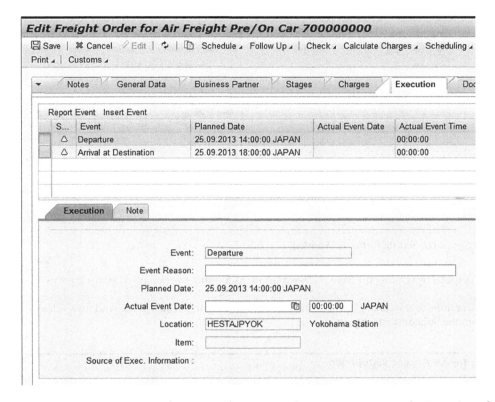

Figure A-215. *Freight order (precarriage): Reporting the Departure event in the Execution tab*

Select the row containing the departure event, and click the Report Event Report Event button.

Save the freight order (precarriage) by clicking the Save ⊞ Save button. In this way, raise the other events, such as Arrival at Destination.

Main Carriage Execution

Let's assume that the consignment has reached the gateway. The gateway operations can now commence. As a first step, the cargo is assigned for loading.

To start freight booking (export), open the forwarding order (export) in display mode. Next, select the Stages tab, and click the freight booking visible in the Document column (stage 3).

This will open the Freight-Booking window. Click the Edit ✎ Edit button to edit the freight booking (export), and then select Set to Loaded from the Set Item Status menu.

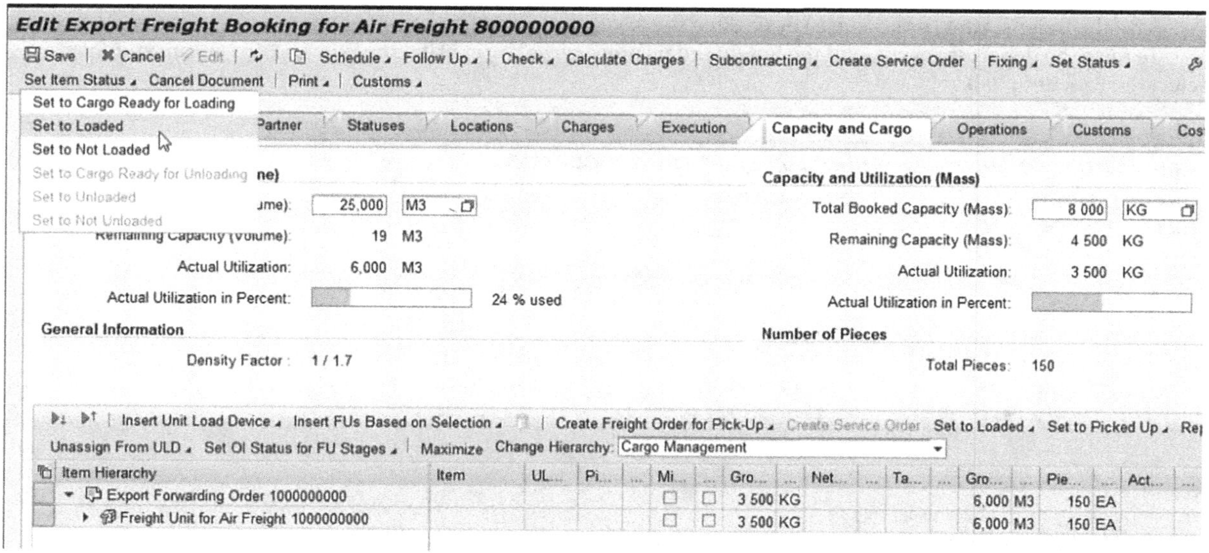

Figure A-216. *Freight booking (export): Setting status as "Loaded"*

Save the freight booking (export) by clicking the Save 🖫 Save button. As a result, the execution status is set to "Loading in Process."

To send the shipping instructions to the carrier, open the freight booking (export) in edit mode, and then select Send Shipping Instruction from the Subcontracting menu.

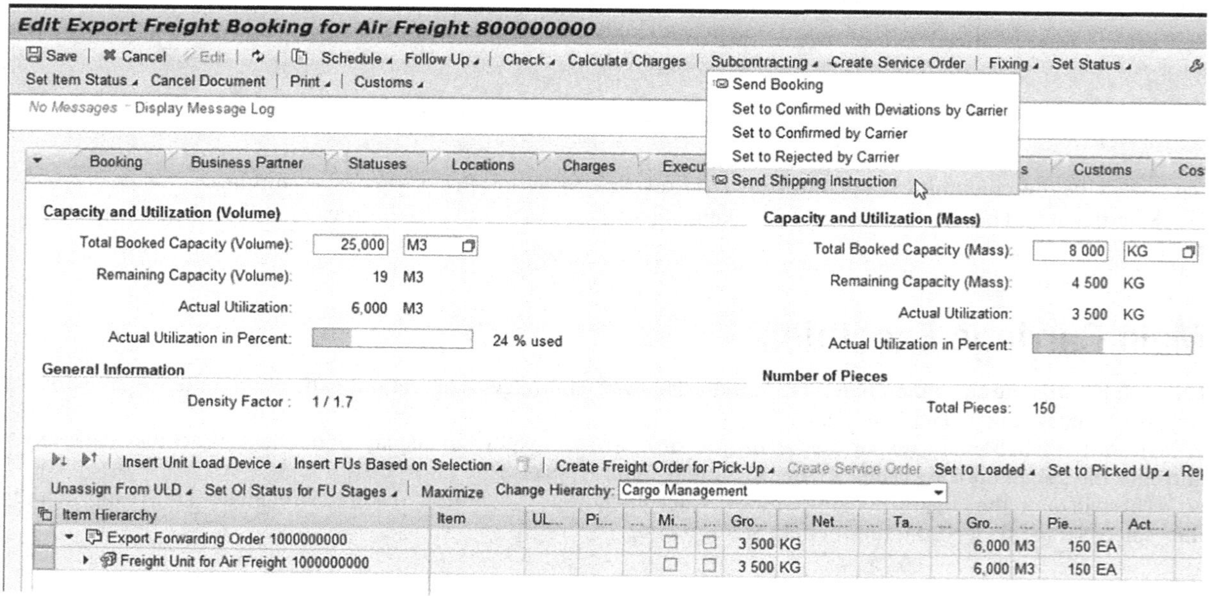

Figure A-217. *Freight booking (export): Sending shipping instructions*

Save the freight booking (export) by clicking the Save ⊞ Save button. As a result, the booking confirmation status is set to "Shipping Instruction Sent to Carrier."

Once the consolidation is over, and the cargo is ready to be transferred to the carrier, drayage to the airport has to be created.

For this, open the freight booking (export) in edit mode, and select the Capacity and Cargo tab. Select the freight units, and then select Create Freight Order for Pickup from the Create Freight Order for Pickup menu.

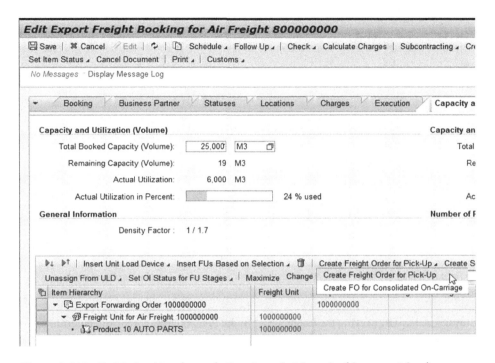

Figure A-218. *Freight booking (export): Creating a freight order (drayage pickup)*

Save the freight booking (export) by clicking the Save ⊞ Save button. The newly created freight order for pickup is now visible in the Freight Order for Pickup column, in the Capacity and Cargo tab of the freight-booking user interface.

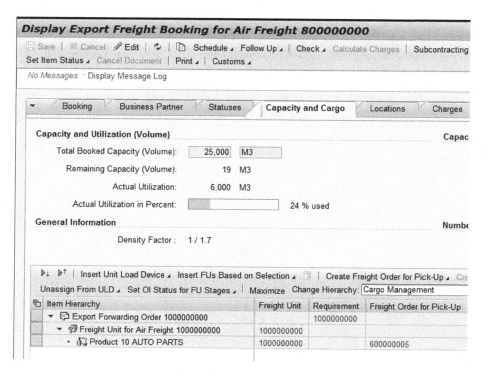

Figure A-219. *Freight booking (export): Display of freight-order number (drayage pickup) in the Capacity and Cargo tab*

Open the freight order (drayage pickup) by clicking the freight order in the Freight Order for Pickup column.

This will open the Freight-Order window. Click the Edit ✎ Edit button to edit the freight order (drayage pickup), select the General Data tab, and enter the data from Table A-165.

Table A-165. *Freight Order (Drayage Pickup): General Data Tab Data*

Field	Value
General Data Tab	
Transportation Section	
Carrier	HE-CR-02
Organizational Data Section	
Purchasing organization	<Enter the organization ID of HEJPFHNAR>
Planning and execution organization	<Enter the organization ID of HEJPFHNAR>

Edit Freight Order for Air Freight Pickup/Del 600000005
Save | Cancel | Edit | Schedule | Follow Up | Check | Calculate Charges | Scheduling | Subcontracting | Fixing | Set Status | Set Item Status
Print | Customs
Notes | General Data | Business Partner | Stages | Charges | Execution | Document Flow | Statuses | Subcontracting
General Information
Document Type: FO01 Freight Order for Air Freight Pickup/Del
Description: Freight Order for Air Freight Pickup/Del
Transportation
Carrier: HE-CR-02
SCAC:
Executing Carrier:

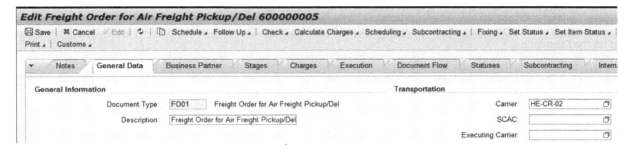

Figure A-220. *Freight order (drayage pickup): Transportation section of the General Data tab*

Organizational Data
Purchasing Organization: 50002849
Purchasing Group:
Planning and Execution Organization: 50002849
Planning and Execution Group:
Person Responsible:

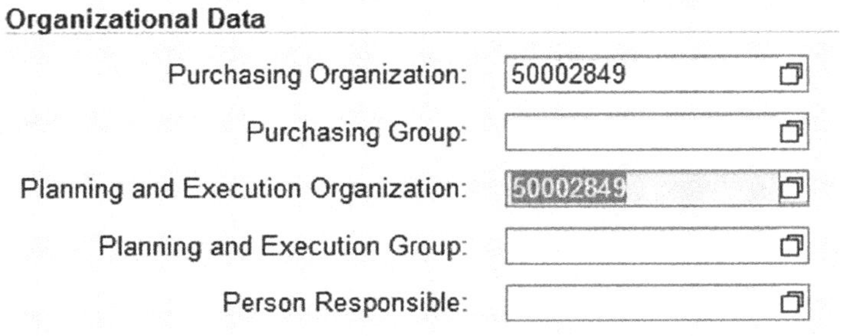

Figure A-221. *Freight order (drayage pickup): Organizational Data section of the General Data tab*

Select the Stages tab, and enter the data from Table A-166.

Table A-166. *Freight Order (Drayage Pickup): Stages Tab Data*

Field	Value
Stages Tab	
Stage type	HE2

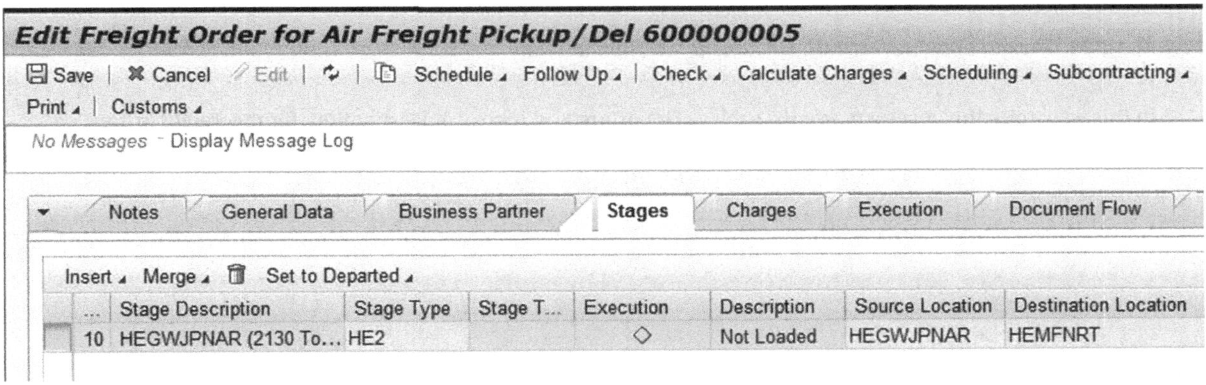

Edit Freight Order for Air Freight Pickup/Del 600000005
Save | Cancel | Edit | Schedule | Follow Up | Check | Calculate Charges | Scheduling | Subcontracting
Print | Customs
No Messages - Display Message Log
Notes | General Data | Business Partner | Stages | Charges | Execution | Document Flow
Insert | Merge | Set to Departed
Stage Description | Stage Type | Stage T... | Execution | Description | Source Location | Destination Location
10 HEGWJPNAR (2130 To... HE2 Not Loaded HEGWJPNAR HEMFNRT

Figure A-222. *Freight order (drayage pickup): Stages tab*

Save the freight order (drayage pickup) by clicking the Save 🖫 Save button.

To generate shipping documents, open the freight booking (export) in edit mode, and then select Print Preview from the Print menu.

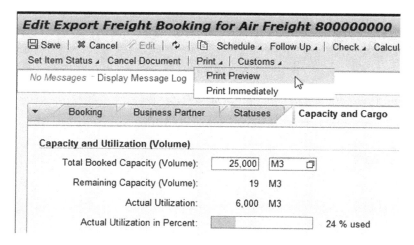

Figure A-223. *Freight booking (export): Selecting Print Preview*

Select the document to be generated in the Print window, and then click the OK [OK] button.

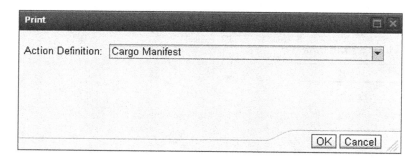

Figure A-224. *Freight booking (export): Document Selection window*

In this way, raise the necessary events, such as Departure and Arrival at Destination, for the freight order (drayage pickup).

Figure A-225. *Freight order (drayage pickup): Reporting the Departure and Arrival at Destination events in the Execution tab*

Now, let's assume that the cargo is loaded onto the plane, the airline has confirmed the count, and the departure (uplift) is confirmed by the export side.

Open the freight booking (export) in edit mode, and then select Set to Uplift Confirmed from the Set Status menu.

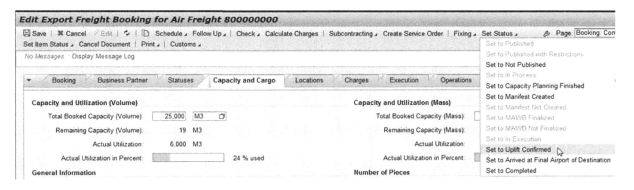

Figure A-226. *Freight booking (export): Confirming cargo uplift*

In the Set to Uplift Confirmed window, enter the date, and click the OK [OK] button.

Figure A-227. *Freight booking (export): Set to Uplift Confirmed window*

Save the freight booking (export) by clicking the Save ⊟ Save button. As a result, the uplift confirmation status of the freight booking (export) is set to "Uplift Confirmed." Also, the freight booking (import) and forwarding order (import) are automatically created, with their life cycle status set as "Draft," and the freight booking (import) is visible in the Document Flow tab.

Figure A-228. *Freight booking (export): Display of freight booking (import) in the Document Flow tab*

Click the newly created freight booking (import).

This will open the freight booking in a new window. Select the Document Flow tab to see the forwarding order (import).

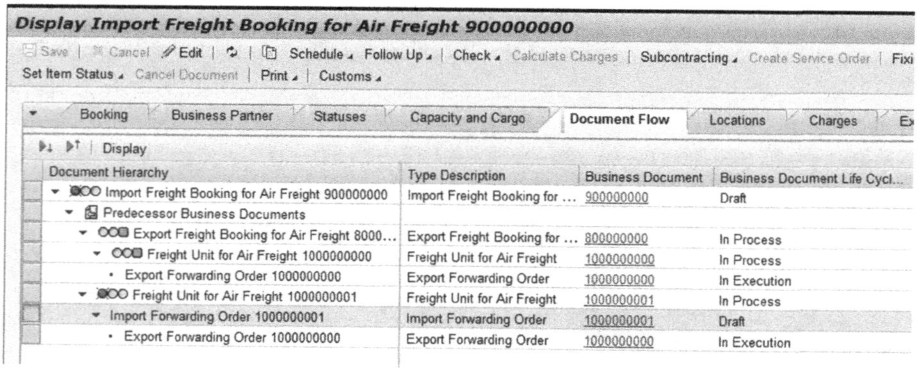

Figure A-229. *Freight booking (import): Display of forwarding order (import)in the Document Flow tab*

Processing the Forwarding Order (Import) and Freight Booking (Import)

To process the freight booking (import) and forwarding order (import), the draft status has to be removed.

■ **Note**   Before the draft status is removed, check whether the business partner, purchasing organization, sales organization, prepaid agreement party, collect agreement party, and so on are correct for both freight booking (import) and forwarding order (import), and make any necessary changes.

To remove the draft status of the freight booking (import), open it in edit mode, and then select Set In Process from the Set Status menu.

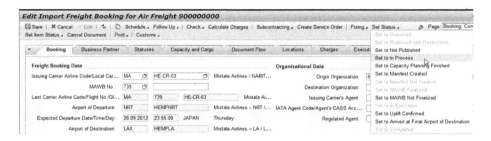

Figure A-230. *Freight booking (import): Setting status as "In Process"*

Save the freight booking (import) by clicking the Save 🖫 Save button.

To remove the draft status of the forwarding order (import), open it in edit mode, and click the Set to In Process Set to In Process button. Save the forwarding order (import) by clicking the Save 🖫 Save button.

Display Import Forwarding Order 1000000001

🖫 Save | ✕ Cancel | ✎ Edit | 🖹 | ✷ | Follow Up ▲ | Check   Confir
HAWB ▲   Forwarding Quotation ▲

No Messages ⁻ Display Message Log

| ▼ | **General Data** | **Business Partner** | **Locations and Dates** |

Forwarding Order Data

* Document Type: FW02

Order Date: 23.09.2013

Life Cycle Status :   In Planning

Figure A-231. *Forwarding order (import): Update of life cycle status to "In Planning"*

Planning and Subcontracting (Import)
Planning for On-Carriage

Planning the on-carriage entails a process similar to the one used for precarriage.

Click the newly created freight order, which is visible in the Document column, in the Freight Orders/Freight Bookings section of the transportation cockpit.

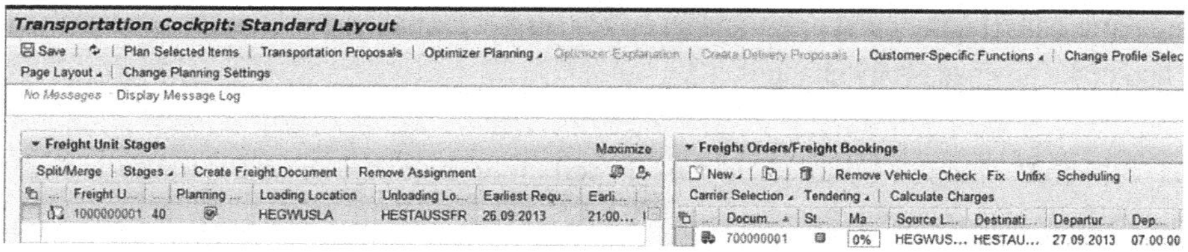

Figure A-232. *Transportation cockpit: Freight order (on-carriage) created through planning*

This will open the Freight-Order window. Click the Edit ✎ Edit button to edit the freight order (on-carriage). Next, select the General Data tab, and enter the data from Table A-167.

Table A-167. *Freight Order (On-Carriage): General Data Tab Data*

Field	Value
General Data Tab	
Organizational Data Section	
Purchasing organization	<Enter the organization ID of HEJPFHLA>
Planning and execution organization	<Enter the organization ID of HEJPFHLA>

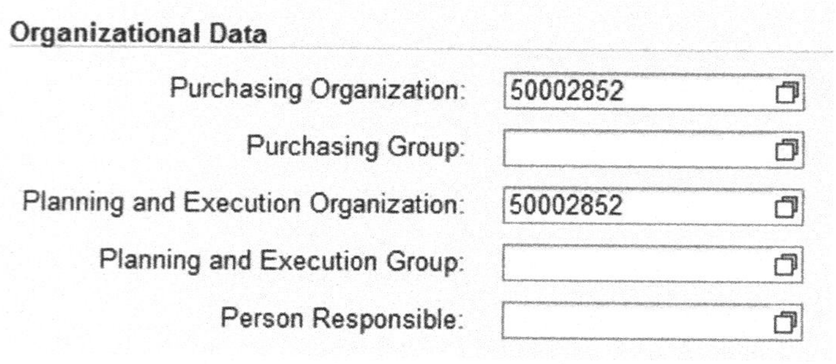

Figure A-233. *Freight order (on-carriage): Organizational Data section of the General Data Tab*

Save the freight order (on-carriage) by clicking the Save 🖫 Save button.

Planning for Delivery

Planning the delivery involves a process similar to the one used for pickup.

Click the newly created freight order, which is visible in the Document column (stage 5), in the Stages tab of the forwarding order (import).

This will open the Freight-Order window. Click the Edit ✏ Edit button to edit the freight order (delivery). Then, select the General Data tab, and enter the data from Table A-168.

Table A-168. *Freight Order (Delivery): General Data Tab Data*

Field	Value
General Data Tab	
Transportation Section	
Carrier	HE-CR-05
Resource Capacity Section	
Vehicle	HEUS_TRUCK
Organizational Data Section	
Purchasing organization	<Enter the organization ID of HEJPFHSFA>
Planning and execution organization	<Enter the organization ID of HEJPFHSFA>

Figure A-234. *Freight order (delivery): Transportation and Resource Capacity sections of the General Data tab*

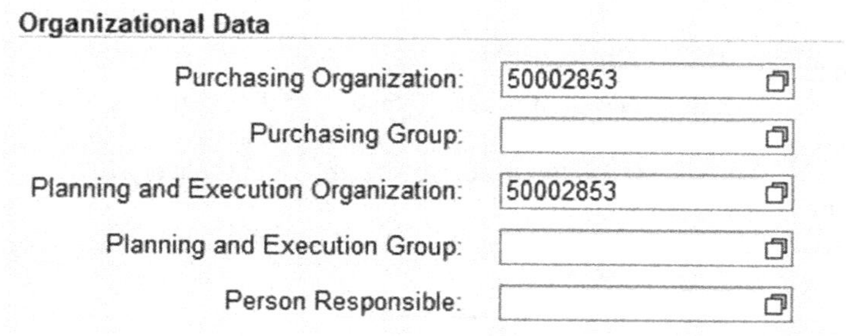

Organizational Data

Purchasing Organization: `50002853`

Purchasing Group: ``

Planning and Execution Organization: `50002853`

Planning and Execution Group: ``

Person Responsible: ``

Figure A-235. *Freight order (delivery): Organizational Data section of the General Data Tab*

Save the freight order (delivery) by clicking the Save 🔲 Save button.

Freight Execution and Monitoring (Import)

Let's assume that the airplane has arrived at LAX.

To capture this, open the freight booking (import) in edit mode, and then select Set to Arrived at Final Airport of Destination from the Set Status menu.

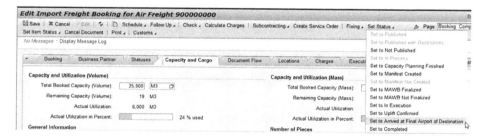

Figure A-236. *Freight booking (import): Reporting the Arrived at Final Airport of Destination event*

In the Set to Arrived at Final Airport of Destination window, enter the date, and click the OK 🔲OK🔲 button.

Figure A-237. *Freight booking (import): Set to Arrived at Final Airport of Destination window*

Save the freight booking (import) by clicking the Save 🖫 Save button.

For drayage from the destination airport to the destination gateway, open the freight booking (import) in edit mode. In the Capacity and Cargo tab, select the freight units, and then select Create Freight Order for Delivery from the Create Freight Order for Pickup menu.

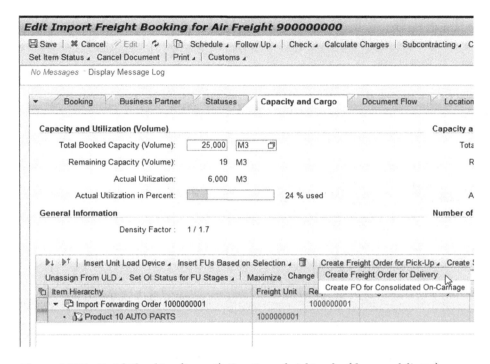

Figure A-238. *Freight booking (import): Creating a freight order (drayage delivery)*

Save the freight booking (import) by clicking the Save 🖫 Save button. The newly created freight order (drayage delivery) is visible in the Freight Order for Delivery column, in the Capacity and Cargo tab.

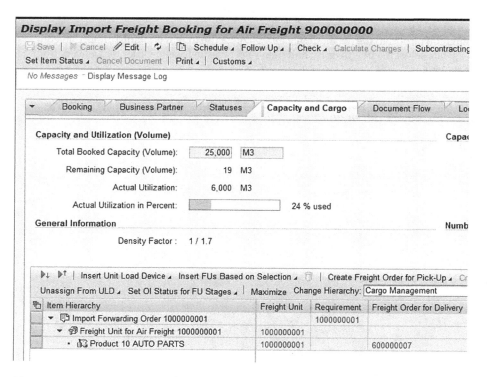

Figure A-239. *Freight booking (import): Display of freight-order number (drayage delivery) in the Capacity and Cargo tab*

Click the freight order (drayage delivery). This will open the Freight-Order window. Click the Edit ✎ Edit button to edit the freight order (drayage delivery). Then, select the General Data tab, and enter the data from Table A-169.

Table A-169. *Freight Order (Drayage Delivery): General Data Tab Data*

Field	Value
General Data Tab	
Transportation Section	
Carrier	HE-CR-04
Organizational Data Section	
Purchasing organization	<Enter the organization ID of HEJPFHLA>
Planning and execution organization	<Enter the organization ID of HEJPFHLA>

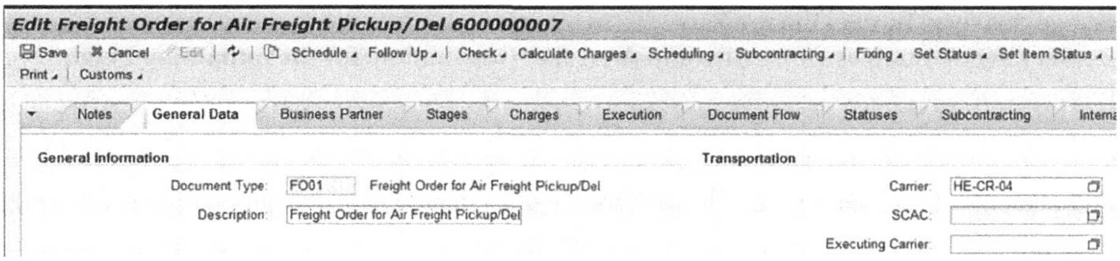

Figure A-240. *Freight order (drayage delivery): Transportation section of the General Data tab*

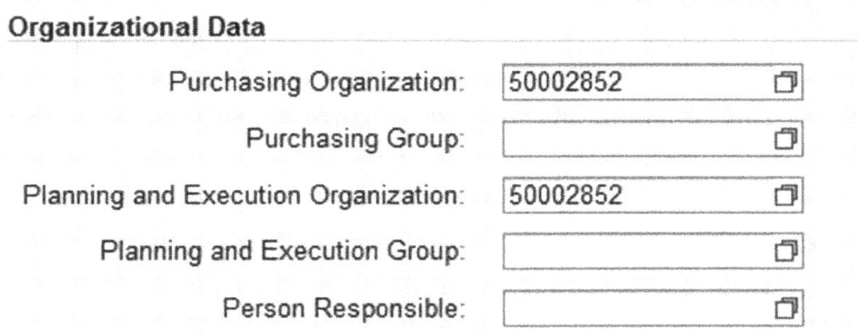

Figure A-241. *Freight order (drayage delivery): Organizational Data section of the General Data tab*

Select the Stages tab, and enter the data from Table A-170.

Table A-170. *Freight Order (Drayage Delivery): Stages Tab Data*

Field	Value
Stages Tab	
Stage type	HE4

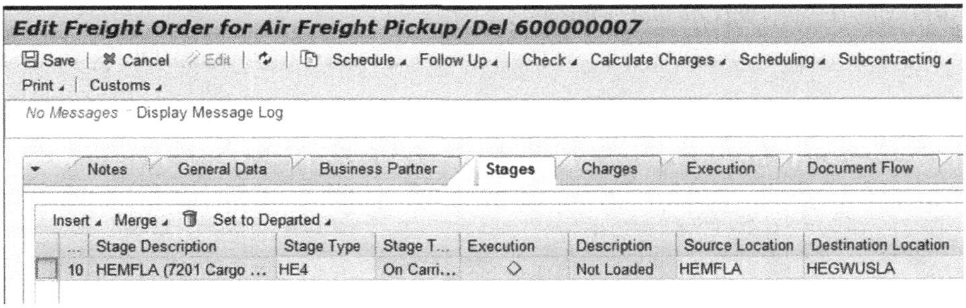

Figure A-242. *Freight order (drayage delivery): Stages tab*

Save the freight order (drayage delivery) by clicking the Save 💾 Save button.

In this way, , raise the necessary events such as Departure and Arrival at Destination, for the remaining freight orders (on-carriage, delivery).

■ **Note**   When the last expected customization event (freight-order type, freight-booking type, freight unit type) is raised, the execution status is set to "Executed."

Customer Billing and Freight Settlement

In this process the accounts department will calculate the charges to be levied on the customer, verify them, and invoice the customer. Similarly, the accounts payable department will perform the freight bill audit, verify the charges levied by the carrier, and do the freight settlement. The forwarding settlement and freight settlement user interface is one of the interfaces provided in SAP TM to perform this process.

Calculating Charges for Billing

For the given scenario, to calculate the charges, open the forwarding order (export) in edit mode, and then select Calculate Charges from the Calculate Charges menu.

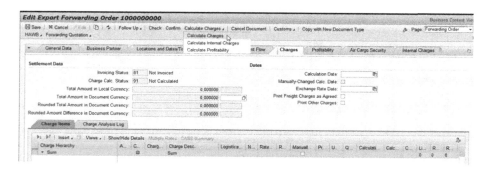

Figure A-243. *Forwarding order (export): Selecting Calculate Charges*

Figure A-244. Forwarding order (export): Display of charges

Save the forwarding order (export) by clicking the Save 🖫 Save button.
In this way, calculate the charges for the forwarding order (import).

Calculating Charges for Invoicing

For the given scenario, the charges for all freight orders (pickup, precarriage, on-carriage, delivery) as well as freight bookings will have been automatically calculated by the system.

Let's assume, however, that for some reason the charges for the freight order (pickup) have not been automatically calculated. To calculate the charges, open the freight order (pickup) in edit mode, and then select Calculate Charges from the Calculate Charges menu.

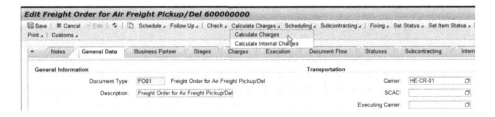

Figure A-245. Freight order (pickup): Selecting Calculate Charges

As a result, the charges will be calculated based on the freight agreement.

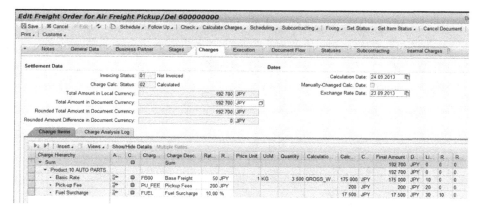

Figure A-246. *Freight order (pickup): Display of charges*

Save the freight order (pickup) by clicking the Save 🖫 Save button.

Check whether the charges are calculated for the other orders (precarriage, on-carriage, and so on). If the charges are not calculated, then calculate them in the same manner.

Billing (Forwarding Settlement)

To create an invoice for the customer, the forwarding settlement document is created and then transferred to a SAP ERP system or any other financial system.

To create a forwarding settlement for the given scenario, open the forwarding order (export) in edit mode, and then select Create Forwarding Settlement Document from the Follow-Up menu.

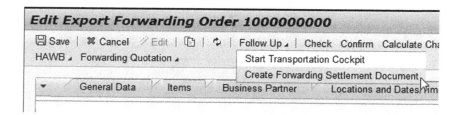

Figure A-247. *Forwarding order (export): Creating a forwarding settlement document*

The program will then ask you to specify the business partner for the forwarding settlement document. Select the appropriate business partner, and click the OK OK button. As a result, the Forwarding Settlement Document window will open, with the life cycle status set to "Ready for Invoicing" in SAP ERP."

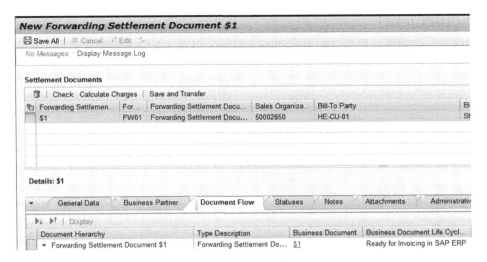

Figure A-248. *Forwarding settlement document: Life cycle status set as "Ready for Invoicing in SAP ERP"*

To transfer the forwarding settlement document to SAP ERP, in the Settlement Document section, select the forwarding settlement document, and then click the Save and Transfer Save and Transfer button.

As a result, the life cycle status of the forwarding settlement document is set to Transferred for Invoicing in SAP ERP, and the billing document will be created in SAP ERP.

Once the billing document is created successfully in SAP ERP, the billing document number will be visible in the Document Flow tab of the forwarding settlement user interface, and the life cycle status of the forwarding settlement document will be set to Invoiced in SAP ERP.

Figure A-249. *Forwarding settlement document: Life cycle status set as "Invoiced in SAP ERP"*

In this way, create and transfer the forwarding settlement document for forwarding order (import).

Invoicing (Freight Settlement)

To verify that the invoice has been received from the carrier, the freight settlement document is created and transferred to the SAP ERP system or any other financial system.

Let's see how to create the freight settlement document for freight order (pickup). For this, open the freight order (pickup) in edit mode, and select Create Freight Settlement from the Follow-Up menu.

Figure A-250. *Freight order (pickup): Creating a freight settlement document*

As a result, the freight settlement window will open, with the life cycle status set as "Ready for Accruals."

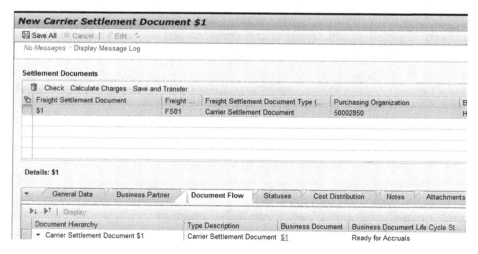

Figure A-251. *Freight settlement document: Life cycle status set as "Ready for Accruals"*

To transfer the freight settlement to SAP ERP, in the Settlement Document section, select the freight settlement document, and click the Save and Transfer Save and Transfer button.

As a result, the life cycle status of the freight settlement document is set to "Transferred for Accruals," and the purchase order and service entry sheet will be created in SAP ERP.

Once the purchase order and service entry sheet are created successfully in SAP ERP, the purchase order and service entry sheet number will be visible in the Document Flow tab of the freight settlement user interface, and the life cycle status of the freight settlement document will be set to "Accruals Posted."

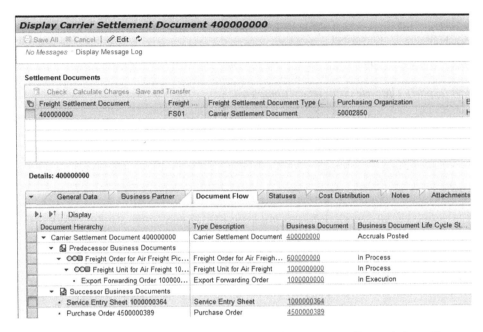

Figure A-252. *Freight settlement document: Life cycle status set as "Accruals Posted"*

Once the invoice is verified in SAP ERP, the invoice number is also visible in the Document Flow tab of the freight settlement user interface, and the life cycle status of the freight settlement document is set to "Invoice Verified in ERP."

In this way, create freight settlement documents for the other orders (precarriage, on-carriage, and so on).

Once the settlement document is created and transferred to SAP ERP, and the last expected events are raised, the life cycle status of the order (forwarding order, freight order, freight booking) is changed to "Completed."

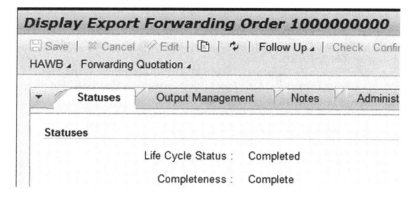

Figure A-253. *Forwarding order (export): Life cycle status set as "Completed"*

Figure A-254. *Freight order (pickup): Life cycle status set as "Completed"*

Index

■ G

■ U, V

■ W, X

■ Y, Z

Get the eBook for only $10!

Now you can take the weightless companion with you anywhere, anytime. Your purchase of this book entitles you to 3 electronic versions for only $10.

This Apress title will prove so indispensible that you'll want to carry it with you everywhere, which is why we are offering the eBook in 3 formats for only $10 if you have already purchased the print book.

Convenient and fully searchable, the PDF version enables you to easily find and copy code—or perform examples by quickly toggling between instructions and applications. The MOBI format is ideal for your Kindle, while the ePUB can be utilized on a variety of mobile devices.

Go to www.apress.com/promo/tendollars to purchase your companion eBook.